Masquerade

# Masquerade

*Essays on Tradition and
Innovation Worldwide*

*Edited by* DEBORAH BELL

McFarland & Company, Inc., Publishers
*Jefferson, North Carolina*

LIBRARY OF CONGRESS CATALOGUING-IN-PUBLICATION DATA

Masquerade : essays on tradition and innovation worldwide /
edited by Deborah Bell.
p.   cm.
Includes bibliographical references and index.

ISBN 978-0-7864-7646-6 (softcover : acid free paper) ∞
ISBN 978-1-4766-1804-3 (ebook)

1. Masks—Cross-cultural studies.   2. Masks—Social aspects.
3. Performance—Social aspects.   4. Masquerades.   5. Disguise.
I. Bell, Deborah, 1952– editor.
GT1747.M376 2015        782.1'5—dc23        2014041847

BRITISH LIBRARY CATALOGUING DATA ARE AVAILABLE

On the cover: *The Bride with the Mask of Herself,* 2002.
Self-portrait © Kimiko Yoshida

Printed in the United States of America

*McFarland & Company, Inc., Publishers
Box 611, Jefferson, North Carolina 28640
www.mcfarlandpub.com*

To my husband, Keith Cushman,
for sharing my love of theatre, opera
and masquerade through the years

# Table of Contents

# Acknowledgments

Special thanks to Keith Cushman and Matthew Teague Miller for assembling the appendix of selected plays, opera, and musicals that involve masquerade. Cushman, a professor of English at the University of North Carolina at Greensboro, is working on his eighth book about D. H. Lawrence, a collection of 16 essays on the fiction and poetry. He has held two Fulbright fellowships and has lectured widely in Europe and Asia. Miller, a graduate of the University of Cincinnati College-Conservatory of Music (musical theatre) is completing his M.F.A. at the University of North Carolina Greensboro (directing). He toured for three years with the original Broadway production of *Les Misérables*, performing with both Colm Wilkinson (the first Broadway Jean Valjean) and Randal Keith (the last). Miller has directed more than thirty regional performances around the country. Thanks also to Jackson Cooper for helping with the Index.

Finally, thanks are due Jim Fisher for encouraging me to embark on this project and for his sage advice.

# Introduction

## Deborah Bell

The essays in this collection examine the art and function of masquerade from a broad range of perspectives. The subject is interdisciplinary in nature and the contributors have various professional backgrounds—as costume designers, museum curators, and scholars in English, theatre, art history, anthropology, African history, critical media, and cultural studies. Several have created versions of masquerade as artists or they have written about versions of masquerade found in their areas of expertise. Their exploration acknowledges traditional notions of masquerade and its forms, but also seeks to define and describe masquerade in new ways as experienced in today's popular culture. The fundamental nature of masquerade and masks will always involve aspects of disguising and transforming identities. But traditional forms of masquerade have dramatically evolved in the past century with the appearance of graphic forms and narration in digital communication found in social media. We even see versions of fashion masquerade on the runway. We still recognize "traditional masquerade" but contemporary opportunities for masquerade have pushed the boundaries of traditional sensibility.

## Defining Masquerade and Masks in the Information Age

In his opulent book, *Masks: Faces of Culture* (1999)—coauthored with Cara McCarty—John Wallace Nunley establishes essential definitions for masquerade and the mask. He describes the "expression of masquerade" as a heightened level found in the ritual performance of maskers as well as in theatrical productions with masked and costumed players. He adds that "as a public event, the social phenomenon of masquerade might include music, food, drama, narration, a stage, or other performance props." Moreover he reminds us about fundamental reasons why we make masks and perform masquerades. "Masquerade performances entertain, distract, provoke, inspire fear, and instruct audiences both descriptively and non-discursively as embedded in memory and ritual. Masking also helps reconstruct social memory."[1]

Nunley defines the mask (a frequent fixture in masquerade) as "a solid form that covers the face and can be removed and put back on,"[2] believing that looser definitions can wreak havoc. He points out, for example, the problem in thinking of a car as a body mask, with the grill as a mouth with teeth and headlights for eyes. We could say that some car fronts appear shark-like and others more benign such as the baby-looking Volkswagen, but most would agree with Nunley that a car does not ultimately function as a mask any more than the face of a Barbie doll functions as a mask. (In correspondence with Nunley, he identified a Barbie doll as essentially a sculptural figure—and as such—reasonably suggested that Barbie functions more as an iconic symbol that possesses a face that looks like a frozen mask but is not a mask. However mask-like her face looks, it does not transform her own persona.)

Yet even Nunley sanctions looser descriptions of masquerade and masks. "Masking at all times, both traditionally and now, has dealt with sliding and multiple identities—even when these masquerading identities are considered rather fixed. An identity which is not fixed tends to gnaw at a traditional mask definition and is fueled with ambivalence and ambiguity. Yet sliding and multiple identities are found in both traditional and contemporary societies—and can become the bridge for traditional and new ways of thinking about the mask and masquerade."[3]

This premise of "sliding and multiple identities" inherent in the mask and masquerade offers new opportunities to think about masquerade. A mask is an object, and admittedly a car is also an object. But unlike a mask, a car resides under the category of transportation however closely it resembles a face. Unlike a successful mask, a car does not function as a way of disguising or transforming the car's "identity," just as Barbie's face ultimately functions as a sculptural iconic symbol rather than as a mask. And yet, using the premise of "sliding and multiple identities inherent in the mask" Barbie's face can, on occasion, function at a higher, transformative level.

For example, when two children assume a blend of their own identities combined with Barbie's iconic identity and present these roles to each other with great earnestness as they "role play," are they not conducting a form of social masquerade? They project themselves to each other as personalized versions of glamorous, grown-up Barbie in a performance setting of sorts—a theatre in the round with improvised dialogue. And are they not presenting "the mask of Barbie" to each other complete with specially selected masquerading costumes in order to help each of them assume more complex identities beyond their own?

*Masquerade* is based on that broader, more inclusive panorama of masking and masquerade. Using Nunley's observations regarding the functions of masquerade, we might even consider carefully selected, personalized photos and declarations on Facebook—or costumed audience members at movie theatres as versions of contemporary social masquerade that can potentially make use of such masquerade accompaniments as drama and narration. For example, a laptop can serve as a "stage" where a virtual community exchanges Facebook narration and dramatic declarations along with specially posed photos in a virtual social masquerade—while the lobby of a multiplex can showcase a literal form of social masquerade with costumed audience members emulating various characters of a featured adventure film.

Furthermore, Vassilis Zidianakis in *Not a Toy: Fashioning Radical Characters* (2011) asserts that "our globalized society does not easily allow for fixed identities,"[4] a situation that ultimately encourages the concept of masquerade to expand in multiple directions. New innovative versions of performance masquerade appear in digital film animation, illustrating exotic adventure stories found in science fiction and comic strips by incorporating the actor's voice and/or motion-captured body with the fantastical graphic effects of digital imagery. Those digital images of characters in computer games actually appear in outfits designed by costume designers employed to explore new looks in which to identify the characters. We can also experience digital masquerade using personal narrative and animated versions of ourselves dramatized in current video games. Even reality television shows project somewhat artificial, exaggerated situations and showcase posing characters as "masquerading" elements of characterization. Nowadays we take for granted the daily flurry of masquerading images that digitally inhabit our homes and entertain us at community, sports, and performance events. As masquerade in contemporary life has become more popular, it has adapted in all sorts of ways—especially in the past several decades with the refinement of graphic technology as well as in new avenues of ritual, social gatherings, and Internet communication.

Across millennia humans everywhere have enjoyed simplified versions of masquerade in child's play. And our sense of masquerade has been deeply embedded in our cultural psyche in the form of long-standing rituals and communal settings—as any child posing with Santa Claus for a photo op will affirm. But these days we see masquerade in so many forms that its appearance is the norm rather than the exception. Multiple versions of masquerade appear in all forms of media, fashion, visual art, photography, popular music performances, film, and television beyond traditional theatre and opera performances. For example, we are obsessed with—and take for granted—altered Photoshopped images of celebrities, conjuring youth, beauty, and idealized physiques on our magazine covers. These technically-altered images are as artificially constructed as the most exotic masquerade costumes. Even fashion spreads inside our magazines regularly depict purely exotic and provocative masquerade-inspired imagery that has nothing to do with fashion.

Indeed, given the extent of masquerade as we now experience it, we might consider our current era as the Age of Masquerade. This Age of Masquerade is the artistic inheritor of the Information Age because never before have we had such a wealth of imagery at our disposal, imagery that we constantly manipulate with the assistance of so many technical resources. Consequently, defining masquerade—and recognizing it in new performance settings—is evolving. Certainly the function and look of western masquerade have broadened exponentially since the early days of Venetian 17th-century carnival street events and elite Jacobean court masques which were rarefied events for the top echelon of society. Nowadays popular global audiences can expect luxurious masquerades such as those produced by Trinidadian Peter Minshall who created several huge televised masquerade spectacle events for the 1992, 1996, and 2002 Olympic Games held in Barcelona, Atlanta, and Salt Lake City.

We no longer require official or sacred holidays in order to experience masquerade's ramifications. If Shakespeare were alive today, he might consider changing his "All the world's a stage" declaration to "All the world's a masquerade." We take for granted many of our masquerade forms—especially those we use in our social role-playing. Daniel Mackay concludes in his book, *The Fantasy Role-Playing Game* (2001), that "life, identity, and meaning are all understood as consisting of nothing more than language games, exercises in role-playing." Mackay adds, "In a world of manifest meaninglessness, devoid of any sense of otherworldliness or metanarrative by which to understand the events around us, it is only through relishing the role one plays that a person can find any sense of satisfaction." Consequently, as we search to validate identities no longer relevant for our ever-expanding cultural sensibilities, we find the art of masquerade in multiple contexts as a handy (and frequently crucial) panacea.

## Universal Functions of Masquerade

Masquerade's potential for heightened spectacle in an exaggerated scale works well for a range of lavish public events that now dominate global exhibitions, pageants, and ceremonies. Whether versions of it appear in a small village or are broadcasted internationally from a sports stadium, successful masquerade can transcend language barriers, allowing us a vivid opportunity to bear witness to the tremendous range of human experience.

Traditional and contemporary masquerade universally function in a number of recognizable ways. First, as Nunley notes, masquerade rituals often function as a way to create a sense of renewal—of abundance, vitality, and fertility. He even suggests that Americans might well consider professional sports as a masquerade ritual that metaphorically supports "national renewal, as regional [uniformed] teams from the same country compete to prove who is the fastest and the strongest."[5] Responding to this commentary in a recent interview, costume designer Laura Crow added that sports uniforms have changed to suit our fantasies. She notes the latest sexy football uniforms with mesh midriffs, and stretch breeches that show off the derrières of magnificent athletes sporting long dreads sticking out of the back of their helmets like plumed knights from the Middle Ages. "And just look at the dramatic changes in Olympic swimsuits."[6] The ritualistic practices of athletic events, complete with costumed attire to identify its participants as part of something larger than themselves, underscore a particularly unique—and popular—contemporary masquerade ceremony. Indeed, the various college football "bowl games" such as the Orange Bowl, Cotton Bowl, Sugar Bowl, and Rose Bowl suggest festivities that celebrate fecundity, rejuvenation, and wealth.

Furthermore, the visual outrageousness of masquerade and its contrasting seductive and potentially terrifying beauty can allow masquerade to safely address controversial topics with anonymity. And masquerade and masking have the power, in part, to control human behavior. We see universal examples of masquerade functioning like this in all cultures. Cheryle Shearer describes the Northwest Peoples' female monster Dzunukwa as a hairy, beastlike, powerful female who will eat children in the forest if they wander too far from home. Dzunukwa's mask has large eyes and an open mouth that makes eerie sounds like the wind.[7] Robert Nicholls lists several West African communities in Liberia, Ivory Coast, and Nigeria, where masquerading "patrols" in numerous ethnic groups serve in various controlling capacities as adjudicators, guards, vigilantes, and executioners.[8] The United States saw its own form of masked vigilantes with the Ku Klux Klan.

Terry Castle explores qualities of masquerade found in 18th-century English culture and literature in her seminal book *Masquerade and Civilization* (1986). While she acknowledges the uniqueness of 18th-century English masquerade (and indeed many cultures have spawned unique masquerade looks and traditions), she suggests reasons for its development by tracing its exaggerated effects back to the Roman saturnalia celebrations which evolved into the medieval Feast of Fools events, which, in turn evolved into the elite Renaissance banquet masquerades culminating with the lush Elizabethan and Baroque staged masques.[9]

Yet one of the triumphs of successful masquerade (as with art in general) is its power to simultaneously project distinctive as well as universal messages. Castle acknowledges this universal characteristic of masquerade, rationalizing that "costumes carry conventional meanings" and that "clothing opens itself everywhere to interpretation by others, in accordance with prevailing systems of sartorial inscription."[10]

Castle also notes the "uncanniness of the masquerade, its sheer, estranging power," describing some versions of masquerade as "inevitably freighted with disturbing symbolic potential" and full of "the possibility of astonishing transfigurations, and a world perennially open to reconstitution." For example, clowns possess both humorous and terrifying connotations. The James Bond sequel *Live and Let Die* (1973) shows clown heads on sticks that guard Mr. Big's sanctuary on the Caribbean island of San Monique. Later in this film Geoffrey Holder portrays Baron Samedi, a voodoo impresario whose make-up suggests powerful and magical black/white imagery of good and evil. James Bond (played by Roger Moore) overcomes Samedi while Samedi leads the islanders in a sacrificial ceremony designed for Bond's cohort. As Bond usurps Samedi by throwing him into a coffin filled with snakes, Samedi's voodoo make-up mask and the menacing clown heads on sticks lose their power to threaten.

While we might assume that contemporary masquerade ceremonies no longer accompany variations on archetypal rites-of-passage, we need only recall elaborate weddings held all over the world. The bride typically masquerades in a white gown and veil, projecting the ultimate symbol of womanhood, while also communicating her own values, personality, and good taste. Similarly, Ann Anderson's book, *High School Prom*, describes in detail another pinnacle masquerade event for most American teenagers who experience prom as a democratic rite of passage into adulthood.

Masquerade costumes found in all cultures satisfy a basic human need to create character with clothing. The mask and masquerade assign meaning and a categorical place in a universe that does not offer labels. Consequently masquerade is always reconstituting itself. While the cognitive side of our brain does not recognize essential hidden truths in the universe, the art of masquerade invariably provokes opportunities for reflecting on our world—outside of its own sphere—as well as within it. Ultimately the universal agency of masquerade has the immense potential to invent and constantly re-invent the essential fabric of culture. Whether masquerade functions to create a sense of renewal, address controversial topics with anonymity, control human behavior, acknowledge and celebrate human rites-of-passage, or simply to reflect on the human experience, we all regularly—and increasingly—experience masquerade's power and variations.

## Masquerade's Evolving Forms

The condensed and exaggerated components of masquerade allow it to suggest more profound, multi-faceted complexities. Often masquerade includes iconic references and implies layers of information and contexts. However when does a costume (and mask) appear more as "spectacle" rather than essentially as an expression of a character? Consider Julie Taymor's Broadway musical *The Lion King*. The show's famous opening pageantry certainly has the look and feel of masquerade spectacle as humans manipulate dozens of puppets to project African wildlife. But in this same production, similar human-operated puppets conjure the meerkat Timon and the warthog Pumbaa, and these staged creations seem less like spectacle and more like characters. As characters they magically blend the mechanics of puppetry with human gestures and voices. Are the humans masquerading as puppets or are the puppets masquerading as humans? By the time we see the masked performers playing Scar and Mufasa, we are artfully prepared to easily accept them as specific characters, rather than as puppets or spectacular moving scenery.

Masquerade has shifted into new forms of "performance art," digitalized film characters, and video games shared by multiple players on the Internet, initiating new ways for us to consider how masquerade currently functions. Consider the Daft Punk musical duo; well-known for the elaborate robot costumes they wear during performances but also while promoting themselves in public. Their masquerade markets them as effectively as Liberace's elaborate theatrical get-ups effectively marketed him decades ago. While these theatrical effects create immediate associations as branding suitable for additional revenue in video games and social media, the costumes pose questions as to how they appear as pure spectacle beyond character connotations.

Masquerade "performances" also continue to evolve into more popular looks with increasingly sophisticated Halloween celebrations, community/tourist-driven carnivals, Renaissance Fairs, and historical reenactments. A huge number of Steam Punk and Cosplay enthusiasts dress up and interact as their favorite cartoon characters at Comic-Con conventions as an annual point of destination for entire families. For decades people in English-speaking countries have ritualistically dressed up as characters from *The Rocky Horror Picture Show* at midnight screenings of that movie. In July 2012 a demented killer masquerading as the Joker massacred people at a midnight screening of *The Dark Knight Returns*, many of whom were masquerading as their favorite Batman characters.

Castle writes that from the 18th century onward, images of the Christian-inspired carnival have especially influenced western civilization's perception of masquerade. Medieval Christian-inspired carnival characters such as the devil, Judas, the Virgin, and angels have continued by way of multiple versions in various carnivals worldwide, particularly where Catholicism has dominated. Conversely, Nicholls describes how Islam and Christianity have "generally discouraged [African] traditional masquerading in its various forms and often actively eradicated it." He notes that "it is a testament to the resilience of masquerades and the need for masquerading in human lives" that some African masquerades have been revived and continue to evolve. He also notes the influence of many African masquerades that have been resurrected or blended with contemporary commercial carnival masquerade traditions—particularly in the Caribbean.[11]

Yet masquerade beyond that found at carnival events can morph in new commercial ways as well. Indeed, Vassilis Zidianakis states that much of current fashion's marketing "actually includes masquerading elements of carnival, particularly in its current obsession with grotesque forms of body and clothing."[12] For example, fashion designer Alexander McQueen designed a stunning jacket with brown pony skin and antelope horns that appeared in the Metropolitan Museum of Art's 2010 "Savage Beauty" exhibition. His Jellifish armadillo boot, which appeared as part of a "masquerading" mannequin figure suggested global (if not universal) assumptions of womanhood, transforming the figure as hunted victim. It also set a new standard for shocking, unnatural footwear.

## *The Convergence of Historic Non-Western and Contemporary Masquerade*

While all of the essays in this book examine and comment on masquerade's evolving forms, Section I focuses specifically on ways in which traditional masquerade continues to evolve and merge with other forms as our world becomes smaller. Historic versions of masquerade have frequently collided with each other even as they have drawn upon and shaped popular taste. Some of the contributors in this section focus on how traditional masquerades have evolved as they align with new contexts. Traditional masquerades have undergone tremendous change, particularly in the last two centuries as they have confronted dramatic global influences and the consequential collision of cultures. Other contributors in this section examine ways in which traditional masquerade—particularly non-western versions of masquerade—have either served in distinctive ways to maintain cultural memory or have significantly evolved due to outside influences beyond their control.

John Wallace Nunley examines the violent experiences of African slaves who responded by assimilating their traditional masquerade forms with New World iconography. New World masquerades recall conditions of slavery even now. He then describes in detail Trinidadian Peter Minshall's profound legacy in carnival masquerade within his home country as well as beyond. Costume designers Loyce L. Arthur and Laura Crow discuss the evolution of contemporary masquerade traditions in Trinidad and Tobago as well as Cuba and the Philippines, often resulting from a wide range of external influences and cultural clashes. Anthropologist and African historian Peter Probst reflects on the *Nyau* images experienced by Chewa contemporary community celebrations in Malawi. Marta Turok highlights imagery found in contemporary Mexican community masquerade and suggests inherent syncretic ritual art motivations that are quickly disappearing as more of its younger citizens leave the smaller villages.

## Public Masquerade Mirroring Communities in Transition

The quest for illusionary transformation remains at the heart of masquerade whatever its guise or venue. Twentieth-century developments in film and television ushered in new realms of spectacle that dwarfed the achievements of the "local" court masque, even as they became more accessible to the public in the form of Busby Berkeley movie spectacles, televised beauty pageants, and rock concerts held in immense stadiums.

Some local community events have become quite massive in scope—especially with the aid of television and we find it difficult to pronounce them either local or global. The 2012 London Olympics opening ceremony exemplifies just how far masquerade has evolved from the elaborate—though quite local—Renaissance/Jacobean court masques which served as exclusive, private showings for the elite. These court masques enjoyed a propensity to display the masquerade monarch (or host) who often appeared as a god or goddess. In contrast, a worldwide television audience viewed the Olympics spectacle. The 2012 Olympic festivities lavishly showcased Great Britain (rather than focusing on honoring and flattering Queen Elizabeth) as a supremely confident nation with a great, distinctive legacy. True, Queen Elizabeth II was in attendance, and a masquerading version of the queen parachuted from a helicopter. But unlike the court masques, which focused almost entirely on elite figures in order to generate political discourse, Britain's floating Mary Poppins figures, winged bicyclists, giant bobbing masked David Bowies, and dancing nurses and jumping children in rainbow colors all showcased a country pleased with its place in the advancement of literature, culture, the arts, and even health care. During these festivities the country could escape its current bad economic climate and bask ritualistically in its former glorious achievements.

The masquerades and masques of 400 years ago invariably utilized allegorical, legendary, and mythic figures. Indeed, masquerading versions of Shakespeare's mythic goddesses can still accompany Prospero's masque in a production of *The Tempest* in order to celebrate the nuptials of his daughter and his enemy's son. And we can occasionally see examples of greatness in masquerade, such as when voluptuous winged angels traverse the contemporary runway, promoting Victoria's Secret lingerie—or when Hollywood celebrities at red carpet events masquerade in *haute couture* gowns and fine jewels as a way of conjuring the illusion of contemporary divine status.

But most of today's popular masquerade celebrations, unlike those of 400 years ago, idealize (or satirize) humans in glorious attire at carnival events or costume masquerade conventions. And this "democratization" of masquerade now encourages each of us to imagine ourselves as heroes, artists, and magicians rather than as gods or angels. Current masquerades, whether local or global, more often champion the heroic qualities of down-to-earth fictional characters like Harry Potter. Mattel's eternally youthful, ever-fashionable Barbie still "masquerades" as the ideal American young woman six decades later (or is the masquerade actually vice versa?).

Moreover, James Wolcott in a 2014 *Vanity Fair* issue ponders our obsession with horror these days, noting our preferences for zombies and vampires—which fall under the democratic category of "everyday" characters rather than elite figures. He adds that:

> Halloween, once mostly a kiddie-costume outing for candy and pranks, has grown into the premier American pagan holiday, an ever mushrooming merchandising bonanza (an estimated $7 billion in sales for 2013) that mirrors how the country has gone completely horror-mad. And not just this country. According to *The New York Times*, Britain has let the Guy Fawkes mask slip in favor of Halloween full-body leotards, because, as we all know, Brits are weird.[13]

First in this section, examining current spin-offs of other local (though obviously urban) community masquerades, British costume designer Hilary Baxter focuses on how London Gay Pride parade figures have morphed from the exotic into versions masquerading more as status quo—reflecting the preference of today's gays to blend into society at-large rather than to stand out as flamboyant. Recent Gay Pride parades have included legions of uniformed male and female police officers, reminding audiences that gays play traditional, respected roles in society.

Kara McLeod, who has worked for three decades in both professional theater and the Halloween industry, then describes contemporary popular Halloween trends that continue to adapt familiar archetypal (and democratic) characters into new forms—and has her own musings on why we still favor zombies as a means of popular community masquerade.

Finally in this section I suggest masquerade motivations behind Dragon Con in Atlanta, Georgia, one of many costume masquerade conventions in a multi-billion industry. Dragon Con's official web site describes itself as "the largest multi-media, popular culture convention focusing on science fiction and fantasy, gaming, comics, literature, art, music, and film in the universe!" While it is ostensibly local (no other center of this industry shares the Dragon Con name and it specifically takes place in Atlanta) it embraces universal themes, covering 37 fan tracks ranging from Tolkien's Middle-earth to Sci-Fi Literature to the Silk Road Cinema and Culture which offer tremendous costume opportunities. This regional masquerade convention vividly illustrates the global influences of masquerade on local popular culture.

## Performance Masquerade as Social and Political Commentary

Masquerade, particularly masquerade when used in performance, continues to present vivid political and social commentary. We see masquerade in a range of performance settings with adventure and fantasy films producing a myriad of masquerading characters. Theatre and opera also continue to support prime examples of provocative masquerade as social and political commentary, some of which I randomly highlight below.

Consider how Broadway flipped cultural contexts when Trinidadian Tony Award winner Geoffrey Holder turned Frank Baum's masquerading fantasy characters (in Dorothy's dream) from rural Kansas in *The Wizard of Oz* (1939) into bold urban African-American renderings in *The Wiz* (1975). Another great performance masquerade took place in London's West End and Broadway with *One Man, Two Guvnors* (2011 and 2012), based on Goldoni's 18th-century *A Servant of Two Masters*. It had James Corden's Arlecchino-inspired Francis Henshall masquerading as two lower-class servants at once, sporting a diamond checkered tie and mixed plaid suiting. This playful romp dramatized age-old distinctions between upper crust societies and the working class. Stephen Sondheim's *Follies* (1971), recently resurrected on Broadway, used thrilling masquerade spectacle as evocative pageantry to present showgirls poignantly recalling their lost youth. Andrew Lloyd Webber's *The Phantom of the Opera* (1986) devotes an entire musical number to masquerade, and populates the stage with a chorus supporting additional puppet figures in an exotic masked ball for upper crust society. Broadway's rock musical *Spider-Man: Turn OFF the Dark* (2011) showcased the masquerading prowess of not only Spider-Man and the Green Goblin, but also the Green Goblin's former employees whom he compels to morph into more masquerading villains. The production also featured the ancient Greek weaver, Arachne, whom the vengeful goddess, Athena, "transformed" into an industrious spider, compelled to weave the fate of the universe while "masquerading" in this arduous condition for eternity.

Gender masquerade in performance has long communicated subtle as well as overt social connotations for its audiences. In ancient Greek and Renaissance English drama men performed the female roles. Male actors still perform the female roles in the *Gèlèdé* celebrations in West Africa, as well as in Japanese *kabuki* and Indian *kathakali* performances. The play (1988) and then film, *M. Butterfly* (1993) features a male Peking Opera singer whose various female impersonations are so convincing that a French diplomat believes he is a woman.

Less frequently, women have masqueraded as men on-stage, but Shakespeare's *As You Like It* and *Twelfth Night* exemplify popular productions where the leading male roles are played by women who masquerade as men. Recall Sarah Bernhardt's famous performance as Hamlet, as well as several female characters masquerading as men in Caryl Churchill's *Cloud Nine* (1979) and *Top Girls* (1982). Furthermore, the 18th-century's *castrati* (castrated male singers introduced in Italy) led to the emergence of women singing male roles. For example, the part of Romeo in Bellini's *I Capuleti e I Montecchi* (1830) is written for a mezzo-soprano. As heroic tenors began to dominate (Donizetti), trouser roles sung by women remained a standard way of maintaining high-pitched "male" voices. Heather Hedlock cites an opera critic in 1833: "We always see the woman who dresses as a man on stage ... as a female in male garb, as if for a joke on a masquerade. Never does she take on the character and the appearance [of a man].... How shall we ever deceive ourselves, seeing a Conquistador, a fearsome warrior, being represented by these figures through the whole performance?"[14] More recently, countertenors—male singers who sing in a soprano voice—have emerged for revivals of Baroque opera. Still, except for trouser roles in opera, audiences are much more likely to see males performing female on-stage rather than vice versa. Regardless, opera has long favored many types of masquerade. Traditional operatic works such as *A Masked Ball, La Cenerentola*, and *Die Fledermaus*, for instance, depend on masquerade to further the plot.

Section III of *Masquerade* devotes special attention to examples of masquerade appearing within the traditional performance formats of theatre, opera, music performance concerts, and film. Literary scholar and editor Richard Fallis describes in detail how three aspects of the irrational and exotic aspects of traditional Carnival—masks, gender bending, and masquerade—have influenced and helped shape operas in the standard repertory, perpetuating opera's power and persistence through four centuries. American studies scholar Vincent Stephens reflects on the continued practice of open secrecy by queer male musicians such as Adam Lambert, Lance Bass, and Clay Aiken as an artistic and commercial strategy. Theatre historian Mary Robinson traces the evolving masquerade of women's suffrage/liberation and political protest with such masquerading feminist groups as the Guerrilla Girls and Pussy Riot. Scenographer Derrick Vanmeter comments on new contexts for Great Britain's Guy Fawkes mask, considered a symbol of the Occupy Wall Street movement in 2011. This mask, popularized by the graphic novel and film *V for Vendetta,* originally symbolized violent rebellion against corrupt authority. The 99 percent movement became a vividly dramatic anonymous public army of masqueraders united against a common enemy.

## *Visual Art's Influence on Masquerade: Graphic and Performance Art, Branding, Photography and Comic Books*

The essays in this section add to the recent work of two richly illustrated books published in Germany which point toward new ways of seeing clothes as art objects. These books present figures in masquerade juxtaposed in a range of unorthodox performance venues. Vassilis Zidianakis' *Not a Toy, Fashioning Radical Characters* (2011) identifies and describes "parading characters" in contemporary society. He presents clothing examples taken from everyday society, but more often displays examples of clothing worn out of context (beyond their intended use) that suggest magnified implications when self-consciously exhibited by both humans and human models. *Doppelganger: Images of the Human Being* (2011) also showcases clothing taken out of traditional function, while emphasizing the artists who wear them as intentional masqueraders.

The artist Yinka Shonibare has created and exhibited headless life-size mannequins in frozen movement, inspired by such paintings as those by Jean-Honoré Fragonard (1732–1806) who illustrates 18th-century European aristocratic characters in frivolous play, oblivious to their reliance on the lower class and slaves for their creature comforts and luxurious fashion statements. Shonibare intentionally leaves off the heads of his masquerading figures as a way of removing "direct connotations of race." He further complicates cultural connotations by combining Dutch wax fabric in bold West African-esque prints and patterns with 18th- and 19th-century European-style fashion. The vibrant, elaborate, highly detailed clothing ironically masks and transforms the sinister side of Europeans (played by these headless mannequins) in leisure pursuits as they dominated world trade and took a disproportionate share of the wealth.[15] Furthermore, Shonibare's artistic signature consistently lies in his sense of bold theatricality, as he uses masquerading elements and masked characters in his photographs, installations, paintings, and film. Robert Hobbs refers to Shonibare's use of African-print cloth as an "updating of the Yoruba *Egungun* masquerades" which utilized layers of cloth to mask all elements of the human body as a means of transforming the body into a spirit.[16]

Dancer and textile artist Nick Cave also references *Egungun* masquerade with his vibrant, dynamic masquerading human forms and accompanying gigantic abstract heads that appear frozen in space. *Egungun* masquerade is a part of Yoruba ritual whereby an elder transforms himself as the spirit of a recently deceased person, using a mask and costume to hide his entire body. Nick Cave's completely covered figures are positioned and appear ready to move, converse, guide, provoke, and dominate. Cave creates these "transformative creatures" by organizing found objects as decorative costume over human-shaped mannequins in rhythmic assemblages. The resulting forms suggest otherworldly spiritual beings that masquerade as humans in an *Egungun* style and this resulting sculptural look in human form blends a poignant combination of Yoruba iconic references with western masquerade sensibilities.

Celebrities have long appreciated the importance of masquerade. Perhaps no celebrity has mutated as much as David Bowie, whom *The New York Times* described as "a man who throughout his career has relentlessly reinvented his persona and his music with astonishing rapidity and unpredictability" and "has both absorbed and anticipated the social and cultural currents of his time."[17] Ian Buruma adds,

> From his red-haired, outlandishly costumed, sexually ambiguous incarnation of glam-rock in his 1972 breakthrough album, *The Rise and Fall of Ziggy Stardust and the Spiders from Mars*; to the Weimar cabaret–influenced persona of the Thin White Duke in 1975; to the surrealist Pierrot figure of the 1980 *Ashes to Ashes*; to the Union Jack-coated master (or is he?)—of all he surveys on the 1997 *Earthling* album, Mr. Bowie has remained eternally mutable and essentially unknowable. Because he never throws anything away and has organized all of his various masquerading costumes throughout his career, the Victoria and Albert Museum exhibited an impressive range of his costumes—along with videos of his shows in 2013.[18]

In preparation for the exhibition, Camille Paglia contributed an essay in the exhibition catalogue which identified him as "a product of Surrealism, of Dada, of the Modernist arts" and "he is body-based, always completely in the role he is playing. His tremendous physical virtuosity, his understanding of costume and how it is an imaginative projection of your body, is part of the biggest thing about him: he is so deeply emotional."[19]

In this section costume designers Marianne Custer and Johann Stegmeir explore new forms of "brand" celebrity masquerade created by stars like Madonna, Beyoncé, and Lady Gaga. These contemporary performance artists enjoy wide audience appeal in their own versions of "voguing," which flamboyant masquerading New York gay transvestites and cross-dressers developed during the late '60s and early '70s (as depicted in the film *Paris Is Burning*).

Fashion magazine photography has also influenced new versions of masquerade—particularly in the range of performance art and its accompanying digital photographic images, which continue to embody the aesthetically beautiful, exotic, bizarre, or grand ways of cultivating, praising, and maintaining our cultural values and fashion trends. Fashion designers including Leigh Bowery, Vivienne Westwood, Jean Paul Gaultier, Karl Lagerfeld, and Alexander McQueen, inspired by dramatic photographic imagery, have moved this "frozen photography" into the realm of theatrical fashion masquerade events that are experienced as performance art—thus creating the "new normal" in the marketing of fashion. John Galliano became well known for his own masquerading bows immediately following his fashion runway shows during his tenure with the House of Dior. By comparing and contrasting highlights of the work of Alexander McQueen and John Galliano, I look at how these giants in the fashion industry have used narrative to influence the effects of masquerade in their fashion shows and in their curtain calls. Both designers illustrate the paradoxical pleasures, transformational power, and attendant dangers of masquerade.

Art historian M. Kathryn Shields examines the significance of "masking" as seen in several generations of feminist photographers starting with Diane Arbus. Recent photographers, no doubt influenced by Arbus' seminal work, have explored film and video masquerading imagery, building on and reconfiguring ancient stories of struggle, rites-of-passage, and good vs. evil in ways that are accessible and compelling for a general audience.

Popular versions of social masquerade such as those seen in Cosplay, Anime video games, or cartoon shows such as *My Little Pony, Rainbow Bright* and *Sailor Moon* are often nowadays inspired by characters coming from comic books. Scenographer Ron Naversen explores one of the comics industry's earliest American masquerading heroes—Superman—and his meteoric rise to fame as a film character. Other heroic and villainous comic book characters regularly masquerade as other personae. Naversen looks at the evolutionary tendencies and motivations for such masquerades by taking a closer look at the cultural background supporting this masquerade phenomenon.

## The Universality of Digital Masquerade for a Global Audience

The inherent global outreach of digital masquerade in the form of animated adventure, folkloric, and sci-fi films suggests that we are on a collision course in confronting competing cultural values, as will be discussed in this section. The fantasy world of digital masquerade illustrates this collision while assimilating divergent cultural themes astonishing ferocity. Some of these divergent cultural values and stories obviously come from century-old sacred traditions.

Even well-intentioned film artists can find the assimilation of time-honored sacred traditions tension-fraught, as, for example, Disney's Pixar Animation Studios discovered when they wanted to secure naming rights for merchandise to create an animated movie inspired by Mexico's traditional "Day of the Dead" holiday celebration. The corporation withdrew a trademark request to the U.S. Patent and Trademark Office after a tremendous onslaught of public criticism and petitions.[20] Conversely, commercial interests are invariably part of any traditional holiday celebration—and can ultimately help to maintain the tradition, long after the sacred motivations behind the holiday have diminished.

But this case exemplifies the potential dangers when commercial interests assume that traditional sacred cultural values can be formulated, "branded," and sold without duly acknowledging the community in which the celebration originated. The encroaching dominance of global commercial tourism has consistently accompanied carnival communities in South America, the Caribbean, Mexico, and New Orleans for decades. Now the global quest to film community masquerade and its attendant traditions out of context (either as documentaries, narratives, or animated effort) becomes a double-edged sword, as commercial interests must balance pecuniary interests with respect for a local community's spirit and spontaneity. Granted, versions of digital masquerade for a global audience can dramatically enhance and enlarge local community masquerade events with the aid of photography, film, and social media. Digital masquerade is at an artistic frontier, poised to encourage new masquerade inventions—at virtual levels—but it also threatens to dilute the profound wonders of traditional indigenous masquerade.

Certainly graphic animators for film have their own exotic spin on all things fantastical and indeed, as illustrators, they easily push the boundaries far beyond what any of us might consider "local masquerade." Innovations in digital animated graphics have dramatically influenced the cinema's bottom line, and increasingly, graphic-inspired fantastic and grotesque characters from comic books found in film have also appeared in theatrical events (such as *Spider-Man* and *Shrek* on Broadway) and included in marketing strategies. Art historian Heather L. Holian looks at how graphic character animation for film can be considered a new form of masquerade, where the graphic animator himself simultaneously serves as both illustrator and as "masked/costumed" performer with the aid of voiceovers. She analyzes some of the artistic implications of these "masked" animators in her interviews with several artists at Pixar. She details how this role as "masked" animator influences and challenges the practitioner, who simultaneously serves as both the illustrator/creator of the character—and as the virtual performer of the character on screen as well.

Rock bands have long used masquerade as a dramatic cornerstone of their performance and personae. Many musicians have experienced the benefits of generating interest in their work via performance music videos, often with enhanced YouTube marketing effects during the past decade. But musicians and celebrities are not the only ones using YouTube for masquerade effects. Ted Gournelos, a scholar of media and oppositional culture, identifies postfeminist comedian and satirist Jenna Marbles as a provocative example of digital gender masquerade. The Jenna Marbles "brand" has influenced legions of the younger generation.

Finally, social media and the Internet have inspired non-performers to get into the masquerade act. Cosplay participation and self-presentations function as contemporary "performance" masquerade because people create their own personae and narratives or carefully edit their work to project favorable aspects of their personae and activities for their "friends" to view. The Cosplay website states, "Cosplay is an art form where the subject attempts to take on the characteristics and mannerisms of a chosen character. Most often this in the form of comic book characters but can range to film/television or video game characters." Costume designer Laura Crow focuses on the dramatic, contemporary character evolution found in this recent form of social masquerade.

In summary, we experience masquerade everywhere in our daily lives—on our television, film, and computer screens; in our theatres, museums, and sports arenas; in our popular magazines; and in a range of frequent community celebrations, reenactments, and masquerade conventions.

*Vanity Fair*'s August 2013 issue showcases nearly a dozen pages of women masquerading in carnival-styled make-up in celebration of Maybelline's make-up sponsorship of the "Mercedes-Benz Fashion Week." In the same issue, a multi-page spread of Tommy Hilfiger models masquerade tongue-in-cheek in fashion attire as archetypal personae identified by names listed above their heads: "The Lucky Break Marlon" (with crutches), "The Field Tripper Julia," "The Professional Student Arthur," "The Social Chair Mrs. H.," along with others. Trudeau in *Doonesbury* finds cause to spoof the outrageousness of any Comic-Con, Anime, sci-fi costume masquerade convention seen in cities the world over—suggesting that even as the masqueraders at these events appear ever more bizarre, the more they all appear essentially the same.[21] True, masquerade will always seem familiar somehow—even as its look is always different.

Masquerade generally demands a certain commercial element for its success—partly because it invariably requires us somehow to go beyond our natural physical selves in order to transform ourselves. But masquerade inherently holds great potential as "big theatre," "big ritual," "big religion," and ultimately "big business" because everyone recognizes the intense value of transcending our limited human condition into something grander or more beautiful, powerful, and humorous, or into something more threatening. Masquerade allows both the masquerader and its witness to feel more inclusive, more aware, and more special as it is shared and savored. We live vicariously, and even transcend death, as we experience the art of masquerade—if only for a moment.

# Notes

1. John Nunley and Cara McCarty (1999), *Masks: Faces of Culture* (New York: Harry N. Abrams), 15, 17.
2. Ibid.,15.
3. John Nunley, correspondence with the author, 16 January 2013.
4. Vassilis Zidianakis (2011), *Not a Toy: Fashioning Radical Characters* (Berlin: Pictoplasma Publishing), 19.
5. Nunley and McCarty (1999), 128.
6. Laura Crow, interview with the author, 7 January 2013.
7. Cheryl Shearer (2000), Understanding Northwest Coast Art: A Guide to Crests, Beings, and Symbols (Vancouver: Douglas and McIntyre Ltd.), 41.
8. Robert Nicholls (2012), The Jumbies' Playing Ground: Old World Influences on Afro-Creole Masquerades in the Eastern Caribbean (Jackson: University Press of Mississippi), 165–7.
9. Terry Castle (1986) Masquerade and Civilization: The Carnivalesque in Eighteenth-century English Culture and Fiction (Stanford, CA: Stanford University Press), 11.
10. Ibid., 55.
11. Nicholls (2012), 231–9.
12. Zidianakis (2011), 34.
13. James Wolcott (2014), "The Collective American Scream," *Vanity Fair,* January (N. 641): 42.
14. Heather Hedlock (2001), "On the Cusp between the Past and the Future: The Mezzo-Soprano Romeo of Bellini's *I Capuleti,*" *Opera Quarterly* 17/3: 400.
15. Rachel Kent, curator (2009), *Yinka Shonibare MBE* (Sydney: Museum of Contemporary Art), 13.
16. Ibid., 34.
17. Ian Buruma (2013), "Ch-Changes of Bowie, Mutating Rock Star," *The New York Times,* 23 March: C2.
18. Ibid.
19. Ibid.
20. Associated Press (2013), "Public Criticism Makes Disney Drop Trademark Request," *Greensboro News & Record,* 9 May: A12.
21. G. B. Trudeau (2013), *Doonesbury,* in *Greensboro News & Record* Comics Section, 15 September.

# Works Cited

Associated Press. (2013.) "Public Criticism Makes Disney Drop Trademark Request." *Greensboro News & Record,* 9 May.
Buruma, Ian. (2013.) "Ch-Changes of Bowie, Mutating Rock Star." *The New York Times,* 23 March.
Castle, Terry. (1986.) *Masquerade and Civilization: The Carnivalesque in Eighteenth-century English Culture and Fiction.* Stanford, CA: Stanford University Press.

Crow, Laura. Interview with the author, 7 January 2013.

Hedlock, Heather. (2001.) "On the Cusp between the Past and the Future: The Mezzo-Soprano Romeo of Bellini's *I Capuleti.*" *Opera Quarterly* 17/3.

Kent, Rachel, curator. (2009.) *Yinka Shonibare MBE.* Sydney: Museum of Contemporary Art.

Nicholls, Robert. (2012.) *The Jumbies' Playing Ground: Old World Influences on Afro-Creole Masquerades in the Eastern Caribbean.* Jackson: University Press of Mississippi.

Nunley, John. Correspondence with the author, 16 January 2013.

Nunley, John, and Cara McCarty. (1999.) *Masks: Faces of Culture.* New York: Harry N. Abrams.

Shearer, Cheryl. (2000.) *Understanding Northwest Coast Art: A Guide to Crests, Beings, and Symbols.* Vancouver: Douglas and McIntyre.

Wolcott, James. (2014.) "The Collective American Scream." *Vanity Fair,* January.

Zidianakis, Vassilis. (2011.) *Not a Toy: Fashioning Radical Characters.* Berlin: Pictoplasma Publishing.

# Section I

---

## The Convergence of Historic Non-Western and Contemporary Masquerade

# Slavery, Violence and Power in African Masquerades

## JOHN WALLACE NUNLEY

Mask performance documents an extraordinary social history of humans, one which developed as a result of a meeting of Amerindian societies of the New World and the experiments in social living created by players and actors from the Old World. While the social life of New World peoples was greatly disturbed by this meeting, another important merging began in the new country taking place among European, African and Asian peoples and it continues to this day. In this respect, this author considers the Indian Ocean trade as an extension of the Atlantic which after Arab-Islamic control was monopolized by European powers. The meeting of Europeans and Africans was largely responsible for the creation of a new economic engine which served as the foundation for the birth of global capitalism. That engine provided the means by which European entrepreneurs leveraged their economic systems, moving from the mercantile format to that of full-blown capitalism.

This engine was the plantation system of the West Indies and South America and its prototype in the Mediterranean and North Africa. As has been said "Man cannot live by bread alone" and so a Creole cultural foundation centering on music, lyrics, dance, festival dress and food, denoting cultural exchange, competition and innovation among strangers, happened. The heroic efforts of these wandering players created meeting places redolent with performance media which in turn, helped to construct new social and individual identities. The new cultural crucible expressed in masking and performance, and literally born of blood, sweat and tears, cradled the new social experiment and its economic alter-ego. Today these playing grounds, descended from Old World practices, thrive, fueled by global tourism.

I have acted upon these new playing grounds starting with my work in Northern Ghana, Sierra Leone and later the Caribbean. Caught up in the heat of 1984's Trinidad and Tobago Carnival, I had my first meeting with *mas* (a Trinidadian term for Carnival bands), through Steven Derrick who had launched a band entitled Clash of Cultures. The name concisely sums up the modus operandi that has given shape to this chapter. I had entered the playing grounds of a major West Indian metropolis. With the heat of the steel band, Soca music, and festival foods from all over the world, Derrick has explored the *mas*, its music and the remaining panoply of the performing arts. This band leader played himself, his heritage, wrapped in a carnival band tapestry of exploration, world cultures, and wonder which came from the global mix that had been cooking forever.

A few years later, I was following a Peter Minshall-band entitled *Jumbies* and as the band made its final lap from the Queens Park Savannah, that beautiful city park where once existed a sugar plantation, the Soca road march *Wet me Down* played on. A dear friend of mine was wining (dancing) in a seething hip rotation, as was the whole city. We were cooling from *Feelin' Hot, Hot, Hot* from the day as well as from the hot plantation days of the earlier settlers. In that same place, today cricket and horse races are held and relaxing Sunday walks are enjoyed by many. Two hundred years before, on these grounds, the original plantation slaves cut cane in extremely hot weather in the claustrophobic spaces composed of the surrounding cane. At the estate factory slaves in the hot, hot boiler rooms produced crystal sugar, molasses and rum. In order that these human combustion engines of the field and factory worked well into the night and the next day, they were wetted down with buckets of water for they too were feeling hot, hot, hot. This cooling technique reduced entropy and thereby extended the life of those human engines.

Meantime at our carnival we were being cooled and healed by performance and masquerade. Raoul Patin, my old friend and editor of the *Express Newspaper*, explained: "I did not play *mas* last year, and for the rest of that year my health faded." At this time, 1987, the *jumbies* and the spirits of Peter Minshall's band restored Pantin for yet another annual cycle of birth, death and rebirth. Unknown to all of us, Raoul would require further cooling and restoration: four years later the newspaper reporter and editor was held hostage by a Muslim faction, the Muslimeen, which staged a violent coup that took the parliament and Trinidad and Tobago Television. As Raoul later expressed, "It was a Muslim *mas*!"

But why were we all together in that time and space playing *mas*?

## Migration! Man, Migration!

In this essay we look at both sides of the Atlantic to see how mask and performance have been used by the African side that is the *supply* side of slavery and on the western shores of the Western Hemisphere, the *demand* side. Both sides have used performances to deal with slavery and later to recall discursively memories of what had happened including the incredible violence. Today on both sides mask performances reenact those days as well as the consequences of the trade.

## The African Side of the Slave Trade: Memory and Compression

The forced migrations of African captives across the Sahara north and to the coast and across the Atlantic to the plantation estates profoundly shaped human experience and the formation of the playing grounds. Africans by the millions as kidnapped victims, captives and those convicted of witchcraft, debtors and those unfortunate to cross the paths of slavers, or slavers on which the tables were turned, experienced the Middle Passage.

Derrick's band members were indeed the distant sons and daughters of those unfortunate ones who happened to encounter hungry slavers. These ancestors or human engines were shackled in cockles, tied to ropes and walked on land over the desert or toward the African coast. Often they were transported by canoes. Occasionally, some individuals were sold at local markets along the way, thus splitting families and mixing ethnicities as other newly acquired slaves were added at these markets. Continuing on foot or boat in herd-like formation, captives felt a great sense of compression which was exacerbated by the nearby dangers posed by leopards, snakes and human predators in the forest, or crocodiles and hippopotami along the rivers and various deltas. People were pinned down and cornered by fear of death. Moreover, Africans from up the coast did not swim! Slaves rested in make-shift cages or huts called *baracoons* at night and continued the journey until reaching the mercantile trade factories on the coast. There, slaves were "stored" in underground bunkers with little or no light and just inches from one another—more compression. Under these violent and chaotic conditions the spirits were blamed or praised by both losers and winners. Spirits both were good and bad depending on whose side they were on. And those spirits could be paid off or entertained by festivals, including masks and performance. On the African continent, protection (both offensive and defensive) made life good for some and hellish for others. The spirits and their plays were instrumental in these matters. Secret associations and the mask plays that sanctioned their trading practices intimidated the general populace by their control of the spirits which reinforced the violence so required of the slave trade.

## The Journey to the Other Side

At the African coastal factories oiled slaves, made to look healthy, were lined up for inspection and sale. Those purchased were loaded onto canoes which passed over the breakers on their way to the ships. The densely packed vessels were unloaded and the slaves were carefully deposited in double level holds, each three to four feet high with no space amongst the chattels. At night spooning was the only way for a slave to stretch out. Compression again!

Fever, dysentery and respiratory disease along with madness cut into the profits of the slavers and their wealthy investors and bankers in Amsterdam, London, Lisbon, Copenhagen, and Paris. To deal with the sanity and morale of slaves, rations of tobacco and rum were occasionally served. For physical maintenance slaves were often brought on deck as well, to exercise to the sound of drums and melodeons, for example, while a threatening whip man shot licks on or near the feet of the exerciser—one did jump to avoid pain. Thus embedded memory of such horrifying calisthenics may well have inspired the Creole dances of the West Indies where high step choreographies, accompanied by whip action are widespread. Chattel was literally whipped into shape. Those Africans who survived the journey usually spent a week on board ship where they were fattened, oiled, and readied for sale in yet another compressed space.

As inhuman and incomprehensible as the business of slavery was, in the Age of Enlightenment, life was just as hard on the estates. People died quickly, the work was brutal and the conditions were just as compressed. The slave cabins were extremely small, like the baracoons and bunkers on the other side and even the hold on the supercargoes. Thus cramped the slaves preferred getting out of their claustrophobic cabins and gather on a piece of open land around which the huts were loosely organized. Most everywhere slave motion was controlled, which allowed no movement from the place of work except to and from, and allowed no visiting other estates to meet other shackled brothers and sisters.

Andrea Stuart in her brilliant book on slavery in Barbados sights French abolitionist Victor Schoelcher on his impression upon visiting the Indies,

> The whip is the soul of the colonies.... It is the clock of the plantation; it announced the moment of waking up and of going to bed, it marked the hour of work; it also marked the hour of rest ... the day of his death is the only one in which the negro is allowed to forget the wake-up call of the whip.[1]

In spite of these conditions decompression offered slaves a little hope and a means of making a life in the new country. A drawing by Richard Bridgens, entitled *The End of the Day* (1820) depicts a Trinidadian slave gang decompressing after a hard day's work cutting cane. The drawing features a metal triangle fashioned from a metal horse stirrup, a metal pot, gourd rattles, a pitchfork and a gong (agoogoo) which establishes the basic tempo of African and the African Diaspora music yet today). Thus the tempos which have driven the masquerades of Africa that promoted slavery and those mask performances that recall it on the American plantations, where the promise of liberation and recollections of slavery are rolled into one, play to each other across the Atlantic. In unison they give experience to the past and present. Yet, as William Faulkner wrote: "The past is not dead. In fact, it's not even past."[2]

## African Mask Performance and the Violence of Slavery: The Supply Side

I will briefly summarize the economics of the African trade in order to demonstrate how directly involved people were at all levels of society. The Saharan, domestic and Atlantic trade formed a dragnet in which credit and the fear of debt all backed by institutionalized violence forced all players into compromising positions. Because of the huge scale of the trade spanning the large continent few players could comprehend the economic system in its immense entirety. Thus warriors, slavers, farmers, craft groups, traders, and kingdoms, states, chiefdoms and tribes and their associates only dealt with the players from whom they received goods including chattel and those with which they traded. Within such a vast economic sea one only understood one's small role and as a result could justify one's economic practices simply as a matter of survival. In such an environment the responsibility of the players was limited to small arenas and the blame and guilt concerning the practice of violence was only seen from a very small perspective, thus limiting a sense of moral responsibility. On this smaller scale one did what one did as a matter of daily life—just getting by no matter what! Masquerades empowered the system and gave it legitimate purpose.

Given that in most African ecological zones the soils are thin, yet in endless supply, the key to capital accumulation is not land, but bodies to work it. Therefore, control of bodies, slavery, was the most valuable commodity in the exchange of goods to, from and in Africa on all fronts. African trade goods included slaves, gold, cloth, animal skins, ostrich feathers, leather, palm oil and shea butter, hard woods, pepper, bees wax, honey, kola nuts, ivory and indigo for examples. Imported goods included beads, cattle, cloth (*lamés,* tapestries velvets, silks) mirror, guns, gun powder, shot, brass, iron and copper, coral beads, cowrie shells, wine, gin, brandy, pewter wares, china, salt, horses, spices and used clothing.

Domestic slaves were crucial to the transportation system which carried the trade, especially with respect to provisions. A caravan of 10,000 camels required the feeding and caring for slave porters, armed warriors, cooks, guides, camp followers and the thousands of slaves. African domestic slaves under state and local control worked the plantations providing staple crops such as millet, sorghum, rice and yams for everyone to make the trip across the desert. On the Atlantic a supercargo could be anchored *in the road* for up to six months in order to fill the slave hold. Thus feeding the cargo off shore required slaves to produce and transport yams, beans and palm oil to feed the growing number of captives aboard and then through the Atlantic passage.

In this brief summary concerning the economic conditions of slavery we note on the African side the strong beliefs in the spirit world which were promoted by ritual practitioners whose correlations, resulting from ritual performances, marshaled those spirit forces. As a result the invisible world of spirits sanctified the visible real world and the practices of everyday life. Thus mask performance and secret societies on all political levels called on the spirits to sanctify the efforts of successful players at the expense of mass human suffering.

## The Bidjogo Peoples and Slavery

We will now focus on the Bidjogo Archipelago on the West Atlantic side of Africa and afterwards the Cross River and delta 2,000 miles to the east to enhance our discussion of slavery and the instrumentality of the masquerade in its practice.

The Bidjogo Islands are located off the coast of Guinea-Bissau. They have been inhabited by seafaring peoples for centuries. Prior to the European maritime expansion initiated by the Portuguese in the early 15th century the Arab-Islamic states from Morocco established trade centers south along the coast. These traders were most likely the first substantial contacts the Bidjogo peoples had with the Mediterranean world and by extension Europe. Because the Arab-Muslim world's commercial success depended on slave labor for industry, agriculture, warfare, and domestic labor, we can assume that the Islanders exchanged slaves, ivory, bees wax, and gold for example, for cloth, beads, metals such as brass, copper and iron, cattle, guns and gun powder and rum with the northern traders. Thus the Bidjogo cluster as we shall call this mix of peoples, was vested with a slavery-based trade economy, along with local fishing; all ran by a sailor-warrior class which raided other islanders and the mainland to sustain their economies.[3]

The Luso- occupation of the region eventually replaced that of the Arab-Islamic powers. Afterwards the inhabitants of the archipelago became involved in a much broader system of international trade. Summarizing Portuguese accounts from 1400 to 1900 CE we see that slave raiding exponentially increased as did the multiethnic Creole culture which both created and resulted from the trade. The social layers included Portuguese traders, mixed bloods of local and European descent, Sephardic Jews and other regional ethnicities such as the Baga, Lebu, Nalu, Kru, Temne, and Sherbro. Powerful land owning women such as 19th-century plantation owner Na Julia ran slave estates (Portuguese word: *pontas*) producing rice, corn, latex, palm oil, cotton and peanuts.[4]

For centuries the islanders were at the vortex of this commercial complex which, again, was based on violence. Archipelago peoples raided coastal tribes for slaves, wives and cattle. They also raided their own kind on the neighboring villages and islands, and even families and clans from the same settlement. Female diviners, working the *ira* shrines, could declare individuals to be witches and as such victims as well as their families could be sold into slavery. More effectively, raiding for captives was the quickest way to assemble chattel for the slave trade- away to make a fast buck.[5]

European travels and traders often commented on the warlike character of these islanders and their techniques of raiding. Warrior canoes with 24 oarsmen and a captain marking the working rhythm of the oarsman could quickly out run an escaping party of fishermen and other travelers and sell them into slavery. Moreover, it has been observed that war canoes often converged upon European vessels and pirate ships that were stuck on shoals or sandbanks making them easy to overtake thus, securing booty and captives.[6] Ingeniously, war canoes in concert with "native submarines" could tip a boat over and "devour" its contents. The "submarines" were made of the trunks of banana and plantain trees. The hollow trunks allowed the swimmers underneath to move the subs across the water unseen. To the intended victims what appeared to be floating logs were actually rams capable of capsizing the target. The approach of the floating trunk suddenly springing into action must have seemed like a shark attack! Shark masks are a primary subject of Bidjogo plays.

Given the pervasiveness of warfare and the introduction of firearms and mounted cannons on board the boats, the mortality rate for young men warrior-sailors must have been extremely high and socially threatening to the life span of a community. With the decline of male populations women took men's roles on the home front both ritually and economically.[7] Significantly, while the sailor-warriors were away the women remained at home. As such they were vulnerable to competing sailors and therefore had to defend themselves and their trade wealth. Thus, performance and ritual of women as well as men reflected the days of slavery then and now.

Informed by this brief narrative of this region we will now turn to Bidjogo masquerades which limn the conditions of the trade then and remembered now. Drawing on Danielu Gallois-Duquette's work, based on the collections of the National Museum of Ethnology, Lisbon we present the experience of slavery through the mask.

To meet the challenge of the survival of the Bidjogo peoples and to further the maintenance of their social-economic practices the Bidjogo incorporated age-grade initiation societies for both genders.[8] In a truly chaotic environment enculturation of the young and the adaptation of a people to market trends and the conflicts therein depended on secret societies. The men had eight age grades to move them from childhood to elder-leader status. Masquerades here have served as a key performative vehicle in the initiations that expresses the people's histories and character. Likewise, the women still have their own version of the age grade system and their performances ritually, non-discursively, limn the world of slavery, conflicts and the chaotic conditions under which human life existed.

Women's masquerades still incorporate bull headdresses and uniquely military accessories such as shields, wooden swords, lances and axes.[9] Initiates are called *defuntus*—that is, deceased male spirits of those warriors who died in the slave raiding battles before completing their initiation cycle. The dances are set in motion to the rhythm of drums played by women—so unique to the gender in Africa and indeed the rest of the world in time and space.[10] Most likely the high mortality rate of men due to trade wars necessitated that women take on male roles in domestic business and the defense of island settlements in the absence of the men. They were especially venerable to sudden attack by neighboring enemies. The colorful scarves worn by female masqueraders convey a visual memory of the slave trade in the early years as it was the Portuguese who imported Indian scarves from the sub-continent on their return from the Malaysian spice trade. Scarves of Indian manufacture and later European production have always been integral to the trade throughout West Africa. They were often included in performance masking rituals.

The primary iconographic motif of Bidjogo masquerades is the bovine creature; next in line are sea creatures, including sharks and saw fish, followed by hippopotami and other aggressive and war like animals. The bull headdress consists of a wood carving of the head with real bovine horns attached to the sides. Trade glass eyes, cord and leather complete the mask. Bull heads are also attached to the head or prow of canoes—a boat mask. The aggressive bull, a perfect symbol of power, strength and violence which characterized the islanders past no doubt was introduced by Iberian settlers who for centuries practiced various versions of bull fighting. Such a sport was descended from Roman animal fights which took place in the coliseums located in the major cities of the Roman Empire. We do know that bull fighting of the *pega* type where several men, *forcadoes,* face a charging bull, whereupon one of the men grabs the head and then altogether the team takes the bull down, was transplanted to the neighboring Canary Islands and as far away as Zanzibar on the coast of East Africa where slavery practices and the economy resembled that of the Bidjogo.[11] The highly acrobatic and out of control behavior performed by the bull masker conveys the unbridled aggressiveness of youth that had to be converted through initiation into behavior that was directed to insure successful trade and raiding for the benefit of society. Most importantly and fundamental to the economics of the Bidjogo slave trade were cows and bulls which generated future stock for trade. In turn Bidjogo men often traded cattle for females and slaves to secure the growth of their own population.[12]

One of the most dramatic Bidjogo masks is that of the Hippopotamus. Native artists capture the immense muscular power of the animal with its massively carved jaw and huge eyes—the largest in the animal kingdom. Like the hippo, Bidjogo sailors too desire to dominate the water ways and strike at will; and like the animal the islanders are very territorial and in the past killed intruders at will. The red paint applied to these masks symbolized the color that hippos turn when provoked. The coloration is caused by a chemical secretion produced by a skin gland when the animal is threatened.[13] Interestingly Hippopotami are the number one killer of humans on the African continent.

Crocodile jaws are sometimes incorporated in Bidjogo masking suits, again to symbolize the strength and cunning of Bidjogo warriors. Most common, however, are shark headdresses and wood dorsal fins that form the masker's suite. The image in motion in the male initiations unleashes a powerful memory of the slave trade. The ominous fin piercing through the water betrayed an invisible enemy—like the submarine tree trunks—which with great speed could suddenly attack. It was a common sight to see sharks trailing the supercargoes which were filled with slaves. Those captives who were sick or had died were thrown overboard and then devoured by the animals. It must be remembered that "taking a slave" in many Creole languages means to be eaten! The big men who took slaves were likened to other animals, like sharks and leopards, that ate humans.

Interestingly, it is the Bidjogo women who still serve as diviners, another role usually assigned to males. They consult the shrines, *ira* and most likely in times past sacrificed goats, chicken and cows to the spirits to insure successful slave raiding and the safety of their warriors. Women were in charge of painting abstract designs such as triangles and spirals which the

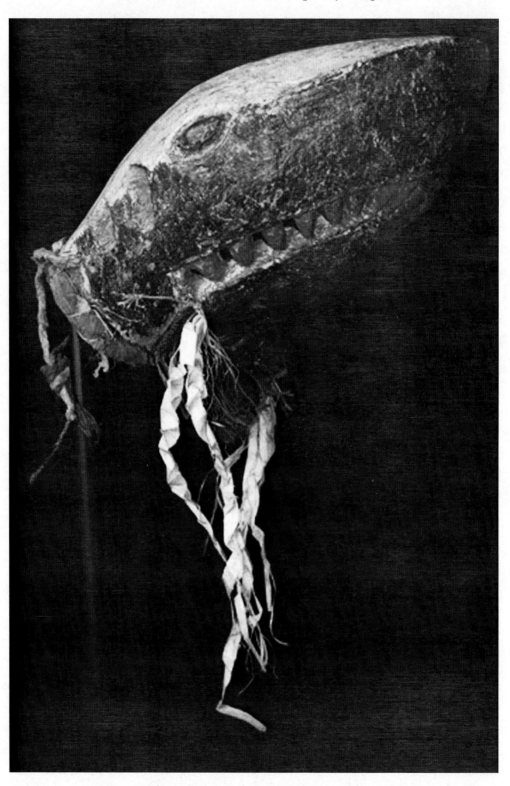

Bidjogo shark mask (courtesy Jeremiah Cole).

masks featured. The symbols, derived from the Jewish Kabbalah, are magic protective devices which as amulets are widespread in Africa. They were transmitted by the slave trade across the Sahara by Jewish-Berber traders and jewelers. The triangle motif in the Kabbalah is known as *abra ka dabra*![14] Such symbols appear on shields, bangles and back ornaments worn by Bidjogo masqueraders.

The switch from slave raiding and fishing to a plantation economy that occurred during the 19th century reduced warfare among the Bidjogo, although slavery continued to serve the *pontas* (plantations). As a result the Bidjogo became more peaceful. Today their mask performances still recall the slave trading days, then and now.

## Slavery in Calabar

As the historical curtain of the 18th century was raised on the Atlantic shores of what is today Southeast Nigeria, the theater of slavery was accelerating. Liverpool, England, enjoying a naturally protected harbor fronted by the Irish Sea would become the world leader in ship building and slaver trafficking. Liverpool ship captains commenced trade along the Cross River Delta of Nigeria and interacted with local big men and a powerful secret society generally known as Ekpe.[15] This secret society controlled the slave trade and most importantly the regulation of credit. The control exerted by credit was a fear, which arose from deep anxieties concerning the punishments and mortal consequences resulting from the inability to honor debt.

The Ekpe worked like a pyramid scheme with branches sold to new players of the trade wishing for a piece of the action. The society depended on spirit-related rituals to enforce its policies and demonstrate its absolute power. Ekpe divided into seven age grades, relied on the masquerade and music coming from the spirit world made manifest by drums, double gongs (*agoogoo*) used in war and merriment, and fancy materials and other goods of the slave trade. Ekpe public pageants and masquerades delighted its spectators on one hand and terrified them on the other.

The economic system was based on what was called "Trust Trade."[16] Venture capitalists in Liverpool and London would form syndicates for building supercargoes and gathering the trade goods that filled the holds. It was hoped that the profits from the trade would be exponential compared to the original investments. Thus on the European side credit risk was established in the homeland where anxieties mirrored those on the Africa side. The ships would drop anchor along the coast, in this case around Calabar and its satellite towns. It took up to six months to fill the holds of the ships with slaves, a very expensive effort considering the equation of time and money. In turn, the African players received trade goods by credit for up to 3,000 pounds sterling—a hefty amount in those days.[17] As a result all players were caught in the dragnet of debt and on the African side the Ekpe was the all-powerful debt broker.

Like the Bidjogo peoples 2,000 miles to the west, Cross River merchants depended on armed war canoes for the trade and like the islanders, they were a mix of ethnicities which included the Ibibio, Eket, Efik, Kwa, Efiat, Moco, Igbo, Oron and Efut. Given the diversity of the population the commercial Ekpe, driven by profit and sanctions from the spirits of African performance, was the glue that held this experiment in social living together.[18]

We are extremely fortunate to have a part of a diary of an African business man from Calabar known as Antera Duke. His remaining and only surviving journal installments cover the years 1785–8, the height of the Liverpool trade. As a member of the top level of Ekpe he was an elite trader whose business impacted all levels of society On November 4, 1786, Mr. Duke writes:

> About 4 a.m. I got up; there was great rain, so I walked to the town *palaver* house and I found all the gentlemen here. So we got ready to cut heads off and at 5 o'clock in the morning we began to cut slaves' heads off, fifty heads off in that one day. I carried 29 cases of bottled brandy, and 15 calabashes of chop for everybody, and there was play in every yard in town.[19]

This passage reveals how powerful Ekpe was in the sense that it could afford the sacrifice of 50 domestic slaves for a celebration of the society. The "play" most likely refers to the masking and music which was supported by the ancestors honored by the mass executions. Any guilt or remorse for the sacrificed and their loved ones was assuaged by the 29 cases of Brandy. Here, we note, that the Efik and Ibibio peoples dominated the trade at Calabar as their ethnic names suggest; for "fik," as in Efik means to suppress the trade of others and "bio" from Ibibio means to cut off heads.[20]

On December 8, 1786, Duke continues:

> ... I went down to the landing to get all the guns ready and we fired 28 great guns ashore, one for each ship. We had shaved our heads first, and we wore fine hats and fine clothes and hand-kerchiefs. All the Captains and we gentlemen had dinner at Esim's house.[21]

In this passage we comprehend the scope of the trade with the salute of 28 guns for as many ships. And to further honor the trade the Ekpe men dressed in their finest for dinner in honor of the European captains. The house of Esim was most likely similar to that of Mr. Duke's having two stories. The upper story where the entertainments occurred were called in Creole "dek" as in the ship's deck-making the Captains feel right at home. Such houses were prefabricated in Liverpool and assembled by ship's carpenters. Sea captains wisely played an active role in Ekpe; as senior society officers they used the organization's social links to insure the collection of debt.

The next day Duke logs in:

> About 6 a.m. at Aqua Landing; there was a small morning fog. I walked up to see an Egbosherry play. We wore new cloth. At midnight Captain Fairweather's tender went away with 280 slaves.[22]

We observe here that the masked performances (*plays* in Creole terms) and celebrations honored the sale of slaves, in this case honoring Captain Fairweather, with the export of 280 chattels. With those bodies secured debts were paid and the next round of credit could be extended in the hopes of getting richer.

In the previous month Mr. Duke noted that Ekpe bush (African wild forest terrain) blew everybody to stay inside their houses after 8 p.m. when the society played all night. The term "blew" refers to striking a drum sound warning all non-initiated to disappear or take cover.[23] Such societies as Ekpe would frequently order all non-members inside their houses, thus denying them access to markets. This action achieved several objectives: (1) people were held hostage and controlled by the play of Ekpe under penalty of death; and (2) the war-like sounds of the double gongs, drums and Ekpe cries—all invisible to outsiders—impressed upon them the efficacy of absolute power sanctioned by the spirit world on behalf of Ekpe. In this way slave trading could be discreetly conducted. It was better that local non-member residents be restricted to their houses under penalty of death. Thus in seclusion they could not see their friends and families, victims of debt, kidnapping, and sorcery being sold out! Victims would simply become missing persons. Thus terror continued to be spread by the invisible forces of mask performance as the slave trade expanded.

## The Face of Ekpe

As a wealth gathering association that depended on credit, ruthless competition, violence and extortion Ekpe required rooms to operate in secrecy. The architectural face of the society was the lodge which was very large running about 40 meters in a square shape with a large open front for "public" display backed by a wall that screened from view the rest of the interior. The front was usually covered by Ukara cloth which was a symbol of power of the society. It was made and imported from the north in Igbo land where many slaves were traded. The cloth was also made by slaves who grew, dyed, and wove the cotton fiber into cloth. The indigo-dyed textile, decorated with white symbols forming a secret language known as *nsibidi,* conveyed the mystery and power of the association. Hung from the lodge, and like a mask, it performed as a veil of secrecy. Members of the upper grades of the society and masqueraders wore the cloth at public and private gatherings.

Although no 18th-century descriptions exist concerning the interior activities of Ekpe, and Mr. Duke smartly does not enter such in his journal, we can assume that ritual performances such as masquerades, sacrifices, and ancestor worship and age graduations were held within. Moreover, such large interiors most likely contained huge stores of trade goods which helped maintain the economic vitality of each lodge and as well could be issued to individual players as Trust Trade.

**Ibibio mask with unhinged jaw (courtesy Jeremiah Cole).**

The social anthropologist Robin Horton photographed a masquerade headpiece of Ekpe at Meinama Village in the middle of the last century. It was placed on its shrine stool where it was ritually fed by a priest. The base of the stool platform features five captives carved in relief. They appear to be attached to one another by a neck nosed rope. The aggressively wide open mouth of the mask exposes a bar of long vertical teeth reminiscent of predators such as leopards and crocodiles which are power symbols of the society. Interestingly Horton includes a photo on the facing page of this plate for which appears to be a bird on top of a small face mask.[24] It is identified as *Oru Ogolo* or "eating fruit." Most likely it is a metaphor for men who cut off heads for power and wealth and in this case for the bird, the head is the fruit that sustains life.

Another Ekpe mask was collected in the late 20th century and it is very revealing about the society on several accounts. First the mask conveys the action of human sacrifice which often, according to Ekpe's fifth sanction declares that a victim should be tied to a tree in the forest and then cutting off his lower jaw or simply disconnecting it.[25] This practice most likely inspired the Cross River masks with unhinged jaws, and it may not be a coincidence that many such masks have a well-defined skull-like appearance. This mask also features the Danish flag in honor of that nation's sea captains who ran the trade across the waters. The mask, itself, is a result of carpentry, learned by Africans from joiners, coopers and European carpenters, all part of the experience of slavery.

Although we do not have written descriptions of these masquerades performed during the slave trade, we may speculate, based on circumstantial evidence that the use of whips most likely added to the performances. Such acts were probably based on the treatment of slaves, its performance. It is recorded that manatees had a special place in Ekpe and that anyone who killed the animal would be automatically promoted to the next age grade or if not a member would become one immediately. Interestingly the skin of this so-called sea elephant was then used to cover a whip (handle?) and also for its "tails." Such whips were highly prized in the society.[26] The skin of manatees is strong and dense and when cured it can easily cut through human skin. Such whips are found in much of coastal Africa. According to Ivor Miller the high pitched voice of the manatee still serves l as a metaphor of the secret voice of the association and as such, cracking the whip becomes an echo of that voice, the voice of violence and suppression![27] Recall the whip on the plantations of Barbados *whose* voice ran the slaves like clockwork until their deaths.

Finally we turn to the *Nyoro* funerary masquerade of Ekpe title holders who through the ritual are replaced by new leaders. Dr. Miller has provided a photo of such a masquerade taken in 2008. The Isim Ekpe performers hold bows and arrows and in their mouths each a red feather. The tails behind the maskers represent that of the leopard and are called *isim*. The spotted peacock feathers which adorn the tails stand for the beauty of leopard's spots. The leopard is the most widespread symbol of high authority in Africa as demonstrated in its inclusion in leadership arts. Suffice it here to say that leopards can quietly enter a village and raid a chicken or goat coral and take a prey off for dinner. During the raid it often kills other occupants of the coral just for the experience of the kill.[28] This "eating of bodies" is again a metaphor expressing the character and power of chiefs and big men who controlled human bodies by consuming them as wealth. Elsewhere in Africa such as in Sierra Leone, Leopard Society leaders wore leopard teeth necklaces and as well hats with crocodile imagery. This animal combination is seen in Ekpe where the power of leopards and the crocodile are joined in the masks and in the architectural decorations of the men's lodge as well as on the Ukara cloth.

Clearly masquerade performances as well as other rituals on the supply side of slavery in

Africa had to negotiate the tensions involved in marketing human bodies and the violence that lent it currency. Rituals were often secretive and held in contained spaces and they often drew on the spiritual power of animals to give the players of this economic system strength to achieve their goals while avoiding the dragnet themselves.

## The Demand Side: West Indies and Trinidad

Two aftershocks that resulted from the slavery explosion in the Caribbean, which began 500 years ago and yet ripples through the region today, were the emergence of a suppressor psychosis and a cultural-social mix which in Trinidad is referred to as a Callaloo Nation. Many artists, participants and leaders of the *mas* groups who perform masked and unmasked in Trinidad and Tobago have in many ways responded to those shocks. Here we focus on *mas* designer Peter Minshall, his rise on the *mas* scene, and his response to those shocking conditions with his extraordinary performance arts of Carnival and later, his contributions to the international scene.

We begin with the thoughts of Raoul Pantin who wrote *Black Power Day* about the movement in 1970. Patin concludes that the enemy of Black protest is the "past of slavery and colonial neglect." The protest in Port of Spain was led by a native son, Stokley Carmichael, who would later make his impact in the movement in the United States. Pantin refers to the conditions of slavery and its relationships to Carnival by quoting another native son of Trinidad and Tobago and noted author V.S. Naipaul:

> The "biggest black people bacchanal, Carnival," Naipaul wrote that Carnival itself "is a version of the lunacy that kept the slave alive. It is the original dream of Black Power, style and prettiness; and it always feeds on a private vision of the world.[29]

Concerning the cultural mix Aisha Kahn points out that the practice of slavery in Trinidad gave birth to a collection of cultural masks' or personalities, that people can don using which ever mask fits the occasion.[30] She quotes anthropologist Daniel Crowley who sums it up:

> A Trinidadian feels no inconsistency in being a British citizen, a Negro in appearance, a Spaniard in name, a Roman Catholic at church, an *obeah* (magic) practitioner in private, a Hindu at lunch, a Chinese at dinner, a Portuguese at work, and a Colored at the polls.[31]

Significantly the observations of these two writers with respect to Minshall's work are (1) that the dream of Black Power highlights "style and prettiness" and (2) that slavery resulted in a collection of masks, so to speak, creating a microcosm of the world's cultures coming as they did down the rivers from their African homelands and crossing vast oceans into captivity. The *Callaloo* soup, a national dish, is made of spices and foods mixed together from all those world cultures, the sources of slavery.

## Peter Minshall

I met Peter Minshall the day after my arrival at the Chaconia Inn located in Maraval, a suburb of the capital. To say that Minch was theatrical would be an understatement. He talked of that year's band called *Mancrab in a Callaloo, The River* (frequently known more simply as *River.*)

Minshall was born on July 16, 1941, in Georgetown, Guyana. His father and his family moved to Port of Spain shortly after and there the future artist grew up. At that time Trinidad was economically in the fast lane with two U.S. Navy bases and a growing oil industry which developed during and after World War II. It was a hot spot of migration. Money was to be made and the Carnival experience with respect to music, the visual arts and the grand scale of the bands, made possible by a developing middle class, created a national street theatre unrivaled. Peter's father created cartoons for a local newspaper and he also was a painter. Many people recall that the cartoonist could be seen at the Savannah with easel and canvas on hand.

Minshall attended the Queen's Royal College and there was very active in theatrical productions. The college, located at the west end of the city's largest park, the Queen's Park Savannah, would be the starting route for all Peter's major bands. This space became a sacred ground for Minshall's creativity. Other major artists and designers such as Geoffrey Holder matured under the tutelage of humanist Rudy Piggott who taught there. Port of Spain was culturally and economically in blossom.

After graduating with honors at the Central School of Art and Design in London, Minshall helped produce West Indian style bands for the Caribbean tourist trade. At the same time Ian Fleming, residing in Port Antonio Jamaica (with Eartha Kitt, Clark Gable and Errol Flynn as neighbors), was writing James Bond spy novels set in the Indies. Things were happening in Minshall's world. In 1974 his mother came to London and requested her son to design a costume for his little Black sister Sherry Ann Guy. This creation, a hummingbird, was a pivotal creation for the artist and for Trinidad's Carnival. Much has been written about this piece. Briefly explained here however, the work allowed its "occupant," its dancer, to move freely and its design translated every movement of the dancer into rhythmic extensions through the bird's wings which made it appear as if it were flying across the stage. It caused a sensation and won Individual of the Year as well as Queen of Carnival. To understand why Hummingbird caused such a reaction we must consider the times.

Carnival in the 1970s was big, vibrant, and obsessed by pageantry. The bands to that point in the post war era were historical, exploring ancient Greece, Rome, Egypt, China; or they were fantastical featuring exotic landscapes and travelers exploring the ends of the earth. Carnival was a colorful dream based on fact and fiction. The top band leaders and designers up to that time had been Harold Saldenah, George Bailey, Stephen Lee Heung and Edmond Hart. The legacy of the era would be transferred to designer and band leader Wayne Berkeley—another great story of *mas*.

In general in the production of individual costumes, kings, and queens the primary materials included velvets, *lamés,* sequined cloth, lavish bead embroidery and other heavy materials. The king and queen productions relied on these materials which when layered became extremely heavy. Moreover, as the scale of these royal characters became 20 to 30 feet in any given direction the weight had to be supported by wheeled steel framed carts. In short the dancer became a beast of burden for a huge, lavish costume that did not move, or as Minshall would say looked and acted like a Christmas tree-stationary and dead. Peter would replace these fancy "things of prettiness" descended from goods of the slave trade and their offspring, with ping pong balls, sun glasses, roscoe metalics, sugar cane stocks, fiber glass poles, bubble wrap, and cardboard, and more. Thus the stationary tree and its quietly performed aesthetic adoration would be replaced by motion and rhythm made visually manifest. This new vision of Minshall's, ironically had its roots in 19th-century Carnival, as we shall see.

The irony here cannot be overstated: Those fancy costumes and what Naipaul called the "style and prettiness" of Carnival were and are made of the same materials that were used in the African slave trade. Slavers, chiefs and kings all wore layers of cloth obtained by selling slaves. The lavish display of fancy materials in the slave trade particularly held prominence in the Cross River-Calabar region as previously discussed. Many of those trade goods were also used in female initiations at Calabar, where the women were secluded, oiled every day, fattened and presented with the fashions made possible by slavery. And, post-emancipation, post-colonial, and post-independence Trinidad championed the liberating effect of Carnival even as it was also weighted down by the burden of wealth. Like slaves on the plantations of Trinidad such as the old Savannah estate, kings and queens and other individual customers were dragging their personae across the stage as did their ancestors who pulled the wheeled carts full of cane to the boiler rooms.

Over time the fancy materials in Trinidad Carnival which originally celebrated liberation were now weighing things down. The stage was set for attainment and personal and social liberation. Along comes ManCrab!

In an article entitled "In Minshall's Words..." (Daily Express, 30) the *mas* man makes two observations: (1) that life is a flutter and like a butterfly one is airborne and carefree on one day and the next is dashed to pieces by the fateful wind, and (2) "My uppermost thought about Trinidad, the most recurring one, is that it is in fact a microcosm of the world: with all the hate, with all the anger, with all the envy, with all the beauty of the world, with all the races of the world, with all the giving and all the taking, with all the glut and all the fasting."[32]

In accord with Minshall, Aisha Kahn pointes out in her book *Callaloo Nation* that Trinidad is indeed a microcosm and one could say as Stephen Derek did in his 1984 band entitled Clash of Cultures the arts of performance celebrated that clash and as well the unifying human condition given that life is a flutter. We may have all come over in separate boats, but we are all in the same boat now.

Essential to our understanding of the power of *mas* and Minshall's creations is the historical context of Carnival-slavery, colonialism and independence—which has shaped the opening event of the street performances held on Monday and Tuesday. This event is called *Jouvay*, which in French Creole means opening day, and it starts around 2 a.m. Monday. Minshall recalls his impressions of *Jouvay* in Port of Spain in childhood. In those days it consisted of people dressed as bats, imps, devils and dragons all with wings. There were also minstrels, *moko jumbies* (stilt maskers who descended from very rebellious slaves ethnically know as Moko from Calabar) wild Indians and donkey riders known as *burrokeets*. These characters all played roles, acting within the performance of Carnival. In those days people played together as individuals. They moved quickly in the dark acting out their roles in the early hours of the morning until sun down. *Jab jabs* and *Jab Molasses* danced though the city streets along with midnight robbers who with skull motifs and whips inspired fear, especially among the young. Jerry Besson vividly describes the significance of these masqueraders:

> The *Jab Molassees* or molasses devil represents the worst thing that could happen on a Cane estate during the days of slavery. A slave falls into a vat of boiling molasses. Its ghost haunts *Jouvay* to this day. Its origins come from the *Cannes Broulées* carnival, 1880s, when an entire cane estate would be portrayed, on fire, with the *Jab Molassees* striding ahead along with the diabs....[33]

Robbers gave speeches in dueling verbal bouts with each other while brandishing whips. The "badder" (fearful) the talk the more applause of the audience and the more money the winner received, money which was thrown into a small coffin offering box which the robber dragged on the streets. A Robber talk line might have been:

> At the age of five, I, this dreaded monarch, was sent to school, but the schooling there was not drastic enough for me.... When it comes to snatching children's faces, ringing their ears, biting off pieces of their nose, I, King Korak, was always on the top.... At the age of two, I drowned my grandmother in a spoonful of water."[34] The characters of *Jouvay* in part evolved from the life styles of slaves who lived under hellish conditions on the plantations. A *Jab Molasses*, for example recalled those slaves who might have fallen in hot tubs of molasses becoming instantly cooked, or those unliked slaves who might have been pushed into the moldered cauldrons in acts of revenge.[35]

Peter Minshall refers to his seminal Hummingbird costume, as a small powerful muscle that performed as a heart beats. Remarkably his description is well applied to *Jouvay* for it is the power source that muscles *mas*. By 6 a.m. the *Jouvay* bands and followers, covered in black oil, soot, clay and chocolate arrive at the heart of the city. They carry chains in memory of slavery and placards denouncing corrupt politicians who have ruled the island since its colonial days. The *Jouvay* peoples' oiled and shiny blackness which catches the light makes them appear as dancing skeletons of death, yet in that death dance liberation is stirred. JUU VAAAAY. Man *Jouvay*! For the moment father time and his son, the Grim Reaper, have been fooled and the flutter feels eternal.

A few hours later after thousands have eaten, drank and danced back to back, belly to belly in the zombie jamboree, people descend on Independence Square. The streets of lower Port of Spain, like blood-carrying arteries, convey these wet, slippery droplets of fluid, these Jouvay players, to the stomach and bowels of the city. The sun lifts itself over the Lavantile Hills delivering its bristling heat. It is hot. *Jouvay* has reached full potential. Jamming, jamming, and jamming. Everyone is moving to all the music. Hands raised toward the sky, the sun, toward freedom, towards the new year to the death of the old year, old loved ones, old experience, between the old and the new in a crossing of times. A genie's magic lantern has been opened and everyone inhales the air of magical release and renewal.

As a boy Minshall's *Jouvay* experience was rhythmically, visually and philosophically cast indelibly throughout his being. Furthermore the mutability of life, the power and delicacy of wings, was pre-figured in the young man in the Carnival by way of the experience of flag waiving which occurs in many events including the introduction and performance of the steel bands on stage at the Savannah and on the streets of *Jouvay*. In one opening blast, in an instant, the bands beat their songs. The complexity of the beats, the nano-second precision, cacophony of sound and the music which has its own life begins to thrill its listeners and dancers who lime on the stands. With the names of the bands printed on flags, flag bearers twist, jump, and turn from side to side on stage, cheering their bands on to victory. The mutable shapes these flags take in responses to the movements of the dancers and the local wind reminds everyone that change is irrefutable. The abstract patterns take on spirit shapes that shift with the raging beat of the music as it nears its climax. The steel band rhythm section is called the *engine room*, the power that moves! This bacchanal embraces in the head, body, and bones. It rolls through the guts as one gyrates on the moving grandstands or on the streets. This event casts a transcendent spell heading one step closer to *mas* and liberation from the past.

*Jouvay* and flags have been primary high affect sources of Peter Minshall's artistic and philosophical sensibilities, the form and content, of his great performances which could have only been born in Port of Spain, Trinidad and Tobago. Never mind Matisse, Francis Bacon and Christo—another side of the artist! For certain their presence is felt.

My initial experience of Trinidad *mas* occurred in 1983, the year Minshall created *Man-Crab*, his first production in a trilogy in part funded by the John Simon Guggenheim Fellowship Award Peter had won in 1982. Much of our discussion thus far has served as the historical context to further understand the artist's work, especially pertaining to the politics and experience of slavery, colonization, and independence. The nurturing days for the works from the 1980s we will now feature would later be presented on the world stage such as in 1992 for the opening ceremonies of the Summer Olympics at Barcelona Spain and those of the Atlanta Olympics in 1996.

## Mancrab in a Callaloo, the River

To obtain a deeper understanding of the 1983–85 trilogy of *River*, *Callaloo* and *Golden Calabash* we explore the designer's and the Trinidadian peoples' cognitive and emotional responses to the entities of crab, *callaloo* and river, how do these things play in the national landscape?

*Callaloo*: It is important to understand the *callaloo* metaphor, because it is central to the *mas* bands created by Minshall in the early 1980s. *Callaloo* is a soup made from a variety of food found or imported to the island. However the dish is prepared diversity is clearly the key to its appeal. Just as the soup improves in taste, becoming sweeter as the various ingredients blend, so does Trinidadian culture become sweeter as its diversity increases. The origins of the soup's ingredients are from five geographically broadly based civilizations: the coconut from India, the dasheen from Asia, the hot peppers and palm oil from Africa, the wheat and chicken from Europe and the crab from the Caribbean.

*Callaloo* is consumed on festive occasions including all the national holidays which celebrate Muslim festivals such and Muharram also known as Hosay, Eid-Al-Adha, Ramadan, and Eid-A- Fitr; Hindu celebrations such as Duvali and Ramleegh; Christian events including Christmas, Easter, and Corpus Christi; and national occasions like Independence Day , New Years, and Emancipation Day. Thus *callaloo* is at once a taste that celebrates a variety of festivals along ethnic, patriotic and religious lines while embracing all festivals across the social spectrum. The soup is a source of national solidarity: everybody loves *callaloo*.

• *River*—River is also an important symbol and metaphor for Trinidadians simply because there are many rivers in the small island country which have been formed by the rains which for millennia have descended the extensive mountain range of the land which is an extension of the Andes of South America. Minshall conceived the sections of his band as the country's various rivers, symbolizing cultural diversity through each section's costumes. To quote Therese Mills, editor of the *Sunday Guardian* at the time of this *mas*, 1983:

> *River*, first act, Monday. Running through downtown Port of Spain, capital, in the Carnival Republic of Trinidad and Tobago, it comprises streams called Maraval, Orpouche, Oropuna, Aripo, Tompire, Tumpuna, Yarra, Oruga, Sana Cruz, Rio Grande, Caroni, and East Dry; as well as creatures and characteristics related to River, like Lizard, Plum, Lagoon, Shark and Marianne. Minshall's River brings together more than 2,500 persons, from all streams of life to enact a two-day drama.[36]

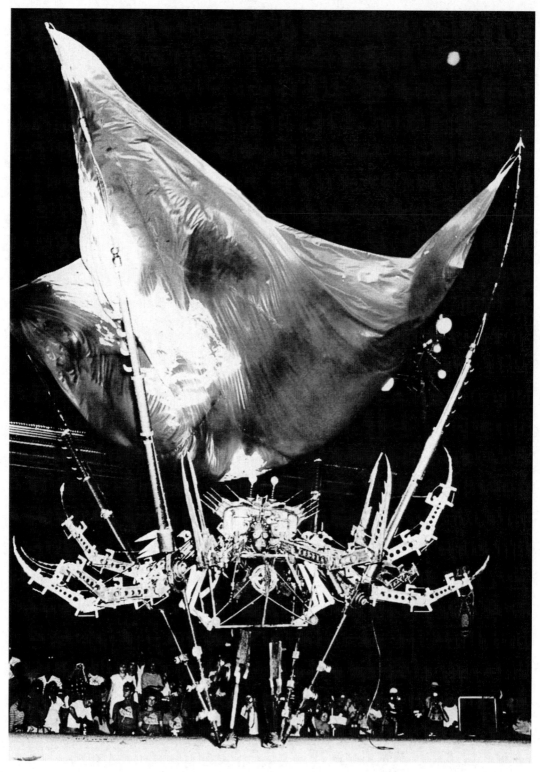

Mancrab with blood-stained shroud from *River* (courtesy John Nunley).

- **Mancrab**—Mancrab is a part biological (human) and part automaton construction that featured six spider-like arms that moved to the motion of the dancer. At the center of the *Mancrab* suit was placed a *papier-mâché* mask of simple construction, looking much like a satellite with antennae. Attached to the Crab's heavy black boots were two poles on each foot. Standing sixteen feet high, the four poles supported a twenty-five foot square canopy of white silk. This costume was worn by Peter Samuels, a longtime associate of Minshall and frequent king of Carnival. Each night of the kings competitions, the creature danced to the music of the East Indian derived *tassa* drums, which included large double-headed wooden drums, smaller ceramic drums and brass cymbals. *Tassa* music is very militant in character, sounding the call to battle in traditional Muslim festivals, such as Hosay which have celebrated the Prophet's struggles and battles concerning the spread of his faith. As the dancing became more violent during the Kings' Competitions the masker released paint from a compressor installed within the costume. Traveling up the tubing attached to the poles the paint, at first, left barely a trace, just a sprinkling. Before the dance was over, however, the silk had turned into a blood stained shroud, symbolizing death, destruction and pollution—an unholy shroud representing a new incarnation of the Devil which from early in the history of Carnival has appeared as Lucifer in old time *mas*. Or the slave owners or those Black headmen they selected to run the various gangs.

  The Mancrab, through the agency of his large scale and menacing claws, visually occupied a big space in the band. Likewise the entire body shell of the crab and its pincer-legs is visually central to the soup. You cannot miss him-her. The crab's exo-shell skeleton is hard, protective and rough; it may scratch its dinner guest. Like Mancrab it attracts, yet can hurt you while eating its sweet and irresistible flesh. Mancrab represents the darker side, the greed and social conflict which are a part of Trinidad. The crab threatens the sweetness of the mix of global cultures represented by the island rivers which by the force of gravity, natural law, flow together as one. In comes Washerwoman.

- **Washerwoman**—Opposed to the frightening character and destructive potential of Mancrab was the Washerwoman, the queen played by the artist's sister, Sherri Ann Coelho. Dressed in a white full-length skirt tied at one end of the waist, this beautiful queen sambaed onto the stage. Two poles arising from her shoulders were used to attach clotheslines, on which were hung pieces of cloth in various abstract shapes. As Washerwoman moved to the music, the cloths shapes waved in the thick night air, created` brilliant flashes of white on the Savannah stage. Carrying a basket of fresh white cloths the Queen continued to purify the river people, protecting them from themselves represented by the crab!

  On Carnival Monday *River,* presented all in white, was performed around the Savannah and on to the stage. The one-half mile canopy above the band symbolized its purity as well as that state of the nation. However, Tuesday, paradise was lost. In the transition to Mardi Gras (Fat Tuesday) the queen died and the king had begun to work his magic on the river people. The river canopy had been dyed blue, yellow, green and red colors that represented pollution and by extension those fancy trade goods once so integral to the slave trade. The river people, who now reveled in the pollution of the river, were about to become agents of self-corruption as well the environment. Self-betrayal drives every holocaust, including slavery.

  The stage was set. The queen's death was indicated by her blood-stained clothes suspended from the clothes lines. In this state she was carried along the streets from noon until

**River Band polluted with color (courtesy John Nunley).**

5:30 while the red shroud of Mancrab, suspended from the four poles was carried in the procession by the king's attendants. This horrifying scene could be seen one-quarter mile away from the Savannah stage. The monster's victory, his defeat of the queen, was amplified by the sound of the *tassa* drums, which gradually increased in volume as *River* moved closer and closer to the stage. The sound was deafening.

Six dancers in white, as maidens honoring the sacrifice, appeared on the stage before the north and south stands. Everyone watched the movement of the priestesses. Slowly they turned to the south and raised their calabashes. They then turned to the north and completed the same movement and then turned back to the south stands. At this moment they raised the calabashes high above their heads then slowly downward over their breasts. Then they tilted the bowls spilling the blood-red liquid all over their pure white garments and skin. *River* masqueraders had made their sacrifice to the god of technology, greed and pollution. Moments later, the triumphal king entered onto the stage, his umbilicus spewing from his guts. Attached to the dead queen was the umbilicus which dragged her across the stage covered in the monster's polluted fluids. The *tassa* drums played their staccato rhythms as the creature moved in triumph. Captured by the joys of technology, the *River* masqueraders entered onto the stage and danced for several minutes, celebrating the victory of their new leader. Bottles of dye carried by the people and compressors of painted showered everyone with color. Thus the stain of technology was shared by all in a three dimensional post–Jackson Pollock chaos of color.

*Opposite*: **Bird of Paradise from the Callaloo band (courtesy John Nunley).**

- *Callaloo*—The second part of the trilogy, *Callaloo*, again portrays the struggle of good and evil. The king in the section entitled *Callaloo Dancing Tic Tac Toe Down the River* was assigned the task of keeping the band people free from sin. *Washerwoman* was now transformed into the character *I have Seen the Bird of Paradise*, and like the former queen represented purity. The Mancrab was replaced by his technical creation Madame Hiroshima, after the Atomic bomb (named A Little Boy) which destroyed that city on August 6, 1945-forty years before. On Carnival Monday the band called Children of the Moon, was pure and free from sin. By Tuesday the band entered a state of sin, thanks to the tricks of Madame Hiroshima; the band was then renamed Callaloo and the Seven Deadly Sins. As the year before the people were soaked in color symbolizing their corrupt state.

  Drawing on the interests of his band's participants, many of which were Afro-descended, the artist has portrayed his hero, Callaloo, as a solidly African character despite the analogy with Christ. The story reads: "Callaloo had plenty sense. Callaloo sense did reach to de sky. Dat Dasheen boy had brains. You could say Callaloo brains were tall as any skyscraper."[37] This skyscraper directly refers to the African-style plank headpiece which Minshall had incorporated into the costume. The abstract shapes on the plank derive from masks of the Bwa peoples of the West African savannah. They once served as magic symbols, borrowed from the magic of the Kabbalah, to protect people from slavery.

  Thus, Callaloo is an African spirit that triumphs over evil, both on the demand and supply-side of slavery. The metallic body of Callaloo also is associated with the African deity Shango, God of Thunder, who has his own body of worshippers and who is popular with the members of certain Trinidad Baptist sects as well. Further, the dasheen plant is used in Afro-American religious ceremonies in Trinidad, thus its inclusion in the Callaloo image. By the same token, Washerwoman may have represented a river sprit associated with the worship of Yemanja, a water spirit that came to the West Indies from Africa during the slave trade. In the Indies, in fact, Yemanja is often considered the mother of Shango.[38] Minshall refers to the dasheen as the magic leaf. The idea that the leaf has the power to keep the band pure is in part rooted in the physical property of the leaf itself, because its oil-like surface repels water. This in turn allows Callaloo to walk on the water, like Christ, just as oil skims across the water's surface.[39] Thus Callaloo is armed in his fight with Madame Hiroshima.

- **Madame Hiroshima**—Madame Hiroshima, the creation of Mancrab, explores another dimension of the Trinidadian character one what would eagerly trade the purity of the land of imported technology. This is represented by the panoply of color, sequins, beads, and various other fancy materials of the Madame's suit. The mushroom cloud itself is made of Ostrich plumes, one of the principal exports from Africa during the slave trade. The fact that she is the offspring of Mancrab and his own technology makes her a product of incest, which in turn symbolically violates the natural order. The power of the nuclear bomb is no match for Callaloo or the Bird of Paradise and on Tuesday the Madame dances in victory while 16 foot standards danced on the stage, representing the seven deadly sins are raised in the color sprayed bacchanal.

- *Golden Calabash*—This 1985 *mas* was the third act of the trilogy. In many ways it suffered from being the last effort, over a three year span, wherein all the key players were wearing down and Minshall had had enough of the decisions of the judges which reflected a bias for the old and worn out carnival of pretty *mas*. The *Golden Calabash* has a very interesting symbolic concept. Its power is its very elusiveness. It may refer to the Golden Calf in the Old Testament, The Holy Grail and the Christ myths; also it recalls Aladdin's Lamp. It was rumored that Washerwoman had drunk from the Golden Calabash to sustain her purity. So how can it be that both good and evil are attracted to it?

*Calabash* was divided into two sub-bands, one called the "Princes of Darkness' and the other, "Lords of Light." Darkness was divided into sections that included Thorns of Cruelty, Hummingbird of Blood, and Bobolee. Bobolee is found on both sides of the Black Atlantic. This Judas character exists as a masquerade in Sierra Leone where it celebrates the death of Christ and In Port of Spain where images of Judas are placed on the streets of neighborhoods on Easter. The section Thorns also makes reference to the Passion of Christ. The Lords of Light included sections such as Wings of Peace-Doves and an individual called Hummingbird of Crystal. The kings and queens were not completed for presentation and so The Adoration of Madame Hiroshima became the central masked character.

*The Adoration of Hiroshima*, played by Hugh Bote Bernard, was a beautifully seductive creature. Its white and golden colors, beads, glitter and sequins sparkled in the sun on the days of the processions. The skull like mask of the character harkened back to the grim reaper. The character carried a scepter with a guided ballistic nuclear warhead missile finial in left-hand and a small world globe in the other. The world was small in the hands of the bomb character conveying the destructive power over the planet. The feathers were, once again, made of Ostrich plums and unlike the colorful plumage of the first Madame, these were pure white, like the mushroom cloud which hovered over the spoils of that Japanese city.

*Golden Calabash* explored the heart of the matter of human nature and though it was not a complete act it did convey the idea that good and evil come from the same source and together they compose human nature. Our struggle of good and evil is an expression of our moment, our flutter, in the wind as Minshall would explain it.

In that year, a contingent of the *Adoration of Hiroshima* would gather in Washington D.C. to protest weapons of mass destruction. It seems unlikely and even surreal today that the band was allowed its theater, its procession round the Pentagon. *Paradise Lost!* This *mas* extending over the National borders of Minshall's native country would prepare the *mas* designer for his presentations in 1992 at the Barcelona Olympics and the 1996 Olympics in Atlanta and much more.

Of all of this master *mas* man's work I believe that *River* was the most aesthetically and emotionally charged production of his lifetime. It raised participants and audiences to new ecstatic heights. When the triumphant Mancrab entered the stage to the *tassa* drums, the crowd roared. Then it suddenly quieted as the priestesses raised their calabashes above their heads. As if first inhaling a mighty breath, the crowd received the Crab, and then in a mighty collective exhaling it quietly watched the blood ritual and then in an even louder exhalation responded to the mad spray of color polluting the river people on the stage. All were unified in a breath, a moment in time with no divisions. The breath was a flutter.

According to Minshall:

> The artist touches the eternal infinite and relates it to the observer, who sees it, touches it himself, and discovers himself in the midst of it. The human moment is evoked infinitesimal, yet momentous and essential, the inevitable link between all that has been and all that will be. The

moment is beyond time and yet continuous time. The vanity of us all, as well as our profundity, are plain in the moment, elucidated by art, *Mas* captures that moment inescapably.[40]

As *River* began to breakup while the Carnival grounds lay at rest, fragments of River people dress floated in the winds and settled on this sacred ground, once a plantation. Where there was once much pain and suffering, release and attainment were allowed their cooling effects of art. This was a sacred place where freedom had replaced the whip. I returned to my accommodations with my camera, hair, and clothes covered with paint. In the shower, the colored water was funneled down the drain, carried by a sewer to a stream, and then to a river and out to sea. Conceptually, the point of the continuing process of pollution was made. Through the years the stains on my camera case have faded as does the flutter of life, and according to the artist Peter Minshall, himself, such fading represents the unfulfilled promise of technology in the face of human worth and understanding. Yet it is faded technology, or built-in obsolescence, as they used to say, which out of the necessity for its own survival must invent new colors to replace the old, and in the pursuit of its goal must further pollute the land. This predicament of culture is the Darwinian knot.

## Postscript

This essay is based on the belief that our species' performances are expressions of life's full blown experiences that are filled with pain and pleasure, the coldness of loneliness and exclusion, the warmth of togetherness and inclusion, the trauma of fear and danger, and other variances of these emotional sensations. These feelings, indelible to our being, can be replayed discursively through written and oral traditions or non-discursively through art and ritual.

Slavery as a production of the African supply side left deeply imbedded traumas in the cultural psyche. The performance of violence, secrecy, compression and exclusion are recalled in African masquerades today where indeed, the practice of slavery remains. On the demand side, plantation life was marked by compression and restriction, but having left the homeland, old ways of control were lost and the master became the source of repression. When human chattel crossed the seas their cultural legs were amputated. Like losing a leg or an arm, in which severed parts are felt by the amputee, those parts long to be remembered. It would take centuries to re-member and also to *forget* in order to *create new memories* for the healing to take place.[41] For the generations of slaves on the demand side the lines were clearly drawn and crossing the line, the abolition of slavery, meant a new sense of freedom where play and performance promised attainment and new experiments in social living.

To paraphrase a speech presented by the, doyen of the arts and humanities and Jamaica's famous son Ralston Milton "Rex" Nettleford at the Smithsonian Institution Symposium for the Christopher Columbus Quincentenary, "Columbus Rediscovered," 1492–1992, Rex explained: We West Indian Blacks faced great hardships and pain on our way through the Middle Passage, but we are now better off than our brothers and sisters we left behind, still caught up in the old ways, the old fights, and those irresolvable cultural differences.[42]

*Opposite*: **The Adoration of Madame Hiroshima from Golden Calabash (courtesy John Nunley).**

# Notes

1. Andrea Stuart (2012), *Sugar in the Blood* (New York: Random House), 181.

2. Ibid.

3. Danielle Grallois-Duquette (2000), "The Bidjogo Peoples of Guinea Bissau," in Herreman, ed., *In the Presence of Spirits: African Art from the National Museum of Ethnology Lisbon* (New York: Museum for African Art), 155–6.

4. Philips Havik (2004), Silence and Soundbytes: The Gender Dynamics of Trade and Brokerage in the Pre-Colonial Guinea Bissau Region (Munster: Lit Verlog), 98, 272–3.

5. Ibid., 109–113.

6. Gallois-Duquette, 156.

7. Ibid., 157–160.

8. Ibid., 159.

9. Ibid., 160.

10. John Nunley and Judith Bettelheim (1988), "Masquerade Mix-Up in Trinidad Carnival: Live Once, Die Forever," *Caribbean Festival Arts: Each and Every Bit of Difference* (Seattle: University of Washington Press), 32–34.

11. Wikipedia, "Bullfighting," 1.

12. Havik, 108.

13. Gallois-Duquette, 116.

14. Labelle Prussin (2006), "Judaic Threads in the West African Tapestry: No More Forever?" *The Art Bulletin* Vol. LXXXVIII, #2 (June): 328–353.

15. D. Simmons (1956), "An Ethnographic Sketch of the Efik People," in *Efik Traders of Old Calabar*, Daryll Forde, ed. (London: Oxford University Press), 4–5.

16. Ibid., 16–19.

17. Ibid., 5.

18. Ibid., 2.

19. Antera Duke (1956), "The Diary of Antera Duke (1785–8)" in *Efik Traders of Old Calabar*, Daryll Forde, ed. (London: Oxford University Press), 50.

20. Simmons (1956), 1; Duke (1956), 74.

21. Duke (1956), 51.

22. Ibid.

23. Ibid., 49.

24. Robin Horton, *Kalabari Sculpture*, no page number, plate 33.

25. G.I. Jones (1956), "The Political Organization of Old Calabar," in *Efik Traders of Old Calabar*, Daryll Forde, ed., 142.

26. Duke (1956), 55.

27. Ivor Miller (2008), *Voice of the Leopard: African Secret Societies and Cuba* (Jackson: University Press of Mississippi), 52.

28. Allen F. Roberts and Carol Thompson (1995), *Animals in African Art: From the Familiar to the Marvelous* (New York: The Museum for African Art), 100.

29. Pantin, Raoul (1990), *Black Power Day* (Santa Cruz, Trinidad and Tobago: Hatuey Press), 114.

30. Aisha Khan (2004), *Callaloo Nation* (Durham: Duke University Press), 23.

31. Ibid.

32. Peter Minshall (1991), "In Minshall's Words," in *Daily Express: The Greatest Show on Earth, Trinidad Carnival: Minshall: The Man and His Mas'* (Port of Spain: Trinidad Express), 30; Debbie Jacob (1991), *Minshall: The Man and His Mas'* ([Port of Spain, Trinidad]: Trinidad Express Newspapers.

33. Jerry Besson, interview with the author, 13 December 2013.

34. Daniel Crowley, "The Midnight Robbers," in *Caribbean Quarterly* (1956): 263–74, 272.

35. Jerry Besson, interview with the author, September 1990.

36. Mills, Therese Mills (1983), "Band of the People's Choice, River, Peter Minshall," *Trinidad Carnival* (Port of Spain: Key Caribbean Publications), 95.
37. John Nunley (1993), *Image and Creativity: Ethnoaesthics and Art Worlds in the Americas,* Dorothea S. Whitten, ed. (Tucson: University of Arizona Press), 303.
38. Ibid.
39. Peter Minshall (1984), *Callaloo an de Crab* (Trinidad and Tobago: Privately Printed), 26.
40. Ibid., 6.
41. Kahn, 65.
42. Rex Nettleford, Smithsonian Institution Lecture, 1992.

# Works Cited

Besson, Jerry. Interviews with the author, September 1990 and 13 December 2013.
Crowley, Daniel. (1956.) "The Midnight Robbers." *Caribbean Quarterly.*
Duke, Antera. (1956.) "The Diary of Antera Duke (1785–8)." In *Efik Traders of Old Calabar*. Daryll Forde, ed. London: Oxford University Press.
Grallois-Duquette, Danielle. (2000.) "The Bidjogo Peoples of Guinea Bissau." In *In the Presence of Spirits: African Art from the National Museum of Ethnology Lisbon*. Herreman, ed. New York: Museum for African Art.
Havik, Philips. (2004.) *Silence and Soundbytes: The Gender Dynamics of Trade and Brokerage in the Pre-Colonial Guinea Bissau Region*. Munster: Lit Verlog.
Jacob, Debbie. (1991.) *Minshall: The Man and His Mas'* ([Port of Spain, Trinidad]: Trinidad Express Newspapers).
Jones, G.I. (1956.) "The Political Organization of Old Calabar." In *Efik Traders of Old Calabar*. Daryll Forde, ed. London: Oxford University Press.
Khan, Aisha. (2004.) *Callaloo Nation: Metaphors of Race and Religious Identity Among South Asians in Trinidad*. Durham: Duke University Press.
Miller, Ivor. (2008.) *Voice of the Leopard: African Secret Societies and Cuba*. Jackson: University Press of Mississippi.
Mills, Therese. (1983.) "Band of the People's Choice, River, Peter Minshall." *Trinidad Carnival*. Port of Spain: Key Caribbean Publications.
Minshall, Peter. (1984.) *Callaloo an de Crab*. Trinidad and Tobago: Privately Printed.
Minshall, Peter. (1991.) "In Minshall's Words." *Daily Express: The Greatest Show on Earth, Trinidad Carnival: Minshall: The Man and His Mas'* (Port of Spain: Trinidad Express).
Nettleford, Rex. (1992.) Smithsonian Institution Lecture.
Nunley, John. (1993.) *Image and Creativity: Ethnoaesthics and Art Worlds in the Americas*. Dorothea S. Whitten, ed. Tucson: University of Arizona Press.
Nunley, John, and Judith Bettelheim. (1988.) "Masquerade Mix-Up in Trinidad Carnival: Live Once, Die Forever." *Caribbean Festival Arts: Each and Every Bit of Difference*. Seattle: University of Washington Press.
Pantin, Raoul. (1990.) *Black Power Day*. Santa Cruz, Trinidad and Tobago: Hatuey Press.
Prussin, Labelle. (2006.) "Judaic Threads in the West African Tapestry: No More Forever?" *The Art Bulletin* Vol. LXXXVIII, #2 (June): 328–353.
Roberts, Allen F., and Carol Thompson. (1995.) *Animals in African Art: From the Familiar to the Marvelous*. New York: The Museum for African Art.
Simmons, D. (1956.) "An Ethnographic Sketch of the Efik People." In *Efik Traders of Old Calabar*. Daryll Forde, ed. London: Oxford University Press.
Stuart, Andrea. (2012.) *Sugar in the Blood*. New York: Random House.

# Playing *Mas* or Mass Playing: Contemporary Carnivals and Street Parades

## Loyce L. Arthur

*Carnival is my life, my culture, my identity.*—*Clary Salandy*

*Our carnival was once hugely broad in the expressions it encompassed; from let-go bacchanal to determined seriousness; from the tawdry to the magnificent; from frenzied to stately and dignified ... from nakedly revealed to fully disguised and transformed ... from rhinestones and beads and sequins to mud and bones and bush; from playing yourself to playing mas.*
—*Peter Minshall*

A definition of carnival is a complex proposition, particularly in contemporary times. Geographically, carnivals are found all around the world. Originally a pre–Lenten festival, there are now carnivals held during every month of the year. Carnivals are Old World traditions that were brought to the New World, transformed, and transported back across the seas to transform again and again, and again. As carnival traditions have expanded throughout the world they have taken on different characteristics, with different meanings for different populations. Carnival traditions have always included elements of masquerade, however.

Whereas some carnival masks originally concealed the hidden motives of dispossessed and disenfranchised black slaves, today carnival masks intentionally reveal all in order to stake a claim on public space shared by a multitude of social, political, and cultural constituents. In the case of carnival in Rio de Janeiro, Brazil, it is as important for people to see the faces of the *bihanas* (women who range from ages 50 to 80 considered the god-mothers of carnival)[1] as it is to see the lithesome young women who are models and TV celebrities on the floats who want to attract media attention.

In Berlin's Karneval de Kulturen, Italian, African, Argentinian, Colombian, and Caribbean immigrants want to be seen as part of the life of this modern multicultural city.

When talking about carnival in Trinidad and Tobago, Richard Schechner gives insights into one of the dominant motivations for contemporary carnival practices as a whole. He states, "[carnival plays out] a dangerous, almost about to come apart, coalition of traditions and socio-political arrangement.... There are tensions and ongoing (if sometimes non-conscious) negotiations ... differences occur at all levels."[2] Milla Cozart Riggio has this to say, (again her words could describe almost any contemporary carnival):

> It is impossible to pin Trinidad Carnival down. Always on the edge, always threatened by commercialization, the festival spins on, twisting and shifting in ways that are neither predictable nor essentially comforting. Nothing characterizes carnival more than its perpetual sense of change. Mostly, whatever one says today will not be true tomorrow. The essence of the event is ephemerality and endless renewal—death and rebirth of many kinds.[3]

It is the transformative, revealing, all-encompassing, dangerous, contentiously collaborative, individual and public expressions of freedom and joy. The highly creative aspects of contemporary carnivals make them some of the world's most unique and captivating forms of artistic expression that enthralls those who practice it and those who witness it.

Carnival designers, who situate themselves in the midst of such highly chaotic creative masquerading spectacles, are rarely recognized as the artists that they are, though critical attitudes are slowly changing. In this article I will examine contemporary trends in several carnivals, with particular emphasis on carnivals in Port of Spain, Trinidad and Tobago; London, United Kingdom; the Cross River State in Nigeria; and Rio de Janeiro, Brazil, in order to show what titanic challenges dedicated, committed, carnivalists in general and carnival designers in particular face, both culturally and economically in order to create some of the world's most fantastic works of masquerade art. I will focus on the work of one carnival artist, Clary Salandy, a Londoner, formally from Trinidad, who is a brilliant example of the artist, activist, community organizer, negotiator, interpreter, politician, global entrepreneur, and educator. At the top of her game, she profiles the type of successful designer who dares to accept the challenges of making carnival today.

## Masquerade Practices Found in Carnivals

An accurate definition of carnival is complex particularly in the present day when the form has undergone radical changes. When talking about carnivals it is useful to think in terms of three categories of masquerade practices: (1) indigenous masquerade,[4] festivals, and rituals; (2) carnival celebrations including European, Latin American, Caribbean and Brazilian diaspora-influenced carnivals; (3) urban street parades including protest parades, and ethnic, diversity, and community parades. Not every celebratory costume street parade is a carnival parade. However, it is not necessary to label one carnival as more authentic than another. Carnival, that encompasses all three categories above and continues to evolve year after year, is difficult to lock into any time, place, or reference point. There are key contemporary carnivals that are as much about a historical socio-political and cultural past as they are about reflecting the realities of today's societies.

Arguably, the most dominant global carnival forms, both in sheer numbers as well as cultural influences come from the Atlantic region. These Caribbean and Latin American carnivals stem from a combination of indigenous rituals: African and Asian influences that were brought to the Atlantic region by slaves and immigrant workers and European traditions brought to the New World by a colonial plantocracy. These carnivals evolved from Medieval pre–Lenten bacchanal with Egyptian and Roman roots,[5] to Caribbean and Atlantic region colonial and postcolonial Creole masquerade festivals, to 20th-century multimillion dollar extravaganzas on the one hand, and community celebratory urban street parades on the other hand. Two of the largest and most influential masquerade events in the world, held in the cities of Port of Spain and Rio de Janeiro respectively, share this evolutionary path. These urban parades spawned a number of diasporic carnivals across the globe, including four that are vying for a top spot in the carnival arena: Notting Hill Carnival in London, Caribana Carnival in Toronto, and the Brooklyn New York Labor Day Carnival Parade.

Less dominant but nonetheless vibrant and culturally invigorating are the carnivals primarily found in Europe (Mardi Gras in New Orleans is an exception), including carnivals in Cologne, Venice, Nice, and Basel, that grew out of Medieval grotesque traditions that mixed with aristocratic pageants, costume balls, and elegant promenades.

Perhaps the most interesting contemporary carnivals, large and small, are those that are a mixture of both Caribbean and/or Brazilian and European forms, such as carnival in Rotterdam, Seychelles in the Indian Ocean, and the Canary Islands (Spain), to name a few.[6] Rotterdam carnival, for example, is a fusion of carnival forms found in Venice, Port of Spain, London, and Rio de Janeiro along with modern street festivals/anything goes masquerades. Victoria, the capital of Seychelles has begun an interesting carnival initiative that demonstrates a different contemporary view of carnival as a multi-cultural celebration. Described as a country that "sells itself as a melting pot of cultures,"[7] the Seychelles Tourist Board invited representatives of carnivals from around the world to the island for three days in March 2011 to take part in a joint parade in order "to create an international melting pot of festivities." Canary Islands has a carnival that has Rio-style costumes along with, in a recent parade, Smurfs and drag queens.

Yes, carnival is difficult to precisely define and describe, which consequently utilizes such exciting, endlessly surprising, and engaging masquerade art forms for people of every ethnicity and demographic. Through limitless invention carnival can be utilized to satisfy social, political, and cultural agendas—for better or for worse.

## Carnival Arts and Aesthetics

In the 21st century the urban street parades known as carnivals are an amalgamation of pageantry and spectacle traditions that seek to recapture and retain the cultural values associated with carnivals of the past, while adapting the practice for today's world. This has led to two hundred plus carnivals that retain masquerade aspects of carnivals of hundreds of years ago married with distinctly contemporary aspects of fashion, ethnocentricities, pop culture, and display. Carnival events and in particular diasporic carnival events in urban areas were first, in the mid–20th century, singularly motivated by the need to show the cultural wealth and the values of immigrants striving to negotiate space within dominant westernized cultures through elaborate carnival masking and costumes. Today carnival celebrations are commercially sidelined by music extravaganzas with Vegas-style costumed participants merely as background, with notable exceptions such as those created by carnival designer Clary Salandy that I will discuss later.

Contemporary masquerade trends towards cookie-cutter, cheaply made costumes have had varying effects on carnival. There is movement away from nuanced, carefully constructed masquerade displays, to cheap, commercial odds and ends and everything in between. Concerned carnivalists worry that simplistic costumes will become the norm. So far, bikini-and-

T-shirts are a fast and easy masquerade costume. Often they are individually styled as seen here at the Zurich Street Parade, 2012, Switzerland. They can also demonstrate group cohesion when designed for a carnival band (courtesy Loyce L. Arthur).

beads costumes, t-shirts,[8] and clown fright wigs sold two for $5, co-exist side-by-side with the large-scale creations that take months and months to make. t-shirt bands[9] are seen in Rotterdam, Notting Hill, and other United Kingdom carnivals. They are popular in street parades such as Zurich's Techno Street Parade that has carnivalesque elements. What was first an easy group costume for school children and young people participating in carnival, allowing them to make a colorful splash without expending a great deal of money, has caught on, blurring the line between everyday clothing and behavior with special carnival masquerade costuming and performance.

Bikini-and-beads costume bands have also become ubiquitous in today carnivals. It is commonly believed by Trinidadian carnivalists that these costumes were imported from carnival in Rio de Janeiro. The race politics surrounding the image of a sleek mixed race woman is highly controversial on a number of levels and is certainly a factor in the response to the costume.[10] The costumes are roundly condemned by older carnivalists, in part because they are so risqué, and in part because they are not authentically part of Trinidad's carnival masquerade traditions. Conversely, pejorative views of the bikini bands can be attributed to the rivalry that exists between Rio and Port of Spain for the top spot as the world's best carnival.

However, Trinidad carnivalists find the promoters of bikini-and-beads bands to be the real threat. A large number of these entrepreneurs have made millions by providing the briefest of costumes to men and women in Port of Spain. These bands entice overseas tourists to the carnivals with pricey package tours promising three or four days of debauchery. Perhaps the most infamous of these bands in recent years went by the name Poison. Critics produced rampant commentary about the poison that this band brought to carnivals in Port of Spain and throughout the Diaspora.

Despite critiques, there are designers who embrace some of the new forms, transforming a t-shirt into an elaborate carnival costume or creating beautiful costumes out of bikini-and-beads. It is in keeping with the carnival spirit to create costumes that are both modern but also evoke the rich traditions of the past. The nature of carnival requires that you make use what you have on hand to make a costume, drawing inspiration from past carnivals or contemporary fashion, art history, magazines, popular films, or television commercials. It is not unheard of to see an 18th-century French hoop skirt, made out of sequin-encrusted African mud cloth, paired with a revealing bodice all together in one carnival costume.

Scholars Judith Bettelheim, John Nunley, and Barbara Bridges use the terms festival aesthetics, aesthetics of assemblage, and aesthetics of assimilation to describe the driving forces that have shaped creative practices in the Caribbean and beyond.[11] These artistic standards reflect a blending process of a multicultural range of cultural influences from Africa, the Americas, parts of Asia, and Europe. Festival aesthetics in action encompass the multi-faceted forms of expression that make up carnival, the inexorably linked combination of masquerades, music, and dance and a multi-media range of materials, from cowrie shells to plastic soda bottles to sequins to natural fibers that are put to use in carnival costumes.[12]

Festival aesthetics aptly describe carnival costuming characteristics in the 21st century. As Bettelheim, Nunley, and Bridges state, "The Caribbean festival arts still revolve around the aesthetics of assemblage. The makers of festival arts attach items both fabricated and found in the urban environment and natural vegetable and animal materials to superstructures in layers resulting in a plethora of textures and colors and collage-like forms."[13]

Festival aesthetics also allow individuals with imagination but few financial resources to

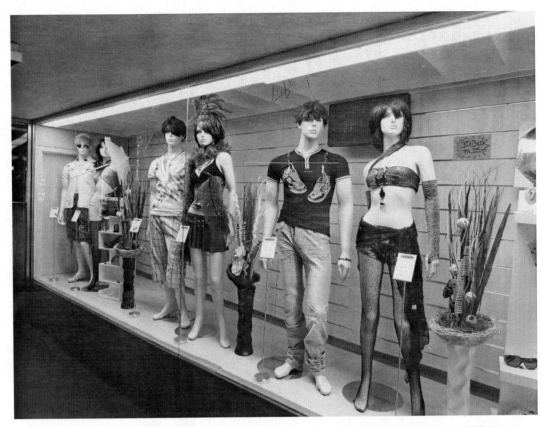

A store in Lucerne, Switzerland, that is just a short train ride away from the Zurich Street Parade in 2012 advertised carnival or street parade fashions popular in cities around the world that rival the large-scale costumes created by carnival designers (courtesy Loyce L. Arthur).

create a costume out of very little. An artful decorated t-shirt or fright wig has to be seen through a different lens when worn by carnivalists from impoverished sections of a city.

A strong case can be made that festival aesthetics have been a key factor in the proliferation of carnival parades across the world. The very transcultural hybridity of carnival allows participants to make individual statements within a collective parade event and allows designers to make multilayered statements in inventive ways. Those individuals and designers aware of the aesthetics of carnival engage in a process year after year in an ongoing cultural and artistic dialogue with each other and with viewers from city to city and country to country, provoking and inspiring more creative masquerading.

In Trinidad and Tobago's major cities where Trinidadians and shared aesthetics have influenced carnival, every effort is made to make the masquerade events more than just a costume parade or a big party. A segment of carnivalists are dedicated to the history and tradition of carnival and believe that they are "playing *Mas.*" Photographer and carnivalist Jeffrey Chock explains:

> To seriously attempt *Mas* is to dedicate one's being to the idea.... All those who take part are *Mas* people.... The true *Masmen* or women are dedicated to the creation they aspire to be. A costume, no matter how splendid, comes alive only when displayed or performed well. The most expensive is not always the best and many an adequate effort rises above itself when skillfully used.[14]

One of the most world-renowned, prestigious, and influential carnival designers, Peter Minshall could be called the master of carnival aesthetics. A source of inspiration for designers in Toronto, London, New York and around the world, Minshall challenges designers to reclaim carnival as described in the quote at the beginning of this article and to continue what he feels is the carnival ideal: *Mas*. He argues passionately that, "*Mas* is the living expression of elemental human energy out on the streets in a celebration of life that dates back to ancient times. *Mas* is a living art." According to Minshall we now experience too many soulless carnival arts that are all too much flash and not enough substance.[15]

The *Masmen* and women that Minshall and Chock describe are a dedicated breed of contemporary carnivalists for whom carnival has a meaningful heritage that must be respected and protected at the same time that this art form as they know it keeps pace with the modern world. An African heritage, in particular, first denied to African slaves

Spandex morph suits have become a very popular choice for urban carnivals and street parades like the one worn by this reveler at the Zurich Street Parade, 2012, Switzerland (courtesy Loyce L. Arthur).

throughout the Atlantic region and later recovered and celebrated in carnivals in 20th-century independence movements, distinctly defines carnivals in Port of Spain as part Caribbean culture,[16] part Latin America culture, and part Caribbean and Brazilian diasporic cultures. As Schechner explains, "No matter how celebratory, Trinidad carnival lives within the shadows of slavery, indentured labor, colonialism, imperialism, and now globalization.... Carnival is a celebration of freedom—yes, but not only or even mostly, individual freedom, but social, collective, national freedom—a liberty that is tenuous, hard-won, and still felt as threatened."[17] For many, carnival is still "a creative path of resistance" even today.[18]

In an article about carnival in the Cross River State of Nigeria Amanda Carlson provides insight into what Nigerian carnivalists call the "trado-originality" of their Calabar carnival, a heritage-based carnival in reverse. By enacting a Port of Spain-style carnival, African masquerade forms that were lost due to slavery are recovered and celebrated at the same time that these Nigerians created a new cross-cultural carnival tradition.[19]

Seeking to increase tourism to the region in order to replace dwindling oil industry revenues Calabar carnival representatives went to Port of Spain to experience carnival. They brought knowledge back with them to their city. Their Cross River State carnival is not a copy. Rather, organizers created their own style of carnival, fusing local traditional dances and costumes with Trinidad-style band competitions and both large and small-scale satiny, sequined carnival costumes. This is more than an act of appropriation. Carlson writes that, "Nigerians are tracing ... the path of their ancestors to the Caribbean, celebrating the interaction and influences their ancestors had in the Caribbean, and then manifesting that history within a new performance style.[20] Wherever you find modern carnivals you find individuals who take the masquerade form and make their own to suit the needs and values of their society.

Carlson gives intriguing insight into the costume making process of the Calabar carnival. She notes that "costume designers and tailors are in abundant supply in Calabar" and that "teams of local tailors [work] around the clock on costumes."[21] There has also been an instance when king and queen costumes from Trinidad were imported for a politician who wanted to make a splash. In 2009 Brazilian designers were brought in to build carnival floats for the parades.[22] The concept of shared aesthetics flourishes in Calabar, and allows citizens, as it does for others in other parts of the world, to step outside the confines of traditional forms in order to simultaneously modernize and protect those forms.

As with carnivalists everywhere, Calabar carnivalists took on the issue of the bikini-and-beads costumes in their parades. In the beginning, the socially-conservative Cross River region did not condone public nudity and consequently its carnival was not the transgressive "celebration of flesh" of other carnivals.[23] Today, however, the official website shows numerous promotional photographs of bikini-clad women,[24] which has led to some media discussions about morality,[25] keeping in step with global trends. Calabar carnival stands as an excellent example of the creative reimagining that is part of a contemporary carnival making process.

## Carnival Designer Clary Salandy—Artist and Creative Entrepreneur

Contemporary carnivals are big business and big artistic ventures demanding both a realistic and hugely creative point-of-view. Clary Salandy, one of only a handful of women carnival designers,[26] is a designer in the thick of it all, designing for the Notting Hill Carnival for the past 30 years. She declares, "When my father played *Mas,* his face filled with joy. This is what he gave me, a love of carnival."[27]

At sixteen years old, Salandy immigrated to the United Kingdom to study at the Wimbledon School of Art. She discovered that carnival in London has a culturally significant but turbulent history. Beginning in the 1930s the migrations before and after World War II brought Caribbean people to the capital to work to repair the economy. Re-settlement was not easy. Racial tensions were high. There are accounts of the hostilities and violent race riots in London in the 1950s, '60s, and '70s.[28] Community organizer and journalist Claudia Jones, whom some call the "Mother of Notting Hill Carnival," presented an indoor carnival celebration with one main goal—to present Caribbean culture in a positive light during a climate of racism and harassment by British whites. In 1966, British/Native American/Russian educator, Rhaune Laslett, took Jones' ideas a step further when she organized a street procession that was a mix of the black and white cultures of Notting Hill to generate "warmth and happiness" in the neighborhood.[29] Lesley Palmer, a Londoner born in Trinidad took up carnival studies in her native country and then brought that knowledge back to Notting Hill for the August Bank Holiday parade in the 1970s, doing her part to firmly establish the Caribbean focus to the parade.[30]

The Orchid Queen, costume worn by Tearea Case employs Salandy's signature forms—graceful swooping shapes that allow for movement at the Grand Carnival Splash, 2005. Alexandra Palace, London (photographer: Michael Ramdeen; courtesy Loyce L. Arthur).

Salandy follows in the footsteps of these female pioneers along with her mentors Nick Lyons, Arthur Peters and Carl Gabriel, and most importantly, Lawrence Noel, all carnival designers and wire sculpture artists that mentored her in the early 1980s.[31] In 1985 Salandy designed her first *Mas* band and in 1989 with partner and fellow Trinidadian, Michael Ramdeen, a wire sculptor who had studied structural engineering, she founded the carnival group, Mahogany, now called Mahogany Community Ventures, Limited.

Salandy feels that, because of the social, political, and carnival history of Trinidad and the United Kingdom, carnival is not a costume parade, it is *Mas*.[32] She takes her role as a designer/community activist very seriously. During the 2011 riots in London and other British cities there was a sense that history was repeating itself. For Salandy, her mission during those times was clear. She passionately stated:

> Look at them. Those boys are making hats, [in the Mahogany workshop]. Those girls are making costumes.... They are creating things. They are not rioting. They like Nike and all that stuff

but they are here working until the early hours and then they go to the shop and buy them. We have seen what some kids do. Carnival will show what our good kids do....[33]

Facing possible cancellation of the carnival parade that year she declared, "Carnival absolutely needs to happen this year. The Caribbean community needs to rekindle its identity. Carnival is an opportunity to demonstrate that we have a creative culture that England can benefit from."[34]

As a Trinidadian Salandy was exposed by birth and experience to festival aesthetics. As a well-versed contemporary artist she is aware and open to exploring and incorporating world artistic traditions into her designs, including pop-culture references. As a resident of an ethnically diverse community in north London's Harlesden area she feels a strong obligation to reflect the cultural richness of her neighbors. Following the political turmoil in China in 1989 Salandy designed a seminal piece for Mahogany, a piece that "helped us realize what the company could do."[35] Called "Shadow of Tiananmen Square," the piece incorporates a towering puppet in black and white that represents the Chinese regime which is manipulated by a color figure that represents the students.

Mahogany is a creative home to people from all walks or life, ages, and nationalities.[36] Year after year a *Mas* family assembles at the Mahogany studios in Harlesden proper to create a masquerade in the Afro-Caribbean sense of the word. Carnivalists and scholars Geraldine Connor and Max Farrar give an excellent framework for both Salandy's work and Notting Hill carnival itself when stating:

> Inherent within the aesthetics of carnival is the seamless fusion of arts practice and community engagement. In particular, carnival is now (2002–4) seen and often used as an effective creative tool for bringing disparate communities together in common celebration. It has repeatedly demonstrated the potential it offers for communication and unification across social, cultural, and political boundaries, and more recently carnival has been seen as a model for artistic and social co-operation, integration and cohesion, ultimately offering creative opportunity for social and political change.[37]

Salandy draws a great deal of inspiration from African masquerade and art forms, including Dogan mask traditions and the Ndebelle women's traditional murals, both of which she has thematically explored in her designs.

In 2000 Salandy designed a series of shields for carnival with the faces of Nelson Mandela, Martin Luther King, and Mother Teresa, whom she calls contemporary warriors. Commenting on this work and her frequent use of shields she says, "I love using the shield because it is a symbol of Africa. It's a symbol of war and I feel that in some ways I am a contemporary warrior.... I am holding onto this culture, protecting it, taking it forward..."[38]

Salandy speaks nostalgically about carnivals of her childhood but is realistic about some of the changes in music and in visual representations that are occurring, welcoming them as inevitable if carnival is to continue and evolve as an art form. Because she feels strongly that contemporary images of carnival are too sexualized, however Salandy strongly opposes skimpy, bikini-inspired costumes. She feels keenly, that skimpy costumes are taking the place of traditional carnival characters and all too often they supplant the artistry and inventiveness of carnival masquerades.

"A *Mas* is glorifying," says Salandy.[39] "Our kings and queens are glamorous, larger-than-life, and ornate because carnival is about art and creativity, exploring shapes and forms, color.

Because the queen's costume Flame/Passion worn by Carolyn Roberts-Griffith embodies the enduring Olympic flame, and the depths of life's passions, Clary Salandy intentionally used concentric forms to represent both flames and the facets of a ruby for *Bling* at the Grand Carnival Splash 2008. Alexandra Palace. London (photographer Andre Harrington; courtesy Loyce Authur).

It is animating sculpture and the sculpture is designed around the human form. Thousands of dollars and hours are spent to make these costumes glorious for the people who wear them."[40]

As a designer Salandy prefers to create sculptural forms that synchronize gracefully and easily with the body of the performer. Her carnival aesthetic, inspired by African masquerades, masks the whole body not just the face and she has, over time, perfected certain forms that are unique signature representations.

Salandy's work balances between tradition and contemporary relevance. Salandy is dedicated to passing on what she knows to the next generation so that they, with an awareness of their heritage, can keep carnival going into the future.[41] She takes great pride in the fact that young people help to make the *Mas* and then perform the *Mas*. She wants them to feel a sense of accomplishment in the work, hoping that the successes that they achieve through carnival can translate into successes in other parts of their lives.[42]

In 2008 Salandy created designs for Mahogany entitled *Bling*. The designs truly exemplify the group's creative and educational mission. With the London Olympic Games four years away, she wanted students to reach for an Olympic-sized personal best. By incorporating Olympic gold, silver, and bronze medals, as well as diamonds and rubies and other faceted jewels into her designs she wanted her participants to feel that they too were as precious and valuable as any prize. The British flag was also an element of the designs and children, whose black faces peeped out behind red, white, and blue shields, made a powerful statement about the UK's future "warriors." The Olympic Flame/Ruby/ "Passion" costumes symbolized individual and collective victories, triumphs, and endurance. Salandy is most proud of the fact that young people wearing these costumes were on stage at the Olympic torch hand-off ceremony to represent the whole of Britain to a world audience.[43]

Clary Salandy and Michael Ramdeen and Mahogany celebrated twenty-five years of carnival tradition and creative innovation in 2014. The band's theme for the year, "Awake!" was designed to call eco-warriors to action to battle climate change. Accompanied by a Greenpeace polar bear puppet, band members wore costumes symbolizing the earth's fauna and flora subsumed by a dead forest and melting ice forms. Knowing Salandy's and Ramdeen's concerns for the future of carnival, they may well have intended to also send a message about carnival's possible extinction as well.

## Commercialism vs. Shared Aesthetics Principles

Carnivals today are huge economic boons and highly profitable enterprises for the countries that produce them. Venice netted approximately $133 million and attracted about 2 million people to their carnival in 2009,[44] compared to Mardi Gras that brought $145 million to the city of New Orleans.[45] Trinidad and Tobago expended 125 million Trinidad and Tobago dollars (TTD) on its event in 2011 and over a million people attended carnival in Port of Spain. The Notting Hill London Parade with 2 million people in attendance generated close to $146 million.[46] Calabar Carnival generated $7 million in worker's revenues, attracted 50,000 revelers, 2 million spectators, and 50 million television viewers in 2012.[47] In 2013 Carnival in Rio de Janeiro generated $628 million in revenues and created 250,000 temporary jobs.[48]

The possibility of increased revenues for carnival cities has proved to be irresistible, particularly with the volatile changes effecting traditional economic development strategies dependent on manufacturing and trade. As Suzanne Burke states: "The more recent focus on the

economic values of the carnival [in Trinidad] can be considered under the pressing need to find alternative vectors for socio-economic development."[49] Burke goes on to explain that Trinidad officials not only set out to make Port of Spain's carnivals "the greatest show on earth" but they have also put considerable resources and efforts into exporting Trinidad's "brand" of carnival to the rest of the world.[50]

Trinidadian economist Keith Nurse puts it this way by commenting, "Caribbean carnivals have grown from being the bane of their respective cities, [*trash, noise, crowds, violence*] to becoming an indispensable feature of popular culture, multiculturalism, and cultural tourism."[51] Carnivals in other parts of the world experience similar polarities as well. Riggio talks about the urbanity of carnivals, including its size and noise, noting that carnival has evolved as cities themselves have evolved and therefore are truly of the cities not a an alien presence.[52] Despite the fact that some locals in Port of Spain, Notting Hill, Rio de Janeiro, Venice, and other cities tend to flee during carnival time, carnival has had to be accepted as part of urban life as important as any other urban festival.

Carnival groups have risen to contemporary challenges, finding ways to keep going year after year. Some small carnivals ask for payment to enter a gated carnival space or ask for donations of support on their event websites. Despite Rio's budgets, participants have to pay for their costumes, with the exception of the Flag Bearers, Muses that lead the *Baterias* (musicians), and some of the elaborate costumes that celebrities wear on the top of the floats. (These are put on display in hotels and department stores, or used in special stage shows, all over Brazil to add to Samba School coffers.)

Mahogany participants either pay a nominal fee, if they can afford it, or work making costumes in exchange for ones they will wear to play *Mas*. Rio and Trinidad and Tobago websites are set up that allow anyone to choose a costume to buy, join a band, and dance in a parade, requiring minimal rehearsals. Participants then get to keep their costumes or throw them away. Enterprising individuals take these discarded costumes in order to sell to tourist or to smaller carnival groups.

Despite efforts of carnivalists to garner funds, clearly a disparity exists between the revenues that city organizers derive from carnival when compared to the financial benefits to dedicated stakeholders. Two participants in Berlin's Karneval der Kulturen went straight to the heart of the matter in 2012 when they explained that since there is no state support to smaller groups in the carnival, they wouldn't be able to take part in future carnivals because they couldn't afford to create costumes and decorate a truck out of their own personal funds.[53]

Even in the well-endowed Rio carnivals groups like Beija Flora, Mangueira, and Salguero (three schools that consistently take top prizes and clearly have budgets high above their competitors), compete with participants from the favelas who must be satisfied with accolades rather than remuneration. This despite the fact that Rio's budgets are bolstered by lucrative TV broadcast contracts as well as corporate sponsorship. Regardless, thousands of Brazilians favor the option of paying for costumes every year as a way of maintaining samba school and national pride.

Of course, no carnival designer anywhere receives a huge salary, even in Rio. However, the popularity of carnivals has meant that the designers and carnival groups have had access

*Opposite*: For *Bling*, Clary Salandy designed costumes for the Britannia section in which young "warriors" like Joshua and Jon-Jon Morgan carried shields to symbolize Black British pride in the Notting Hill 2008 Carnival Parade, London, United Kingdom (photographer Andre Harrington; courtesy Loyce L. Arthur).

to more grants and more corporate support in some carnival cities and more opportunities to create interesting work for wider and wider audiences.

Clary Salandy, Michael Ramdeen, and the Mahogany staff exemplify some of the success stories. Mahogany is a limited company run as a not-for-profit social enterprise with an approximate annual $170,000 grant from the United Kingdom's Arts Council.[54] The company has managed to get contracts like the Harrods Department Store's Christmas Pageant and a corporate event at the London Zoo to help to cover costs. Mahogany even has a contract with Greenpeace that helps to pay the bills but also aligns with their social mission by providing polar bear and orangutan costumes for protesters.[55]

While the business of contemporary carnival is booming, the effects on the aesthetics carnivals have become more and more corrosive in some respects. Economic downturns and rampant commercialism have led to an imbalance between the music, dance, and masquerade elements of carnival. Carnivals in London and Berlin, and to some extent Port of Spain and New York, have become more music-driven street festivals than masquerade events. Some revelers are only interested in following sound trucks, semi-trucks that haul fifteen to twenty-foot high speakers blasting Soca club music, a wildly popular style of Caribbean music form. Other participants crowd around static sound systems, banks of speakers planted on street corners with DJs or popular singers performing for crowds, which clog parade routes. Law enforcement officers and carnival bands alike find masquerade participants more like audience members who prove to be a tremendous headache. Both of these groups of participants seem to actually prefer the pure music carnival events to the parades because they can wear make-up or a drugstore mask or second-hand clothes and they don't have to waste money on expensive costumes.

## Conclusion

Despite the global social, political, and economic challenges, carnival continues to flourish driven by determined individuals and groups that are willing to give all that they have to ensure carnival's survival. Newer carnivals join the ranks and older carnivals evolve with the times. Trinidadian carnivalists in Port of Spain and London continue to embrace principles of re-invention while employing a rich tradition of masquerading. Rio de Janeiro continues to champion carnival as an essential and valued part of Brazilian contemporary culture. As other communities, such as the Cross River State in Nigeria, embrace carnival they quickly find that they must struggle with complex social, cultural, and economic factors which play out on the streets in grand, dramatic, and creative ways.

## Notes

1. Brazil Carnival Ooah! http://brazilcarnival.com.br/culture/de-baiana-de-carnaval-of-brazil.

2. Richard Schechner (2004), "Carnival (Theory) after Bakhtin," in *Carnival: Culture in Action—The Trinidad Experience,* Milla Cozart Riggio, ed. (New York: Routledge), 7, 11.

3. Milla Cozart Riggio (2004), "Time Out or Time In? The Urban Dialectic of Carnival," in *Carnival: Culture in Action—The Trinidad Experience*, 45.

4. Trinidadian scholar Jeff Henry provides a useful explanation when stating that the Pre-Lenten festival known as carnival is European in origin, going back to Roman and Medieval times. In contrast, "masquerade" refers to African forms of mask performance brought by slaves to the islands and banned

by authorities. See Jeff Henry (2013), "Carnival/Masquerade in Trinidad: Resistance through Performance," in *Carnival: Theory and Practice*, Christopher Innes, Annabel Rutherford, and Brigitte Bogar, eds. (Trenton, NJ: Africa World Press).

5. Modesto Mawulolo Amegago (2013), "Interrogating the Roots, Elements, and Crossovers of the Caribbean Carnival: A Case of West African Celebrations," in *Carnival: Theory and Practice*, 26–34.

6. A complete list of carnivals is available on Wikipedia: http://www.trinijunglejuice.com/carnivalcalendar.html.

7. The WHL Travel Group (2011), "Top Five Carnival Celebrations Outside Brazil," *2 February, http://www.thetravelword.com/2011/02/02/top-five-carnival-celebrations-outside-brazil/*.

8. Bikini and beads bands is the phrase describing the hordes of skimpily costumed men and women found in contemporary carnivals; t-shirt bands use t-shirts all of the same color, sometimes with a logo, like followers of a particular team sport or music band. Some London and UK bands allow participants to cut shapes into the t-shirts and add beads and other decorative elements, allowing individuals artistic license within the restrictive limits of the use t-shirts instead of costumes.

9. Carnival parades can have 20 to 60 bands, each one with its own themed costumes that may be split further into visual variations on the theme.

10. The image throughout the Atlantic region relates to the glorification and exploitation of mixed race women, called *mulatas* or *mestizos* in Brazil. A *profissao mulata* are women of African descent who make a living dancing samba or advertise carnival. From a lecture by Maria J. Barbosa, "From Mucamas to Mulats/Globeleza," University of Iowa, 6 June 2012. See also http://brazilcarnival.com.be/muses.

11. John Nunley, Judith Bettelheim, and Barbara Bridges (1988), *Caribbean Festival Arts: Each and Every Bit of Difference* (Seattle: University of Washington Press).

12. Ibid., 35.

13. Ibid., 36.

14. Jeffrey Chock (2013), in *Carnival: Theory and Practice*, 93.

15. Peter Minshall and Christopher Innes (2013), in *Carnival: Theory and Practice*.

16. Not every island in the Caribbean has carnival traditions.

17. Schechner, in Carnival: Culture in Action—The Trinidad Experience, 6.

18. Henry, 67.

19. Amanda B. Carlson (2010), "Calabar Carnival: A Trinidadian Tradition Returns to Africa," *African Arts*, Winter.

20. Ibid., 44–45.

21. Ibid., 48.

22. Ibid., 53.

23. Ibid.

24. http://www.carnivalcalabar.com/category/image-galleries/2011/adult-carnival.

25. "Calabar Carnival Has Now Become Sexual—Photos" (30 December 2012), http://news2.onlinenigeria.com/headline/233391-pictures-from-the-2012-calabar-international-carnival.html.

26. Rosa Magalhaes has been a *carnavalesco* (designer) in Brazil since 1971. Karen and Kathy Norman are two up-and-coming fashion and carnival designers in Trinidad and Tobago. Rosalind Gabriel is a noted Adult and Junior carnival *Mas* band leader and designer among several female junior band designers in Trinidad and Tobago. More work needs to be done in order to identify female carnival designers around the world.

27. Clary Salandy interview by Loyce Arthur (2013), "Mahogany Artistic Director and Notting Hill Carnival Costume Designer," 3 May.

28 Geraldine Connor and Max Farrar (2004), "Carnival in Leeds and London: Making New Black British Subjectives," in *Carnival: Culture in Action—The Trinidad Experience*, 256–257.

29. Connor and Farrar, citing Cohn (1993).

30. Connor and Farrar (1993).

31. Salandy also credits Errol Hill's book, *A Trinidad Carnival: Mandate for a National Theatre*, as one of the works that has shaped her work as a carnival designer.

32. Clary Salandy interview by Loyce Arthur (2013), University of Iowa.

33. "The Importance of the Notting Hill Carnival," (25 August 2011), *The Guardian*, http://www.u.tv/articles/article.aspx?cat=news&guid=f744d109–98dc-4315–8285–84fbd8bfbe76.

34. Alexandra Topping (19 August 2011), "Notting Hill Carnival: Fraught with Risk, but the Show Goes On" *The Guardian*, http://www.theguardian.com/culture/2011/aug/19/notting-hill-carnival-london-riots.

35. Ibid.

36. While Notting Hill Carnival is dominated by Trinidadians, it actually brings together Caribbean people from multiple island nations including Grenada, Barbados, Jamaica and others.

37. Connor and Farrar (1993), in Carnival: Culture in Action—The Trinidad Experience.

38. Leslie Ferris (2013), "Designing for the Diaspora: Images of Africa in Contemporary British Carnival," in *Carnival: Theory and Practice*, 184.

39. Ruth Tompsett (2002), "Wings Soar, Sequins Shimmer: Textile Arts in the Notting Hill Carnival," *Embroidery* Vol. 53, No. 5.

40. Clary Salandy interview by Loyce Arthur (2013), University of Iowa.

41. _____. 2013. A Biography of Clary Salandy.

42. Clary Salandy, interview by Loyce Arthur, April 2013. University of Iowa.

43. Ibid.

44. Teresa Machan (13 February 2009), "Venice Takes off Its Mask: Two Social Networking Groups Have Organized a Street Party to Reclaim Carnival for Venetians," *The Guardian*, http://www.theguardian.com/travel/2009/feb/12/venice-carnival-local-street-party.

45. Jaquetta White (2009), "Study: Direct Economic Impact of Mardi Gras Is $145 million," *The Times-Picayune, http://www.nola.com/business/index.ssf/2009/12/study_direct_economic_impact_o.html*.

46. See Keith Nurse (1988); Jo-anne Tull (2005), "Globalization in Reverse: Diaspora and the Export of Trinidad Carnival," in *Carnival: Culture in Action—The Trinidad Experience*; "Money Matters—Trinidad and Tobago Carnival 2005," (22 April 2005), presentation at Reflections on Carnival 2005, Carnival Institute of Trinidad and Tobago, http://www.academia.edu/326827/_Money_Matters_in_the_Trinidad_Carnival_.

47. Titus E. Amalu and Anim O. Ajake (2012), "An Assessment of the Influence of Calabar Carnival on the Economy of the Residents of Calabar Metropolis, Cross River State, Nigeria," *Global Journal of Human Social Science: Geography & Environmental GeoSciences* Vol. 12, Issue 10, Version 1.0; "Calabar Carnival" (19 December 2012), *Royal Times of Nigeria*, http://royaltimes.net/more/tourism/carnival-calabar/.

48. Holly Ellyatt (11 February 2013), "Even the Carnival Can't Save Brazil from a Slump," http://www.cnbc.com/id/100449508.

49. Suzanne Burke (2013), "Policing the 'People's Festival': State Policy and the Trinidad Carnival Complex," in *Carnival: Theory and Practice*, 111.

50. Ibid.

51. Keith Nurse, in Carnival: Culture in Action—The Trinidad Experience.

52. Riggio (2005), "Time Out or Time In? The Urban Dialectic of Carnival," in *Carnival: Culture in Action—The Trinidad Experience*.

53. Berlin carnivalists interviews with Loyce Arthur (2012), Berlin, Germany.

54. Robert Plummer (23 August 2011), "Notting Hill Carnival Spirit Boosts London's Economy" BBC, http://www.bbc.co.uk/news/.

55. "Group Action Day at Shell Station Hamburg," (16 July 2012), http://www.greenpeace.org/usa/en/multimedia/slideshows/Group-Action-Day-at-Shell-Station/Group-Action-Day-at-Shell-Station-Hamburg/; and Kate Magee (26 March 2010), "Taking Action: Greenpeace vs. Nestle," *PR Week,* http://www.prweek.com/uk/news/992445/.

# Works Cited

Amalu, Titus E., and Anim O. Ajake. (2012.) "An Assessment of the Influence of Calabar Carnival on the Economy of the Residents of Calabar Metropolis, Cross River State, Nigeria." *Global Journal of Human Social Science: Geography & Environmental GeoSciences* Vol. 12, Issue 10, Version 1.0.

Brazil Carnival Ooah! http://brazilcarnival.com.br/culture/de-baiana-de-carnaval-of-brazil.

Carlson, Amanda B. (2010.) "Calabar Carnival: A Trinidadian Tradition Returns to Africa." *African Arts*, Winter.

Connor, Geraldine, and Max Farrar. (2004.) "Carnival in Leeds and London: Making New Black British Subjectives." *Carnival: Culture in Action—The Trinidad Experience.*

Hill, Errol. (1972.) *A Trinidad Carnival: Mandate for a National Theatre.* Austin: University of Texas Press.

Innes, Christopher, Annabel Rutherford, and Brigitte Bogar, eds. (2013.) *Carnival: Theory and Practice.* Trenton, NJ: Africa World Press.

Nunley, John, Judith Bettelheim, and Barbara Bridges. (1988.) *Caribbean Festival Arts: Each and Every Bit of Difference.* Seattle: University of Washington Press.

Riggio, Milla Cozart. (2004.) *Carnival: Culture in Action—The Trinidad Experience.* New York: Routledge.

Salandy, Clary. Interview by Loyce Arthur, April 2013. University of Iowa.

Tompsett, Ruth. (2002.) "Wings Soar, Sequins Shimmer: Textile Arts in the Notting Hill Carnival." *Embroidery* Vol. 53, No. 5.

Tull, Jo-anne. (2005.) "Globalization in Reverse: Diaspora and the Export of Trinidad Carnival." *Carnival: Culture in Action—The Trinidad Experience.*

# Colliding Cultures in the Carnivals of Cuba and the Philippines

LAURA CROW

This essay on Cuban and Filipino carnival traditions and masquerade is the result of various visits to both Cuba and the Philippines between the years of 2002 and 2013. The second of three trips to the Philippines was generously sponsored by a Fulbright Senior Scholar grant, and the others were partially sponsored by the United States Institute of Theatre Technology (USITT), the Organisation Internationale des Scénografes, Techniciens et Architectes de Théatre (OISTAT) and the University of Connecticut, where I am currently a professor of costume history, design and technology. The results of extensive research, along with on-site observations and many informal interviews in both countries with performers and designers, has led to the following conclusions that explain dramatic changes in the experience of carnival in both of these countries that reside within evolutionary historical contexts. Of paramount interest was the mixture of cultures that comes about at times of festival, augmented with the aid of masquerade, giving a certain license to make emboldened theatrical and political statements. These activities provide a much-needed outlet for the individual to express sentiments in an unthreatening manner, helping to bring about a cultural understanding that in other circumstances might be in conflict. Even though tourist-centric commercial events reflect a deceptive gloss, underneath is an ethnic blend resulting from decades of conflict in the case of both countries. Both Cuba and the Philippines have Spanish domination in their pasts with the heavy burden of Catholicism carried on their backs—sometimes literally. Masquerade and Carnival are at the center of these cultures that have a history of poverty, corruption and injustice. Both are hot and humid tropical climates, and both have been affected by the rampant capitalism of the United States.

Since the dawn of time, mankind's most basic instinct has been to decorate the human form. No place offers greater freedom in this endeavor than Carnival. Initially, the mask gave the freedom from inhibition needed for this theatrical gesture, but now an uninhibited costume is lauded as an acceptable form of self-expression with or without the mask. These marvelous fantasies express the inner soul of the wearer and not the mundane reality.

## Cuban Carnival Masquerade

Carnival celebrations, in particular, tend to blend multi-cultural looks. In the Caribbean countries, there are diverse cultural influences, most particularly European (Spanish and French with some English), African (Nigeria and the Congo), and American (USA, Mexico and Brazil). All of these countries have lavish yet very different Carnival traditions, and most of them are celebrated in the winter months, most particularly late February/early March, just prior to Lent. Cuba is the exception since the Carnival in Santiago has stayed centered around the Celebration of Saint Iago (James) on July 25th and in Havana in early January.

The social anthropology side of masquerade comes out in countries that have various cultures coming together at times of festival. Cuba's two large festivals have dress up parades. Both include influences from 17th-century slave owners and their slave's cultures from the Congo and Nigeria (Yoruba). These are combined with elements of traditional Mardi Gras masquerade, Chinese horn players, fifties Las Vegas style Tropicana dancers and celebrations centered on the revolution of Fidel Castro.

The traditional Mardi Gras style festival in Havana changed after Fidel Castro took control and emphasized only non-religious aspects of the culture. *Carnival* instead commemorates the departure of the dictator Fulgencio Batista who fled from Cuba to Spain, just after New Year's Eve in January 1959. The commercial focus attracts more tourism, and does not directly conflict with other traditional Carnival celebrations such as those in Trinidad and Brazil.

The second huge celebration honors Fidel Castro's *26th of July Revolution* in Santiago de Cuba. The date commemorates a failed attack on the Moncada Army Barracks that began the revolution in 1953, and today it is a clever diversion when workers are laid off from the banana and sugar cane plantations and at their most restless.

The parades in Santiago de Cuba are complete with white wigged Granmas and Granpas who represent the cabin cruiser named *Granma* that brought Fidel Castro, Raul Castro, and Che Guevara among 82 revolutionaries from Tuxpan, Veracruz in Mexico two years after the 26th of July attack. The overburdened boat made it to the Playa las Colorados, in what is now Granma Province, just over the mountains from Santiago de Cuba. Those white wigged "Granmas" and "Grandpas" are a mainstay of the celebration. They represent not only the revolution, but also the slaves wearing hand-me-down clothes and white wigs from their 18th-century masters.

As early as the 17th century, slaves were granted liberty for a day so they could celebrate in the streets. Many of the slaves came from the Congo, so the celebrations naturally involved lots of drum playing and dancing. Initially *Carnaval* in Havana was held at the traditional time, just before lent as opposed to Santiago de Cuba where the 25th of July was a celebration on the feast day of their Catholic patron St. James (St. Iago). In fact Castro began the revolution with an attack planned for daybreak on the 26th knowing that the people of Santiago would still be celebrating and the invasion of the armed revolutionaries would go unnoticed.

The wealthy landowners in Santiago traditionally carried the effigy of Saint James though the streets and then went to the Cathedral for mass. Following behind their masters, and free for the day, their slaves would sing and dance in the parade and then party on while their masters were in church. Soon the masters tired of the parades since the after-parades were more entertaining. Subsequently the slaves, in a role reversal, wearing their masters' cast off clothing, began to lead the parade. The street dancing followed on with various drummed rhythms. The lines between the rich and the slaves were once again obscured just as they were in the 18th-century Venice *Carnevale*. The masks and white wigs blurred the racial lines. In Cuba, ladies wore white gloves and shawls while men wore white gloves and high-necked cravats along with their white wigs and masks. Today, the Granmas and Granpas, the social leaders of the city, wear 18th-century clothing while also symbolizing the Revolution. They no longer wear masks because they are now the social leaders of the community, and wish to be seen.

Along with the Congolese slaves, there were slaves from the Yoruba culture in Nigeria. The *òrìsà*, the guardian saints of their Santeria religion, bear a striking resemblance to 18th-century ladies in high pompadour wigs. When masquerading as an *òrìsà*, most women wear high shiny turbans and similar fancy pastel satin gowns with ruffled trimming. Color-coding identifies various *òrìsà* costumes. The most commonly depicted *òrìsà*, Obbatalá wears white and correlates with the Catholic Virgin of Mercy, often intertwined with a dove. Ochun dresses in yellow and represents fertility and prosperity. She shares characteristics with Cuba's patron saint, Our Lady of Charity (*La Virgen de la Caridad del Cobre*). Even though Catholic religion and rituals are banned in Cuba, these *òrìsà* are tolerated, and have become a cross between the two.

Each festival has a distinctive look that has evolved over the years and each one has typical stock characters from year to year identified with bright colors. Kings, queens, and dignitaries lead the parade, moving at a slower pace. They wear clothing loosely based on the 18th-century silhouette worn by the original street-dancing slaves in their master's cast-off clothing taking on the Identity of those who enslaved them. Masquerading beauty pageant princesses appearing in their own gowns add to the mix with voluminous gowns, although without wigs or hats. During the most commercial phase of *Carnaval* in Cuba in the first half of the 20th century, socialites created beauty queen pageants, and corporations sponsored lavish floats to market their products. Today the young beauties stroll behind the Kings and Queens.

Street-dancer designs draw inspiration from Flamenco as the basis for their costumes, with a plethora of ruffles that enhance their rhumba and samba movement. Each group consists of as many as 300 dancers, who move in carefully choreographed movements and they share one persona Instead of individual masqueraders. They are judged by their response to the theme chosen by the organizing group each year, as well as on the precision and timing of their presentation. The influence from the flamenco fashions, the culture of Spain, and commercial tourism is especially noticeable in Havana. The Malecon weaving its way along the retaining wall by the seaside is one of the longest pedestrian paths in Central America and perfect for festival parades with cool sea breezes blowing off the water and generating a mellow atmosphere.

Santiago de Cuba also presents choreographed routines, and often with costumes sporting the large ruffled *rhumba* sleeves and pants that have a vaguely flamenco feel, tight through the thighs and from the knee down. The routines, however, are much more about African rhythms and hip-hop on very hot steamy summer nights. The dancing clubs (called *samba* schools) in Santiago de Cuba are made up of younger performers for the most part aged 12 to 18, and they dance passionately all night long.

The Contra Dance, a line dance that has inspired much of the street dancing of both Trinidad and Cuba, was originally from the festivals in Normandy. The French brought it to the islands in the 18th century and it became the basis for a popular dance in Trinidad. The dance filtered over to Cuba during various migrations and by the mid–19th century it had

Granma costume combines the "Granma" look with a basket full of crops to honor the harvesters who began the revolution. Granma Key played an important part in the Revolution of Fidel Castro. The boat named *Granma* brought the revolutionaries from Mexico to Cuba. The unemployed cane workers were a ready force to help in the fight. This costume glorifies both the farmers of Cuba and the Granma name. They represent not only the revolution, but also the slaves wearing hand-me-down clothes. Santaiago de Cuba, Cuba, 2004 (courtesy Laura Crow).

evolved into the Cuban Contra Dance that was mixed with African movements. In Santiago de Cuba, a musician named Pepe Sanchez with no musical training, created the *samba*; the first complete synthesis of African rhythms and Spanish tunes. The Africans in Cuba took the *samba* sound and by placing the emphasis on the hips, the *rhumba* dance was born. The Chinese immigrants from the early 19th century added a third musical component; the Chinese horn creates a shrill sound that rises above the drumming and *rhumba* music.

As the wealth and stability of the groups grew, the parades became more formalized with built costumes and an increasing number of stock masquerade characters. Saint Iago (James), a stock character usually in white face, can appear in various ways throughout the parades. Devil bats appeared in the early part of the 20th century carrying the chains from the slaves as a reminder of their bondage. Skeletons are a part of these devils too, along with a full range of masked devilry. Lucifer was imported as a stock character from Germany in the 1920s. He wears fancy satin clothes, again reminiscent of the 18th-century plantation owner with his *papier-mâché* mask. Devils wear masks in Santiago, but there are also giant *papier-mâché* devil heads worn on top of the heads of individuals covered in a curtain of fabric that masks the wearer. Similar masked characters in the Yoruba culture are frequently covered in straw thatching. The "big heads" traditionally initiate the parade in Santiago de Cuba. Roughly 100 of these giant *papier-mâché* heads spin and dance along the parade route while children in the stands reach out, overcoming their fear, to touch the heads for good luck. Initially these were devil characters, but now they are more often giant Disney cartoon figures thrown into the mix.

*Kalinda*, or stick fighting, came by way of the Dominican Republic and figured heavily in the revolutions of the 1880s. In Vigan in the Philippines they still do elaborate stick-dancing routines in massive groups with syncopated rhythms striking their sets of sticks (much like drum sticks) on the ground and against each other. In that case they represent the sticks used to beat the cotton from the seeds. The French planters in the Dominican Republic would dress up as slaves and wear rag costumes and black face in their own exclusive carnival. Now in a double role reversal, the young Afro-Cuban men of Santiago dress up in rags with the sticks that have become flag poles, and run along before each group signaling their arrival. They rush around and do acrobatic tricks as teams.

Torches representing *Cannes Brulées* are carried for illumination and theatricality in Santiago de Cuba. This stems from the torches used by the slaves for cane burning in Trinidad and Tobago. It was a time when all of the plantation slaves would gather together, so it is not surprising that in the 1830s they were used to celebrate their release from slavery. It became a carnival for the slaves in the dead of night, wearing African masks as a representation of freedom. The African masks and the dark night provided safety through anonymity. In the New Orleans Mardi Gras parades the *Cannes Brulées* still exists. For a small coin donation a parade watcher can hire the fire to provide warmth for a few moments, but they are no longer carried by masqueraders, and for many they have lost their meaning.

The street dancing to the rhythms from the Congo and Nigeria and especially the *rhumba*, have become synonymous with Cuba. The *rhumba* was made famous during the 1950s prior to the Revolution, at the famous Tropicana Nightclub in Havana. The Tropicana has been reborn and migrated to Santiago de Cuba at the opposite end of the island, despite the squashing of all influences "American" by the Communist regime. A large open theatre operated as a tourist attraction presents the "tits-n-ass" Las Vegas of another era while focusing on their famed lighter-skinned and taller *Mulata* women. More statuesque than most showgirls in the United States these women are selected at a young age for their great beauty, represented by their lighter skin and tall stature. The Tropicana advertises their theatre for the tourists by sponsoring floats that display those *Mulata* on platforms as figurative goddesses to be worshipped for their beauty in the streets of Santiago de Cuba. As everyone basks in the beauty of the *Mulata*, the equally beautiful, but shorter rhumba dancing women are featured in the floats all around them. The contagious rhythm encourages dancing crowds along the route.

The scantily clad *rhumba* dancers are part of the culture, but they do not look as provocative as the dancers in Las Vegas. The women are muscular and great dancers without an inch of jiggling fat. Though the costumes are skimpy, they function well for the heat of the summer nights. When there is no escaping the heat, movement cools the body and the larger the mass of exposed

*Hombres Carrozas* (Men Floats) combine African, Mayan and Mardi Gras themes. The Cuban government pays for everything, so the flamboyance of the parade is largely constrained by economic conditions in Cuba. This "man float" is an example of what can be done with hangar wire and mylar fringe hand-cut into small sequins. Santiago de Cuba, Cuba, 2010 (photographer: C. Otis Sweezey; (courtesy Laura Crow).

skin, the more the flow of air can intersect with sweat to refresh the skin. The *rhumba* performed on the floats is often in contrast with the modern hip-hop seen in the street dancing.

The costume designer takes a paramount role everywhere that there is carnival in Cuba. Carnival designers tend to be paid professionals, along with the director/choreographers. Maria Luisa Bernal, perhaps the foremost designer from Santiago de Cuba prefers to stay with traditional historical forms, but she takes them into the world of theatrical exaggeration. There are many references to the ruffled rhumba costumes that pre-date the Castro regime when times were seemingly freer.

Designer Elio Meralles Rodriguez has invented the popular *hombres carrozas* or "man floats." The masqueraders for these floats wear masks and extensive costumes that represent the *òrìsà* as well as the magical nature that surrounds Santiago de Cuba. The *òrìsà* have special powers to control fate and replenish the soul in hard times. They represent a higher power than the government and even though Catholic religion is abolished, Santeria is tolerated. Elio Meralles uses untwisted wire hangers to construct the frames, and small wheels allow the frame to be carried along with the central character. They reflect a modest version of the enormous framed costumes made so popular by Peter Minshall in Trinidad. These wire hangers and glitter combined with enormous creativity from recycled objects make for a wonderful moving dancing spectacle that is worthy of worship.

All of the volunteer performers are most often young people under thirty years old. The other participants are people of social position within the neighborhoods or *samba* groups, who promenade before the dancers, and often they will make their costumes at home and repeat their special look year after year. Street vendors benefit financially from *Carnaval*, as do those seamstresses in the area who work triple time against impossible odds to finish costumes. For some local Cuban women who sew, this is their only guaranteed income each year.[1]

In general, armies of volunteers create the carnivals in Cuba. As it is the off-season for plantation work in Santiago, there are always plenty of bodies available to wear the costumes and those willing and able to dance in the hot and humid summer nights. In Havana, it is the students who are the main performers since it is during the school holidays and the designers and builders are a little bit more professional, or at least they have the benefits of larger budgets that pay for some labor. There is a roughness that is common to all carnival costumes and a heightened reality in the excitement of the parade. Larger than life details are often rather crudely put together by hand for a one or two-night event. The splashes of carnival color serve alongside thematic ideas to create street theatre that is achieved through exaggeration, more than authenticity. The outward appearance is a fun and colorful for the sake of the tourists who don't realize that there are hidden symbols in almost every aspect of the parade, and despite the fact that its roots have strong political implications.

## Filipino Carnival Masquerade

The Philippines is comprised of 7,100 islands stretching over 1,000 miles north to south near the equator in the Southern Hemisphere and claims to have more beachfront property than any nation in the world. On the edge of the Pacific Ocean, this cultural melting pot is the gateway to Southeast Asia with festivals and masquerade at the core of their social history. After Magellan first landed there on his circumnavigation of the world, the Philippines had 400 years under Spanish rule. After the Spanish American War, they came under the rule of the United States. In this way the history of Cuba and the Philippines is remarkably similar. The United States, took their colonialism very seriously and English-speaking public schools were instituted in the Philippines. After a five-year occupation by the Japanese during World War II, and a return to American rule, they finally became an independent country after 600 years in 1952.

During the pre-historic times, the islands originally had the name *Tanik*. In the 13th century ten *Datus* (Lords) from Borneo came to Miagao, on the island of Iloilo in search of more fertile farming lands. One gold necklace and one *Sadok* (Golden Hat) from Borneo were enough to buy all of the lowland farmable land from the native Ati. The *Datus* divided the land into three districts and the peace loving and retiring Ati were driven inland to live. These volcanic islands are very dramatic, much like the islands of Hawaii with tropical vegetation.

The population today is made up of native Polynesian, Chinese, Spanish, American, Japanese, Siamese, Bornean, Arab and Eastern Indian bloodlines. Along with the fascinating blend of ethnicities, Catholic, Protestant, Muslim and Pagan religions are thrown into the mix. The Pagans are generally animists who still sacrifice chickens and pigs. There has been a huge population movement in the Philippines since the Second World War contributing to cultural mixing. Many are drawn to Manila just as most of the world's urban centers attract a diverse population. The large Chinese population has been a constant, since the northern most islands, the Batanes Islands, are only a short boat ride away from Taiwan. The Chinese New Year's Festival in Manila is quite spectacular with many men masquerading as one giant dragon to thrill and delight the crowds.

Carnival and masquerade are a huge part of the cultural heritage of the Philippines due to the Spanish domination for so many years. Much of the carnival activity happens in the Visayas; the middle islands of the archipelago that make up the Philippines. The Visayas are located between the two main islands of Luzon and Mindanao, but further west, closer to Malaysia. They abound with festivals that combine the many cultural and ethnic traditions that surround them. The traditional costumes of the Visayas have a South Asian appearance with draped and wrapped garments made from brilliantly colored fabrics. However when masquerade happens, all of the countries, cultures, and religions that have influenced the *Gateway to Asia* combine to create a more theatrical vision.

On the large island of Panay the emphasis is on the tribal heritage of the Filipino people. Since the original trade, in a festival titled *Ati-Atihan,* the Malay settlers celebrated the event of the purchase of the islands from the Ati by smearing their bodies with charcoal mixed in palm oil and acting out the trade. This soon became a ritual and for the past 200 years "tribes," called *tribu* of male only dancers have formed to compete with each other.[2] The men gather together to dance very intricate choreography in very strict unison, wearing scanty, but highly decorative costumes on top of the black painted bodies.

The look of the original *Datus* can be seen best on Mactan, a small island separated by a narrow channel from the larger island of Cebu. Annually they recreate Lapu-Lapu's victory over Magellan. Lapu-Lapu was the native leader who cleverly lured Magellan and his men to a place where the water was waist deep and the men in steel armor were helpless against the lightly clad native Indonesians in their brightly colored silks. The silk costumes of today are much more colorful and elaborate with much more golden bling than the originals wore, and the conquistadors have peroxided yellow hair to indicate that they are European, even though they keep their natural black beards.

The original *Ati-Atihan* festival was in Kalibo, Aklan on the island of Panay, where it has continued uninterrupted since the first celebration. Following the dancing *tribu* are hoards of people dancing and "merrymaking," similar to Mardi Gras. The inspiration for the street dancing that follows the black painted *tribu* was a wish to bear children. Young couples would pray to Santo Niño (the baby Jesus) for a child. Both the husband and the wife carrying their replica of Santo Niño would follow in the wake of the tribes of dancers in hopes that their wishes would be fulfilled.[3] The Santo Niño is a replica of the original carved wooden baby Jesus in a red cloth cloak given by Magellan to the tribal leader of the Philippines on the island of Cebu.

When Magellan arrived, he gave the Santo Niño in hopes of converting the Malaysian Muslims to Catholicism. The Spaniards were successful and moved from island to island reaching Panay in rather short order, where they also converted the native Ati tribes to Catholicism. The church celebrated this event each year and they combined it, as they so often did, with local rituals. The combination is intriguing with frenetic drum beating pagan rituals followed by dancers bearing the very Christian image of Santo Niño.

Iloilo's *Ati-Atihan* parade started in 1968 and quickly became the rival of the original *Ati-Atihan* festival in Kalibo three hours away. Many people see both, since Kalibo always occurs on the 2nd Sunday in January and Iloilo always occurs on the 4th Sunday in January. The entire ritual in Iloilo has become more commercial. It has lost its pre–Lenten meaning and become more of a tourist attraction in a two-day event titled, "*Dinagyang.*" This festival specializes in group dancing to percussive rhythms. The Ati were quite petite, more like the Aboriginal people from the Australian Outback than the African-feathered masqueraders that dance in the streets at the *Dinagyang* Festival in Iloilo today. Today's look has an African appearance combined with the theatricality of Mardi Gras, but the rhythms are all percussive with sticks pounding against hollowed bamboo drums.[4] Iloilo's *Dinagyang* Festival is one of the largest masquerade parades in the Philippines and the focus is purely theatricalized African, even though often the headdresses are made of paper feathers.

The *Ati-Atihan* ritual became mixed up with Santo Niño, so the population would gather each year to see the Santo Niño, paraded through the city. Now we can see a confusing cultural contrast between large groups of scantily clad men covered in black body make-up dancing pagan rituals that are Afro-Centric and those dressed in colonial fashion worn at the end of the five hundred years of Spanish domination. In addition, a fair number of contemporary princesses or beauty queens escort small children who masquerade as Santo Niño. The rituals are worlds apart from each other. Their origins in Africa and Spain are equally far from the Philippines where both worlds collide in *Dinagyang*. Iloilo City is on the large island of Panay, the same island where Kalibo is found.

In the 1980s, after the tourism possibilities became obvious, a third festival came along in the Visayas on the island of Cebu to celebrate *Ati-Atihan* and is even more mixed with Mardi Gras including the use of large *papier mâché* images carried on poles and the use of floats. The floats are called *carossa*, the same name as the wagons that are used to carry the saints in various religious processions.[5] Most of the *carossa* in these parades hold a local beauty in a glamorous gown holding a replica of the Santo Niño statue. *Sinulog*, the festival held in Cebu, the largest city in the Visayas, is a big commercial event on the 2nd Sunday in January

*Opposite*: *Dinagyang* Festival, Iloilo, Iloilo Province, Philippines, 2002 (courtesy Laura Crow).

at the height of the tourist season. Many popular tourist destinations that have white sand beaches and aqua seas are on the 20 islands in the Visayas. The drier, somewhat cooler winter months are the best time to feature parades and *Sinulog* functions like a commercial venue with the sponsors' name for each *tribu* prominently displayed. All of these Mardi Gras festivals do not actually happen when Americans celebrate Mardi Gras in February, but rather at a time of national holidays around Christmas and New Years. Christmas is a very religious holiday in the Philippines, so this is a chance to break out after a very spiritual time.

At the *Sinulog*, a pop song is chosen that symbolizes that particular year's carnival. This song is played over and over throughout the Carnival and becomes a memory key, reminiscent of those special days of Carnival. Their masquerade costumes look much more like the circus with spandex and sparkle.[6] Other groups in the Philippines rely only on live music as in Cuba, where the percussion bands each have their own special sound to play for their particular *tribu*. Much as in New Orleans, the *Sinulog* Mardi Gras costumes sharply contrast with the theatricalized Visayan ethnic costumes.

Ethnic Visayan costumes are also represented at *Sinulog* and comprise some of the best examples of typical masquerade folk costume. Because women as well as men participate in this parade, the costumes are by mandate, modest and appropriate for the celebration of Santo Niño, but the authenticity is highly theatricalized.

Traditional Visayan costume is based on peasant clothing from the turn-of-the-century. The women wear a wrapped skirt like the traditional Muslim dress of the region, called a *patadyong*.[7] With that they will often cover the top of the body with a skin colored body suit and many beads along with their triangular shaped Indonesian Muslim hats. There are young men who wear complete body suits all printed with tattoos and a small wrapped skirt with their triangular straw sun hats or wrapped turbans. These are the traditional Filipino warriors, called the *pintados* who went to China to be tattooed after each successful battle.[8] They have a slight political edge, but smile and wave just as everyone else does.

There are also peasant costumes that proudly represent the local weaving businesses and are known for their colorful exaggerated plaid fabrics in particular, but the wrapped skirts are the same as any found in Southeast Asia. For the parades today they weave a far more colorful version than the true garments from the period. Sometimes the young men wear costumes reminiscent of Mexican peasants with straw sombrero hats, and others wear the triangular straw sun hats with their blousy shirts with colorful neck scarves and waist sashes worn over pajama style pants. These are also very heightened in color—the myth of the happy dancing peasant.

Another group goes for the more aristocratic look from Colonial days. They wear the *patadyong* wrapped higher on the body and a sheer jacket with "butterfly sleeves." The unique butterfly sleeves were first popular among aristocrats in the 1890s at the end of the Spanish era, when leg o'mutton sleeves were in fashion. The stiff *piña* cloth made from the fibrous leaves of the pineapple plant is gathered into big sleeves that look almost like wings when pressed flat. They did this after being washed, since they were stored folded and not hung on hangars.[9]

This is a great example of a combination of cultures creating a new look. The resulting new ethnic costume had a very Asian wrapped skirt and a cropped blouse with a sleeve that resembled a butterfly whose origin was the Western turn-of-the-century leg o'mutton sleeves. These were very popular due to the "Thomasites," the 540 volunteer schoolteachers who came to the Philippines in August of 1901, on the USS *Thomas* cargo ship to establish an English public school system that functions to this day. Using Abaca fiber that was cheaper than piña and even stiffer theatricalized the butterfly sleeves for dress up. The Abaca fiber is from a plant that is related to the aloe plant, whose fibrous leaves are dried and stripped, then woven into a stiff fabric. The abaca made it possible to create a gauzy, more open weave while maintaining its shape, thus the very theatrical "butterfly" wings. Imelda Marcos, wife of the president in the prosperous period during the 1960s and the 1970s, made the butterfly sleeves fashionable in the rest of the world and it ultimately caused the large leg o'mutton sleeve revival in the 1980s all over the world.[10]

Some of the women wear long aristocratic flowing skirts called *sayas*, and shawls called *panuelos* over their *Maria Clara* jackets made of transparent *silamay* woven from a pineapple fiber mix. The shape, however, looks closer to the *sayas* of the '20s and '30s inspired by Hollywood's bias cut figure-hugging gowns.[11] Whether inspired by Spanish flamenco dancers or glamorous Hollywood movie stars, the look has become distinctly Filipino. They tend to dance in flowing and circling formations reminiscent of the aristocrats in Spanish colonial days from over one hundred years ago. This colonial masquerade is similar to the white wigged 18th-century Cubans, but from a different time period. The underlying irony is that these people have been freed from that dominance, yet still glamorize it. There is power that comes from playing the other side.

The more formal male dancers wear the *barong*, a sheer embroidered shirt with the tail worn out, and made of *piña* or *silamay*. The *barong* was required for the Filipinos by the Spaniards. With the sheer shirts and tails worn untucked, it was clear who was bearing weapons.[12]

As in Las Vegas, *Sinulog* has to be bigger and bolder. Using natural feathers mixed with tissue paper to make an outrageous silhouette, designer Kenneth Yamas used Indonesian trousers to cover the body rather than traditional palm oil and charcoal, a crown with peacock feathers and gold filigree everywhere.

Pagan populations live high in the rice terraces on the main island of Luzon and they have different ethnic influences. The Ifugao, are somewhat akin to the Ati, but dance much like Native Americans decked out in feathers and loincloths. They pride themselves on their monkey skulls integrated into their headdresses representing the unconquered people of the Philippines. The monkey skulls led to the myth that they were cannibals with shrunken heads adorning their costumes.[13]

Ironically this distinctly pagan group has an Easter ritual where their entire village hikes the five kilometers up to the top of their mountain village in scratchy burlap costumes, meant to represent hair shirts. This theatricalized Christian ritual representing the trials of Jesus Christ includes even the most elderly members of the community, yet appears juxtaposed with their animist beliefs and their connection to the land. After they reach the top of the mountain, they change into theatrical bright red loincloths and dance masquerading and moving much the way Native Americans perform at a powwow. There is chanting and lots of shaking pieces on their costumes, like shells, bells or nuts that create the distinct powwow sound of this theatrical event. They even title this theatrical performance the "Eagle Dance"; a name that sounds Native American. During this event they feel comfortable wearing very skimpy clothing that would be not be appropriate in their everyday lives, but because it is masquerade, it encourages a different mindset and harkens back to the pride of the only "unconquered" people in the Philippines. The costume today is a much exaggerated form of the original dress.

The Filipino heritage is rich with all of the cultures that pass through the "Gateway to Asia" and blend in wonderful theatrical ways to create a new looks. The newly branded industry

*Pana-ad* Festival 2003. *Mandugay* team with body paint make them resemble snakes. Bacolod City, Negros Occidental Province, Philippines (courtesy Laura Crow).

of street carnival/masquerade hopes to spark tourism in many areas, at many times during the year. The lengthy Spanish Catholic domination granted each community their own personal Saint, consequently each town celebrates their Saint's Day along with other festivals. The Saint's Day festivals tend to show off the local agricultural products in a theatrical way. In Vigan, far north on the Island of Luzon, not far from China, they parade in costumes made from tobacco leaves, while Sagay, a city in the Visayas, takes advantage of its sea shells, lentils and soybeans.

The *Pintaflores* event in San Carlos, on the island of Negros Occidental, celebrates horticulture and particularly flowers, but now they manufacture costumes from exaggerated synthetic flowers that light up for the evening with small fairy lights. These are accompanied with fake tattooed body suits. *Pintaflores* is coined from the words *Pintados*, the name for the tattooed warriors of the Philippines and *flores* the Spanish word for flowers; again a cultural combination that produces a theatrical masquerade of the two. The masquerade event started in 1992 and happens in early November on multiple evenings and looks very much like New Orleans or Rio de Janeiro Mardis Gras, but with the emphasis on street dancing and no floats. The rhythmic dances glorifying good over evil are from ancient warrior rituals and the flowers represent man's appreciation for the environment.

Beyond this other groups have masqueraded simply in body make-up. The *Mandugay* group from the *Pana-ad* Festival have painted their bodies to look like the snakes that keep the rats away from the corn. Others decorate in a more fantastic way as butterflies or flowers. Body painting competitions are very popular.

In the Philippines, the dancing carnival groups usually represent various *barangays* or neighborhoods. Year after year the last group teaches the routines to the newcomers becoming more and more theatrical in scale. Separate from the dancers are the *Conga* bands of drummers. They have a personality all to themselves, projecting a rock band look. These super slick young men wear sunglasses and the latest shoes. They form their own entity and delight in making improvisational music for the crowd of onlookers. They limit their masking to sunglasses and they often bleach and dye their hair. Their radical hairstyles and colorful scarf headbands recall the look of the revolutionaries, who fought so hard for their freedom, but they serve a more pragmatic function to keep their sweat under control in the extremely hot weather. The t-shirts match in usually vibrant color and always project some theme. The music seems to vary a great deal from region to region. It is borderline rock-and-roll in the *Sinulog* carnival, and more native percussive rhythm for the *Ati-Atihan* carnivals.

Street dancing remains the realm of the young and the young at heart. In the subtropical temperatures of Cuba and the Philippines, the youth are more capable of maintaining this rigorous pace. Their dances, despite a tendency to follow the style of modern hip-hop, are done in costumes that move and sway based on the ruffled flamenco costumes from Spain. In addition the Muslim/Moro influence combines that look with their traditional triangular hats woven in straw that offer protection from the blistering sun, much like a parasol would, but these also symbolize the legendary triangular hat traded to the original *Ati*. A number of Malay Costumes in full Moro style with triangular hats exist in the parades alongside the Spanish Christian look. The Festival exudes a sense of unity and participants display many signs praying for peace and harmony. They wish for religious conflicts to be resolved.

All of the carnival designers cross ethnic lines and transform taste for a short, but magical, period of time. They allow a wonderful freedom of expression and encourage the participants to escape from their gray day-to-day existence. They take their imagination into the streets energizing connections between the various ethnic and religious groups. These odd juxtapositions make old ideas fresh. The World Costume Festival at Vigan in the Philippines in May of 2013, sponsored by Mayor Eva Medina, had wonderful examples of these cultural clashes.

"Masskara" from Bacolod City is an example of cross-cultural fertilization. The cut glass mosaics, designed by Emiljune Bantolo, show the influence of India and the Sultanates of Indonesia. Myriad particles of shiny objects are embroidered into the costume. The trouser has a South Asian look, draped and wrapped from brilliantly colored silks where the people are generally of the Muslim faith. They wear the now generic dancing shoes, sneakers, made popular by basketball players from the United States. The brightly colored feathers are pure artistry borrowed from Las Vegas or Brazilian Carnival.

The "Masskara" Festival uses the term mass indicating a multitude of people mixed with *cara* the Spanish word for the face. It's also a pun on the Filipino word for mask, *maskara*. Their faces are always smiling to symbolize the overcoming of grief. The festival began when the use of artificial sweeteners were eroding the sugar cane business and their economy. During the same period, on April 22, 1980 there was a giant oil tanker collision with an inter-island ferry, and 700 people died including many prominent family members. There was a decision to commemorate the event with a celebration of smiles, since the nickname of Bacolod City was the "City of Smiles." This symbolized their victory over hardship and pain. Along with the drums and beauty queens and food festivals, there lays at the heart of the festival a very Christian celebration to commemorate the passing of the lost lives into heaven, and since it occurs around Easter, it all blends in together.

The Indonesian group from Java who came to the World Costume Festival had very eclectic looks that combined Chinese opera gods with flags on their backs, native weaves, batiks and richly colored silks. The women who were Muslim had exotic head coverings. One even had a sort of Carmen Miranda fruit basket on her head, but that was mixed with a tabard that had Thai winged shoulders, and a skirt that looked like one Marie Antoinette might wear in the 18th century. One of the goddess figures had an elegant tattooed forehead, with a headdress made from Indonesian shadow puppets, and a hairstyle that was reminiscent of a Japanese geisha.

Afif Ghurub Bestari designed the masquerade festival costumes from Indonesia for the World Costume Festival—2013. He designed twenty costumes to show the cultural diversity of Indonesia using ethnic crafts, music, traditional dance choreography with Indonesian flora and fauna. The costumes represented traditional fashions from many regions such as Java especially in Yogyakarta, Sumatra, Borneo, Bali, and Papua. Western metallic fabrics were blended with traditional textiles such as Batik, Balinese Prada, and Sonket—an Indonesian woven textile.

The Tawo-Tawo Festival from Bayawan on Negritos Orientale, had designs by Manlangit, reflecting the ties to Southeast Asia and Thailand, Vietnam, Laos and Cambodia. The hats have the Moro/Moslem silhouette that comes by way of Indonesia and are triangular.

On the southern island of Mindanao costumes for the *Kaamulan* harkened back to the traditional styles, but are more theatrical. The *Bukidnon* maintain their tribal look for all their animist rituals. Like the *Ifugao* they emphasize the color of red almost exclusively in the traditional clothing. Their costumes cover quite a bit more than the *Ifugao,* but these are tribes are often lead by women, so they dictate the style of dress. The trim appears as many intricate patches of black, yellow and white. Beyond that they wear beaded jewelry, not unlike the Native American Sioux from the plains of the United States, made from seed beads. Next to this the men wear Muslim turbans and the women wear a fan headdress that looks more like

*Masskara* Festival, 2013, Bacolod City, Negros Occidental Province, Philippines. Costume designed by Emiljune Bantolo (courtesy Laura Crow).

**Indonesian tattooed head (courtesy Laura Crow).**

Chinese. As with many cultures, including Native American, they have an oral tradition of passing down their heritage from generation to generation.

Davao City is in the heart of the Muslim island of Mindanao. They have taken the traditional busywork crosshatch embroidery and exaggerated the shapes with larger embroidery floss. It is woven in traditional colors, but the shapes are more abstract flowing across the body in horizontal waves. Designer *Dodjie Batu* complemented the costumes for the World Costume Festival—2013 with jewelry that looks more south Asian as in India or Pakistan.

As everyone grapples with the reality of less cash flow, the aesthetic of theatrical carnival

*Tawo-Tawo* **designs from World Costume Festival, 2013, Vigan, Ilocos Sur Province, Philippines (courtesy Laura Crow).**

made with recycled objects has more and more appeal. Rolando de Leon from Manila, is the king of recycling art, creating amazing floats from plastic coke bottles cut into petals and shaped with a blowtorch. He has also created a whole system using foam rubber for making huge three-dimensional costumes,[14]

The Filipino parades have a longstanding history of taking advantage of the fine art of cross-dressing. Frequently men will masquerade as women in the street dancing. Traditionally gay men will parade at the end of each *tribu*. The crowds readily accept the reversed roles and these men actually compete in beauty pageants, suggesting the ultimate in masquerade.

Probably the most extreme costume made of recycled foam painted red, is that representing the goddess Freya created for the World Costume Festival—2013 in Vigan. Considered the most beautiful and sensual, Freya, the Norse goddess of love, had a skirt looking like a 16th-century Spanish farthingale, a bodice with filigree that looked like a 17th-century court ballet from Louis XIV, and high fashion-looking gloves. The headdress was at once goddess-like, but with multiple heads that look distinctly south Asian, along with the very South Asian-looking male attendants. The ultimate fantasy masquerade has to culminate with any male participant who transforms himself into a female love goddess.

Gay beauty queen as Freya at the 2013 World Costume Festival in Vigan, Ilocos Sur Province, Philippines (courtesy Laura Crow).

*Special thanks goes to my OISTAT colleague, Joy Rago, who traveled around much of the Philippine archipelago as my friend and guide.*

# Notes

1.  Maria Luisa Bernal de Figaroa (July 2004), Carnival, Santiago de Cuba, interviews and Carnival performances.
2.  Joy Rago, interviews with the author, November 2001 and January-June 2002, Manila and Davao City, Philippines, and other assorted locations in the Philippines.
3.  Rolando De Leon, interviews with the author, January-June 2002, Manila, Iloilo, and Davao City, Philippines.
4.  Rago, interviews with the author, November 2001 and January-June 2002.
5.  Rolando M. De Leon, interviews with the author during workshop tour and Sinulog Festival performances, January 2002, Cebu City, Philippines.
6.  Eric Piñda, interviews with the author during workshop tour and Sinulog Festival performances, January 2002, Cebu City, Philippines.
7.  José "Pitoy" Moreno (1995), *Philippine Costume* (Manila: J. Moreno Foundation), 44–47, 139–142.
8.  Ibid., 34–37.
9.  Ibid., 162–165.
10.  Ibid., 280–291.
11.  Salvador Bernal, Georgina R. Encanto, and Francis L. Encanto (1992), *Patterns for the Filipino Dress: From the Traje de Mestiza to the Terno, 1890s-1960s* (Manila: Cultural Center of the Philippines), 40–57.
12.  Moreno (1995), 44–47, 152–155.
13.  Ibid., 64–77.
14.  Rolando M. De Leon (May 2013), interview, workshop tour and World Costume festival performance, Vigan, Philippines.

# Works Cited

Bernal, Salvador, Georginia R. Encanto, and Francis L. Escaler. (1992.) *Patterns for the Filipino Dress: From the Traje de Mestiza to the Terno, 1890s-1960s*. Manila: Cultural Center of the Philippines.
Bernal de Figaroa, Maria Luisa. (July 2004.) Interviews and Carnival Performances, Carnival, Santiago de Cuba.
De Leon, Rolando M. (January 2002.) Interviews with the author during workshop tour and Sinulog Festival performances, Cebu City, Philippines.
De Leon, Rolando M. (January-June 2002.) Interviews with the author, Manila, Iloilo and Davao City, Philippines.
De Leon, Rolando M. (May 2013.) Interview, workshop tour and World Costume Festival performance, Vigan, Philippines.
Moreno, José "Pitoy." (1995.) *Philippine Costume*. Manila: J. Moreno Foundation.
Piñda, Eric. (January 2002.) Interviews with the author during workshop tour and Sinulog Festival performances, Cebu City, Philippines.
Rago, Joy. (November 2001 and January–June 2002.) Interviews with the author, Manila and Davao City, Philippines, and assorted other locations in the Philippines.

# Sublime Images:
# Masked Performances and the
# Aesthetics of Belonging in Malawi

PETER PROBST

---

## I

This essay is about a popular masked society called *gule wamkulu* (literally "great dance") for outsiders and *nyau* (for members) among the Chewa people in southeast Africa. The ethnographic data stem from fieldwork I conducted between 1994 and 1996 in the Chewa village of Kalumba, Lilongwe province, Malawi.[1] At night one could see the lights of Malawi's capital Lilongwe in the distance. Kalumba was about 40 miles from Lilongwe and ties between the village and the city were close. Kalumba's headman for example still maintained a house in Lilongwe and came to the village only on certain occasions. People in the village were ambivalent about this. As much as they favored to have an educated chief who was able to deal with the government they were careful to make sure that he observed the village tradition, a obligation which meant first and foremost to respect *nyau*.

The conflicts resulting from this situation were considerable and sometimes led to difficult moments. Not everybody supported *nyau*. In fact, *nyau* was very much a subject of debate. Christians considered *nyau* as a matter of the devil, an allegation informed by *nyau*'s assumed proximity to the realm of witchcraft and cannibalism. Yet there were also more mundane objections. During the time of the Banda regime (1966–1994) *nyau* was collaborating with the government to harass and sanction critics. And even with the end of the regime the close ties with Banda's party remained. And yet despite all these tensions, frictions, and reservations it was never any question that *nyau* needed to be seen as a key feature of people's feeling of belonging and ethnic identity.[2] In what follows I will thus focus on the some of the aesthetic concepts people in Kalumba employed when talking about *nyau*. The aim is to get some understanding for the attraction and popularity *nyau* performances enjoyed among the people of Kalumba and its neighboring villages.

## II

Before I begin let me clarify a few structural features. *Nyau* needs to be seen as three things at once: a ritual institution, a performance, and a mask.[3] With regards to the institutional dimension, *nyau* masking societies in Lilongwe province were part and parcel of a wider ritual complex. As representations of local village authority they corresponded with the *chisumphi* rain cult as the representation of territorial authority on the more encompassing level of chiefdoms. As such, both institutions, *nyau* and *chisumphi* are historically, ritually and cosmologically closely linked with one another.[4] While the rain cult takes responsibility for the wellbeing and the fertility of the land and its people in general, *nyau* is first and foremost a matter of the village, or to be precise, a matter of the male half of the village for membership to *nyau* is—with few exceptions—restricted to men only.

The closeness of *nyau* to the rain cult is perhaps best expressed by a riddle whose answer each novice has to memorize when initiated into *nyau*. It alludes to the Chewa creation myth according to which the primal harmony between God, man, and the animals was destroyed by man's invention of fire which resulted in the coming into being of both death and *nyau* and asks for the way of *nyau*. The answer consists in listing the various stages of *nyau*: from the very beginning of its construction, by gathering maize husks after the maize had been harvested, till the end of the figure when it is burned at the graveyard. The life cycle of the figure which the riddle describes is thus embedded in the seasonal cycle and the calendric rituals of the rain cult which means that the world constructed by *nyau* is part of the world constructed by the rain cult and at the same time an inversion of it.

Contrary to the importance that anthropological research attached to the creation myth, people in Kalumba had only a vague knowledge of it. The story existed only in fragments. No one in Kalumba had a particular interest in seeing them as elements of a larger, coherent narrative. From a local point of view much more attractive was *nyau* as a source of astonishment, wonder, and excitement. Everyday life in the village did not offer many distractions and *nyau* certainly was a distraction. Shrouded in mystery, the masked dancers seemed to have come from another world. In fact, for non-members they represented wild animals (*zirombo*) who came from the bush into the village in order to accompany the difficult passages from youth to maturity and from life to death to the realm of the ancestors. The imagery used in this context ranged from crocodiles, elephants, and lions to bicycles, trains, missionaries, and politicians. Insiders confirmed this notion of difference. They did so however from another perspective. Thus they used the word *kusanduka* (to change, to change into something) to express the idea of transformation. When men dance *nyau*, so they said, they cease to be human beings and become instead embodiments of *mizimu* in the sense of spirits or spiritual entities.

## III

In 1995 the inventory of *nyau* masks in Kalumba counted roughly 20 figures. The complete *nyau* pantheon of central Malawi, however, already contained over 200 characters at that time.[5] While I feel it safe to say that there was a great deal of consensus as regards people's feelings towards *nyau*, the knowledge of the figures' meanings varied greatly. *Nyau* meant different things to different people. The plurality and heterogeneity corresponded to the multiple perceptions and levels of connection within and to *nyau*. Differences existed between dancers and audiences, *nyau* members and non-members, initiates and their tutors, children and adults, men and women, people from the city and from the village, Christians and non–Christians. In other words, the perceptions and understandings of *nyau* varied with the different social groups and individuals. Not everyone was able to name a given *nyau* mask on demand. In fact, both the masks and their dances were often comprehensible only to a few. Furthermore, *nyau* was not always *nyau*; that is to say, the use and meaning of the masks was anything but uniform. The masks had various roles, and these roles were in turn dependent on the time and place of the *nyau* performance.

Within such a dynamic and multi-levelled word of experience of *nyau*, nonetheless certain over-arching realities existed. In retrospect it seems quite revealing to me that when people in Kalumba spoke about *nyau* in English they did not talk of a mask dance (*gule wamkulu*, literally "great dance") but instead used the English term "picture dance." The phrase stems from the experience that, over the years, *nyau* had become a tourist attraction of sorts. In both the nearby capital Lilongwe and in the area of Lake Malawi, the country's greatest tourist attraction, hotels offered *nyau* dances for their European and American customers. In Kalumba, too, it was common knowledge that the announcement of a *mkangali* (girls' initiation) or a *mphalo* (ceremony in remembrance of the dead) had the power to draw *asungu*, white people, who travelled about the countryside on weekends to take pictures of *nyau* dances.

Men and women stood on opposing sides of the dance ground, with the women serving quasi as the choir of *nyau*. Through the songs they sang to the dances of the masks, they produced a particular acoustic space clearly separated from the sphere of everyday life. In an alternating call and response song between the women participating and the various *nyau* figures, old ritual codes from the world of the mask society, comprehensible only to the initiated, followed gossipy stories about everyday life in the village, and vice versa.

The consistent motif throughout was that of lust. The explicit naming of the body parts and sexual acts involved corresponded to the lewd, no less explicit dances of the masks. The dramatic nature of their performances bound audience and actors in a shared surrender to affects. In normal village life, depicting such things so openly and candidly would certainly have resulted in a court case (*mlandu*). Yet within the context of *nyau*, the open depiction of indecent behavior marked the ritual quality of the event, which was considered to lie beyond the legal and moral spheres of everyday life. What appeared to flash up was the wonder of the extraordinary as it manifested itself in the masks and, for the duration of their presence, shone on the world of man.

# IV

Let me dwell a little bit on the phrase "picture dance." The Chichewa word for photograph, *chinthunzi*, is the same as the one for picture, image, or form. Now, *chinthunzi* turns out to be a highly interesting concept. It stems from the noun *mthunzi* meaning shade or shadow. As a synonym for spirit the notion of shadow is widespread among Bantu speaking groups in Africa. Among Chewa the word for spirit is *mzimu* but the term *chinthunzi* is closely related to this realm.

When people in Kalumba talked about *chitunzi* they described it as a person's double or other. A person, so it was said, consists of their body (*thupi*), their life force (*moyo*) and their double or other (*chitunzi*). All three develop over time. A newborn child grows into a social person through the care provided by its parents. With time the person matures, developing character (*kalidwe*), heart and feeling (*mtima*). Both heart and character appear as expressions of *moyo*, or life force. *Moyo* begins with the act of conception, in the mother's womb. After birth it is manifested in the *chitunzi*, the double or other. Only death (*infa*) puts an end to this concept. When a person dies, his or her image or form (*chitunzi*) leaves the body. The life force (*moyo*) which had resided therein does not cease to exist; rather it initially transforms into a spirit of the dead (*chiwanda*). In this potentially dangerous state—in Kalumba, people said that spirits of the dead are "hot"—it flits about the village until it has attained the normative status of a "cool" ancestral spirit (*mzimu*), either through the completion of a ceremony in remembrance of the dead or through other actions displaying respect and reverence towards the deceased. These commemorative acts were of key importance, as they not only guaranteed the safe transition and transformation of a spirit of the dead into an ancestral spirit; they also made it possible for the spirit to be reborn and return to the land of the living.

What follows from the above outline is the realization that Chewa ancestral spirits have no form, no image, no *chitunzi*; only the living do. Yet, if the ancestral spirits possess no *chitunzi* what, then, are *nyau* who after all are said to be both the embodiments of these spirits as well as that of the wild animals which had left men as a result of the primal fire? The answer appears to lie in the concept of *fano*. *Fano* also means image, however not in the sense of a direct representation of reality, but rather as a product of imagination.

The verb from which it is derived is *kufana*, which essentially means "to resemble." Therefore, *fano* is more an internal image; it is perceived more with the heart than with the eyes, and its relation to the object it represents is more one of affective similarity, not of visual identity. Possessing this quality as it does, *fano* is associated with the idea of spatial expansion and extended action, an action which can perhaps best be illustrated with reference to the experience of dreaming. The creation of new *nyau* masks in Kalumba, for example, was at times the result of dreams. Some, though not all dreams were seen as being the work of doubles or ancestral spirits. The latter travelled and visited the living, making them see things. In the eyes of the people of Kalumba, then, dream images were not produced, but rather passively received, an idea similar to that which lies behind the expression "it came to me in a dream." The idea of spatial expansion may further be seen in the sensual force *nyau* masks were thought to hold. When pressed to reflect on the masks they produced, *nyau* mask-makers sometimes claimed that the masks were images (*fano*). Here they emphasized the special power or force which resided in the figures or images as a form of *moyo* in the sense of life force. What appeared to be a particular characteristic of this power was their ability to penetrate, comparable to that of air and wind, and the presence of which could be sensed in the rustling of the leaves in the cemetery, the home of *nyau* and the spirits of the dead.

# V

The findings are reminiscent of Lienhard's classic study of Dinka religion.[6] Almost 50 years ago, Godfrey Lienhardt used the Latin term *passiones* in order to arrive at a better understanding of the religious experiences and imaginations of the Dinka in Southern Sudan. For Lienhardt, referring to the Latin *passiones* seemed an adequate way to express and translate these experiences. Following Dinka reports on how people were chosen by deities, he recognized the difficulties inherent in attempting to express the underlying experience in his own language.

"It is perhaps significant that in ordinary English we have no word to indicate an opposite of 'actions' in relation to the human self. If the word "passions," were still normally current as the opposite of "actions," it would be possible to say that the Dinka Powers were the images of human *passiones* seen as the active sources of those *passiones*."[7] In other words the Dinka deities, which is to say the powers or forces which take hold of and possess the Dinka, are to be seen as active images of human experience, active in the sense that they affect a person as independent agents and therefore represent a source of action which lies beyond the individual's control. The places where the images and objects of these *passiones* are to be found are numerous. They may be present in the field of the visible or of the invisible. As such, they may refer either to dominant impressions existing beyond and apart from the person, or to experiences within the person.

Some years ago, Fritz Kramer extended the anthropological use and fruitfulness of Lienhardt's concept of *passiones* by coupling it with the equally antique concept of mimesis.[8] In Kramer's view possession can be understood not only as a non-autonomous action but rather as a compulsion to imitation, as an assimilation to an other as being different from the subject seeking to attain representation. The argument is based on a thorough comparative study of both African cults of masking and possession. In Kramer's view there exists a structural analogy between the two.

A case in point might be the figure of *kapoli*, one of the most common and probably oldest figures of *nyau*. It appears with feathers around the head and with strips of cloth around the waist. It is a friendly and talkative character which mainly functions as a messenger. Yet kapoli also dances. The name of the dance is called *kulapasa*.[9] As a dance *kulapasa* is a space oriented body motion stressing the two lateral directions. The centres of motion lie in the legs and feet, quick step sequences shovel away large amounts of dust wrapping the dancer in a red coloured cloud of dust so that only his silhouette remains visible. The dance has thus a certain resemblance with the verb from which the dance stems. *Kulapasa* means "to scratch," or "rake out," like to rake out a fire, movements which explicitly evoke images of the movements of a fowl. Accordingly then, also the dance of *kapoli* can be seen as imitating the movements of a bird.[10]

Thus, following Kramer, we might say what *kapoli* in *nyau* represents is not an animal in its concrete corporeality and materiality but the image of an experience in the sense of *passio*. In other words, when the dancers of *nyau* dance the name of a figure, what they dance is not the external image associated with the name but the imaginations and affects stemming from and linked with this image. It is in this way then that we can speak of possession in the context of dancing *nyau*. As mentioned above, *nyau* are said to be embodiments of spirits (*mizimu*). Yet, it seems what grabs the dancers in the act of performance and transforms them is not the spirit (*mzimu*) but rather its image (*fano*).

# VI

The temporal element of *nyau* was part of the set dramaturgic rules for the masks' performances in Kalumba. Although one knew full well of their presence, their appearances were just as unexpected as were their movements. Seeming to come from nowhere, they appeared from behind a house or from a banana grove and quickly swept toward the village meeting place, always causing the women and children there to scatter wildly as a result. While the whole process certainly had its playful aspects, they were also mingled with an undercurrent of fear and danger radiating from *nyau*.

The suddenness and sentiment corresponded with the word frequently used in Kalumba to describe one's feelings upon encountering *nyau* masks: *zizwa*. Translatable as amazement or astonishment, *zizwa* denoted the extraordinary, fantastical character of the mask dance that bordered on the realm of deception.[11] A moment of hesitation and of indecision was interwoven into this feeling. What appeared in encounters with the figures of *nyau* was on the one hand a sign of the existence of a world beyond the visible, and on the other the latent scepticism as to the validity of that sign. But *zizwa* also alluded to the feelings of cold, fear, and dread, a semantic spectrum that echoes the Latin word verb *terrere*—the root of our word terror—meaning "to shiver" or "to be afraid." At stake is the indifference as to the cause and effect of terror. That is to say, terror is both that which produces fear and the fear itself. It both moves and paralyzes. Suddenness belongs to the aesthetics of terror.[12]

Seen in this light, the imaginations of evil the people of Kalumba associated time and again with *nyau*, as well as those of the mask society's closeness to witchcraft and cannibalism, might be understood as a reference to the notion of sublime 18th-century philosophers were writing about. In 1757 Edmund Burke noted: "Terror is the ruling principle of the Sublime."[13] Surely, Burke understood this insight as a marker of difference between beauty and sublimity. For people in Kalumba such difference did not exist. On the contrary, what the ethnographic material points to is the possibility of thinking, understanding, and experiencing the two realms as belonging together. The corporeal power of such experience might explain the attraction and popularity of *nyau* among the people in whose midst *nyau* is dancing.

# Notes

1. See Peter Probst (2005), *Kalumbas Fest. Lokalität and Ritueller Wandel in Malawi* (Berlin and Münster: Lit. Verlag). In terms of style, as the reader can see I have refrained from the so-called "ethnographic presence," and instead kept my analysis in the past tense.

2. In 2005 UNESCO awarded *nyau* the status of "Intangible World Heritage." See Mapopa Mtonga (2006), "*Gule Wamkulu* as a Multi State Enterprise," *Museum International*, No. 229–330, 59–67.

3. Matthew Schoffeleers (1968), "Symbolic and Social Aspects of Spirit Worship among the Mang'anja," Ph.D. diss., University of Oxford; Deborah Kaspin (1990), "Of Elephants and Ancestors: The Legacy of Kingship in Rural Malawi," Ph.D. diss., University of Chicago; Laura Birch de Aguilar (1996), *Inscribing the Mask: Interpretation of Nyau Masks and Ritual Performance among the Chewa of Central Malawi* (Fribourg: Editions Universitaire).

4. Schoffeleers (1968); Kaspin (1990).

5. See Birch de Aguilar.

6. Godfrey Lienhardt (1961), *Divinity and Experience: The Religion of the Dinka* (Oxford: Oxford University Press).

7. Ibid., 151.

8. Fritz Kramer (1993 [1989]), *The Red Fez* (London: Verso).

9. Gerhard Kubik (1993), *Makisi, Nyau, Mapiko* (München: Trickster), 159.

10. It is significant that within the *mashave* possession cult among the Shona in Zimbabwe there exists a figure equally called *kapoli*. See David Lan (1985), *Guns and Rain: guerrillas and Spirit Mediums in Zimbabwe* (Cambridge: Cambridge University Press), 160. Even though the latter is not a mask, it can be argued that there exists a relationship of similarity between *kapoli* in *nyau* and *kapoli* in *mashave*. In both cases *kapoli* belongs to the category of alien and animal spirits. The situation calls to mind Kramer's argument (op. cit.) of the intimate connection between masking and possession as outlined above.

11. For similar findings in other masked traditions see William Murphy (1997), "The Sublime Dance

of Mende Politics: An African Aesthetic of Charismatic Power," *American Ethnologist* vol. 25, no. 4: 563–582; and Mary Nooter Roberts and Andrew Roberts (1998), *A Sense of Wonder: African Art from the Faletti Family Collection* (Phoenix, AZ: Phoenix Art Museum).

12.  Karl Heinz Bohrer (1994 [1981]), *Suddenness: On the Moment of Aesthetic Appearance* (New York: Columbia University Press). For a fuller discussion of these issues see Peter Probst (2004), "Schrecken und Staunen: Über Nyau Masken der Chewa im Kontext der Konjunktur des Okkulten und der Medialisierung des Schreckens," in *Africa Screams,* Tobias Wendl, ed. (Wuppertal: Hammer Verlag), 115–126.

13.  Edmund Burke (1958), Philosophical Enquiries into the Origin of our Ideas of the Sublime and the Beautiful, J.T. Boulton, ed. (London: Routledge and Paul), 58.

# Works Cited

Birch de Aguilar, Laura. (1996.) *Inscribing the Mask: Interpretation of Nyau Masks and Ritual Performance among the Chewa of Central Malawi.* Fribourg: Editions Universitaire.

Burke, Edmund. (1958.) *Philosophical Enquiries into the Origin of Our Ideas of the Sublime and the Beautiful.* J.T. Boulton, ed. London: Routledge and Paul.

Heinz Bohrer, Karl. (1994 [1981].) *Suddenness: On the Moment of Aesthetic Appearance.* New York: Columbia University Press.

Kaspin, Deborah. (1990.) "Of Elephants and Ancestors: The Legacy of Kingship in Rural Malawi." Ph.D. diss., University of Chicago.

Kramer, Fritz. (1993 [1989].) *The Red Fez.* London: Verso.

Kubik, Gerhard. (1993.) *Makisi, Nyau, Mapiko.* München: Trickster.

Lan, David. (1985.) *Guns and Rain: guerrillas and Spirit Mediums in Zimbabwe.* Cambridge: Cambridge University Press.

Lienhardt, Godfrey. (1961.) *Divinity and Experience: The Religion of the Dinka.* Oxford: Oxford University Press.

Mtonga, Mapopa. (2006.) "*Gule Wamkulu* as a Multi State Enterprise." *Museum International* No. 229– 330.

Murphy, William. (1997.) "The Sublime Dance of Mende Politics: An African Aesthetic of Charismatic Power." *American Ethnologist,* vol. 25, no. 4: 563–582.

Probst, Peter. (2004.) "Schrecken und Staunen. Über Nyau Masken der Chewa im Kontext der Konjunktur des Okkulten und der Medialisierung des Schreckens." In *Africa Screams,* Tobias Wendl, ed. Wuppertal: Hammer Verlag.

Probst, Peter. (2005.) *Kalumbas Fest: Lokalität and Ritueller Wandel in Malawi.* Berlin & Münster: Lit. Verlag.

Roberts, Mary Nooter, and Andrew Roberts. (1998.) *A Sense of Wonder: African Art from the Faletti Family Collection.* Phoenix, AZ: Phoenix Art Museum.

Schoffeleers, Matthew. (1968.) "Symbolic and Social Aspects of Spirit Worship among the Mang'anja." Ph.D. diss., University of Oxford.

# Fiestas, Dances and Masks of Mexico: Community Masquerade and Ritual Art

## Marta Turok

Flute and drum musicians lead the way with their ancient syncopated high pitch and pitter patter sounds. At the end a five-instrument brass band begins to play loudly, announcing that the *fiesta* is about to begin. A group of dancers, each with a distinct costume and mask, has assembled outside of the home of the *mayordomo*,[1] the cargoholder in charge of the event. Children start running, the adults hurry to finish their chores and line up along the road, whether they reside in a mountainous village or a flat township. There is an air of expectation and excitement. Everyone knows the script, they have grown up with it, yet every year they flock and wait to see if the tradition will be up-held, if new ideas will be introduced and accepted. This occasion appropriately encourages celebration with the children, family, and neighbors as the *fiesta* unfolds.

The first stop will be to the church to pay respect to the patron saint or the virgin, or perhaps a Christ figure or a particular saint whose saint's day is being celebrated. Sometimes the church stewards have filled the church with wreaths, flowers and candles beforehand. Sometimes the procession carries them into the church as an offering as the band silently waits outside. The church might have a permanent priest or a priest visits to initiate a program for that day. Before mass, the group prays by themselves. Hats, and masks are set aside, and the flute and drummer enter the church. When they begin to play again, the group leaves the church, the band awakens, and the *fiesta* can begin.

## Fiestas *as Ritual Cycles*

Every indigenous and *mestizo* community has a festivity cycle with one or more *fiestas* occurring during the year. Some are in honor of the Patron Saint while others for saints or the Virgin who represent a *barrio* or neighborhood. The Christian cycle of the Nativity of Christ,

Candlemas (*Candelaria*), Carnival, Holy Week (*Semana Santa*), the Holy Cross Day (May 3), Pentecostés, Saint John (June 24), *Corpus Christi*, Saint Michael (September 29), and All Soul's Day (*Dia de los Muertos*) have also been reinterpreted to fit the ancient agricultural cults which paid homage to the sun and rain gods. Certain rituals programmed for special occasions might occur in and around the town with processions going up to sacred mountains, the edge of springs, or the bowels of caves with underground rivers. The time of year, the type of celebration, the region and ethnic group determine the specific kind of ceremony and dances that take place.

To understand each *fiesta* is it important to note that it is a community event. A *mayordomo* receives status and respect within the community in exchange for the great expenditure of organizational duties. He obtains assistance from friends, family and *compadres* (godparents), who in turn will also help out when it is their turn, establishing a rite of reciprocity at the core of *fiesta* organization. Throughout the year as well as on the celebratory day, the *mayordomo* offers candles, fresh flowers, music and fireworks for the saint. He frequently offers food to the musicians and dancers, to the organizers, and many times to the whole community, sacrificing and stewing a cow, various sheep or turkeys. Communities "dress-up" for *fiestas*, ephemeral paper cuts are strung on the streets, flower or seed arches are placed at the church entrance, and different firework "castles" with complicated displays lite up the night. No two *fiestas* can ever be identical. Each offers a unique visual experience.

Participation in a *danza* (dance-drama) is considered an *ofrenda* (ritual offering) and dancers make a *manda* (pledge) for a certain number of years or perhaps a lifetime. Many times the principal character passes on from father to son. Participating becomes an individual act of purification that contributes to the collective offerings and rituals that give the *fiesta* its significance. Thus the cultural and historic wealth of Mexico's almost sixty ethnic groups who speak over 300 languages greatly influence the beauty and diversity of the pageantry. The person wearing a mask transforms into the character he incarnates, which tends to be part of a dance or a ritual that is, in turn, part of a ceremony or a celebration. Together, through the dance and with the mask as a disguise, dancers and spectators recreate the sacred myths and legends of their people while they simultaneously authenticate the pageantry and theatrics of the public performance.

## Origins of Mexican Masquerade and Dances

Masks appeared widespread in pre-conquest (Hispanic) times, although it has not always been possible to comprehend their exact function. Funerary masks made from stone or wood with fine turquoise mosaics were superimposed on the faces in the burials of important personages in or near pyramids. Using body, facial decoration, and masks theocrats assumed the characteristics of gods such as *Tlaloc* or *Chaac* (Aztec and Maya God of Rain), Huitzilopochtli (Aztec God of War), Quetzalcóatl or Kukulcán (Aztec and Maya Plumed Serpent) or the mythical white-bearded man who brought wisdom, left and promised to someday return. Warriors wore eagle and jaguar helmets and costumes, absorbing the identity and power of these animals. Some masqueraders wore bird, insect or reptile masks. Comic and droll acts were performed with masks of little old men and women. Dramas and satires made fun of members of the community or ridiculed neighboring ethnic groups. Murals, painted vases and stone-sculpture reliefs offer a visual testimony of that past, combined with 16th-century Spanish chroniclers who described a series of costumes and masks used by Aztec and Mayas in their processions and for warfare.

*Idols behind Altars*[2] best describes what occurred during the process of evangelization after the Spanish conquest of México. Pre-Hispanic religion and beliefs based on a cyclical concept of the Universe where duality, opposing forces, and polytheism converged. They contradicted a more lineal European Judeo-Christian monotheism that pitted good against evil, heaven against hell. Most indigenous groups accepted the new religion without giving up their own beliefs, substituting their ancient deities with Christian saints, often using the name and attributes of a saint for an ancient god. Five hundred years after the Spanish Conquest, Mexican festivities still reflect the blending of cultures and ancient traditions that emerged as a new, albeit syncretic belief system.

## The Role of Music and Dance

The importance of music and dance is almost universal and sets the stage for rituals and festivities. In Mexico ancient instruments, such as the drum and reed flute (used together) have survived along with various rattle percussions. Brass bands and string instruments came with the Spanish and add great fanfare to processions and during dances, where specific *sones* (tunes) are played to accompany and separate each part of the dance-drama. Consequently the musicians know the script and its parts.

Within the diversity of expressions there are patterns that emerge and allow us to identify eight categories of dances that I will briefly describe.

- **Cosmogonic and solar cult dances** —These dances keep the cosmic forces of nature in balance, coupled with the solar cult. They are some of the most spectacular rituals of pre–Hispanic origin. In the Flying Pole ritual, a masked figure accompanied with music, selects and cuts down a 20 to 30 meter tree. He sacrifices black chickens and other offerings to the oldest tree, which he determines to be the Spirit of the Forest. The tree is then taken down to the village, set up, and five men climb to the top. Four wrap a rope around their waists and jump off head first, arms stretched as birds, and each one does 13 revolutions, which multiplied by the four add up to 52, corresponding with the years of the pre–Hispanic "century."

  As an agricultural society, the sun plays a vital role. There are basically two seasons in Mexico: dry and rainy. Therefore during the dry season many rituals relating to the solar cult coincide with Carnival, Holy Week and Holy Cross Day. These related rituals of purification with body and facial paint involve flagellation with ropes, battles to draw blood, and sacrifices of animals, offerings, and prayers.

- **Agricultural rituals and rain petitioning dances**—The importance of the center of origin, discovery, and development of maize in Mesoamerica (Mexico and Guatemala) is constantly recognized through agricultural rituals of pre–Hispanic origin where animals and humans interact. Dances related to the pre–Hispanic cycle of agriculture and hunting take place during various times of the year. They overlap with the solar cult during Carnival and Holy Week during the time when the land is prepared for planting. The Holy Cross festivity on May 3rd relates to the ancient rain god Tlaloc, marking the onset of the rains while some animal/jaguar cosmic "fights" take place. Other dances take place during the rain cycle asking for rainfall and a successful harvest.

- **Dances during Carnival that petition and serve in role reversal**—The 365 day solar calendar was divided into 18 months of 20 days and the last five were the "lost days" where the reversal of roles and order marked the beginning of the solar cults, a festivity that paralleled the European Carnival in time but not meaning. It corresponds with a moveable date in the Christian calendar, coinciding approximately with the beginning of the pre–Hispanic year, around February 2 (*Candlemas*). This important syncretism takes place at the beginning of the "year" which commences the agricultural cycle. Many Carnival dances are in fact a rain petitioning ceremony marked by purification, differing with the European tradition of frenzy and chaos.

In Carnival and Holy Week, indigenous communities apply facial and corporal paint

The Danza de los Paragüeros (Umbrella Dance). Amaxac de Guerrero, Tlaxcala, Mexico (photographer: Ruth D. Lechuga; courtesy Marta Turok).

which functions as a means of transformation because the resulting masquerade takes on new attributes or because it erases the external facade. Often ritual objects have hidden meanings, such as those associated with using a wooden snake, a rope, or an umbrella in different ritual dances that promote thunder and rain.

- **Dances for the cult of the elders**—Elders are especially respected in a society where oral tradition and important rituals still serve as paramount community participation. The characters may be serious or witty, representing wisdom or the ancestors. Sometimes the elders also separate from the other groups of dancers and act as ceremonial clowns, being indecent and scandalous. In some dances their character and features are humorous. They might act as if they can barely walk and then break into vigorous dancing and provoke lots of improvisation and impromptu comments about local gossip and social and political critique.

  Once considered ancient gods the elders were revered as part of the ancestor cult and as the gods of fire. In the Huasteca region (western states of Hidalgo, Veracruz) the dancers who represent the *Huehues* (elders) go the edge of the town as the Day of the Dead begins (October 31) and lead the souls of the deceased through the village, church, homes, and cemetery while the families pay them homage with altars and offerings . At the end of the festivity on November 2 the elders lead them back out, with the same fanfare and masquerade, lest they should want to stay.

- **Dances of the Conquest**—At the time of the Conquest the Spanish had created the *Dance of Moors and Christians,* an important historical *drama-dance* that recreated the epic battles of the united Christian Spaniards against the Islamic Moors and their expulsion from Spain at the end of the 15th century. The apostle Santiago (James), also known as Santiago *Matamoros* or ( James the Moor-killer), inspired the re-conquest of Spain, appeared as a masked figure, as did the captains and the vanquished Moors. Indians were enchanted with the legendary battles and performed them in their own way with masks and costumes, mixing biblical and historical characters of different epochs. In the indigenous version Santiago is the main character, appearing on "horse-back" with a tiny horse tied to his waist, a reminder also that at first Indians thought that men and horses were one and the same, for they had never seen them before. In San Andrés Tzicuilan, a Nahuatl speaking community of Puebla, the horse structure is venerated, candles are lit and flowers abound. Other characters might include Poncius Pilatos, Moors, or the historical French invaders of 1855–1858. Men dressed as women also appear, mostly representing la "*Malinche*," the Indian who served as Cortes' translator and mistress, facilitating the conquest of Mexico by helping the Spanish ally with the Aztecs enemies.

  The different dances of the Conquest, especially the *Dance of Moors and Christians* served the purpose of the Spanish conquerors to remind the local population that they had been vanquished and converted to Catholicism. But they never imagined the ability of the communities to reinterpret the Christian teachings and adapt them to their pre–Hispanic beliefs. The masks and their wearers would turn history upside down and the vanquished would have the last word—and in a sense revenge the conquerors and other exploiters by means of satire and mockery.

- **Historical events and lifestyles celebrated by dances**—Through the masks and costumes satire and humor are important aspects of many characters that reflect painful historical events that Mexicans and Indians transform into forms of mocking the landlords that kept them in virtual slavery together with their black Afro-descendent chief cowherders, the rich, the city "dandees," and even oppressing priests, politicians and recently intruding tourists. Other dances relating to lifestyles include Mules and mule-train dances, miners, sowers, and harvesters. Some of these dances occur during Carnival or during Patron-Saint festivities. Chiapa de Corzo in Chiapas also has a famous and tumultuous fiesta known as the *Parachicos* (for the child) that reenacts the 17th-century story of a miraculous healing of a Guatemalan child whose mother pledged to help the community after a cholera outbreak.

- **Dances that pay homage to mock battles**—Regional and local events over various centuries can be transformed as reenactments memorializing mock battles. The defeat of the French invasion in the 1860s is a reminder of the constant struggle to maintain Independence during the 19th century and is reenacted during the Carnival in Huejotzingo, Puebla.

- **Dances celebrating evangelization**—The *fiestas* discussed earlier include numerous dances and rituals that most frequently reflect European influence. However, in the majority of indigenous communities the resulting festivities and dances are totally syncretic.

- **Easter Holy Week (Semana Santa)**—Formally, Easter or Holy Week represents the death and resurrection of Christ, yet it coincides with purification rites and rain petitioning ceremonies that alternate with Carnival. After Christian teachings were adopted the Passion Play represented the fight of good against evil, a vision contrary to Indian belief of duality as part of the life-cycle.

    The Cora Indians, in keeping with syncretic fashion the Christian passion events, have substituted the theme of the struggle of the sun against the forces of the nights. Christ is transformed into the sun and his persecutors, known as Romans, Jews, Devils and the Pharisees, who are the forces of the night. The masks are made out of *papiermâché* and traditionally get thrown into the river the last day of the *fiesta* to represent the triumph of the Sun.

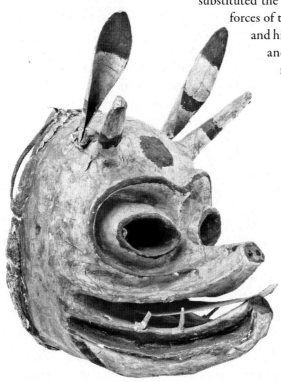

- **Christmas plays:** *Pastorelas*—The reenactment of the birth of Christ with

Cora ritual mask (made in 1970) in the form of Jurio or Fariseo (Pharisee) style: *papiermâché* and aniline dyes. The Cora peoples live in the mountains of the state of Nayarit in Mexico. They come together in the Jesús María, their religious and political center, during Holy Week to reenact the ritual of death and rebirth of the Sun. All the young men must participate in the ritual and wear body paint that remains hidden until the last day. As the Sun rises victoriously, the body paint is washed away. The masks are thrown into the river to disintegrate (photographer: Michel Zabé; courtesy Ruth D. Lechuga/Franz Mayer Museum).

masked characters is played mostly in Central and West Mexico, where various characters with masks represent shepherds, animals, the devil, death and other characters who are following the northern star to reach the new born child. Bartolo or Lucas, both serve as the town fools and as narrators of the story. The devil plays tricks and tries to convince them to give up their quest.

- **Totemic and ritual transformation dances**—Dances celebrating the Deer Hunt in Northwest Mexico harken back to the times of totemic filiations and human transformation while those representing the Jaguar Hunt in the Southern Pacific region recall aspects of the force of the jaguar as the Lord of the Night.

- **Other animal masquerades and dances**—In accordance with the pre–Hispanic concept that men and animals need one another to survive, many myths express versions of how animals showed humans fire and the secret of maize. If an animal must be hunted and eaten, a special ceremony is held to ask its forgiveness or to thank it. Animals also represent the "*tona*" or spirits that accompany each individual and are representative of a person's personality, therefore they must be protected to ensure health and life. A third category involves animals who represent totems and clans, such as the Aztec Wolf, Jaguar, and Eagle-knights who wear elaborate costumes and helmet-masks in their likeness. The masquerading animals participate in these dances to remind humans that animals and nature must be acknowledged.

- **Totemic and ritual transformation dances involving the deer and jaguar (or *tiger*)**— As a figure in dance rituals, the jaguar is one of the most important. Among the Aztec Gods, the jaguar (popularly referred to as a *tigre*) was the "tona" or animal spirit of Tezcatlipoca or Smoking Mirror. Simultaneously revered and feared, he serves as protector and as a threatening symbol of nature and the unpredictability of the future.

He appears in a set of related dances throughout Mexico, the *Tecuanes* of Puebla, the *Tejorones* of Oaxaca and the *Tlacololeros* of Guerrero. The characters include the jaguar, the hunters or farmers, the dog who leads humans to the jaguar, and other animals which the jaguar attacks and kills. In turn the jaguar must be hunted and killed because he is a threat to domestic animals and the maize cycle.

Jaguar (Tiger) mask. The jaguar was one of the most venerated and feared animals since pre-Hispanic times, as the largest feline of the region. The dances that evolved where the jaguar is included usually are related to agricultural propitiatory festivals. Mask: Leather with paint created by Nahuatl peoples. 1940. Zitlala, Guerrero. Mexico. Photographer: Michel Zabé. Photograph courtesy of Ruth D. Lechuga/ Franz Mayer Museum.

## The Mask Maker and His Materials

Mask making tends to be a specialized activity. Some mask makers are also *santeros* (wood carvers), who use fine techniques and finishes and also make figures of saints, the virgin, and angels. Others, although specialized, alternate carving with agricultural activities and commercial handcrafted carving. Moreover, some make their own masks for a dance or a *fiesta* simply for the joy and satisfaction of making it.

The simple tools contrast with the masterful skills of the carvers, who wield them. Only a metal *machete*, a knife, chisels, perhaps a saw, an engraver, and plenty of sandpaper, make up the workshop of the mask maker, who spends long hours searching for the right material that "speaks to him."

Unlimited creativity in mask making somewhat depends on the endless number of materials used. The most common material for traditional Mexican masks is wood, however mask makers also use bones, horns and deerskin, and other endemic animals, no doubt having pre–Hispanic origins, although the skins of goats and cattle are frequently used today. The use of clay was an ancient practice that survives in a couple of communities. Organic materials include dry gourds, leaves, and the *quiote* or heart of *maguey* (a material considered to contain spiritual forces), and even turtle shell. Before the word recycling entered our vocabulary some masks were made from tin cans preserving the original stamps of the commercial brand.

The masks with European features have thick eyebrows, hair and beards either carved from wood or applied with curled and frizzed horsehair or *ixtle* (agave fiber). Indians are generally beardless. The great majority of masks are enhanced with decorations such as ribbons, rattles, glass, metallic paper, full-length *ixtle* or horse hair and other local fibers, and goat or bull horns.

## Change and Continuity

The indigenous world has been resilient to changes for more than 500 years. Today young Indians, both male and female have more opportunities to study in higher education. Since globalization began in this century thousands of young Indians have migrated to the United States and look for new opportunities they could not get locally. Many have sent money back to Mexico and the countryside is dotted with American style homes where thatch homes once stood. Frequently the money is invested in the *fiestas* to perpetuate the *mayordomías* and *fiestas*.

Sometimes they are able to come back for a *fiesta*, and when they do they come with different haircuts, clothing, and ideas. Increasingly they stay in the United States, frequently finding ways of recreating their dances in a strange land as is happening in and around New York with the Tepehua, Totonac, and Otomi immigrants.

In certain regions traditional masks are being replaced with industrial rubber, *papier-mâché* or plastic mold masks due either to the lack of wood or specialized carvers. In other regions the *mayordomías* are dying out due to the vast number of men leaving the country. The outer spectacle changes, while the pageantry remains and we have yet to see how tradition will hold up in future decades.

## Notes

1. *Mayordomo* is the spelling for México, in Europe it is *majordomo*, both refer to the person who is the chief organizer.

2.  This is the title of a book by Anita Brenner first published in 1929 that explores the substitution of pre–Hispanic deities for Christian saints leading to syncretism and the intrinsic relationship of art and religion.

# Works Cited

Brenner, Anita. (1929.) *Idols Behind Altars*. [New York]: Payson & Clarke.

# Section II

Public Masquerade Mirroring
Communities in Transition

# Masquerade, Pride, Drag, Love and Marriage

## Hilary Baxter

---

*The first, called the anti-masque, was performed by professionals and regularly presented a world of disorder or vice, everything the ideal world of the court masquers was to overcome and supersede. When the moment of transformation arrived, the dancers in their splendid costumes descended from the stage ... merging the ideal world with the real, took partners from the audience, concluding the theatrical performance with a grand ball.*[1]

"Do we still need Gay Pride?" was the recurring question in the British media in the week leading up to the London Pride March in June 2013.[2] Activities built anticipation through the week with planned parties, decorated banners, and completed costumes. Christie's released five Andy Warhol photographs of the 1984 Gay Pride for an online auction.[3] Central London would be closed and the volunteer stewards ready, repeating a familiar pattern since the early 1990s. But something important in the social and cultural contexts was changing, not just in the UK but also in European countries and across the world. Twenty-first century governments in Western Europe and North America have begun to legalize same sex marriages, formalizing public recognition of partnerships, starting with the Netherlands in 2001 and since followed by many other countries and states. In London, a similar law is in mid-progress and despite spirited opposition, should be passed later in 2013.[4] In June 2013, Ben Summerskill, the Chief Executive of Stonewall[5] claimed that the 3.7 million British gay people would no longer be second-class citizens in their own country. On June 26, 2013 (four days before Pride London) the U.S. Supreme Court struck down a law denying federal benefits to gay couples, clearing the path for same-sex marriages in California,[6] a state that had already briefly allowed these to take place in 2008.

Taking these changes in the social and cultural contexts of Gay Pride into consideration, the starting point for my article on masquerade and Gay Pride is first, whether "Pride" could be considered as a form of masquerade and following on from that, the consideration of the changes in costuming used by the Gay Pride marchers over the past decade. I will correlate the importance of masquerade in its relation to the juxtaposition of "vice and disorder" as well as "law and order" in costume.

The designation of "Pride" as a form of masquerade may seem superficial to some, even derogatory given the underlying politics and the "reconceptualisations of gender which emerged from the activism and scholarship of the 1960s and '70s" that were summarized by Harry Brod in his essay "Masculinity as Masquerade."[7] Gender and queer theory is a complex and interesting area of debate though not pertinent to my primary interest as a costume designer. I work to understand the use of clothes as explicit expressions of personality in familiar and challenging contexts, using both the familiar and recognizable together with confrontational and theatrical choices. In this regard, since the 1980s Gay Pride may seem to have developed from the historical background of the masquerade as outlined by Terry Castle who cites in *Masquerade and Civilization* the masquerade balls in English pleasure gardens (Ranelagh, Vauxhall) and the assembly rooms as vestiges of the "ancient and powerful world"[8] of carnival.

The masquerade projected an anti-nature, a world upside down, an intoxicating reversal of ordinary sexual, social and metaphysical hierarchies.[9] Castle links 18th-century masquerades to a carnival tradition and listing their primary classic features such as "sartorial exchange, masking, collective verbal and physical license."[10] She compares this function to the early modern "festivals of misrule" and disregards any link with the Jacobean Court masques: "Such aristocratic fantasia—the elaborate allegorical productions of Inigo Jones and others—probably had little direct impact on the popular resurgence of carnivalesque behavior in the 18th century."[11]

Castle rightly maintains that the Jacobean court masques were a "highly articulated, self-conscious artistic fantasy" and "a performance for the few" (in one sense it was a performance for the King alone who had the best seat in the house, from which all the design perspective was realized.) But I suggest that Castle has presented an incomplete picture. If we consider the whole structure of the masque and all its contributors then we can see a different interpretation and a more direct link with other forms of masquerade. In the Jacobean court masque, the evening would start with an anti-masque performed by actors showing the world in chaos. The playwright Ben Jonson, working in collaboration with designer Inigo Jones, took responsibility for developing this structure while also writing plays for the playhouses, meaning that the two forms of performance were inextricably linked. The masque demonstrated a profound truth for the court participants, emphasizing the unassailable nature of their right to rule.

Not enough information exists to be clear about the anti-masque in terms of costume or design but as this was the only part that was scripted, the text survives. This world of disorder was always rectified by the appearance of the court participants who did not speak and only danced, playing themselves as the naturally ruling class enhanced by visual symbolism. In Shakespeare's *The Tempest* the masque goddesses[12] (who are actors and therefore speak) herald the beginning of an ordering where all strangeness or upside-down-ness of the natural world is resolved into a reasonably satisfying ending. I am drawing attention to the basic structure of anti-masque (vice and disorder) followed by the masque (law and order) as being of particular interest in my investigation into "Pride" as a Masque(rade).

As a costume designer, I engage with the fantastical dressing that can be found in some of the expression of characters both as individuals and as part of a community. It may seem that in the year 2013, Gay Pride has recently become less outrageous than in previous decades, lacking more obvious spectacle or brilliance in costume design and construction, but is this true? My investigation here will start with the clothes for the very first marches in the 1970s, look briefly at Warhol's images in the '80s and the Australian Gay Mardi Gras. But I will primarily focus on my photographs taken at London "Pride" in 2004 and 2013 respectively.

The common impression of the London Pride march, portrayed by the UK mainstream media is one of frivolous excess with colorful exaggerated costuming and frequent use of drag elements. These images accompany Paul Burston's article in *Timeout*[13] with the headline "TWO, FOUR, SIX, EIGHT, IS THAT COPPER REALLY STRAIGHT?" showing a montage of 44 highly colorful photographs of costumed revelers: smiling policemen, drag queens, mad headdresses, funky sunglasses, penis balloons and handsome young men and women wearing a kaleidoscope of rainbow colors. There is one tiny picture of a placard and one large one of a sloganed t-shirt. The reality of the London Gay Pride march is somewhat different, as I shall explain later.

Modesty of dress is one of the key descriptors mentioned by photographer Suzanne Poli[14] in an NBC interview while discussing her photographs of the New York Gay Pride Parades taken from her apartment window documenting every year since the first New York march in 1970. Poli comments that in this first parade, these were just "neighborhood people ... residents, people believing in this cause ... coming together ... with just a truck and a few balloons."[15] The march was a very public "coming out" using the methods of street activism by an invisible and oppressed minority, and was considered dangerous at the time, with the braveness of marchers being emphasized by Poli's photograph of a line of six black uniformed police walking behind the parade, following them out of the picture. This is a very obvious example of the forces of law (masque) establishing control over the chaos of the marchers' world (anti-masque). The first London march, originally "The UK Gay Pride Rally" through Central London, was held in London on July 1, 1972, chosen to be close to the anniversary of the Stonewall riots in New York in 1969, the circumstances of which are widely considered to be the catalyst for gay rights in the U.S.[16] and the formation of lesbian, gay, bisexual, and transgender (LGBT) movements across the world. One of the photographs of this march shows the nature of the "on duty" police presence almost blocking the view of the marchers with cars still driving alongside. Placards are held aloft: "Homosexuals are Revolting," "Total Equality or Bust."[17] The photographs seem to predominantly show male marchers, although the longer hairstyles of the '70s can be misleading and the higher angle of the photographer over the police might have obscured shorter figures. The dress is fashionable, smart, and modest with casual shirts open at the neck (without ties) generally light in color. Lots of marchers are wearing sunglasses, none of the policemen are. In fact the most noticeable group are the police who wear white shirts with black ties, no jackets but traditional "custodian" helmets, walking alongside. The uniform may be less oppressive than the dark cops of New York, but essentially the message is the same. The law will subdue chaotic movements.

In the five Warhol photos taken in New York in 1984 here again we see casual marchers in t-shirts, jeans, shorts and sunglasses enjoying themselves, smiling with decorated trucks and more balloons, but one of the photos shows an elaborately costumed band of around twenty, all dressed in matching exaggerated outfits with large white headdresses, *lamé* skirts, and excessively flounced bell bottomed trousers, indicating that the costumes may be meant for dancing rather than just marching. The juxtaposition of the ordinary clothes alongside the bizarre band costumes and the overtly demonstrating interest groups have come to be, a dominant theme of the Pride marches.

The Sydney Mardi Gras (held annually in March) has long held a reputation for extravagant costuming with floats, group displays, and warm weather. But the first Sydney Pride in June 1978[18] ended in an unexpected response of police violence with serious repercussions for those marchers who were named and shamed in the press. Reports suggest that some had come in fancy dress, and others just dressed warmly. Subsequently a decision made to move the event earlier in the year into the warm summer months allowed for more revealing and sexier clothing. By the early 1980s the Sydney Gay Pride Parade had become Gay Mardi Gras (name carried over from the Lenten Carnival Fat Tuesday—the day of indulgence before fasting) presumably to fit within the February timing of Lent. I would suggest that this most closely aligns with the medieval carnival tradition of the "world turned upside down" where women dress up as men and men as women. The Mardi Gras is highly visible and costuming plays a key role and special feature of this parade not just through the photographs but also in the many reports of those who have attended.

As the name has deliberately changed from Gay Pride to Mardi Gras, I would suggest that this has somewhat colored expectations in terms of moving away from a march and more into a carnival event. It might be difficult to tell the difference at this point, particularly from using readily available press and Internet photos. The film *The Adventures of Priscilla, Queen of the Desert*[19] has inspired many Gay Pride outfits, and in 2007 I interviewed Tim Chappel, one of the Oscar-winning costume designers for this film. He had based the drag costumes on his own experience of the Sydney scene and shared recollections about the Sydney Gay Mardi Gras:

> I've done costumes for the shows for Sydney Mardi Gras before. The whole thing of the Mardi Gras is it's a real blessing to Australia because it really made being gay something that was ... because it was so bright and colorful and fun to watch, and cheeky and funny which is such a part of the Australian identity, it made the idea of people who were gay different, and an easier pill to swallow.[20]

He goes on to comment that in Los Angeles (where he now works) they have the Gay Pride march "and it's so dull and political, just marching down the street holding banners." Clearly that he much prefers the costume making, dressing up, and partying. He also suggests that in Australia there are less resources to choose from so marchers and performers can have an idea of what they want but then tend to work with what they can find. That generates a much broader range of materials including found objects and junk. Chappel suggests that the exuberance and general wittiness of the costuming has tended to mask the more challenging ideas surrounding the gay scene, regarding sexual preferences and practices. In other words exciting costumes will distract and ultimately be persuasively acceptable.

Drag queens have widely copied one of the costume ideas from *Priscilla,* a feather boa wrapped round the face. When I put this to Chappel, he said that he had borrowed the idea from a George Michael video, where Linda Evangelista had worn a white one. But he had also seen it on a background person in the musical *Sweet Charity.* He wanted it to look like a *Waratah* (a New South Wales national flower) in the film. This is very much how the drag queen scene works, with ideas copied from culture into life and back again into culture. I suggest that this gives a strong sense of shared identity, whether copying a film, a music video, or another drag queen. For example, the substitution of feathers for hair and the creation of a headdress is a very common part of drag queen culture. Chappel considers the act of "seeing drag" as a "very intimate form of gay theatre" experience, consequently the drag queens didn't really have to look exactly like women, a whole different thing altogether. Working closely with the actors, he had to convince them of these subtle differences between drag queens and pretend women, so he did not use fake breasts at all for the "queens" only for the transsexual characters. He used this principle in developing the eventual style for the costume scheme. Chappel's background as a costume designer was evident as he went onto explain that:

What I try to do is I try and work with really basic visual dynamics; I try to limit the colors that each character wears and the visual elements, like for instance, when they climb up Kings Canyon they all wear these different headdresses ... and I went and found ... bits of pieces that would really give an insight into the character."[21]

This element of control so enjoyed by him as a costume designer means that his final picture has narrative and drama as well as visual logic and balance. This effect does not naturally occur in a random grouping, however good or exciting individual costumes might be.

In the UK the general impression of Gay Pride, as I have explained, is one of frivolous excess with colorful fetish wear. Some march in drag and resemble Chappel's Priscilla designs. As yet, no one can recall and identify the first person to march as a drag queen at "Pride" but by the end of the 20th century many were marching. To the casual observer it might seem that the cross-dressers are an obvious group of masqueraders, often known as the "Drag Queens." Although seemingly absent from the early marches in terms of wearing their female clothes in public, we can assume that they also attended the event in more androgynous apparel. The most famous 20th-century British cross-dresser Quentin Crisp, whose early years in the '30s and '40s are dramatized in film[22] is reported to have said that he did not believe in rights for homosexuals, vastly preferring to be a singular eccentric rather than part of an emerging community, which Gay Pride has always offered.

The connotations of the word "drag" seem to be theatrically-based, referring to dressing in the clothes of the opposite sex (skirts dragging on the floor), and has often been seen in the UK as an acceptable form of mainstream entertainment. Perhaps this is partly due to the tradition in previous centuries of short-coating male infants and dressing them as girls until they were put into breeches, or perhaps drag has always simply been a familiarity of cross-dressers in traditional family entertainment. Annual Christmas Pantomimes could typically include a man playing an old woman character known as the Dame and the young male lead (Principal Boy) played by a girlish woman. John Lithgow, the American actor, writes in the foreword to the anthology *Ladies or Gentlemen?*[23] about his experiences as an eleven-year-old when he performed as a damsel-in-distress with a flowered tablecloth skirt and discovered the humor in playing up to the audience. Lithgow has gone on to play several cross-dressing roles, some humorous and others very serious and he comments:

> So what have all these adventures taught me? That the sight of a man playing a woman can indeed be hilarious. But it can also be horrific. And it can be deeply moving. Switching genders is the most potent tool an actor has to startle an audience whether his intention is to amuse, to frighten, or to move them.[24]

"Men as Women,"[25] a section of *Masks: Faces of Culture* by Nunley and McCarty examines different cultural forms of males masquerading as females and uses a broadly classical definition of womanhood as having three stages of life (Maidens, Mothers, and Crones) to look at ritual masquerades in each stage. Conversely the cross-dressing at "Pride" clearly expresses "self" as well as a burgeoning cultural phenomenon. The references are complex and personal and as a costume designer I am most interested in the visual presentation as it relates to the outsider's view (the audience) rather than deconstructing the "complex act of appropriation and representation."[26] None of the male to female drag marchers in Pride London were referencing the middle stage of womanhood so the "mothers" were solely represented by lesbians. Drag queens dressed as either "maidens" or "crones." Usually older women are attributed wisdom, but Nunley suggests that this is regarded negatively in patriarchal societies, where older women project witch-like appearances. Moreover, cross-dressing has generally suggested satirical connotations with a humorous costume and played for laughs.

The public arrival of the ultra-stylish drag queen in mainstream culture, a version of the showgirl and a highly stylized "theatrical maiden" is relatively recent and exemplified in the photos of Leland Bobbé. In one of his recent projects he has taken photographs of drag queens with half their female make up and half their unmade up male face.[27] These extraordinarily glossy glamorous portraits show good looking young men expressing their femininity through heavily stylized stage make-up, colorful full wigs, and painted pouts. This "full-on" stage glam-our look would have distinctly retro at the turn of the 21st century, looking back towards the 1960s glamour dressing of Danny La Rue. But recent contemporary fashion trends for young women which now include fetish-inspired platform shoes, sequins, and other glitter, false eye-lashes, short skirts and tiny shorts brings both girls and queens closer together in their choice of clubbing attire. A podcast with Ongina,[28] a New York drag queen, explains that "costumes help us be the people we want to be." Ongina does not usually use wigs or fake breasts but decides each morning to explore what he wants to wear each day and he has outfits with names such as "the Barbie Doll." This is not unusual. In many ways a "queen" will "read" (interpret) clothes in the way that a costume designer does, and expends a great deal of time and effort in devel-oping and maintaining "her" look.

Ongina says that he feels more approachable as a drag queen; he loves being recognized and also thinks that he is "nicer" when dressed up. A recurring theme when talking to drag queens is their fear of how they are portrayed. They want control at all levels about their image. I would suggest that the queen's personal experience of image is particularly important and might vastly differ from the image experienced by the viewer. This sets up a contradictory ten-sion. The drag queen courts publicity and attention, but then has to personally negotiate it, as the public view can be harsh, moralistic, and misrepresenting.

In Britain in the mid–20th century, Danny La Rue became famous and had a long career as a female impersonator. Others such as Lily Savage (drag queen), Dame Edna Everidge, and Eddie Izzard have all been accepted into mainstream entertainment as cross-dressers. The most recent celebrity is artist Grayson Perry who came to public notice when he collected his 2003 Turner Prize on National Television dressed as his alter ego "Claire" in a short full-skirted satin dress decorated with bows and jumping rabbits accessorized with white ankle socks, and red button shoes—a new public exposure on alter ego cross-dressing. Perry gave the prestigious Reith Lecture sponsored by the BBC in 2013.

In 2004, in order to investigate a less celebrity version of drag, I interviewed "Queen Naz"[29] who is a London drag queen and quite happy to publically talk about being at Gay Pride. He commented that all the queens dress themselves individually, each trying to outdo the other with a sense of camp rivalry, although no prizes are ever given. He has developed his own par-ticular style of dress, favoring high-feathered headdresses which make him over seven feet tall from heels to plume tips. In his words, "I'm a big girl." Naz's photo had been used in the Sunday press the previous year as one of the colorful parade images, in a rainbow-feathered headdress riding a rickshaw. He obviously enjoys the attention from his recognizable image.

In everyday life Naz was a costume student, and consequently he created and constructed his own costumes. This was slightly unusual at that time because many of the queens were com-missioning outfits from specialist costumiers, such as "X" who always dressed as "Batgirl." This professional designer also creates costumes for Grayson Perry. Naz commented that his "queen" friend had two completely separate lives. One life spent a professional week with family, but during weekends his other life always appeared in drag at festivals. The two lives were strictly segregated. Queen Naz explained that he personally uses drag as a form of escapism where he can experience more fun and less shyness. He does not intend to pass himself off as a woman. At least six foot tall, even without heels, he considers his look to be simultaneously fun and grotesque, and his costumes suggest an asexual image rather than the traditional pantomime Dame. He often wears the same dress more than once to all the marches in a season. His most favorite outfit is the latest one he has created, generally recycling elements. Petticoats, for example, or feathers start out white and then he dyes them into colors as they become dirty. At the time I interviewed Naz he had twelve dresses. He loves lots of glitter and pretty things. Like many drag queens, he enjoys using non-costume materials; sometimes incorporating flashing lights into the ensemble, with the battery pack stuck in his bra. Seeing a swan plant pot he thought, "I could stick that on my head," and so he constructed a headdress out of it.

This use of the everyday, mundane item is echoed in other drag costuming reflected in Chappel's work for *Priscilla* where flip-flops (thongs) were used to create a Courrèges-styled outfit. Queen Naz credits being influenced by videos of Sydney Mardi Gras, performer Leigh Bowery, and styles displayed in *Priscilla*. Queen Naz marched in the London Pride in 2004 and then again in 2013.

Each Pride is meant to have its own costume workshop, which works on some of the costumes for the march. It is, however, generally open to all and the interpretation of the theme quite broad. In 2004 the theme was "All Communities Together" celebrating the diversity of the British population. People of all ages marched, often in particular interest groups. Interestingly the distinctive features of the costumes were not so much the styles or finishes but rather the rationales for each individual group's choices in order to identify themselves.

The gay community tends to have a slightly higher income than average, in this affluent country, yet this characteristic was not particularly evident in the costumes. We might initially assume that the culture of long working hours, which is so dominant in the British workplace, implies that Pride marchers simply don't have the time to devote to making outfits for their presentation. However I later formed the idea that the participants were no longer looking to disguise their participation. The most noticeable addition to the "Pride" in 2004 was that of the policemen and women who marched as a group in their own uniforms, albeit rather awkwardly.[30] The previous year some police forces had marched as a group, in their own clothes with permission, but not all were allowed. In 2006 the armed forces began to follow suit first with the Royal Navy, then the Royal Air Force and finally in 2008, more controversially, the Army finally allowed serving men and women to march in their uniforms.[31]

London Pride attendance numbers dramatically increased in 2013 from 2004. The weather was also significantly better, which in the UK really motivates the public mood. In 2004 I stood in Whitehall on the other side of Trafalgar Square, watching a slightly dispersed series of marchers parade down a very wide formal street. Those that had made it that far were clutching umbrellas and looking a little cold. Most of the interest groups, (such as Amnesty International, Gay Catholic Walkers, and Shoe Fetishists) were still parading, with an occasional drag queen, although apparently many had taken the tube from Trafalgar Square heading north for a subsequent Party in the Park. Consequently my photos are an incomplete record. The photographs show lots of individuals marching together, carrying banners, and waving colored flags. Groups are either identified by dressing identically such as a group of young males marching in pink underwear with headbands or wearing the same colored t-shirts as the rugby team did.

The key difference here from the later 2013 "Pride" is that by 2013 it was relatively easy to print individual t-shirts. Ironically corporate sponsors may have sponsored elements of the march but were not encouraging their gay workers to be identified.

My reaction to the 2004 Pride, in response to the police marching in their uniforms, many of them for the first time, was one of surprised admiration. My photograph shows a slightly hesitant group of serious men and women in full uniform, in stark contrast to the smiling, waving and playful group marching in 2013. However, I reiterate that we focus not on the polish and finish of the costumes or even the design of them, but rather on how each group has chosen to self-identify.

How could this "bring-your-own-clothes" event relate to masquerade? If people march as themselves, in their own clothes this is surely just a political demonstration. But even in the early days when most marchers wore ordinary clothes, there have always been masqueraders. Where were the drag queens and the trans-people, the anti-masque figures representing vice and disorder? No one thought to ask the policemen featuring so prominently in photographs as the upholders of the law whether any were gay. As the law keepers, symbols of the state, their part of the event was the "masque" of law and order so to speak, resolving chaos into order. It is unknown how many gay police officers might have been involved in those marches, but it is reasonable to assert that there were police officers masquerading as the status-quo heterosexuals during the earlier parades.

Pride 2013 conversely had advanced the social masque (masquerade) to a new standard, clearly involving inclusivity for all walks of life. LBGT communities from every profession and interest group plus their friends, families and supporters now have more opportunities for "masquerading" at a more authentic level.

From the big man who worked for the Bank of America, to the little girl in the green fairy dress on the shoulders of her "South London Lesbian" mother, the parade of interest groups represented not only drag queens but socially-accepted lawyers, doctors, students, transport workers, counselors, teachers, actors, boy scouts, bankers, charity and insurance workers, the civil service, trade unionists, ambulance and fire crews as well as the community-based interest groups. There were also marchers from well-known corporations representing restaurant chains, supermarkets, food shops, and department stores. There were Sikhs, Muslims, Jews, Catholics and other Christians as well as marchers from the Philippines, Turkey, India, and American Democrats. There were bikers, Christian walkers, roller skaters and hockey players, and a choir singing "I'm getting married in the morning," drawing attention to both the 2013 "Love and Marriage" Pride theme and the imminent change in the law.

Festival organizers led the parade, followed by the armed forces marching in their uniforms, a familiar sight on "official" celebrations. Then came groups in matching outfits, homemade costumes, along with trans-people in normal clothes and drag queens in their favorite frocks. At least one marcher appeared to be a Sister of Perpetual Indulgence, judging by the nun's wimple headdress and exaggerated white face make-up together with a neatly trimmed beard. There were "toppers" and funny hats, large headdresses, tail-coated grooms with or without trousers, and groups of Barbie brides wearing big white meringue dresses and huge blond wigs. Traditional showgirls paraded in dresses made from newspaper, or modeling balloons, fake tattoo sleeves (and real tats too), traditional native costumes and Scottish kilts, large plastic headdresses decorated with champagne glasses, others made from colored pipe-cleaners, jeweled tutus, grass skirts, an orange butterfly outfit, and a "real" pink poodle. One man wore half of an elephant costume and several appeared in rubber dog masks. A drag queen looked remarkably like old Queen Mary circa 1920. One marcher wore a large stylish hat decorated with blown-up condoms; another wore a union jack mini dress, while yet another wore a pale blue baby-gro accompanied by a pale blue surgeon. A black clad group of submissives chained together walked in front of the Christians. There were garlands, wings, huge wigs, and rainbows on flags, on umbrellas, and on crinoline dresses. There were face paints and full body colorings, but all of these were accompanied by hundreds of different colored t-shirted groups, specially printed with logos or statements with lots of placards and many, many balloons.

There was a restriction on vehicles, so that most participants had to walk with only a couple of red London buses and a "milk float." Professional costumes were at a minimum. The majority were gloriously handmade and the overall effect of the matching groups together with the individuals was a marvelous jumble as if to state that the more cost-efficient, the better to enjoy oneself. The image was less important than the feeling of the apparel. Participants obviously preferred being in the moment; not looking at it.

Pride traditionalists deplored the involvement of business, considering it too commercial and too mainstream. The participants, however, no longer seemed intent on confronting viewers or hiding behind the actual masquerade, worried that family, friends and colleagues might recognize them and reject them for their sexual preferences.

In terms of costume design, the spectacle might not be as flamboyant or as controlled as seen in film, theatre, or even Mardi Gras, but this masquerade style of costuming reflects the changing nature of British culture. Every person marching as himself or herself in Pride still masquerades in flamboyant, imaginative attire that effectively enhances his/her own place in society, whatever clothes they choose.

The anti-masque has now become the masque proper. The need for multiple disguises as protection or for anonymity is nearly over, with all participants now able to play as multiple versions of themselves. Let the celebratory dancing begin.

# Notes

1. J. Stephen Orgel Harris and Roy Strong (1973), *King's Arcadia: Inigo Jones and the Stuart Court* (London and Bradford: Lund Humphries), 36.

2. "Pride in London" is the registered name of the company that organizes the LGBT Gay Pride parade and associated parties, but it is referred to by many other variations of name. I have used the term Pride or Pride London to refer to the Gay Pride Parade throughout this chapter, as this is how it is most commonly referred to in the UK. http://londoncommunitypride.org/.

3. www.gaystarnews.com/article/andy-warhols-photos-1984-new-york-gay-pride-parade-released210613.

4. "Gay Marriage Bill: Peers Back Government Plans" (5 June 2013), BBC News, www.bbc.co.uk/news/uk-politics-22764954.

5. A professional lobbying group to prevent the stigmatization of gay people.

6. "U.S. Supreme Court in Historic Rulings on Gay Marriage" (26 June 2013), BBC News, http://www.bbc.co.uk/news/world-us-canada-23068454.

7. A. Perchuk and Helaine Posner, eds. (1995), *The Masculine Masquerade* (Cambridge, MA: MIT Press), 13–19.

8. Terry Castle (1986), *Masquerade and Civilization* (Stanford, CA: Stanford University Press), 11.

9. Ibid., 6.

10. Ibid., 11.

11. Ibid., 19.

12. Juno, Ceres and Iris.

13. Paul Burston (2013), *Time Out* magazine, no. 2233 (25 June to 1 July): 15–16.

14. Suzanne Poli, a New York–based photographer who has published photographs documenting the New York Gay Pride march.

15. http://www.youtube.com/watch?v=LTqTzLInlPg

16. The Leadership Conference (22 June 2009), "Stonewall Riots: The Beginning of the LGBT Movement," www.civilrights.org/archives/2009/06/449-stonewall.html.

17. http://lib-1.lse.ac.uk/archivesblog/?tag=gay-liberation-front.

18. http://www.mardigras.org.au/about/history/.

19. The Adventures of Priscilla, Queen of the Desert (1994), Stephen Elliot, director.

20. Tim Chappel, interview with the author, 23 April 2004.

21. Ibid.

22. *The Naked Civil Servant* (1975), Jack Gold, director.

23. Jean-Louis Ginibre (2005), Ladies or Gentlemen: A Pictorial History of Male Cross-Dressing in the Movies (New York: Filipacci Publishing).

24. Ibid., 6–7.

25. John Nunley (1999), *Masks: Faces of Culture* (New York: Harry N. Abrams), 167–177.

26. Ibid., 160.

27. Leland Bobbé, photographer (2012), "Portraits-Half Drag."

28. http://feastoffun.com/podcast/2009/02/24/fof-937-a-taste-of-ongina-022409/

29. Queen Naz, when I interviewed him in June 2004, was a 25-year-old drag queen who had taken part in the Gay Pride Marches for the past six years, five of which he marched in drag.

30. "Gay Police Head Pride March" (20 June 2003), BBC News, http://news.bbc.co.uk/1/hi/uk/3007918.stm.

31. "Army Lifts Gay Pride Uniform Ban" (15 June 2008), Metro UK, http://metro.co.uk/2008/06/15/army-lifts-gay-pride-uniform-ban-188750/.

# Works Cited

*The Adventures of Priscilla, Queen of the Desert.* (1994.) Stephen Elliot, director.

"Army Lifts Gay Pride Uniform Ban." (2008.) Metro UK (15 June), http://metro.co.uk/2008/06/15/army-lifts-gay-pride-uniform-ban-188750/.

Burston, Paul. (2013.) *Time Out* magazine, no. 2233 (25 June to 1 July).

Castle, Terry. (1986.) *Masquerade and Civilization.* Stanford, CA: Stanford University Press.

Chappel, Tim. (23 April 2004.) Interview with the author.

"Gay Marriage Bill: Peers Back Government Plans." (2013.) BBC News (5 June), www.bbc.co.uk/news/uk-politics-22764954.

"Gay Police Head Pride March." (2003.) BBC News (20 June), http://news.bbc.co.uk/1/hi/uk/3007918.stm.

Ginibre, Jean-Louis. (2005.) *Ladies or Gentlemen: A Pictorial History of Male Cross-Dressing in the Movies.* New York: Filipacci Publishing.

Harris, J. Stephen Orgel, and Roy Strong. (1973.) *King's Arcadia: Inigo Jones and the Stuart Court.* London and Bradford: Lund Humphries.

The Leadership Conference (22 June 2009), "Stonewall Riots: The Beginning of the LGBT Movement," www.civilrights.org/archives/2009/06/449-stonewall.html.

*The Naked Civil Servant.* (1975.) Jack Gold, director.

Nunley, John. (1999.) *Masks: Faces of Culture.* New York: Harry N. Abrams.

Perchuk, A., and Helaine Posner, eds. (1995.) *The Masculine Masquerade.* Cambridge, MA: MIT Press.

"U.S. Supreme Court in Historic Rulings on Gay Marriage." (2013.) BBC News (26 June), http://www.bbc.co.uk/news/world-us-canada-23068454

# Halloween Masquerade: Contemporary Trends and Hidden Meanings

## Kara McLeod

When most Americans hear the word masquerade, they think of elegant ladies and gentlemen in elaborate, Venetian-style masks, looking like the masquerade scene in *Phantom of the Opera*, or Carnival celebrations in Rio. It is sophisticated and exotic, something foreign. Our homegrown holiday of Halloween isn't the first thing to come to mind. However, in contemporary America, Halloween is our masquerade; one of those rare moments during which anyone- children, teens and adults alike, can participate publicly in fantasy fulfillment, openly masking as their alter ego or desired, idealized states, for an audience. That audience, in turn, will positively respond to and reinforce the masked state with both observation and participation. At Halloween, maskers can try on different aspects of personality and assume unaccustomed social roles. We can mock our own mortal nature and our fear of the unknown future in a psychologically safe space. We can mock the "betters" of society, upending the social order, albeit temporarily, without fear of reproach or consequence. We can mask our ordinary public face and reveal our true selves, or the selves we wish we could be, but only one day a year. During this brief period, we can play.

As kids we understand how to play and are not ashamed of it. Childhood play, both active and role-playing, is encouraged and supported. Adults, however, are expected to grow out of the need for play, particularly the need for role-playing which is often characterized as practice for adulthood. Therefore, as we become part of the adult world we feel pressured to discard role-playing as a sign of social maturity. Those who do not discard role-playing are ridiculed as socially inept, childish and emotionally arrested. Many of us embrace the rising popularity of video games, MORPs (Multi-player Online Role Playing games) and Cosplay events like Comic-Con and The Labyrinth of Jareth. Yet such entertainment is considered juvenile and lacking seriousness. We view any adult pursuing these games beyond his or her early twenties with suspicion.

Yet Halloween persists. This open display of people expressing, even flaunting, the pretend state has not diminished. In fact, it grows in popularity among adults and that popularity is accelerating. In 2012, a record 170 million people planned to celebrate Halloween: seven out of every ten Americans. Halloween is now the second most popular holiday in terms of spending and is expected to reach 8 billion dollars in 2012. National Retail Federation President and CEO Matthew Shay said, "By the time Halloween rolls around each year it is safe to say Americans have already spent two months preparing for one of the fastest-growing and most widely-loved holidays of the year."[1] While still paling in comparison to the 35.3 billion spent in the November-December holiday shopping season,[2] Halloween retail growth has been substantial. It has transformed from its earliest origins as a celebration of the harvest, to a holiday primarily for children, to a modern exercise in fantasy fulfillment and escapism, while still incorporating elements of masking our fears of mortality.

So, what is Halloween and where does it come from? The popular conception holds that Halloween originated as the Celtic festival of Samhain, a holiday devoted to the spirits of the dead. However, this widely accepted tradition is only partly true, and this ancient festival is not the only contributor to our modern holiday. In his work on the history of Halloween, Nicholas Rogers points out that "there is no hard evidence that Samhain was specifically devoted to the dead or ancestor worship"[3] but more importantly:

> What was especially noteworthy about Samhain was its status as a borderline festival.... In Celtic lore, it marked the boundary between summer and winter, light and darkness. In this respect, Samhain can be seen as what anthropologists call a liminal festival. It was a moment of ritual transition and altered states.[4]

This aspect of the Samhain Festival, the idea of a special time not bound by normal rules, most informs the modern practice of Halloween. Still, Halloween is not the Samhain Festival, but a polyglot of several traditions. In the 17th-century Hallowmas was the beginning of the Christmas season in Europe and was celebrated with elaborate masques and dance recitals. In London, lawyers of the Middle Temple put on these events as "major social events, and included the rich display of feathers and finery." In the 18th century, the word "Halloween" first appeared in the ballad "Young Tamlane: "This night is Hallowe'en, Janet. The morn is Hallowday." Robert Burns' 1875 poem "Halloween" records the folk customs of telling the future, mostly one's romantic future, with apples and nuts.[5] Halloween was not widely celebrated in the United States until the 19th century, where it was a festival celebrated mostly by the Irish and Scottish in both family-oriented gatherings and larger public balls. However, by 1874 advertisements representing local shops in the Ontario (Canada) *British Whig Weekly* marketed Halloween masks.[6] Halloween was making its mark in the larger mainstream community, and would soon be divorced from its ethnic identity in North America.

At the turn of the 20th century, Halloween was widely known as a night of pranks and mischief-making, primarily by children. The film *Meet Me in St Louis* (1944), introduced the young character of Tootie and her friends who express themselves in what can only be described as a riot of destruction: the children set fires, try to crash a streetcar, and fantasize about mayhem and homicide. This vividly portrayed a fairly common type of Halloween celebration. By the 1920s we see efforts to tame and control the holiday. Halloween booklets for entertaining started to give more space to children's entertainment, and by the 1930s they were almost entirely so. The fortune-telling games played by adults were now dismissed as old-fashioned superstition.[7] The *Halloween Fun Book* (1937) advises in its introduction, "Instead of condemnation for pranks which too often have overstepped the line, youth should be given the co-operation of their parents and leaders in making Hallowe'en a gala, carefree holiday."[8] Halloween was now a commercial holiday for children, one that was not reclaimed by adults for decades. But in the process of its commercialization and its many changes, it became a peculiarly American and secular holiday. It even offers us a sense of community. Speaking on the popularity of haunted houses, cultural critic and author David Skal writes:

> As American communities become more transient and impersonal, more virtual than visceral and as civic participation wanes at all levels, the appeal of Halloween rituals may not be so mysterious after all. However empty your neighborhood may appear, at least in a haunted house there's *always* somebody home.[9]

Halloween in fact, has become such a quintessentially American observation that it was the subject of much debate in 2001, in the aftermath of the September 11th attacks. While some argued that Halloween celebrations should be toned down or suspended entirely, others saw the loss of Halloween as downright un–American. Angus King, Governor of Maine, commented that terrorists could "mess up the postal service, but they had better stay away from trick-or-treating."[10] Even a woman who had lost her own mother in the World Trade Center attack, when asked about the holiday for her children answered, "The kids need something to be afraid of that they can control. The kids can control Halloween-scary; it's not real, like the other."[11]

Certainly the idea of control appeals to adults as well as children. We are all reassured by the familiar and the quantifiable. These two ideas, the desire to conquer our fears by acting them out in a controlled setting compounded with the limited opportunity for role-play in our lives as adults, suggest why we most appreciate about Halloween.

We can at least partially illuminate this phenomenon by examining it in terms of the masquerade personae that people adopt. Fred Davis, in discussing the nature of fashion, addresses the clothing code, the meaning we attach to forms of dress. He writes,

> ... we know that through clothing people communicate some things about their persons, and at the collective level this results typically in locating them symbolically in some structured universe of status claims and life-style attachments. Some of us may even be so bold as to assert what those claims and attachments are [such as] a tramp presuming the hauteur of a patrician, as a *nouveau riche* ostentation masking status anxiety but ... the actual symbolic content that elicits such interpretations eludes us. Lacking such knowledge we can at best only form conclusions without knowing quite how we derived them; this is something we often have to do in everyday life.[12]

We all know that a code of sorts informs our perceptions of dress, both the dress we choose and the dress we see on others. In masquerade costume the code is far clearer and more overt in its message. Davis refers to Halloween events as one category of several "ritualized and special ceremonial occasions in which men are permitted to do 'funny things' with their appearance and clothing."[13] In everyday life, the messages we send with our clothing have to reflect our serious adult personae. On Halloween, the conceit of masquerade gives us latitude to make bolder statements.

Consequently, I suggest some ways in which to decode some of the messages people send and receive in their choices of costumes, because I have seen them over many years working in the business of selling Halloween. Thousands of costumed customers later, these are some of my observations.

My first experience as a Halloween professional was in 1985, working in a small rental/retail costume shop. The pace was fast and "reading" a customer meant the difference between a sale and an unhappy walkout. Our job, in a very real sense, was to find the secret identity of each person who walked in the door, show it to them, and send them out satisfied with that choice. Some customers were more challenging than others, but it was unusual that a customer left empty handed because we couldn't figure out what they wanted, even if we didn't have it. A truly remarkable transformation occurs when people see themselves in costume—the right costume—for the first time.

I recall from several years ago, a woman who had rented a bumblebee costume. Her family was hosting a Halloween party for her 85th birthday and she came to the shop to get ready, "just for the kids you understand, it was a little silly," she told me. A bit reserved at first, she dressed and I put on her make-up: black and yellow stripes, black-lined eyes, little, pouty black "bee stung" lips and a shiny black pageboy wig. When it was all complete, she looked at herself in the mirror and gasped with delight saying, "Look at me! I'm so cute!" She minced and posed and batted her false eyelashes, and practically danced out to the car with her daughter. She had license to behave in a way she would not "as herself," but that behavior was now acceptable because she was *not* herself—she was a cute bumblebee. The mask let her be what she wanted to be: adorable, charming, and fanciful.

Year after year, the same sorts of characters appear at Halloween parties. These perennial favorites (aside from being predictable profits for Halloween merchandisers) are icons that the masqueraders can adopt and adapt to their needs and desires. Look at any Halloween catalog, merchandise rack or costume shop stock and you'll find these archetypes: the vampire, the pirate, witches and wizards, sexy characters, devils and demons, zombies, ghosts, clowns and comic characters, along with an infinite variety of animals. Over my 28 years in the Halloween field, I've seen this cast of characters over and over again, with slight shuffles in popularity ranking and a few pop culture incursions from whatever movie, television franchise or newsmaker is trending in any given year. The data backs up my observations: The 2012 National Retail Federation (NRF) survey lists the most popular adult costumes of that year, in order, as: witch, vampire, pirate, Batman, zombie, vixen, princess, ghost, nurse, cat, and Superman.[14]

Instinctively, different people gravitate toward different characters based on their own secret or not-so-secret-selves. Once examined, we see that these characters are totemic representations of powerful dream states, idealizations, and wishes. Those characters and the ideals of our society that they represent allow individuals to access and manipulate their own projected self-image as a way to address "the stranger within" in an emotionally safe and socially acceptable way. Each character type has a different *crasis*, a composition of personality/character traits that the masker then takes on as his or her own. If we break them down individually we can see what each of these masks conjures for the wearer and the viewer.

- **The Vampire:** Vampires are the embodiment of power, sexuality, and immortality. Men find this role especially appealing because it allows them to role-play without straying too far from the conventions of masculinity in Western culture. The vampire role, essentially a more virile version of men, makes them mysterious and compelling to the opposite sex. Women also find the vampire role appealing because as a sexual role, it allows for more power, even a sexually dominant position, than other sexy female archetypes. More recent vampire versions have become more sympathetic, even more romantic, as exemplified by the character, Angel, from *Buffy the Vampie Slayer.* Angel is a vampire with a soul, a hot body, and a romantic streak. As a classic doomed lover, a Romeo figure of sorts, he's still an animal that possesses hypnotic and dangerous sexual appeal.

Masqueraders also discover the idea of immortality as a powerful draw to the vampire character. Its invulnerability is reassuring in a holiday that brings to our attention death and its attendant indignities. By emulating a creature that transcends death, and manages to stay attractive while doing so, the masker can sample the Vampire's fearlessness of mortality.

- **The Pirate:** Pirates represent freedom from authority as well as domination and the power that comes from access to wealth. Part of the pirate fantasy includes adventure and conquest. We fear—and yet admire—pirates because they defy conventional authority and standards of morality. Pirates have their own hierarchy that they enforce. They live by their own will and strive for ruthless pursuit of gain, without apology or guilt. Moreover, the pirate is not limited by modern 21st-century society, by law, social mores, expectations, or career.

  This crasis speaks to our inner rebel. Halloween pirates are rarely truly dangerous criminals. They are lovable rapscallions, even Robin Hoods, in a hedonistic world of adventure and freedom. It is not socially acceptable indulge in one's excesses in ordinary life, but a pirate is expected to do so. Bring on the rum and wenches.

- **The Witch or Wizard:** This archetype embodies magical and spiritual power, that which is supernatural and transcendent of ordinary mortality. Witches have power over nature and ordinary mortals. They have access to hidden powers and knowledge. The world of the witch is mysterious and, again, powerful. This character ranges across a wide morality spectrum, from malevolent to benevolent, even harmless; from the evil witches of fairy tales to contemporary iterations of the magical like the characters of the Harry Potter series.

  Witches often involve themselves in larger struggles in secret, unseen worlds, where ordinary concerns are abandoned for a larger, more purposeful quest. Masqueraders choosing to emulate this character pattern do so to escape normal, conventional boundaries. The fantasy here allows for the gain of one's desires with a wave of the wand or a muttered incantation. Witches are the elite few, who know special secrets, making them part of a larger reality of great significance. This larger reality is invisible and inaccessible to ordinary mortals.

- **Sexy Characters:** Sexy characters have a variety of iterations, often novelty inspired, but essentially they all represent feminine power, as either the seductress or the sexual object, and sometimes they are both simultaneously. She is the much sought-after female, the Venus/Aphrodite goddess who has the ability to bestow, or not bestow, her favor on her many suitors.

  This character has wide appeal; it supports cultural values associated with femininity such as attractiveness, youth, and fertility. In many cases, there are elements of feminine submission and coy pubescence. Sexy costumes often incorporate juvenile elements juxtaposed with sexuality, such as the classic examples of the baby doll and the French maid. Their brief, short-skirted, waist-nipped, cleavage-baring dresses, often with frilly ruffled petticoats, are occasionally referred to in the trade back rooms as "slutoween" costumes. They carry a huge variety of themes, including jokes and puns ("Dirty Martini"), career-based costumes ("Naughty Nurse"), culturally-based and often racist costumes ("Sexy Squaw") historically-based ("Sexy Marie Antoinette") and variations on classic fairy tale females like Little Bo Peep, Cinderella, or Little Red Riding Hood.

Additionally, the sexy costume, in its special space created by Halloween, is accessible to a more diverse range of body types than "normal" clothes would be. Women who would not dream of wearing a bikini in the summer or a short skirt don't shy away from the sexy costume rack. Hot Firewomen or Sexy Schoolgirls are for anyone who wants them.

Masqueraders find the sexy characters appealing because women's clothes are especially judged in terms of how much sexual availability they advertise. Clothing judged as trashy or too revealing in everyday life loses its negative association on Halloween and instead brings the wearer admiration. "Asking for it" or even "demanding it" (sexual attention) is acceptable in the masquerade environment. This is a reversal of the status normally accorded women wearing such openly sexualized clothing; it transforms a woman from whore to goddess.

- **Devils and Demons:** The devil or demonic character evokes a darker personality whose crasis speaks to forbidden impulses. Like the pirate, devils are free from convention but they combine with that the supernatural power of the witch. The devil is law unto him or herself, the ruler of the underworld, a force more powerful than death. Devils and demons are beyond the mortal as well as highly sexualized and utterly profane.

  Maskers emulating devils or demons give themselves permission to express darker emotional states and desires. Devils punish, subdue, conquer, and tempt. They are always attractively "bad" and can be naughty tricksters, especially sexually, because a large part of the devil persona emphasizes the devil as seducer. The trope is so well known it is even used to humorous effect, exemplified by the devil-clad neighbor in *Hocus Pocus* (1993) who tries to masquerade as Lothario to the visiting witches, until his wife intervenes.

- **Zombies, Ghosts and the Undead:** These characters who defy death actually have a fear of the dead and dead bodies. This masquerade is a source of fright that, at the same time, allows both masker and participant to treat lightly that which we most fear: what lurks in the darkness outside and in the darkness of death.

  The current surge in the popularity of zombies may partly stem from a larger trend in Western culture that pop culture entertainment has capitalized on: fear of contamination. The zombie represents the violation of self by a corrupting, unconquerable force. The various zombie apocalypse scenarios in vogue all speak to the fear of the loss of individuality, identity, and the security of one's own person. Even one's own body is not safe. Indulging in the zombie as a mask empowers the masquerader to subdue and control that fear.

  In film and television, the foundational myth is George Romero's *Night of the Living Dead* (1968), which not only spawned a series, but an entire film genre. We are now in a pop culture renaissance of sorts for the zombie story and the oeuvre has expanded to encompass straightforward tales of terror like *28 Days Later* (2002) and *World War Z* (2013), satirical takes like *The Cabin in the Woods* (2012), comedies like *Shaun of the Dead* (2004) and *Zombieland* (2009) and even romance, as in the retelling of Romeo and Juliet as a zombie story, *Warm Bodies* (2013).

  The zombie has recently become such a phenomenon it has spread outside its Halloween boundaries. Aside from its appearances in movies and television, zombies have invaded the world of exercise. Southern California is the home of the 5 kilometer obstacle race "Run for Your Lives," which bills itself as the "original zombie infected 5k."[15] There are other similarly themed events in other states, of course. Those training on their own can buy an app for their smart phones, "Zombies, Run!" featuring "zombie chase interval training."[16] Not only can you mask as a zombie for Halloween, you can adopt the persona of "survivor of the zombie hordes" in the off season.

- **Clowns or Comic Characters:** Often projecting personifications of the wise fool, this mask allows the wearer to mock the foibles and sacred cows of society without fear of reprisal. These lighthearted masks are a counterpoint to the darker and more serious themes and characters of the holiday. Who fears death when wearing a giant hot dog suit? The absurdity of it is cathartic and freeing.

  This group of characters includes political caricatures. Mocking those in power levels the playing field and is psychologically satisfying. For example, clowns can direct their humor against those who share or oppose the masker's individual political values. The clown's message can be a kinder, gentler form of political protest, a statement of solidarity, or a way to express a desire to have a more prominent position of power and influence. During every Presidential election, costume shops invariably have a last minute rush to stock enough of the final candidates, without having so much on hand that you are stuck with too many of this election cycle's loser. The one exception: Nixon. Tricky Dick is a reliable seller every year.

- **Animals:** Animals embody primal energy. Each animal has its own individual personality but broadly they express primitive, unfiltered, and sometimes childlike impulses. Cats are by far the most common animal mask chosen (and most typically chosen by women). Cats are attractive, sensual and dangerous. They are fully self-absorbed, hedonistic characters. A subset of cat masquerade includes Catwoman, combining attributes of the cat and sexy archetypes. Catwoman is more than a cat—and more than a woman. She's a vixen—a sleek, high-powered seductress with claws. And frequently carries a whip.

  The animal masquerade empowers the masker with the attributes of the selected animal, be it the glamorous cat or bat, the powerful lion, the cuddly dog, the dangerous wolf, or the comic but affable, ever-popular pig. An animal costume also functions as an easy transition for people who might not feel completely ready to commit to the expense or effort of a more elaborate mask. Animal costumes often come as inexpensive packaged kits of ears and tail and are readily adaptable to different wardrobe choices. A bunny kit can just as easily furnish a child playing the Easter bunny as it can a woman looking for a sexy, provocative "bunny."

All these character archetypes have something in common. They tap into the collective cultural myths familiar to all of us, and this familiarity makes them perennial. "What gives the myth an operative value is that the specific pattern described is everlasting; it explains the present and the past as well as the future."[17] Is that what we are doing with our Halloween masks—exploring our past and our future, trying to attach ourselves to the larger mythic cycle? Or is it simple fantasy, an ephemeral entertainment? Perhaps it is both. Folklorist Jack Santino calls Halloween "polysemic," having different meanings in different places and times, or to different people, even in a given place and time. Halloween is what we make it, because it is "defined by art and imagination."[18] At Halloween, we are all artists, and our masking is our art. It is our imagination that rules the day—or the night. David Skal concludes that:

> The Halloween machine turns the world upside down. One's identity can be discarded with impunity. Men dress as women and women vice versa. Authority can be mocked and circumvented. And, most important, graves open and the departed return. Of course, the 'return of the

dead' is an evocative allegory for the return or expression of just about anything that's been buried, repressed, or stifled by the living.[19]

So, how will you masquerade for Halloween?

# Notes

1. National Retail Federation (2012), Halloween 2012 Consumer Spending Survey, http://www.nrf.com/modules.php?name=News&op=viewlive&sp_id=1430, 25 September.
2. Todd Haselton (2011), "Holiday Spending Jumps 15% from Last Year to $35.3 Billion," http://bgr.com/2011/12/28/holiday-spending-jumps-15-from-last-year-to-35-3-billion/, 28 December.
3. Nicholas Rogers (2002), *Halloween: From Pagan Ritual to Party Night* (New York: Oxford University Press), 19.
4. Ibid., 21.
5. David J. Skal (2002), *Death Makes a Holiday: A Cultural History of Halloween* (New York: Bloomsbury Press), 25–26.
6. Rogers (2002), 53.
7. Lisa Morton (2012), *Trick or Treat: A History of Halloween* (London: Reaktion Press), 165–166.
8. Morton (2012), 167.
9. Skal (2002), 121.
10. Christopher Noxon (31 October 2002), "Time to Take Back the Night," *Los Angeles Times*.
11. Rogers (2002), 168.
12. Fred Davis (1992), *Fashion, Culture and Identity* (Chicago: University of Chicago Press), 4.
13. Ibid., 40.
14. "There's No Spooking Spending as Seven in 10 Americans Plan to Celebrate Halloween this Year" (2012), National Retail Federation, http://www.nrf.com/modules.php?name=News&op=viewlive&sp_id=1432, 25 September.
15. www.runforyourlives.com
16. https://www.zombiesrungame.com/
17. Claude Levi-Strauss (1955), "The Structural Study of Myth," *Journal of American Folklore* Volume 68, Number 270 (Columbus, OH: American Folklore Society), 430.
18. Morton (2012), 153.
19. Skal (2002), 17–18.

# Works Cited

"There's No Spooking Spending as Seven in 10 Americans Plan to Celebrate Halloween this Year." (2012.) National Retail Federation. 25 September. http://www.nrf.com/modules.php?name=News&op=viewlive&sp_id=1432.

Davis, Fred. (1992.) *Fashion, Culture and Identity.* Chicago: University of Chicago Press.

Haselton, Todd. (2011.) "Holiday Spending Jumps 15% from Last Year to $35.3 Billion." 28 December. http://bgr.com/2011/12/28/holiday-spending-jumps-15-from-last-year-to-35-3-billion/.

Levi-Strauss, Claude. (1955.) "The Structural Study of Myth." *Journal of American Folklore* Volume 68, Number 270. Columbus, OH: American Folklore Society.

Morton, Lisa. (2012.) *Trick or Treat: A History of Halloween.* London: Reaktion Press.

Noxon, Christopher. (2002.) "Time to Take Back the Night." *Los Angeles Times* (31 October).

Rogers, Nicholas. (2002.) *Halloween: From Pagan Ritual to Party Night.* New York: Oxford University Press.

Skal, David J. (2002.) *Death Makes a Holiday: A Cultural History of Halloween.* New York: Bloomsbury Press.

# Dragon Con as a Hip
# Spiritual Destination for
# Geeks and Pop Culture Lovers

### Deborah Bell

Popular culture masquerades have taken place for centuries, especially in Catholic countries celebrating versions of pre–Lenten carnivals. These have allowed participants from all economic and social backgrounds some moments of glee and an excuse to escape life's daily pressures at the height of the winter doldrums. Italy's Venetian population has a long history of sporting masks and masquerades at their own distinctive carnival festivities that hearkens back to the 12th century. We also find carnivals in Spain, Bulgaria, Switzerland, Bolivia, Brazil, Trinidad and Tobago, and Haiti.[1] The United States stages masquerades during its annual Mardi Gras celebrations in New Orleans and surrounding cities, while Day of the Dead masquerading inspired by Mexican Catholic and indigenous religious traditions and their festivities regularly occur in California.

Perhaps it was just a matter of time before the mid–20th-century Renaissance Fair celebrations and Society for Creative Anachronism events—as well as the community-sponsored historical reenactments of the '80s—would morph into the huge costume masquerade industry conglomerate known under various sub-headings such as Comic-Con, Sci-Fi Con, Star Trek Conventions, Cosplay, Anime, Wondercon, and Alternative Press Expo. *The New York Times* regularly reports on the local SantaCon phenomenon, where masqueraders appear as "naughty santas" with license to drink excessively and behave badly—within limits. It started in the mid-'90s (probably in San Francisco) and now "takes place in more than 300 cities in 44 countries."[2] Secular versions of community masquerade have morphed in all sorts of new ways, beyond the traditional Catholic-inspired carnival events.

Dragon Con (formerly Dragon*Con), an annual commercial masquerade convention in Atlanta, was no doubt a spin-off of these earlier secular masquerading events. The founders of Dragon Con describe it as "an outgrowth/evolution of the local Science Fiction and gaming group (the Dragon Alliance of Gamers and Role-Players [DAGR])." But they also suggest that the name "Dragon" was derived from co-founder Ed Kramer's "Dragon Computer (a European version of Radio Shack's venerable Color Computer)" that initially was capable of serving as "a central hub [for the DAGR members.]"[3] In this essay I compare—more than contrast—the similar organizational structure and quest for spirituality that commercial masquerade conventions and religious institutions hold in common with each other, using Dragon Con as a case in point.

Over the course of the past 27 years Dragon Con has unquestionably become one of the largest eclectic masquerading events of its kind in the United States. CNN reported in August 2013 that,

> San Diego Comic-Con might draw more ticket-buyers, press, and bigger Hollywood names, but Dragon Con appeals to a broader spectrum of subcultures from a more passionate fan base ... the convention has built a reputation of acceptance and appreciation of all things nerdy, growing from a crowd of 1,400 in one hotel in its first year [1987] to an event spread out among six hotels in the heart of downtown Atlanta. Organizers say Dragon Con is expected to draw at least 55,000 people this year based on pre-ticket sales alone.[4]

Dragon Con has become a sort of annual Mecca for nerds; it has taken on traditions and rituals that seem remarkably enthusiastic in its mission to welcome new participants. Moreover, the Dragon Con experience encourages a general quest for—and acknowledgment of—spiritual themes found in popular literature, games, and film.

The remarkable success of Dragon Con and other masquerade conventions that thrive in urban centers everywhere affirms our global fascination with the phenomenon of masquerade on a grand commercial scale. Why? Even recent major world economic recessions have not discouraged this type of masquerade. In fact, perhaps economic stress makes many of us want to escape its pressures by exploring identities and worlds beyond our own. The exotic world of Hollywood movies placated Americans suffering during the Great Depression. While fantastic adventure and animation films continue as popular forms of escape, the masquerade conventions are dramatically expanding in scope as ticket sales rise exponentially and these conventions rapidly replicate themselves in major cities.

Surely our contemporary fascination with masquerade has much to do with the Information Age in which we live. The impact of the explosion of Internet information has produced multiple shards of written, oral, and visual data which often stimulate and challenge us to grasp new ways of thinking. We must react to these dense shards of information with incredible immediacy.

Masquerade allows us to "try on exotic appearances" and to play a range of roles representing new identities and cultural values without overly committing ourselves. Masquerade, especially at Dragon Con and similar masquerade conventions, becomes a seductive way for audiences to experience new thoughts and concepts in free fall. The instant gratification of masquerade is most appealing. And instead of seeing and practicing masquerade only once a year at carnival or during Halloween, more people witness and practice masquerade regularly, via television and the Internet as well as at countless other costume conventions, Renaissance Fairs, SCA events, historical reenactments, and Disney World.

Dragon Con taps into this rampant social urge to masquerade. While its participants meet collectively only once a year, entire families spend months in advance planning for the event by carefully inventing or duplicating figures they can masquerade from popular culture. Like other masquerade conventions, Dragon Con encourages grand collective public discourse and individual commentary on a multi-cultural span of spiritual values. Dragon Con loyalist Sean Cannon underscores this sentiment with his own story of how he became involved.

> My family has always had geeky tastes and high interest in science-fiction fantasies. We have always liked Renaissance Fairs and dressing up together. Almost everyone at Dragon Con wears a costume and the quality standards for these costumes are remarkably high. Three years ago my 12-year old sister went to panel hosted by the Comic Book track. She asked such insightful questions, the moderator was incredulous. Later, my family and I became fast friends with this moderator. In fact, typically I find myself surrounded by strangers—but the communal ambience implies that actually, I am surrounded by best friends—I just don't know them yet! At Dragon Con your day job doesn't matter and your expertise really doesn't matter either. Here, you can't tell the geeks from the gays and it doesn't matter. By that I mean that these two groups aren't separate at Dragon Con; it doesn't matter what your background, ethnicity, or sexual-orientation are, Dragon Con welcomes you.

He also reports that his "family regularly meets fifteen other participants from across the country—participants who, at this point, have become part of our family."[5]

Freddy Clements, a costume designer and professor at Jacksonville State University in Alabama, who went to his first Dragon Con in 2004, observes that it has the "largest costume parade in the southeast, if not the entire country." Clements has been one of the costume judges at Dragon Con for many years and has also given numerous workshops on various costume crafts. He believes that Dragon Con has grown relatively quickly because "it has it all—the gaming, guest star performance and crafts artists, vendors, walk-of-fame stars of fantasy, costume parades, costume balls, and costume expo merchandise."[6]

I asked Clements to elaborate on what makes this convention so popular. He credits the convention's annual major guest artist appearances, referencing in Dragon Con web site's detailed description of the first convention in 1987:

> Dragon Con '87 featured Guest of Honor Michael Moorcock.... Robert Asprin and Lynn Abbey, Robert Adams, Richard "Lord British" Garriott, the creator of Ultima, and Gary Cygaz, co-creator of Dungeons and Dragons. Just over 1,200 fans joined in on the fun, a notable number for a first-year convention. Miramar recording artist Jon Serrie delivered his keyboard arrangements from within a real NASA flight suit, with helmet, during the Masquerade/Costume Contest. Michael Moorcock and longtime friend Eric Bloom, Blue Oyster Cult's vocalist/guitarist, even jammed onstage, performing the Moorcock-written BOC tunes "Veteran of the Psychic Wars" and "Black Blade." This launched live concerts as an annual Dragon Con tradition.

Clements also recalls that, "When Barbara Eden appeared in 2011, hundreds of people in "I Dream of Genie costumes" paid $25 per photo to have Barbara Eden pose with them."[7]

Clements also credits Dragon Con's lively party atmosphere while other conventions are more sedate. "While Gen Con participants might play board games all day, or other conventions close the doors to hotel meeting rooms when filled to capacity, Dragon Con participants will often spontaneously spill out into the hallways, leaving the large meeting rooms empty." Another crucial aspect of Dragon Con's success derives from "its sole emphasis on costumes and masquerade—not lighting, scenery, or sound." Dragon Con's emphasis on diversity also holds wide appeal. Clements describes how five people can be in the same elevator masquerading as Wonder Woman, with one of them gay and one of them African-American.[8]

Clements observes that, "People have mundane jobs and Dragon Con is like a pilgrimage event. It offers its participants excitement in terms of its predictable rituals such as parades,

Freddy Clements posing in the kilt he created for the 2012 Dragon Con kilt-making workshop. Atlanta, Georgia, United States (courtesy Freddy Clements).

costume balls, and contests, as well as spontaneous masquerading surprises." Some participants create and construct their own costumes, while others carefully replicate character looks, and some simply buy costumes at the expo when they arrive. "We can be five year olds again at Dragon Con," Clements says, "experiencing the wondrous states of masquerade as both audience members and as participants." He believes that Dragon Con works for entire families because the kids are included in conversations about the various tracks and genres. The kids have their own skills and desire their own kind of creative experiences.[9]

Carnival masquerade does not dwell on religious concepts the way it used to, but Dragon Con masquerade caters to popular tastes even as it often takes advantage of the spirituality and humanity themes surrounding our great popular literary and sci-fi stories, myths, and legends. Masquerading versions of characters from various *Harry Potter*, *Star Wars*, *Star Trek*, or *The Hobbit* film series abound while admittedly Steam Punk or Pokémon-inspired versions of individual personalities flaunt whimsical, highly original masquerade extremes.

Regardless, masquerade for carnival as well as masquerade convention events are increasingly commercial in their objectives. Sean Cannon hesitates to estimate how much he and his family spends at Dragon Con, but he recalls the $1,000 his father plunked down this year for five toy "light sabers" for each of his kids and Sean's girlfriend. "You can get these things online, but it's so much easier to buy them at Dragon Con's dealer's room," he says. "You can spend a fortune on food but some people bring coolers and food with them. You can easily spend $200 per night on a nearby hotel room and often 4 to 6 people share a room which cuts down on the cost. But the five or six official Con hotels will charge $500 per night."[10] Clements acknowledges that a Darth Vader costume can easily cost $1,000—and even more if you purchase the costume from a vendor rather than sculpting and making your own molds to fit.[11]

Dragon Con's versatile themes attract all sorts of artistic personalities, especially designers and performers. In 2007, Clements met Lee Cox, who currently serves as the Costume Track Director. This track, one of the largest fan tracks of Dragon Con, emphasizes a broad range of costuming techniques, such as fabric dyeing and manipulation as well as elaborate sewing and craft techniques, including mold-making and metal crafts for making armor. The Dragon Con website features 37 Fan Tracks, allowing for potential opportunities in masquerade genres such as Robotics, Independent Films, Science Fiction," Anime-Manga, Star Wars, Horror, Urban Fantasy, XTrack, Paranormal, and the popular Kaleidoscope track (emphasizing Disney-type themes). Dragon Con additionally offers planned entertainment, such as Talloolah Love performing in "Dragon Con Burlesque: A Glamour Geek Revue" as well as a myriad of contests, including the Star Wars Costume Contest, the Miss Star Trek Universe Pageant, From Page to Stage—Comic Book Pageant, and Robot Battles.[12]

I asked Lee Cox to elaborate on the challenges of his work for Dragon Con. "My greatest challenge is coordinating 14 educational costume panels, some of which are presented to groups of 300 people and more as well as nine or ten Q&A panels with guest artists. We're actually in the process of cutting back the number of panels with the intent of improving their quality." He explains that he is responsible for some of the most popular costume panels that range in topics from corset-making techniques, to techniques for making costume accessories, to vacu-form- and mold-making techniques as well as presentations by SCA (Society for Creative Anachronism) costumers. In 2013 he planned for 24 panels and also coordinated several costume events and contests including The Makeup Makeover Challenge (one of his largest contests—and Dragon Con's version of SyFy Channel's FaceOff), Dragon after Dark (naughty),

Steampunk night masqueraders Kristina Leigh Howard, Chris Mueller, Rainer H. Clements and Freddy Clements outside the Weston on the way to the Time Travelers Ball, Dragon Con 2012, Atlanta, Georgia, United States (courtesy Freddy Clements).

Project Cosplay, and the Friday Night Costume Contest. Cox also coordinates related costume program planning with Dragon Con personnel responsible for running the Vendor Room, the Dealer Room, and the "Mom and Pop" handcrafted show room. He also coordinates costume programing themes associated with the Art Room currently run by John and Ann Parise. (The Art Room involves paintings, drawings, and sculptures relating to fantasy themes.)[13] Obviously Lee Cox engages at full speed immediately before and during Dragon Con.

The costume balls can feature Steam Punk style morphing into Diesel Punk style, or even elaborate inventions of pirate, zombie, angel, and hero styles. When I asked Cox what initially attracted him to Dragon Con, he mentions the exhilaration of the event as a celebration of self-expression. "Costuming at Dragon Con brings out people's true nature," and he added his insight into how Dragon Con encourages this self-expression with its costume ball events:

> Each year a committee decides an overall theme—not as an intentional mirror of society—but as a way to investigate various approaches to how the costumes for that theme might be created. This committee consists of members of the Special Events team, under the leadership of Robert Rector. My team pulls together costumers and costuming (sold for charity) for the event. For instance for our angels and demons theme, we'd be interested in how people might create wings. We want more of a sense of honesty to each successful costume approach, which incidentally will be viewed by someone two feet away. We don't need exact looks like Luke Skywalker at the Balls. We like a thematic project that requires some input and personal interpretation. The topics of "pirates" or "steam punk" are great themes for that reason—our own personalities are incorporated. Of course, there is something quite powerful about 100 storm troopers appearing

out of nowhere and looking exactly alike—and we have opportunities for that sort of display at Dragon Con as well. But you could never have a Star Wars Ball or a Star Trek Ball because it is not individual/self-expressive enough.[14]

Like so many Dragon Con loyalists, Cox found out about Dragon Con by word of mouth. A friend wanted him to hang out at registration but then his friend immediately got distracted. So Cox pitched in. He eventually helped with lots of TV advertising in 2004 and did lots of other volunteer work such as helping with projectors, hotel space coordination in terms of stages and ballrooms, and administrative fees. He admits to being "hooked ever since."[15]

Cox believes his love of clowning was his original inspiration for his love of masquerade. He had performed as both a magician and as a clown during his high school years. He delighted in creating many of his own clown costumes and moved to Atlanta at age 32 to make his start professionally. When he realized that magicians were more popular in the Atlanta area than clowns, he decided to focus on developing his magic skills. "I sold my clown costumes and went to my initial 'Con' in 1998 or 1999. That first year, I had attended on the convention's last day (Labor Day) and it was basically winding down at that point. But during my second year I saw the Saturday parade; experienced the night balls, and thought, 'Wow. I have underestimated this world,'" and soon after he was volunteering. He initially volunteered his heavy

Mandalorian armor costumes from Star Wars exhibited at Dragon Con 2005, Atlanta, Georgia, and worn by Freddy Clements and Chris Mueller, both costume designers and longstanding participants at Dragon Con. Mandalorians are warriors (courtesy Freddy Clements).

responsibilities as director of the Costume track (and in helping with administration-related aspects like hotel planning), but he discovered that he often easily spent $2,000 to $4,000 of his own money to satisfy his costume "habit" and realized he needed financial compensation for his major contributions as director.

"Now I have my own volunteer staff, but am still just as busy, if not more so," he acknowledges. Dragon Con provided the inspiration for masquerading in a manner that clowning always had for Cox. It now serves as a medium for both of his primary passions—clowning and magic.

Arguably and perhaps surprisingly, masquerade conventions generally rely on organizational structures that function much as a church functions for Christians. The conventions and churches also enjoy similar types of general patronage. First, Dragon Con operates with surprisingly few paid staffers. While some people like Cox are paid salaries for major responsibilities, Dragon Con and other masquerade conventions greatly depend on the aid of dozens of volunteers—all at the service of its corporate founders. Also, churches and costume masquerade conventions connect with huge categories of popular themes, consequently attracting a remarkable range of groups and participants as members.

Second, geeks and their families appreciate Atlanta's Dragon Con and other masquerade conventions as their "point of destination" in a way similar to Muslims and Christians who make pilgrimages to Mecca and Jerusalem or to Mormons who make pilgrimages to the Salt Lake Temple in Salt Lake City.

Third, like many religious institutions, Dragon Con is one giant commercial, artful enterprise, showcasing annual rituals and "rites" (in the form of masquerade balls and parades) as a way of generating significant profits earmarked for charities while also creating a grand culmination of cultural and spiritual values. Dragon Con has given away hundreds of thousands of dollars to charities, including the Leukemia and Lymphoma Foundation, the American Diabetes Association, the American Heart Association, the National Multiple Sclerosis Society, the Amyotrophic Lateral Sclerosis Association, and A World Fit for Kids. Furthermore, the Robert A. Heinlein "Pay It Forward Blood Drive" is one of the most prevalent third-party groups at Dragon Con.[16] Dragon Con also generates millions of dollars in revenue for the city of Atlanta. (CNN reported that "by 2011 Dragon Con was bringing in more than $40 million ... primarily through dining and lodging, according to the Atlanta Convention and Visitors Bureau."[17])

Finally Dragon Con brings people together much as churches do. People enjoy mingling socially with like-minded people. Rock star singer/song-writer Alice Cooper was an exceptionally popular guest artist at the 2012 Dragon Con. Cooper had gone "through some rough patches in his life and eventually turned to Christianity." Sean Cannon said that Cooper's panels were very well attended by "people who not only loved his music, but were also inspired by his life story."[18]

Dragon Con's geek membership inevitably enjoys the camaraderie of other geeks, who otherwise sometimes feel like social misfits. Dragon Con accepts everyone—but particularly creative technocrats. Just as churches enthusiastically welcome people from all social spheres and backgrounds, Dragon Con's membership pointedly welcomes all political parties, ethnic groups, minority groups, and people from all religious affiliations. Dragon Con and its cohorts—as do churches—reach out especially to families with children.

However, even as many mainstream churches have experienced decreasing membership in recent decades, Dragon Con and other masquerade conventions continue to attract rapidly expanding participation. CNN describes it as a "privately held company that has declined to disclose its total revenues, but a four-day ticket in 2013 cost $130,"[19] and over 57,000 attended.[20] Yet unlike churches, which traditionally have not encouraged masquerade events—other than via versions of carnival in Hispanic countries—Dragon Con showcases masquerade—all types of pop cultural masquerade—as its primary, supreme experience.

# Notes

1. Barbara Mauldin (2004), *Carnival!* (Seattle: University of Washington Press), v.
2. Jason O. Gilbert (2013), "Bring Drunken Santas Under Control," *The New York Times*, http://www.nytimes.com/2013/12/13/opinion/ban-santacon.html.
3. http://dragon-con.pbworks.com/w/page/39624764/History%20of%20Dragon*Con .
4. Ann Hoevel (30 August 2013), "Dragon Con: The Birth and Growing Pangs of a Nerd Pilgrimage," CNN Living, http://www.cnn.com/2013/08/30/living/dragon-con-2013/.
5. Sean Cannon (2013), interview with the author, 26 September.
6. Freddy Clements (2013), interview with the author, 4 January.
7. Ibid.
8. Ibid.
9. Freddy Clements (2013), interview with the author, 5 January.
10. Sean Cannon (2013), interview with the author, 26 September.
11. Freddy Clements (2013), interview with the author, 5 January.
12. http://www.dragoncon.org/?q=content/cosplay-contest-0.
13. Lee Cox (2013), interview with the author, 5 January.
14. Ibid.
15. Ibid.
16. Sean Cannon (2013), interview with the author. 23 October.
17. Lee Cox (2013), interview with the author, 5 January.
18. Sean Cannon (2013), interview with the author. 23 October.
19. Ibid.
20. http://en.wikipedia.org/wiki/Dragon_Con.

# Works Cited

Cannon, Sean. (2013.) Interviews with the author, 26 September and 23 October.
Clements, Freddy. (2013.) Interviews with the author, 4 and 5 January.
Cox, Lee. (2013.) Interview with the author, 5 January.
Gilbert, Jason O. (2013.) "Bring Drunken Santas Under Control," *The New York Times*. http://www.nytimes.com/2013/12/13/opinion/ban-santacon.html.
Hoevel, Ann. (2013.) "Dragon Con: The Birth and Growing Pangs of a Nerd Pilgrimage," CNN Living (30 August). http://www.cnn.com/2013/08/30/living/dragon-con-2013/.
Mauldin, Barbara. (2004.) *Carnival!* Seattle: University of Washington Press.

# Section III

---

# Performance Masquerade as Social and Political Commentary

# "Exotick and Irrational": Opera, Masquerades and Carnival

## RICHARD FALLIS

Artificiality and extravagance are two of opera's hallmarks. In a sense, every dramatic presentation is a masquerade, but opera probes the limits of probability. Here we have characters, often with archetypal associations, who *sing* their thoughts and feelings. An orchestra supports their expression and may well tell us more about them than they themselves know. Plots range from myth to melodrama and farce. Elaborate costumes, sets, and stage machinery may add to the sensory overload. The result, as Lawrence Kramer writes, is that "opera is legendary for superlative states of being, both high and low: supremacy and debasement."[1] By its joining of all the arts, opera makes claim to being the highest of high culture. As historian G.W. Bowersock has written, "It uniquely combines theater, narrative, music and the human voice in extravagant and paradoxical ways.... But for its devotees, opera provides an aesthetic and emotional experience unlike any other."[2] Yet for another learned observer, Samuel Johnson in the 18th century, it was "an exotick and irrational entertainment, which has always been combated, and always has prevailed."[3]

There are many reasons for what Johnson recognized as opera's prevalence. Part of its power over audiences derives from its roots in the rituals of European Carnival. Carnival, as an event and a state of mind, creates a site for self-projection, disguise, and social transgression. The "carnivalesque," with its mocking challenge to authority and social hierarchy, breaks through the orderly fabric of things not only in the Carnival season but in many operas. In particular, three aspects of traditional Carnival—masks, gender bending, and masquerading— affect and give definition to operas in the standard repertory. They will be the focus of this essay—and with more emphasis on opera's plots and structures than on its music. It will also explore historical contexts to suggest the significance of these carnivalesque moments in their own times. Ultimately, Dr. Johnson was right in seeing opera as "irrational" and "exotick," but in its exotic and irrational elements lie opera's power and persistence.

## Carnival and the "Carnivalesque"

Opera began with high-minded purposes. At the turn of the 17th century, some Florentine humanists wondered how the ancient Greek dramas they admired on the page were originally performed. They persuaded themselves that the plays had originally been sung. Thus Jacopo Peri, the first opera composer, invented what we now call *recitative*: a solo voice producing sung speech. As musicologist Tim Carter notes, "music, not speech, formed the natural language of the gods."[4] The first opera for which both words and music have survived is on the theme of Orpheus and Eurydice. Presented to celebrate a royal wedding, it helped set the pattern for how acting, singing, and accompaniment could be joined to architecture and costume in a new art form. Even early on, the cost of producing an opera required aristocratic, if not princely, resources. Gorgeously arrayed and barely separated from the stage action, the elite audience became part of the *mise-en-scène*. In effect, the new form invoked the ancient world through a new kind of music and praised its princely and aristocratic patrons, the sources of social order and munificence.

Rapidly, though, opera and the passion for it spread beyond Florence. Venice, with its culture of ducal processions, *commedia dell'arte*, and carnival, took up opera as public entertainment as early as 1637. Opera moved beyond palaces to become public entertainment for paying audiences in theatres. From 1637 until the end of the century, 388 new operas were produced in seventeen theatres in Venice.[5] In all this activity, opera changed: star singers emerged who required arias to display their virtuosity; sets and stage machines became elaborate and essential to the spectacle; plots moved away from classical models. Monteverdi's Venetian operas used elaborate stage machines—ships labored on the seas; gods were airborne in chariots—and added "scurrilous and comic characters, nagging nurses (often played by men in transvestite garb), flirtatious servants, and regular recourse to magic and disguise."[6] The English diarist John Evelyn went to an opera in Venice in the middle of the 17th century. He had never seen one before and thought "it is doubtless one of the most magnificent & expensefull diversions the Wit of Men can invent":

> The historie was *Hercules* in Lydia, the Seanes chang'd 13 times, The famous Voices *Anna Rencia* a Roman, & reputed the best treble of Women; but there was an *Eunuch*, that in my opinion surpass'd her, and a *Genovese* that sang an incomparable Base: This held us by the Eyes and Eares until two in the Morning."[7]

Evelyn responds to what opera audiences of the last four hundred years have also responded to: the visual excitement of elaborate scenes; the comparisons of star singers; the intense absorption of "Eyes and Eares" in the entire spectacle.

The origins of much of what we expect in opera are in Carnival, the season prior to Lent when many European cities had—and still have—elaborate and earthy celebrations of the flesh. Carnival begins in January and reaches its height the week before Fat Tuesday, the day before the beginning of Lent. By the 17th century, Venice was the unquestioned capital of Carnival, not least because its version ran on much longer than elsewhere, starting even before Christmas. In Venice, as elsewhere, Carnival had its ritualized aspects, but it was a time of excess when the world seemed turned upside down. As Katerina Clark and Michael Holquist observe: "Carnival is a gap in the fabric of society. And since the dominant ideology seeks to author the social order as a unified text, fixed, complete, and forever, carnival is a threat."[8]

The degree of threat can be seen in the many descriptions of Carnival in cities across Europe. Goethe, in Rome in 1788, observed, "The difference between the social orders seems to be abolished for the time being; everyone accosts everyone else, all good naturedly accept whatever happens to them, and the insolence and license of the feast is balanced only by the universal good humor."[9] Goethe, in the year before the fall of the Bastille, seems complacent about Carnival, but a contemporary German saw more risk:

> Carnival is a dangerous time. Many a virgin has lost her innocence and many a matron her virtue at this time. How could it be otherwise when, in those lovers' hours, flushed with wine and dancing, a couple find themselves alone in a closed carriage going home and, having arrived there, the cavalier escorts his lady to her bedchamber ... while her strict father, her vigilant mother or her jealous husband ... is otherwise engaged in pleasure.[10]

For some modern interpreters, Carnival's excess seems to be a safety valve for the tensions that build up in a highly structured society. Especially in the week before Shrove Tuesday, many people wore masks that hid identities and gave the lower classes temporary equality with their betters. There were elaborate parades and other public entertainments with plenty of parodies of the rich and powerful. Historian Edward Muir notes that Carnival's "rituals allow subjects to express their resentment of authority but do not change anything and, in fact, strengthen the established government and social order."[11]

In contrast, the Russian literary theorist Mikhail Bakhtin argued that Carnival has a riotous life of its own that continues eternally under the surface of the dominant social structure:

> Carnival with all its images, indecencies, and curses affirms the people's immortal, indestructible character. In the world of carnival the awareness of the people's immortality is combined with the realization that established authority and truth are relative.[12]

For Bakhtin, the overturning of hierarchies permits mingling the sacred with the profane and the sublime with the ridiculous. Carnival encourages alternative voices to undermine the authority of official culture and has revolutionary implications.

Both points of view are helpful in understanding opera as a Carnival form. On the one hand, opera itself is highly ritualized. The processions, spectacles, and dramatic presentations of Carnival and non–Carnival civic life carry over to the operatic stage: in *Aida* we see and hear the purported religious rites and secular triumphs of ancient Egypt; in *Carmen*, we participate in the rituals of bull fighting and smuggling. Rituals around marriages and wedding nights inform *The Marriage of Figaro, Lucia di Lammermoor, Lohengrin, Otello,* and *Madama Butterfly*. Early on, opera absorbed the masks, stock characters, violence, and social satire of *commedia dell'arte,* long a constituent part of Carnival. Most Italian comic operas from the first half of the 19th century have highly ritualized plots, often involving an elderly guardian, a pert young woman, an incompetent physician, a smart servant, or an unfaithful young wife, all elements from *commedia dell' arte.*

Opera's musical forms may also be highly ritualized. In the heyday of *opera seria* in the 18th century, a work might include as many as thirty arias. Most were A-B-A structures in which the first section expressed a theme, the second offered a complementary or conflicting one, and the third repeated the first with ornamentation and elaboration by the singer. Even the choice of keys to reflect certain emotions became standardized: D minor for rage; D major for pomp and bravura; G minor for pastoral effects; and E flat for pathos. Likewise, the *convenienze* of Italian opera in the first half of the 19th century meant that each major singer would have at least one aria in two parts. The slow *cavatina* provided a chance to reflect on a situation; the following, more rapid, *cabaletta* resolved the problem and often led to action. Thus Violetta in Act I of *La Traviata* first broods on whether to give herself to love, then spiritedly proclaims that she wants always to be free. Fixed forms, together with strict rules of versification, gave audiences a sense of where they were in the action—and what emotions to feel.

On the other hand, opera also participates in Carnival's lusty pleasure in disorder, verbal and physical abuse, and adolescent pranks and jokes. Carmen herself is the archetypal figure of the carnivalesque woman exploding into an orderly, ritualized world. In Act II of *Der Rosenkavalier*, Octavian presents to young Sophie a silver rose symbolizing her engagement to Baron Ochs in a highly ritualized scene set to gorgeously lush music. Within moments, however, Ochs himself stomps on stage, musically belching and bellowing. With his entourage of bumpkins, he reduces Sophie's father's mansion to chaos. *The Barber of Seville* parodies not only romantic notions of love but Spain's military, physicians, and church officials. Mozart's Don Giovanni, Rossini's Figaro, Verdi's Falstaff, Donizetti's Malatesta, Puccini's Gianni Schicchi, and Stravinsky's Nick Shadow are all carnivalesque "lords of misrule," wildly varied as they may be.

## Masking

In some operas, characters associated with carnivalization literally mask themselves. For Bakhtin, the wearing of masks blurs fixed identity and indicates that the existing order of society is arbitrary and can be overthrown.[13] In Venice, where opera first flourished, wearing a mask was more than a Carnival disguise. As James H. Johnson writes of the 18th-century city:

> For six months of the year, beginning in early autumn and ending with Lent, masks dominated the city. They reappeared periodically throughout the summer for civic festivals and ceremonies. Nobles greeted foreign emissaries masked. Venetians entered private receptions and public theatres masked. They heard concerts, watched plays, and danced at formal balls masked.[14]

The period of masking coincided with Carnival and the opera season. From the 1690s until a century later "the cape and mantle combination called the *tabaro* and *bauta*, with its characteristic white mask and black hat, was a common feature of the urban landscape."[15] While the costume and mask helped limit the display of aristocratic wealth, foreigners and doubtless some Venetians associated masking with crime, this adding to the city's reputation as a dangerous place. However, most Venetians sensed that wearing a mask provided for modesty as well as concealment, with both to be valued in a crowded city famous for spies and intrigue. Maskers were generally accorded considerable respect: to take off someone's mask was a prime insult From behind a mask, one could say whatever one pleased—or dared. Masks also supported a certain degree of equality in a city in which the ruling aristocracy made up only a tiny but very conspicuous minority. As John Rosselli notes: "Venice, ruled by a discreet aristocracy that held power for a thousand years, found a useful way to keep reveling crowds in order was to exploit the fashion for wearing masks.... A masked usher at the opera house shared in this anonymity, and might hope to outface a truculent member of the upper classes. In Italy to this day a theatre or cinema usher is called a *maschera,* though the mask has long since gone."[16]

Countless operas and operettas have plots that turn on masks, unmasking, and a moment of truth-telling. Masks hide identities in countless *bel canto* operas and 19th-century operettas.

Sometimes, simple deception is the goal. The courtiers who kidnap Gilda in *Rigoletto* are masked. Rosalinde in *Die Fledermaus*, pretending to be Hungarian to fool her husband at a Carnival ball, not only wears a mask but sings a *czardas*. The plot of Carl Nielsen's *Maskarade* revolves around two young people who meet at a masquerade ball. They fall in love; are distressed to learn they are expected to marry others; and, at a second ball, realize the pre-arranged marriages are to each other. Derived from a play by Ludvig Holberg, *Maskarade* neatly turns its plot on both literal and figurative masking. Some other operas, notably Ruggiero Leoncavallo's *I Pagliacci,* take a twist on the masking in *commedia dell'arte*. Reflecting the tensions among the players of Canio's troupe, the second act consists mostly of a play-within-a-play in which his wife, acting the role of Colombina, schemes with Arlecchino to run away. Overhearing them, Canio, playing Pagliaccio, stabs Colombina and tells the shocked audience that "*La commedia è finita.*" The rituals of *commedia dell'arte* collapse into chaos under the pressure of jealousy and realization of the truth.[17]

Occasionally, masks and unmasking are means to wisdom. In the final scene of Verdi's *Falstaff* the common people of Windsor come masked to the woods at midnight to terrify the lecherous aristocrat, Sir John Falstaff. After a riotously carnivalesque scene, Falstaff gets the last word when he tells the maskers and the audience that everyone, himself included, is a fool. The opera's final pages offer the kind of comic resolution Shakespeare often provides as the world reverts to order and new possibilities. To represent this, *Falstaff* ends with a highly ritualized musical form, a fugue on the theme that "all the world is a joke."

Masking came easily to the mind of Mozart's best librettist, Lorenzo da Ponte, who had spent his early adulthood in Venice. In *Le Nozze di Figaro,* the climax of the plot arrives when the self-righteous and hypocritical count has to seek forgiveness from his countess. In *Così fan tutte,* two young men who are testing their lovers' fidelity supposedly are called away for military service. Disguised as Albanians, they return to Naples and try to persuade both women to fall in love with the wrong men. Towards the end of Act I of *Don Giovanni*, three masked characters come on stage seeking vengeance. Don Giovanni has attempted to rape Donna Anna and has killed her father. She and Don Ottavio, her fiancé, have realized that their fellow aristocrat is the attacker. Together with Donna Elvira, one of Giovanni's many earlier conquests, they come to his palace just as he is hosting a party during which he plans to seduce Zerlina, a peasant girl. Ironically, they wear masks in their effort to unmask Giovanni's villainy; the honor of the aristocracy will be vindicated through deception. They pray for safety and success in what William Mann calls "a solemn yet very florid trio with woodwind accompaniment." It provides a moment of repose between the thickening of the plot earlier in Act I and the excitement of Giovanni's peasant party.[18] Towards the end of the last act, Anna's father returns from the dead as his own burial monument to drag Giovanni down to Hell. Yet the opera goes on past that tremendous scene to end with a seemingly trivial sextet in which the surviving characters complacently tell us that good has triumphed and proceed to plan their futures as if nothing much had happened.

David P. Schroeder in *Mozart in Revolt* provides a plausible explanation. He sees the opera's underlying conflict as between the forces of Carnival and Lent. Giovanni is a Carnival prankster *in excelsis* who "thumbs his nose at religion, marriage, the law, and honest or decent dealings with one's fellow beings." The opera as a whole "brims with the most basic features of Carnival: especially seduction, masquerading, lies, coarseness, ascent of the lower classes, gender equality, abuse, disorder, grotesqueness, drinking, emphasis on the physical, foolishness and fascination with sexuality.[19] For audiences of the Romantic Age, Giovanni seemed the embodiment of the demonic, and Gustav Mahler, among other conductors, insisted on ending performances with Giovanni's descent into Hell. Most performances these days respect Mozart's intentions, however. The conventional-seeming conclusion ironically asserts that Lent has won; we return to a life based on common-sense and sobriety. The eruption of the demonic and carnivalesque into all the characters' lives is already yesterday's news.

## Gender-Bending

Forms of gender-bending, one of the frequent features of Carnival, appear almost as frequently in opera as in mardi gras. Most frequently, female singers perform male roles. Reflecting the rules of Shakespeare's theatre, sometimes male singers perform female roles, and a few operas include actual cross-dressing. Perhaps the two most famous travesty figures in the standard repertory are Cherubino in Mozart's *Marriage of Figaro* and Strauss's Octavian in *Der Rosenkavalier*: both supposedly young men; both sung by women. In both as well, the female impersonating a young man has the "indignity" of being dressed for a while as a girl. In *Figaro*, the women see Cherubino more as a toy than as a young adult, and there is something kittenish about him throughout. Not yet ready to be a soldier, as the Count and Figaro command, he is also not taken seriously by the women as a sex object. Kittens have claws, however, as Cherubino shows when he seeks to take his aristocratic rights on Barbarina, a twelve-year-old servant girl.

We first meet Octavian in Der Rosenkavalier in a post-coital musical haze. He is seventeen and delighting in an affair with a married woman; she, the wife of an absent field marshal, is thirty-two. Despite the female voice, there is a masculine swagger to him—and, we also realize, a young male's inability to understand the emotions of his partner. The gap in their ages provokes a great deal of thought from her about the aging process. She can be playful with her toyboy, but her conversations and ruminations in Act I also reveal her to be one of the wisest and most endearing characters in opera. In Act II, Octavian is almost at a loss for words when he presents the silver rose symbolizing engagement to young Sophie on behalf of her suitor, the gross Baron Ochs. Yet he also shows a young male's rambunctiousness in the practical jokes on Ochs in Act III and adolescent male insensitivity when he chooses Sophie as his bride and leaves the Marschallin, his former lover, to chat with his prospective father-in-law.

Strauss and his librettist, Hugo von Hofmannsthal further explored gender-bending in two later operas. In *Arabella*, Zdenka, the younger daughter of Count Waldner in 1860s Vienna, has been passed off as a boy since childhood because her profligate father cannot afford a dowry for her. The action is set at Carnival time with "Zdenko" having to help his friend Matteo in his pursuit of the older Waldner sister, Arabella. After several twists, the last act offers bedroom farce in the style of Arthur Schnitzler. Matteo learns that the woman whose bedroom he has just visited is not Arabella but Zdenka, who now appears in the hotel lobby in her negligee. The Carnival setting provides not so much liberation as ditzyness, but the motivation for the trouser role—the Count's shortage of cash—offers a sardonic commentary on the dancing Vienna of the Johann Strauss era and its operettas' plots.

The young male Composer in *Ariadne auf Naxos* provides a soprano voice of idealism as well as a dab of satire. A wealthy man in the 18th century has hired for his guests two forms of after-dinner entertainment, an *opera seria* troupe and a *commedia dell'arte* crew. As both rehearse, the news comes that the time for entertainment is short and that both sets of performers must go on simultaneously. More-or-less ignored by his own opera's stars, the Composer becomes aware of Zerbinetta from the comedy troupe. Despite her worldly-wise advice, he remains a Romantic idealist, insisting that Music is a sacred art. Carnival has been brought onto the stage itself in the confusion as the *opera seria* cast intrigues and the *commedia* troupe zips around. The Composer's teacher may be right in telling his protégé to do whatever is necessary to get his fee for his opera. But the young man wins our hearts with his passionate insistence on art as more than entertainment even as we smile at his naiveté.

The convention of men playing female roles began early. In one of the first operas still performed, Monteverdi's *L'incoronazione di Poppea*, the loathsome Nero is a male soprano while Poppea's nurse is a man in drag. Handel's operas regularly showcased the talents of *castrati*, men who had been castrated early on so that they retained soprano or alto voices but with the power of male lungs: The immensely famous *castrato,* Senesino, created leading roles in seventeen of Handel's operas. However paradoxically, *castrati* usually played heroic roles as generals, gods, and emperors. In *Giulio Cesare*, Caesar is a male alto to Cleopatra's female soprano and in *Serse*, the role of the Persian emperor was written for a soprano *castrato* with two other male roles taken by male altos.

As the age of the *castrati* ended in the early 19th century, "trouser roles" emerged. Frequently sung by female mezzo-sopranos masquerading as men in tight pants, they offered visual as well as aural pleasure to an audience. Reflecting, perhaps, that he grew up towards the end of the *castrato* era, in Rossini's *Tancredi*, the trouser role is the protagonist; in *La Donna del Lago*, he is the heroine's true love; and in *Semiramide*, he is the queen's much-desired object. By *Guillaume Tell* at the end of Rossini's career, however, the only trouser role is Jemmy, Tell's young son. Overall, Rossini was more given to breeches roles in his serious operas than his comedies, though the mischievous page Isolier in *Le Comte Ory* is a hilarious exception, nowhere more so than in the scene in which he, his master, and the lovesick Countess Adele share a bed.

Breeches roles continued through the Victorian era, but in most cases, they were less important than they had been in the heyday of Rossini. Still, from Donizetti's *Lucrezia Borgia*, through Gounod's *Faust* and Meyerbeer's *Les Huguenots* to Verdi's *Un Ballo in Maschera*, they abounded on the lyric stage. However, as the Meyerbeer and Verdi examples suggest, women in breeches increasingly became asexualized pages. The breeches role of Nicklausse in Offenbach's *Les contes d'Hoffmann* is more complicated. Like the co-star in a buddy movie, he must rescue Hoffmann from his passions for an operatic soprano and a singing doll. In the version of the score most commonly played today, there is the further complication that the singer who portrays Nicklausse also plays Hoffman's female Muse. The Muse clearly loves Hoffmann deeply, but is her love also a desire to consume him? Or a displaced death wish? And the Muse, clearly, is female even as Nicklausse assures us of his masculinity.

## Masked Balls

Only the aristocracy came masked to Don Giovanni's ball, but masking was expected of all participants in the masquerade balls of the eighteenth and nineteenth centuries. In Italy—and often elsewhere—masked balls marked the climax of the opera and Carnival season. The main floor of the opera house became a space for dancing; a banquet would be served on the stage itself. John Rosselli reports that there could be as many as a dozen masked balls in a row at some Italian theatres. Men and women regularly ate, gossiped, looked for sexual partners, and arranged assignations at ordinary performances, but the balls, with fancy dress and masks hiding identities were especially titillating—and open doors to immorality. As early as 1724, when the fad had reached London, masquerade balls were denounced as immoral: "very commonly the ruin of ladies of the first quality."[20] Around the same time, William Hogarth published an engraving called "Masquerades and Operas or The Bad Taste of the Town" showing two theatre entrances facing each other. A large and mostly fashionable audience swarms in to see an Italian opera featuring Francesca Cuzzoni, one of Handel's stars. Across the street, devils rope another crowd into a masquerade ball. Between the crowds, the plays of Shakespeare, Ben Jonson, and Dryden are piled up as waste paper. The lesson is clear: the corrupted taste of the town now prefers exotic and irrational entertainment.[21] By the early 1800's, public masquerades in London had taken on what Rosselli calls "an aura of lowlife and drunkenness: the burning down of Covent Garden [opera house] in 1856 during one such ball leads to much moralistic head-shaking, even though the fire started on the roof."[22]

Sometimes masquerades take on clear political meaning. Mozart's *Figaro* opens as Figaro and his bride-to-be are setting up their new room in their master's palace. Gullible Figaro notes how convenient it is that they will be adjacent to her mistress's bedroom as well as his master's. Shrewder Susanna, knowing the Count's philandering and aware of the ancient aristocratic *droit du seigneur*, observes that he could just as easily send Figaro away to have Susanna to himself. Through the scene—and throughout the opera—the orchestra comments on the action, frequently ironically. The beauty of the music persuaded Emperor Joseph II to permit it to be performed publicly even though he had recently forbidden a performance of the Beaumarchais play upon which da Ponte based his libretto. For all its musical delights, *Figaro* is a deeply political opera. Obviously, it satirized the aristocracy. Susanna and Figaro, the servants, are far cleverer than their employers or the hangers-on around them. As with Shakespeare's *Much Ado About Nothing*, its plot is also clearly about sexual politics and the inequalities of gender. Beyond that, as Volkmar Braunbehrens has argued, the opera's emphasis on equality supported a basic element of Joseph II's domestic policy: "the elimination of aristocratic privilege, and judicial equality for all subjects."[23] By the end of the opera, there is no question in an audience's mind about the status of the characters. The final scene occurs in the dark garden of the Count's palace and with Susanna and the Countess masquerading as each other. The Count eventually tries to seduce his own wife, thinking she is Susanna, and has to bow to seek forgiveness for his jealousy and arrogance from the Countess. As William Mann describes it, the Count "falls on his knees before his wife, his chattel in the eyes of church and state, before all his servants, and begs her pardon."[24] It is a truly revolutionary moment in operatic human relations.

A few years after *Figaro*, events at an actual masked ball startled Europe. On March 16, 1792, the Swedish king Gustav III was assassinated during a Carnival ball at the Stockholm opera house. He had been warned of a threat on his life but chose to disregard it. When he entered the masquerade, wearing the traditional domino, tricorn, and mask, he was surrounded by three conspirators. They greeted him with "*Bonjour, beau masque*"; then one stepped behind him and fired a shot into his back. The king did not die immediately and was taken to his nearby palace.

The story of the assassination seemed almost an opera plot in itself.[25] In the 1830s, the French composer Daniel Auber took up the tale after Eugène Scribe had turned it into a five-act libretto. Auber was writing for the Paris Opera, the grandest house in Europe and one that specialized in huge productions with startling technology. His *Gustave III* was a success, especially because of the ball scene and ballet in the last act. As a contemporary described it:

This *salle de bal* is overlooked by boxes, these boxes are filled with masks, who play the part of spectators. At their feet, constantly moving, is the circling crowd, disguised in every imaginable costume, and dominoes of every conceivable hue. Harlequins of all fashions, clowns, peddlers, what shall I say? ... Peasants, marquises, princes, monks, I know not what, mingle in one rainbow-hued crowd. It is impossible to describe this endless madness, this whirl, this *bizarrerie*, on which the rays of two thousand wax tapers, in their crystal lustres, pour an inundation of mellow light.[26]

Even after the popularity of the opera waned, its fifth act was often performed for the sake of its elaborate ballet. Ten years later, a leading Italian composer, Saverio Mercadante, took up the story. His *Il reggente* transfers the setting to Scotland and converts Gustav into the regent for the young James VI. In both Auber and Mercadante, the tale of regicide is set within operatic conventions. The ruler is in love with his best friend's wife; she gradually recognizes her love for him. When her husband realizes the situation, he swears vengeance, orders her to kill herself, and, disguised, assassinates the ruler at a masked ball.[27]

Verdi's *Un Ballo in maschera* repeats essentially the same story. Verdi, already the leading Italian opera composer, had signed a contract with the San Carlo opera house in Naples in 1857 to provide a new opera for the next Carnival season. His original plan was for a work based on Shakespeare's *King Lear*, but that came to naught. To fulfill his contract, Verdi eventually wrote to the management of the San Carlo: "Let me scrounge around among other plays, and it will be fine when I finally find a subject."[28] His scrounging led to the story of the assassination of King Gustav III, what Julian Budden calls "one of the most hackneyed solutions imaginable: a plot fifteen years old, already set by at least three composers of note."[29] Presumably, Verdi took this expedient because of the press of time. However, the libretto for Auber's *Gustave III* was a vast five-act affair specifically intended as spectacle for Paris. Verdi needed it quickly reduced to a three-act Italian melodrama.

Further complications arose when Verdi sent a synopsis of the libretto for review by the Naples censors. They would not permit Sweden as the setting, and Gustavo could not be a king. Italy was in the turmoil of reunification; the Bourbon monarchy in Naples was shaky, and Italians had recently sought to assassinate the French emperor. The censor would not approve the protagonist's passion for his best friend's wife; the presence of a fortune-teller; the drawing of lots to choose an assassin; and the on-stage murder. Eventually, Verdi wrote to his librettist:

> I'm in a sea of troubles! It's almost certain that the Censorship won't allow our libretto.... They've suggested to me—out of the kindness of their hearts—the following modifications:
>
> (1) Change the protagonist into a lord, taking away any idea of sovereignty.
> (2) Change the wife into a sister.
> (3) Modify the witch's scene, transferring it to a time when this was credible.
> (4) No dancing.
> (5) The murder off stage.
> (6) Cut out the scene where the names are chosen by lot.[30]

When Verdi refused to meet the censor's demands, the theatre sued him for breach of contract; Verdi counter-sued. After the suits were settled, Verdi offered the opera to the Teatro Apollo in Rome. Determined to see the opera performed, it became Verdi's turn to make emendations to the libretto. The setting was moved from Sweden to colonial Massachusetts of all places!

The Swedish king became a count named Riccardo, the warm-hearted British governor of Puritan Boston. Rome did not resist either the drawing of lots for a murder (which Verdi considered the most striking situation in the plot) or the assassination at a masked ball.[31]

When, after all this, the opera finally premiered, what was the result? The protagonist, Riccardo, is willful, high-spirited, and charming, the Duke of Mantua with a conscience and a sense of humor. The leading lady is earnest, troubled, and repressed. Together, they sing the most passionate of all of Verdi's love duets, but Riccardo is often as amused by the world as Amelia is troubled by it. Her husband, Renato, may seem a stock villain when he demands his wife's suicide and murders his friend, but he is a complex figure, seemingly betrayed by his wife and best friend. In Act II, when Amelia's mask slips off, he is humiliated to recognize his wife together with Riccardo on a barren field after midnight and in front of some low-life conspirators. He obsessively seeks revenge, demands his wife's death as though she were his property, and rejoices when he draws the lot to kill Riccardo. Unmasking here starts a downward spiral towards revenge, a primordial urge that overcomes Riccardo's Enlightenment optimism. The action up to the unmasking could be an operetta tale, the more so because of the presence of Riccardo's page, Oscar, a coloratura soprano trouser role. Oscar's music, tripping, superficial, and sarcastic, separates him from the main characters and fits uncomfortably with an opera that otherwise is so melodramatic. Ulrica, the contralto fortune teller is his opposite. Associated archetypally with death and the underworld, she is, like Riccardo, deeply self-obsessed even as she claims to see others' futures.

Consequently, the opera tries to balance between the dark side of carnivalesque superstition and revenge and a courtly setting of sophistication and playfulness. The real Gustav III, an admirer of Voltaire and nephew of Frederick the Great, sought to be an enlightened despot like Mozart's Joseph II. He brought Enlightenment values to Swedish society, limiting the death penalty and torture and providing some civil rights for Jews and Catholics. A patron of the arts, he founded the Royal Swedish Opera and Ballet and built Stockholm's opera. Yet he held down the nobility, and conspiracies against him among the nobility were frequent.[32] Some of this comes through in *Un Ballo in maschera*, but the opera, like its protagonist, teeters between superstition and reason. From our perspective, it is a puzzling work. The powerful throb of the passionate music tells us one story; Riccardo's almost giddy rejection of Ulrica's prophecy and Oscsar's ditties tell another. Is the strange mixture of frivolity, desire, and revenge simply a Romantic melodrama with some odd accretions? Is it a commentary on the failure of the Enlightenment to suppress human evil? Or is the music's mixture of tragedy and laughter a Shakespearian take on a much-told story?

To invoke Glen Bowersock again, Verdi's opera, like so many others, "uniquely combines theater, narrative, music and the human voice in extravagant and paradoxical ways." *Un Ballo* clearly has conflicting elements of the carnivalesque, but so do many other operas. Some operas, especially comic ones, can seem to be harmless carnivals on stage. Others, far darker in tone, take more paradoxical positions towards carnivalization, that sense of ambiguity heightened by opera's inherent emotional and presentational extravagance. Masks hide true identities but also sometimes reveal them in startling ways as with Falstaff or the singing animals and furniture of Ravel's exquisite *L'Enfant et les sortilèges*. To bend gender is to risk Dr. Johnson's protests about irrationality and exoticism, but in opera's complex rhetoric of communication, it also offers more deep truths about human nature than titillation. Octavian is a particularly rich portrait of an adolescent, in part because he sings with a female voice. A *bal masque* on the operatic stage reinforces opera's inherent ambivalence about the social order. We are dazzled by what we see but also rightly suspect that disruption is afoot, whether it is in the swirl of Hoffmann's tales or the menace of Don Giovanni's hired band. When Riccardo is stabbed in the last act of *Un Ballo in maschera,* the stage band keeps playing for the masked dancers. Carnivalesque wildness has invaded the royal ballroom, but the courtly dance goes on. In many of these ways, opera can indeed seem "exotick and irrational," but it persists in part because its Carnival elements—together with music, singing, and spectacle—play powerfully on our minds and hearts.

# Notes

1. Lawrence Kramer (2007), *Opera and Modern Culture* (Berkeley: University of California Press), 1.

2. G. W. Bowersock (26 May 2013), "Opera Is Not Dead," *New Republic,* http://www.newrepublic. com/article/113095/opera-not-dead.

3. Quoted in Richard Luckett (1984), "Exotick But Rational Entertainments: The English Dramatic Operas," In *English Drama: Forms and Development,* M. C. Bradbrook, Marie Axton, and Raymond Williams, eds. (Cambridge: Cambridge University Press), 123.

4. Tim Carter (1994), "The Seventeenth Century," in *The Oxford Illustrated History of Opera* Roger Parker, ed. (Oxford: Oxford University Press), 8–9.

5. Donald J. Grout (1947), *A Short History of Opera: One-Volume Edition* (New York: Columbia University Press), 84.

6. Carter (1994), 23.

7. Quoted in Carter (1994), 23.

8. Katerina Clark and Michael Holquist (1986), *Mikhail Bakhtin* (Cambridge, MA: Belknap Press), 303.

9. Quoted in David Schroeder (1999), *Mozart in Revolt* (New Haven, CT: Yale University Press), 30.

10. Quoted in Schroeder (1999), 32.

11. Edward Muir (1997), *Ritual in Early Modern Europe* (Cambridge: Cambridge University Press), 90–91.

12. Mikhail Bakhtin (1968), *Rabelais and His World,* trans. Helene Iswolsky (Cambridge, MA: MIT Press), 256.

13. Ibid., 39.

14. James H. Johnson (2011), *Venice Incognito* (Berkeley: University of California Press), 47.

15. Ibid., 49.

16. John Roselli (1994), "Opera as a Social Occasion," in *The Oxford Illustrated History of Opera,* Roger Parker, ed. (Oxford: Oxford University Press, 1994), 465.

17. Leoncavallo's *verismo* competitor, Pietro Mascagni, had less luck with his opera, *Le Maschere,* which uses traditional characters from *commedia dell'arte* entirely. With much fanfare, it premiered simultaneously in seven Italian cities in 1901 and was a failure in each.

18. William Mann (1977), *The Operas of Mozart* (New York: Oxford University Press), 486.

19. Schroeder (1999), 40–41.

20. Roselli (1994), 474.

21. British Museum (2011), "William Hogarth: 'The Bad Taste of the Town,'" http://www. britishmuseum.org/explore/highlights/highlight_objects/pd/w/william_hogarth,_the_bad_taste.aspx.

22. Roselli (1994), 474.

23. Volkmar Braunbehrens (1990), *Mozart in Vienna 1781–1791,* trans. Timothy Bell (New York: Grove Weidenfeld), 215.

24. Mann (1977), 435.

25. Ironically, the attempted assassination of a ruler was an important element in Mozart's last opera, *La clemenza di Tito,* which premiered only four months before Gustav's murder.

26. Jules Janin quoted in Ellen Creathorne Clayton (1865), *Queens of Song* (New York: Harper and Brothers), 324–325. There is an enlightening discussion of the political implications of *Gustave III* in Sarah Hibberd's *French Grand Opera and the Historical Imagination* (Cambridge: Cambridge University Press, 2011).

27. Julian Budden (1984), *The Operas of Verdi, Volume 2* (London: Cassell), 365.

28. Mary Jane Phillips-Matz (1993), *Verdi: A Biography* (Oxford: Oxford University Press), 370.

29. Budden (1984), 363.

30. Ibid., 369.

31. Many recent productions have moved the setting back to eighteenth-century Sweden, the setting in Puritan Massachusetts seeming too preposterous even for opera.

32. For an overview of the period, see H. Arnold Barton (1986), *Scandinavia in the Revolutionary Era, 1760–1815* (Minneapolis: University of Minnesota Press).

# Works Cited

Bakhtin, Mikhail. (1968.) *Rabelais and His World*. Trans. Helene Iswolsky. Cambridge, MA: MIT Press.

Barton, H. Arnold. (1986.) *Scandinavia in the Revolutionary Era, 1760–1815*. Minneapolis: University of Minnesota Press.

Bowersock, G. W. (2013.) "Opera Is Not Dead." *New Republic* (26 May), http://www.newrepublic.com/article/113095/opera-not-dead.

Braunbehrens, Volkmar. (1990.) *Mozart in Vienna 1781–1791*. Trans. Timothy Bell. New York: Grove Weidenfeld.

British Museum. (2011.) "William Hogarth: 'The Bad Taste of the Town.'" http://www.britishmuseum.org/explore/highlights/highlight_objects/pd/w/william_hogarth,_the_bad_taste.aspx.

Budden, Julian. (1984.) *The Operas of Verdi, Volume 2*. London: Cassell.

Carter, Tim. (1994.) "The Seventeenth Century." In *The Oxford Illustrated History of Opera*, Roger Parker, ed. Oxford and New York: Oxford University Press.

Clark, Katerina, and Michael Holquist. (1986.) *Mikhail Bakhtin*. Cambridge, MA: Belknap Press.

Clayton, Ellen Creathorne. (1865.) *Queens of Song*. New York: Harper and Brothers.

Grout, Donald J. (1947.) *A Short History of Opera: One-Volume Edition*. New York: Columbia University Press.

Hibberd, Sarah. (2001.) *French Grand Opera and the Historical Imagination*. Cambridge: Cambridge University Press.

Johnson, James H. (2011.) *Venice Incognito*. Berkeley: University of California Press.

Kramer, Lawrence. (2007.) *Opera and Modern Culture*. Berkeley: University of California Press.

Luckett, Richard. (1984.) "Exotick But Rational Entertainments: The English Dramatic Operas." In *English Drama: Forms and Development*, M.C. Bradbrook, Marie Axton, and Raymond Williams, eds. Cambridge: Cambridge University Press.

Mann, William. (1977.) *The Operas of Mozart*. New York: Oxford University Press.

Muir, Edward. (1997.) *Ritual in Early Modern Europe*. Cambridge: Cambridge University Press.

Phillips-Matz, Mary Jane. (1993.) *Verdi: A Biography*. Oxford: Oxford University Press.

Roselli, John. (1994.) "Opera as a Social Occasion." In *The Oxford Illustrated History of Opera*, Roger Parker, ed. Oxford: Oxford University Press, 1994.

Schroeder, David P. (1999.) *Mozart in Revolt*. New Haven, CT: Yale University Press.

# Open Secrecy: Self-Presentation by Queer Male Musicians

## Vincent Stephens

In September 2010 Dan Savage initiated the "It Gets Better Project" after the mainstream media increased its reportage of gay harassment directed toward lesbian, gay, bisexual, transgender and questioning (LGBTQ) youth. The project encourages LGBT people and allies to create videos that "show young LGBT people the levels of happiness, potential, and positivity their lives will reach, if they can just get through their teen years. The It Gets Better Project wants to remind teenagers in the LGBT community that they are not alone—and it WILL get better." As of this writing the project has generated thousands of responses as well as the 2011 book *It Gets Better*. But it seems more accurate to tell teens that "it gets complicated," rather than "better." This reasoning is especially germane in the realm of popular culture.[1]

Veiled secrecy, coyness, allusions, and other forms of sexual masquerade were an outgrowth of political and social circumstances, but their role as compelling structures in queer performance extends well beyond the pre-liberation era of the 1950s. The careers of queer '70s era male icons like Freddie Mercury and Elton John are clear examples of this teasing dynamic. Furthermore almost every male performer who eventually came out during the 1990s, including Pet Shop Boys and George Michael, began their careers as nominally heterosexual acts, even if traces of queerness pervaded their music and personas. The issue is not the reality of their sexual orientation but their latent queerness. There are inevitable tensions between artists and audiences, and sexual intrigue is part of the pleasure of this interaction. We cannot presume audiences enjoy these acts less now that these performers are "out." But I want to explore what compelled audiences to pursue these performers from the outset. The musicians' performances of gender and expressions of sexual desire are significant in this regard.

In the early 2000s several mainstream male pop performers came out including Lance Bass (of *NSYNC), Clay Aiken, Mika, and Ricky Martin. Adam Lambert, first runner-up during the 2009 season of *American Idol*, projected sexual ambiguity and came out after the season ended. These performers have expressed diverse reasons for not beginning their careers as openly gay. The sexual ambiguity they initially projected masked their sexual orientation technically. Yet audiences, who can both distort artists' identities for personal fantasies and often look beyond artists' self-definitions, did not punish them as liars. Rather audiences looked beyond their partially hidden sexuality and located intangible aspects of their personas as part of their appeal. Their initial reluctance to level with their fans defies recent political expectations and warrants our critical attention. Musicians continue to use the glass closet as a kind of masquerade. It represents a reality for queer performers that may seem difficult to comprehend in an era when visibility and transparency are current queer buzzwords on the ground.

This essay explores the enduring role of open secrecy in the careers of contemporary queer male musicians. D.A. Miller's argument that secrecy functions as the "field of operations"[2] and Eve Sedgwick's argument about the allure of the "coming out story that doesn't come out"[3] are not references to arcane events eradicated by politics. Their statements address cultural production aesthetics and interpretations as specific realms that politics can inform but will never fully define. My discussion employs a postmodern historical lens to illuminate the perspectives that Bass, Aiken, Lambert, and Martin have provided regarding the gradualness of their official coming out processes.[4] Their careers differ but there are detectable parallels in their journeys toward "outness," including fears of commercial vulnerability, pressure to be cultural representatives of mainstream gay politics, and the expectation that they present sexually cohesive images as gay, rather than bisexual, omnisexual, or queer. While this is not a gay "heritage" discussion their contemporary careers clearly indicate how the cautiousness that shaped the original "proto-queers" of the 1950s—Liberace, Johnnie Ray, Little Richard and Johnnie Mathis—has morphed to include cross-generational boundaries.[5] Over time musicians have accumulated the vocabulary to more clearly define (or not define) themselves within various political and social milieus. Ultimately the public masquerade of the closet is an enduring form of expression among queer musicians that transcends political trends.

The modern gay and lesbian movement has primarily organized itself around visibility, with "coming out" serving as its dominant metaphor. Implicit to the metaphor is the notion that personal authenticity provides mental clarity for queer people. Such authenticity can potentially motivate their communities to humanize "homosexuality," a transformation that could create a more accepting society. If visibility were the primary social gesture required of gays and lesbians for political and social liberation the movement would be nearly over. Since the gay liberation movement began, multiple forms of political organizing, the AIDS crisis, and increased media representations have made gays and lesbians more visible.

Yet even in the context of these and other important developments queer musicians still present themselves to the public as half-hidden. It is historically inaccurate to dismiss the men of the 1950s as self-loathing "closet cases" since they were partially obscure for complicated individual reasons. The queer male performers of the 1970s (i.e. Mercury and Sylvester) were perhaps the boldest generation in their defiance of mainstream gender norms, but their struggles can be attributed to the newness of the gay liberation movement. Presumably though contemporary performers would have fewer reasons to not be "out" in this age of gay visibility and yet there remains a persistent recalcitrance to transparency.

## Delaying Disclosure

Four male singers came out publicly from 2006–2010 including Lance Bass who came out to *People* magazine in 2006 and published the memoir *Out of Sync: A Memoir* in 2007.

Aiken, first runner-up on *American Idol's* second season, also came out to *People* magazine in 2008. In June 2009 Lambert came out in *Rolling Stone* at the end of *American Idol's* season. Finally, in 2010 Martin, a former member of Menudo (and one of the Latin pop singers to cross over to English pop in 1999), came out on his website and in his 2011 memoir *Me*.

Each of these singers performs in a different musical style and has a distinct persona, but they share several important characteristics. First, each began his musical career as a mainstream act that recorded for a major record label and had access to broad commercial channels for production, distribution and promotion. Second, the genres in which they record are integral to their mainstream status. Bass performed in a teen pop boy band during the commercial resurgence of teen pop. Aiken recorded in an adult contemporary/soft rock vein. Lambert's style is very rock-oriented with traces of glam and pop; and Martin recorded in a broad pop style including romantic ballads, dance pop, and Latin-influenced pop. By definition these genres (pop, rock, soft rock) are encoded with broad appeal and have greater commercial potential than "niche" genres, consequently making the performers more commercially viable.

None of these musicians was "out" publicly at the beginning of his career, even if rumors circulated regarding their sexual orientation. These performers came out in very different contexts. Bass had performed in *NSYNC since 1998 and he came out in 2006 after eight years of visibility. Blogger Perez Hilton's public suggestions that he was gay also prompted his decision. Four years passed between Aiken's commercial debut and his coming out. His disclosure was preceded by tabloid rumors, and his eventual coming out coincided with the announcement that he and a close female friend had conceived a child together. He rationalized his coming out partially by noting that lying would have been hypocritical for him as a parent noting, "It was the first decision I made as a father. I cannot raise a child to lie or to hide things."[6] Lambert's stylized appearance, sassy personality, and bold musical interpretations (such as a falsetto-laced performance of Johnny Cash's "Ring of Fire") may have suggested queerness to many viewers.[7] But he came out after the season ended and in response to a picture of him kissing an ex-boyfriend circulating on the Internet to clarify rumors. Martin's sexual orientation had long been a subject of speculation and like Aiken, becoming a father prompted him to come out. He asked himself, "How could I teach my kids to lie?" Moreover, "How could I teach them not to be themselves?"[8]

Most importantly, these performers demonstrate several common themes regarding their reasons for delaying discussions of their sexual orientation. These themes have particular importance for understanding the relationships that "proto-queers" queer performers of the '70s and this new generation of "out" performers have to secrecy. In each of these historical periods, which roughly correspond to pre-liberation, liberation, and post-liberation politics, the performers and their managers carefully negotiated sexuality as a significant aspect of their identity. Whether musicians communicate blatant sexual orientation or keep it secret, once they are "out," anxieties about homosexual identity continue to surface as highly salient factors in the public personas of queer male musicians. These patterns are essential in illuminating the complicated nature of "progress" in gay cultural history.

Visually their appearances complimented their musical roles as default sexual idols. The performers' visual presentations, especially hair and costuming, are relevant textures for understanding their relationship to sexual objectification more so than signifying specifics about their sexual orientation. Lambert and Martin have more overtly sexual costuming that invite sexual objectification. Bass and Aiken have more benign visual images. The effect of this blandness almost deters interest in them sexually. Bass was primarily photographed as a supporting player in *NSYNC, especially compared to default lead singer Justin Timberlake. Bass still lacks a strong visual persona that would signify him as an overtly gay man. Clay Aiken's February 2003 *American Idol* audition photo features him wearing a white striped shirt and baggy jeans. Though he wears a sleek suit and make-up, and sports more sculpted hair in his May 2003 finale photos, his image has never been overtly sexual.

Ricky Martin was always marketed as a sexual idol with a taut body draped in form-fitting clothes. His December 1999 and March 2011 concert photos both feature him posing erotically in leather. He has a beard and stylized highlighted hair, and shows more of his torso in the 2011 photo. Regardless of year, a pansexual erotic look remains endemic to his solo persona. Adam Lambert's spiked haircut, heavy eye make-up and leather outfits borrow from glam rock and punk which have always signified a more radical, iconoclastic image than typical *Idol* contestants. This look probably suggested his queerness early on, especially in relation to his flamboyant vocal style.

## Post–Coming Out Themes

**#1: Gay identity as commercial risk:** All four performers express fears that an openly gay identity could offend their established audiences and negatively impact their commercial appeal. Genre expectations are especially influential in their concerns.

As male teen pop icons, Bass and his band mates had to convey sexual appeal and availability to their primary fan base of teenage girls. A 2007 story on Bass notes, "As more of his close friends learned his secret, Bass began to come to terms with his sexuality, but he still feared that going public would jeopardize "*NSYNC's popularity with female fans."[9] In the 2006 *People* magazine "coming out" article he acknowledged concern that his sexuality could be a commercial liability noting, "I knew that I was in this popular band, and I had four other guys' careers in my hand, and I knew that if I ever acted on it or even said [that I was gay], it would overpower everything."[10] Though many figures from the 1950s probably appealed to women precisely because they seemed more like friends than sexual or romantic partners the illusion of availability was part of the exchange. Bass feared that sexual openness could have disrupted this relationship. He also seems anxious that his sexuality would have dominated press coverage of the band and potentially undone the band's commercial stature.

Martin's commercial rise as an English-language performer was also attributable to the image of him as a heterosexual idol for teenagers and adults. Furthermore he was also perceived as the face of a new Latin pop music boom, which also included Marc Anthony, Enrique Iglesias and Jennifer Lopez. His debut album was a broad pop set featuring up-tempo dance pop ("Livin' La Vida Loca"), adult contemporary ballads ("She's All I Ever Had"), and songs sung in Spanish.[11] Its diversity aimed to make him a crossover act who could achieve success with diverse audiences in many different markets. In a 2009 *Out* magazine interview he addressed the decade-long coming out process, "I didn't do it earlier because of fear, and bottom line, it was all in my head. I was seduced by fear, and I was sabotaging most of my life—my music, my relationships with friends, with my family, with everybody."[12] Like Bass, fears of rejection pervaded his experience.

His role as a Latin pop star also informs his delayed coming out. "'I am a minority twice,' he says. 'I am Hispanic, and I am a gay man, and they both struggle. Is it a big responsibility?

It can be as big as I want it to be, and I believe there's a lot still to come.'"[13] In a parallel to Little Richard, Johnny Mathis, and Sylvester his commercial appeal was shaped by demands for certain kinds of visibility among ethnic minority performers. *Out* notes that his coming out was different from white singers since "none had to contend with the dual responsibilities of being gay and a crossover Latin music star—or [as] a 'symbol of the new status of Latin culture holds in mainstream America,'" as *The New York Times* dubbed him in 1999.[14] A 2012 article in *Latina* magazine depicts the positive but complex cultural fallout of Martin's life after coming out. The story describes his family, his forthcoming role in *Evita* on Broadway and Martin's sense that the age range of his audience is broadening. It also notes how, "In one particularly vicious verbal attack, a female pastor said that Martin's openness about his sexuality was condemning people to hell."[15]

Aiken is a crooner who performs in the soft rock/adult contemporary style of performers like Barry Manilow and Richard Marx. Older and more affluent listeners comprise the primary audience for this adult contemporary radio format. Its audience tends to be perceived as having more conservative tastes.[16] Aiken also conveyed a gentle, non-threatening image that generated a sizable female teenage audience ("Claymates") who visibly embraced him as an idol. After coming out he addressed this potential impact telling writer David Caplan, "Whether it be having a child out of wedlock, or whether it be simply being a homosexual, it's going to be a lot."[17] His comments also feature a sense of resignation regarding the potential fallout, "The fans, if they leave, they leave. But if they leave, I don't want them to leave hating me. I don't want them to live feeling that I lied to them, because I didn't. I'm not lobbying to keep them being supportive. I sure hope they do. But I am more interested in them knowing I care about them, even if they don't care about me."[18] Though his interview suggests contentment with his decision an element of fear also creeps in at certain moments. He primarily differs from Ray and Liberace in his decision to breach the exchange element of the "open secret" integral to his career by coming out and directly challenging the expectations of conservative members of his audience.

Lambert spent the shortest amount of time in the closet among these four figures but his coming out must still be regarded seriously as a genuine disclosure for many in the audience he developed on *Idol*. Like Bass, he expresses concerns that his sexuality will overly define him in the public's eye. *Rolling Stone*'s profile of Lambert notes, "He thought about coming out in the press, but he didn't want audiences to focus on the issue. 'I was worried that coming out would be so sensationalized that it would overshadow what I was there to do, which was sing,' he says. 'I'm an entertainer and who I am and what I do in my personal life is a separate thing. It shouldn't matter.' He sighs. 'Except it does.' He shakes his head. 'It's really confusing.'"[19]

Clearly fears of losing audience members are not just confined to previous generations from a less "liberated" era. Contemporary popular performers continue to assume that homophobia could limit their appeal. But there's also a new strand of this skepticism toward disclosure, notably that it will sensationalize their careers, hence Lambert's sigh. David Bowie used homosexuality as a form of titillation but Lambert, who borrows liberally from glam rock, seeks greater detachment of sexuality from his identity as a performer. Surely increasing gay visibility has de-stigmatized it in many respects. But curiosity, anxiety, and a fascination with homosexuality have generated fears from musicians themselves that their homosexuality will overly define them as queer performers. Lambert explained why he declined to come out until after the *American Idol* finale noting, "I didn't want to acknowledge it as a mistake [when photos of him kissing his ex-boyfriend circulated] or something I was ashamed of—I'm not. It's part of who I am, but because our nation is the way it is, it's an announcement. If I lose some fans, fuck it, I need to be happy too."[20] He insists that his sexual orientation is a significant factor in his identity but acknowledges that this might define him as a "gay singer" and could hurt his appeal.

    **#2: Gay performers as cultural representatives:** One of the outgrowths of the gay political movement and the increased cultural visibility of queerness in popular culture is an expectation that "out" performers will use their "celebrity" to help organizations dedicated to gay political and social issues. "Out" performers often participate in public advocacy efforts like the It Gets Better Project and endorse initiatives by organizations like the Gay and Lesbian Association Against Defamation (GLAAD), which recognizes gay-inclusive popular media, and the Human Rights Campaign (HRC).

    For example HRC awarded Bass the Visibility Award in 2006 and gave the Vito Russo Award to Martin in 2011. These performers have also supported various organizations publicly. Aiken promotes the Gay Lesbian Straight Education Network (GLSEN) on his website, and participated in an educational video for the "Give a Damn" campaign sponsored by Cyndi Lauper's True Colors Foundation. Bass is featured on a GLSEN PSA for the annual Day of Silence. Though Lambert has been cautious about identity politics, he filmed the video, "It Gets Better" in 2010.

    The willingness of these performers to collaborate with these organizations indicates their investment in using their sexual identities to advance social equality. But some have expressed concern about overstepping their boundaries as entertainers. Lambert told *Rolling Stone*, "I'm trying to be a singer, not a civil rights leader."[21] He has obviously wavered on this issue in many respects yet his statement is significant because by doing so he defines himself primarily as an artist rather than as a spokesman for causes. I detect the feeling of a tacit pressure particular to queer artists in his statement. Two years earlier Bass addressed this issue more elaborately noting:

> I knew last year that when I came out. If I said, "OK I'm going to lead every parade and I'm going to speak at every engagement," half of the community would say, "Screw you! Who are you to come out and start speaking for everyone?" He adds, "That's why I held back and was like, OK, I said my piece now; I'm just gonna lay back and get way more educated about myself, about the community, and not pretend I know what I'm talking about." He laughs, "Then, of course, the other half of the community is like, 'Why don't you do more?' So it's very hard to please everyone."[22]

Clearly from his statement the concept of being "out" does not necessarily imply an individual decision but as a statement of membership within a community. This is a new expectation specific to the post-liberation movement. In the '70s openly gay singer-songwriter Steve Grossman viewed himself as representing gay liberation ideals, whereas Bowie dismissed the group mentality and rigidity of the political movement.[23] Over two decades later, the mainstream gay political movement is more centralized and organizes consistently around issues like marriage and partnership rights, military inclusion, and various anti-discrimination initiatives. This provides an almost automatic set of issues or causes for "out" performers to embrace.

    There are several potential limitations to this imperative. For example many performers might feel a sense of obligation rather than a sense of personal motivation to serve in an activist capacity. Moreover, the public holds a lot of general skepticism toward the credibility of "celebrities" who posit themselves as activists and leaders. Another hazard is the related expectation that gay performers act as "role models" which sets them up for even greater public scrutiny whether in their public behavior or their intimate relationships. Another factor, the prominence of mainstream gay and lesbian advocacy groups and the issues they advocate, has alienated many sectors of the queer population. Many individuals and organizations in LGBT communities view the institution of marriage, U.S military service, and other civil issues as limited efforts that do not eliminate homophobia, and actually assimilate gays by eradicating queer cultural differences. Finally, activists frequently criticize mainstream gay and lesbian political organizations for limited attention to people-of-color, trans-issues, and alternatives to marriage. Eaklor places this issue in context by noting:

> Like the militants before them gay liberationists rejected the idea that only those willing to be straight, act straight, or say they were straight deserved to be treated decently. Philosophically gay liberation, sexual liberation, and political liberation were part and parcel of each other, and building coalitions with other movements was one strategy. When they began organizing though, they also confronted old dilemmas in attempting to unify theory, practice, goals, and actions.[24]

Considering these longstanding debates it is unclear if "out" performers who hold more radical views can express these countercultural perspectives without being dismissed as contrarian or self-loathing.

Debates over the objectives of gay politics also relate to the social expectations associated with sexual disclosure. In the current political landscape many in gay activist and media circles expect "out" artists to participate in community efforts and to publicize their personal lives. Romantic partnerships, children, and other intimate areas are considered standard information once celebrities come out. Thus Aiken and Martin have publicized their fatherhood roles and mainstream and gay media have reported on Lambert's various boyfriends. It seems doubtful that performers could come out and decline to share their personal lives without inspiring puzzlement or even ire for going against the grain. For example Morrissey's decision to be celibate and to not declare his sexuality continues to confound many because this is a standard expectation of celebrities, especially queer ones.[25]

The fact that "out" queer celebrities are encouraged to share their personal and political views seem like markers of progress because these steps represent transparency over secrecy and shame. But outness and transparency do not necessarily signify confidence or triumph over shame and fears of stigma. It is possible that musicians who hesitate to appear out and political worry that audiences may feel more comfortable accepting gay artists but have less interest in gay issues related to romantic or political concerns. We have not clearly arrived at a cultural moment when performers can come out without feeling obligated to participate in certain tropes of outness like romantic disclosures or political involvement.

**#3: Pressure to present a sexually cohesive image:** These four musicians began their careers singing songs directed toward female listeners, and who presumed these artists were heterosexual-oriented. After coming out these men experience pressures that they must express homosexuality in coherent ways that conform to the essentialist notion that people or either gay or straight, as opposed to bisexual or pansexual. These issues of authenticity dominate their careers regarding the public's assumptions about their ability to perform songs credibly using heterosexual content and expressions of sexual desire.

Ricky Martin interestingly exemplifies the dilemma of this issue since heterosexuality was directly encoded into his public image. In addition to a female reference in the 1999 lyrics "Livin' La Vida Loca," the video featured a woman pouring hot wax on his body. "Nobody

Wants to be Lonely" was originally a solo album track on 2000's *Sound Loaded* but was re-recorded as a duet with Christina Aguilera when it was released as a commercial single. Two of his biggest singles were "*She's* All I've Ever Had" and "*She* Bangs." Martin defended his status at the time noting, "'A lot of people go, "Wait a minute, so 'She Bangs' became a 'He Bangs?'"' —he laughs—'No, I never lied. That was my truth at that moment. And when you are on stage you just are. Mind you, as an entertainer if you make a move and get a reaction, trust me, you are going to make that move again—that's what we entertainers live off. Do I think it's going to be the same now? I don't know, and,'—his voice drops to an urgent whisper again—'it doesn't matter. It feels good that it can't be wrong.'"[26]

His comments are pertinent because he essentially makes amends for any perception that he was dishonest or insincere in his performances before he came out. Martin elaborates on this in *Me* noting, "I am the artist I am thanks to the many experiences that have influenced me along the way, and this has absolutely nothing to do with my sexuality. Even though I know very well that all my music and performances have a 'sexualized' component, inasmuch as I dance with women, move my hips, and enjoy the rhythm, that doesn't mean it is an expression of my sexuality, regardless of whether I feel attraction from women or for men."[27] Obviously, like many male figures his performances made him an object of desire for men and women. And his songs could be appropriated by listeners to fulfill their fantasies and desires regardless of his orientation. But the gesture is important, especially since female fans were highly visible during his commercial rise and probably remain central to his commercial audience.

The second issue relates to his identity as an "entertainer" as opposed to a "straight" or "gay" entertainer. His comment suggests that performance is almost genderless and that the thrill of the spectacle inspires the repetition of the successful performance aspects including its sexualized aspects. His coming out may have released the tension regarding his true identity but it may also complicate his status among heterosexual female fans. Visibility has personally liberated individual musicians but also fostered the persistence of the music industry's double standard. The heterosexuality of straight musicians goes unnoticed but singers who come out are labeled "gay singers" and the rules of performance seem to change. Rarely are "straight" musicians expected to address how they might cater to the desires of gay audiences but "gay" musicians are pressured to consider how their expressions of homosexuality might impact heterosexual audiences.

We can deduce from Martin's individual case that performers who are initially marketed as heterosexual and/or viewed as sexually ambiguous might have more access to the commercial mainstream. This access is informed by record label resources, musical genre, and commercial trends, not just qualities of sexual orientation. But performers who come out later in their careers clearly have to renegotiate their images which can potentially reduce their commercial appeal. In 2011 Martin released the mostly Spanish album *Musica + Alma + Sexo* and went on tour—proving that he is still commercially accepted as an "out" singer though he is less prominent.[28]

The commercial impact of coming out, and changes in their commercial strategies are difficult to assess since these performers have diverse commercial status. Lance Bass does not currently play an active as a solo recording artist and it is not clear if *NSYNC will reunite. Aiken's debut album *Measure of a Man* (2003) and his follow-up, *Merry Christmas with Love* (2004), were multi-platinum sellers with several radio hits. *A Thousand Different Ways* (2006), an album mostly featuring covers of hits from the '70s to'90s, was a modest commercial success and the pre-coming out set *On My Way Here* (2008) was also only a mild hit. He also supplemented his recording career performing on Broadway in Monty Python's *Spamalot*. Aiken left RCA in 2009 and signed with Decca Records. 2010's *Tried & True* was a cover album of pop standards from the '50s and '60s. It debuted at #9 but was not a hit and he has since left Decca.[29]

Adam Lambert's commercial potential remains an open-ended issue since it is not clear how he will define himself beyond the initial catapult provided by *American Idol*. Lambert's 2009 debut *For Your Entertainment* peaked at #3, and had three singles, including the top 10 hit "Whataya Want from Me" which earned him a Grammy nomination for Male Pop Vocal Performance.[30] He has been "out" early enough in his career that his strategy needs less alteration than Martin, Aiken or Bass. Lambert is also a candid personality who has noted his unwillingness to appeal exclusively to men. In reference to *American Idol* he admits, "'I loved it this season when girls went crazy for me,' he says. 'As far as I'm concerned, it's all hot. Just because I'm not sticking it in there doesn't mean that I don't find it beautiful.'"[31] In the same interview where he discussed being gay he felt comfortable acknowledging that "lately, you know, there's part of me that's almost bi-curious the other way around. I've made out a few times with girls at nightclubs when I had way too many drinks. I don't know if it would ever happen, but I'm kind of interested."[32]

Among these performers he has occupied the shortest distance between open secret and disclosure, which makes him truly contemporary and potentially representative of a generational shift. But this remains an open-ended issue. His outness suggests confidence in his self-understanding and public image. But the controversy surrounding his risqué performance at 2009's American Music Awards, aired on ABC, raises questions about the boundaries of what's acceptable in mainstream media. During his November 22, 2009 performance of "For Your Entertainment" he kissed his male bassist, grinded a dancer's head against his crotch, and also grabbed the crotch of another dancer. He was scheduled to perform on *Good Morning America* but after the Parents Television Council complained to the Federal Communications Commission (FCC) the show cancelled his scheduled appearance. CBS's *Early Show* invited him to perform in response to ABC's cancellation. Interestingly only a few days prior to his performance he told the Associated Press his performance would make a statement and noted an interesting double standard: "We've seen female pop and rock performers do that for the last 10 years. They've been very provocative, owning their power and sexuality. You just don't see men doing it very often. And I'm hoping to break down that double standard with this number."[33]

Lambert's experience is instructive in many ways. Contemporary performers regularly lace their performances with sexually explicit elements. Despite his initial acceptance by *American Idol's* broad audience, the "controversy" exemplifies how certain boundaries emerge around homosexual displays of sexuality as opposed to *suggestions* of gayness via signifiers. He is arguably the most modern "out" performer recording in terms of musical genre, image and persona. The AMA incident suggests he may have to subdue aspects of his personality to remain commercially viable.[34]

This temperance would be unfortunate since Lambert has also stated desire for people to move beyond homogenous notions of sexual identity. He notes, "Clay Aiken's gay, and I'm gay, and we couldn't be more different. The only thing that's the same about everyone in the gay community is that we're gay. Do we have anything in common besides the fact that we like dick? Why can't we just talk about a human community?"[35] His stance acknowledges gay sexuality but connects it to identities and connections beyond other gay people and speaks to a cultural horizon beyond identity politics. Though his statement is blandly pluralistic it suggests a longing for a perceptual understanding that includes sexual transparency yet is flexible enough to move beyond the artificial stability of identity. Embedded in this statement is a desire for popular audiences to embrace a more panoramic understanding of sexuality, the kind hinted at among "proto-queers" when queerness was visible but unnamed in the mainstream. Identity politics has provided a social philosophy and political movement for queer people to strive for legal equality, seek cultural inclusion, and pursue social justice. Yet queer desire remains the engine of how queer people live and experience the world. Desire and identity must align with queer politics to be able to resonate within queer culture.

# Notes

1. Urvashi Vaid (2011), "Action Makes it Better," in *It Gets Better: Coming Out, Overcoming Bullying, and Creating a Life Worth Living,* Dan Savage and Terry Miller, eds. (New York: Dutton), 24–26.

2. D.A. Miller (1988), *The Novel and the Police* (Berkeley: University of California Press), 207.

3. Eve Kosofsky Sedgwick (1990), *Epistemology of the Closet* (Berkeley: University of California Press), 248.

4. Vicki Eaklor notes, "A nonlinear or postmodern history of sexuality based on its social construction does not merely deny that progress has occurred; it denies that progress is a viable concept. Once irrelevant, progress can no longer be assessed in the past, present, or future" (2008, *Queer America: A People's GLBT History of the United States* [New York: The New Press], 293–94).

5. "Proto-queer" describes the social positioning of four individual male musicians (Liberace, Johnnie Ray, Johnny Mathis and Little Richard) who debuted as recording artists between 1950 and 1956. They emerged before the liberation movement popularized the terms gay and lesbian and are not accurately describable as gay. "Proto-queer" signifies how these artists expanded the possibilities for gender expression and affectivity to their audiences in a highly public manner through their status as popular musicians.

6. David Caplan (2008), "Clay Aiken: No More Secrets," *People* (6 October): 72.

7. Lambert performed "Ring of Fire" during "Grand Ole Opry Week."

8. Aaron Hicklin (2010–2011), "Man in the Mirror," *Out* (December/January): 161.

9. Kyle Buchanan (2008), "Why Wasn't this the Year of Lance Bass?" *The Advocate* (15 January): 31.

10. Marisa Laudadio (2006), "Lance Bass: 'I Feel Like Myself. I'm Not Hiding Anything,'" *People* (7 August): 87.

11. Joel Whitburn (2006), *The Billboard Albums,* 6th ed. (Menomonee Falls, WI: Record Research Inc.), 663.

12. Hicklin, 86.

13. Ibid., 87.

14. Ibid., 87.

15. Damarys Ocaña (2012), "Amazing Grace," *Latina* (February): 73.

16. Christina Baade (2012), "Adult Contemporary," in *Continuum Encyclopedia of Popular Music of the World, Volume VIII,* David Horn, ed. (New York: Continuum), 10.

17. Caplan, 72.

18. Ibid., 78.

19. Vanessa Grigoriadis (2009), "Wild Idol," *Rolling Stone* (5 June): 54.

20. "Adam Lambert: Breakthrough of the Year," (2009–2010), *Out* (December/January): 62.

21. Grigoriadis, 57.

22. Buchanan, 31.

23. Grossman's 1974 debut album *Caravan Tonight* (Mercury Records) was acclaimed as an authentic representation of homosexuality. See Stephen Holden (1974), "A Gay Minstrel," review of *Caravan*

*Tonight* by Steven Grossman, *Rolling Stone* (23 May): 73–74. Bowie differentiated himself from the politics in Mick Rock (1972), "David Bowie Is Just Not Serious," *Rolling Stone* (8 June): 14.

24. Eaklor, 158–59.

25. Nadine Hubbs (1996), "Music of the 'Fourth Gender': Morrissey and the Sexual Politics of Melodic Contour," *Genders* 23: 268–269.

26. Hicklin, 87.

27. Ricky Martin (2010), *Me* (New York: Celebra at New American Library), 141.

28. "Ricky Martin," http://www.allmusic.com/artist/ricky-martin-mn0000359026.

29. *Measure of a Man* reached #1 on the Billboard 200 Albums Chart in 2003 and had three hit singles on the Hot 100 singles chart: "This is the Night" (#1), "Invisible" (#34) and "Solitaire" (#4). After 2004 Aiken's albums consistently peaked in the top 10 but did not have Hot 100 singles (http://www.allmusic.com/artist/clay-aiken-mn0000147468).

30. "Adam Lambert: It Gets Better," http://www.advocate.com/news/daily-news/2010/10/18/adam-lambert-it-gets-better.

31. Grigoriadis, 52.

32. Ibid., 57.

33. "Adam Lambert to Perform on 'Early Show,'" http://www.cbsnews.com/2100–500185_162–5762324.html.

34. On May 15, 2012, Lambert's album *Trespassing* debuted at #1 on the Billboard 200. None of its singles reached the Hot 100 ("Adam Lambert," http://www.allmusic.com/artist/adam-lambert-mn0001532591).

35. Grigoriadis, 57.

# Works Cited

"Adam Lambert: Breakthrough of the Year." (2009–2010.) *Out* (December/January).

Baade, Christina. (2012.) "Adult Contemporary." In *Continuum Encyclopedia of Popular Music of the World, Volume VIII*, David Horn, ed. New York: Continuum.

Buchanan, Kyle. (2008.) "Why Wasn't this the Year of Lance Bass?" *The Advocate* (15 January).

Caplan, David. (2008.) "Clay Aiken: No More Secrets." *People* (6 October).

Eaklor, Vicki. (2008.) *Queer America: A People's GLBT History of the United States.* New York: The New Press.

Grigoriadis, Vanessa. (2009.) "Wild Idol." *Rolling Stone* (5 June).

Hicklin, Aaron. (2010–2011.) "Man in the Mirror." *Out* (December/January).

Holden, Stephen. (1974.) "A Gay Minstrel." Review of *Caravan Tonight* by Steven Grossman. *Rolling Stone* (23 May).

Hubbs, Nadine. (1996.) "Music of the 'Fourth Gender': Morrissey and the Sexual Politics of Melodic Contour." *Genders* 23.

Laudadio, Marisa. (2006.) "Lance Bass: 'I Feel Like Myself. I'm Not Hiding Anything.'" *People* (7 August).

Martin, Ricky. (2010.) *Me.* New York: Celebra at New American Library.

Miller, D.A. (1988.) *The Novel and the Police.* Berkeley: University of California Press.

Ocaña, Damarys. (2012.) "Amazing Grace." *Latina* (February).

Rock, Mick. (1972.) "David Bowie Is Just Not Serious." *Rolling Stone* (8 June).

Sedgwick, Eve Kosofsky. (1990.) *Epistemology of the Closet.* Berkeley: University of California Press.

Vaid, Urvashi. (2011.) "Action Makes It Better." In *It Gets Better: Coming Out, Overcoming Bullying, and Creating a Life Worth Living,* Dan Savage and Terry Miller, eds. New York: Dutton.

Whitburn, Joel. (2006.) *The Billboard Albums* 6th ed. Menomonee Falls, WI: Record Research Inc.

# Behind the Mask: Guerrilla Girls and Others Exposing Unfair Practices and Voicing Protest

## Mary Robinson

Since their inception in 1985, the Guerrilla Girls have waged war on the visual arts world. With their signature gorilla masks, posters, and biting satire, these anonymous women have addressed the shortcomings which kept marginalized artists from exhibition and success. *Guerrilla Girls on Tour*, which branched off from the original activities, juxtaposes activism and performance by focusing on re-habilitating feminism and re-inventing theatre.[1] Based in New York, this collective serves as a prominent example of feminist masquerade; however, they do not stand alone. New models of masked activism have risen to tackle issues affecting women on a global and diverse scale.

While the *Guerrilla Girls on Tour* (GGOT) will be the locus of this discussion, a variety of internationally-recognized groups have adopted masquerade as an effective tool for protest and reform. Originating in Israel in 1988, Women in Black (WIB) expanded their brand of activism to over twenty-four nations. Concealing their identity by wearing black and donning headpieces, WIB highlights human rights abuses, including rape and ethnic cleansing. In Mexico, *Zapatista* began in 1994 as an indigenous movement fighting injustice, but it soon transformed into a mainstream rebel militant endeavor with masked women demanding social change by taking to the streets with signs, cries, songs, and dances. Pussy Riot, masked in colorful *balaclavas*, has achieved iconic status in Russia and international attention due to their arrest stemming from their *Punk Prayer* performance. Afghan women appear on the television show *Niqab (The Mask)*, behind plastic masks, to discuss taboo subject matter, such as domestic violence, rape, and child-trafficking. Masks, however, no longer need a physical representation. Avatar and other digital masking, such as the Twitter-feed Feminist Hulk, allow users to express ideas and take bold stances.

Masquerade emerged as a third-wave feminist strategy and serves as a vital discursive component of each group's protest, intent, and sustainability. Each group draws attention to the issues in a creative and provocative manner, with masks and masquerade that function on three levels: pragmatic, symbolic, and theoretical.

The GGOT seeks to dramatize discrimination in the world of theatre and film through performance. The members maintain 'day jobs' as performers, designers, or writers, adopting the names of dead theatre and literary artists, such as vaudeville star Fanny Brice, dancer Josephine Baker, and director Eva Le Gallienne, for their activist work. "Aphra Behn," artistic director, states that members "choose their own name and the name must be someone whose spirit and herstory you want to carry with you into your activist work ... because we talk about who we are wherever we go."[2] This act of naming reclaims the original artist and rewrites history to reinforce the legacy of female artists historically discarded from the theatrical canon. In *Feminism and Theatre,* Sue-Ellen Case states "initial observations about the history of theatre noted the absence of women within the tradition."[3] Because of the integration of gorilla masks, naming also differentiates each member during interviews and performances. The individual personae represent achievements by under-acknowledged women, but the group collectively pursues activist principles.

The work of GGOT illustrates and exposes the failures of the theatrical industry in regard to power and gender dynamics. The visibility of stage actresses leads many to erroneously assume that sexism does not exist in theatre, but scholarly studies unveil the staggering reality. Marsha Norman discusses a three year study by the New York Council for the Arts (2002), revealing how

> [w]omen are welcome at the front door of the theatre but not at the stage door. This goes for actresses, costume and lighting designers and directors as well as writers.... One of the most horrifying facts to emerge from this study was that women have a better chance of reaching production if they write about men than if they write about themselves.[4]

Norman further expands upon the idea of discrimination, noting that in 2008, "theatres around the country did six plays by men for every one by a woman, and a lot of theatres did no work by women at all, and haven't for years."[5] Reinforcing the need for activism, Emily Glassberg Sands contends that discrimination has remained relatively constant in American theatre for over a century. Her extensive study on discrimination conveys that women playwrights wrote fewer than 12.8 percent of Broadway shows produced in 1909, while in 2008 the figure declined to 12.6 percent.[6] Despite the lower figure, shows by female playwrights earned 18 percent more revenue than the plays of their male counterparts.[7] Sands argues that discrimination leads artistic directors and literary managers to believe that scripts written by women have lower overall quality and artistic merit. In an interview when asked what evidence exists regarding the marginalization of women and gender inequity in theatre, "Aphra Behn" mentions and endorses the merits of this study:

> Last year an amazingly brilliant economist, Emily Glassberg Sands, did a study to try to prove that there is discrimination in theatre.... When women artistic directors and literary managers read the scripts they rated those written by women as less likely to 'fit with their theatre's mission statement' than the identical play when it had a male pen name attached.... This kind of prophetic discrimination was a shocking conclusion of the study.[8]

Female directors and managers maintain power and agency, but when evaluating scripts by women they do not wish to jeopardize their position. Helen Krich Chinoy explores one possible explanation: "women have not easily or regularly come into positions of importance or power in the major institutions. They have been restricted by ... their socialization into a passive but emotional self-image."[9] The simple labelling of a script with a male or female name impacted the consideration for production, questioning whether quality and construction are considered. Guerrilla Girl member "Frida Kahlo" acknowledges this struggle for artistic equality noting, "Women had to fight to become professors, doctors and lawyers. For some reason people believed the art world was above it all."[10] The same rules should apply to the creative realm, but women continue to fight for equality and voice in this venue.

Masks, therefore, serve as a prominent feature and discursive tool in the fight against social, economic, and political injustices, and exist on three intrinsic planes: pragmatic, symbolic, and theoretical. The pragmatic level represents the external value of the mask. Performers can conduct their activities without fear or hesitation, allowing more depth to the process of exploration and critique. Masks also guard against accusations of self-promotion as the ultimate goal, and protect each member from any retaliation from peers as well as authority. Masking unifies the group, linking each member to the collective and their activism. By presenting themselves to the public in such an anonymous manner, this disguise presents a romanticized notion that they could be anyone, anywhere.

The unconventional masquerade utilized by the GGOT shocks and generates reaction. The group's unique presentation juxtaposes a humanoid body with an animal face, maintaining the focus on issues rather than the character or specific performer. In addition to wearing the trademark gorilla mask, the group also adopts a variety of styles and personae, including half masks, humanoid masks, and celebrity masks.

Practical affordability of masquerade is similarly employed in other feminist efforts. Women in Black (*WIB*), an international organization of women for justice and against war, traditionally wear black, while adopting a silent demeanor and a non-violent approach. The group communicates non-verbal protest by using placards. The black ensemble, dress, leather gloves, ski masks, and veiled headpieces show solidarity during the vigils. The readily accessible components conceal the individual identity but provide disguise for any woman who rejects war and its destruction. Similarly, the Muslim veil and burka, while not traditional masks, have been adapted for protest purposes. For women participating on an Afghan television show, *Niqab,* a masking technique was developed to conceal identity. Sami Mahd, the creator of *Niqab*, elaborates on the necessity of the mask by explaining, "I was always desiring to have something like the mask, like this show, in our media. I was not very sure about the concept and the format, but I was very sure about the mask, you know. Because in Afghanistan, it's very difficult for women to talk about their difficulties and their problems, and the violence they are facing in their home."[11] This masking allows them to participate in this public arena without risking their lives. A colourful Russian *balaclava* was meant to obscure the identity of the all-female punk rock band, Pussy Riot. The guitar-playing masked members typically set-up, perform, and depart quickly. This disguise serves the obvious practical purpose against police detection, as they appear at venues such as churches and malls, overtly calling through their music for religious and governmental reform. Maria Chehonadskih identifies the *balaclava* as possessing an inherent Russian quality, "behind which a unique 'Russianness' appears."[12]

Masks have been employed for practical purposes across time and geographic lines and often appropriated into a cultural niche. Masquerade offers protection and elicits attention, creating the novelty of an out-of-the-ordinary draw. They assist in unifying a collective and are the mechanism for easily identifying intended goals. These groups recognize that their pursuit of change is made more viable by incorporating masks and masquerade in their performances.

The symbolic nature of feminist masquerade requires a subtext of deconstruction. Harkening back to the ancient Greeks, the Guerrilla Girls appropriate the use of masks as a commentary on the Western origins of misogynistic practices and the exclusion of women in the canon.[13] Moreover, the gorilla masks add to the group's activist mystique as masked avengers, who electively find power in what the masks represent. Suzanne Lustig states that the mask proves to be "an ironic and empowering declaration of war."[14] The mask allows these performance artists to fight back and add a new dissonant narrative to the stage, invalidating the notion of the unseen, unheard, invisible women. According to Trinh T. Minh-Ha, "If the act of unveiling has a liberating potential, so does the act of veiling. It all depends on the context in which such an act is carried out, or more precisely, on how and where women see dominance."[15] While veiling differs from masking by choice, the GGOT has the agency to don masks as an apparatus to refuse silence in a male-dominated profession. Embracing this 'maskulinity' gives license for activism and potentially positions women to undermine the dominant practices with an 'attitude' that creates an explosion in the social code. Furthermore, Julia Kristeva finds marginalization empowering if women accept and lay claim to it.[16] This masking acceptance is in direct contrast to "past anonymity [which] had been a curse on female artistic creativity, but the Guerrilla Girls embraced the strategic benefits of covert existence."[17] GGOT initially targeted local theatrical and film discrimination, but has since extended their cause into the international theatrical arena, addressing world issues, such as war, rape as a tool of war, male violence against women in domestic life, human rights abuses, and ethnic cleansing, eventually embracing issues of interest held by other masked avenger groups.

All of these groups use masks and color as signifiers to bring the subtext forward, allowing tangible physicality, providing power and voice, and ultimately exposing the underlying failures and shortcomings of society. WIB recognizes that masculine cultures are especially prone to violence when women's voices are silenced. In the West, black signifies mourning, and this veiling reinforces this sentiment. Rather than adopting an abrasive approach WIB uses silence to symbolize the end to the cacophony of empty statements that go unheard. Moreover, Afghanistan's television show *Niqab* uses the mask as a mechanism for addressing issues of women's rights as well as persecution in Afghanistan. The mask is pale blue on one side, representing oppression, while the other half is white, representing innocence. A cultural resonance is built into this color-palette. Therefore, the mask represents the turmoil women face on a day-to-day basis. A female viewer can identify with the wearer of the mask, while men are compelled to consider their interactions with women. The plastic mask does not blend with skin tones but with the contours of the face, allowing the women to speak freely without fear of reprisal. The mask allows emotions and turmoil to be discussed openly. A female viewer can identify with the wearer of the mask, while men are compelled to consider their interactions with women. This is just a step in progress from a traditionally closed society.

While the Zapatista masking strategy symbolizes a collective resistance toward Mexican policies, Pussy Riot represents a struggle of dissidents against oppression in Russia. This political tension unites not only the group but serves to portray them as a symbol of Russian protest, and a representation of universal discontent. Slavoj Žižek, a Slovenian philosopher, argues:

> They are conceptual artists in the noblest sense of the word; artists who embody an Idea. This is why they wear *balaclava*; masks of de-individualization, of liberating anonymity. The message

of their *balaclavas* is that it doesn't matter which of them are arrested—they're not individuals, they're an Idea. And this is why they are such a threat; it is easy to imprison individuals, but try to imprison an Idea![18]

Abstract ideas, though, need concrete, tangible images that can more immediately reveal these ideas. That is where the masquerading activist can aid in symbolically identifying/branding the need for change.

Each mask style, thus, symbolizes intent. While the mask is worn to fight a cause, it also serves to visually represent that very cause. Consequently masquerade allows for reaction and resistance. The groups choose masks that relate to their given culture, which resonates with their intended audience. As visual signifiers of the problem, the symbolism helps compel people to think. A mask, like ideas, can be abstract unless it is visually imbued with meaning.

American philosopher Kenneth Burke's early 20th-century theories provide a framework for each group's tactics, approaches, and practices. Burke explored a theoretical aspect which he identifies as incongruous social, cultural, and political issues which can align when groups desire to initiate change. Burke's perspective explores ways that incongruous issues effectively recast or juxtapose unrelated phenomena by re-contextualizing issues, words, images, or ideologies. This theoretical component materializes in the masked antics of the GGOT in several ways. Gorilla masks on a human body subvert expectation and startle the audience. Moreover, the rhetoric of gorilla and guerrilla evokes a dual imagery. Stemming from an inadvertent misspelling, the terms "deliberately refer to the aggressive, uncivilized behaviour of untamed animals as well as the subversive, underground activities [which align] with their taking on the cultural mainstream."[19] Guerrilla means "little war" in Spanish. Guerrilla fighters prefer small, targeted attacks instead of large military operations. Similarly, the displaced term parallels the way GGOT accosts mainstream theatre through performing in nontraditional spaces, such as the street, universities, and other intimate venues. This striking imagery goes against the grain of the day-to-day assumptions seen in the mirror or in newsstand images. The audience sees the image of a gorilla-masked performer, followed by a small gap of time before finally constructing meaning to the jarring performative event. This Burkean response is similar to Brecht's *Verfremdungseffekt* creating heightened awareness in the audience.[20] In addition to the jarring effect, masks provide paradoxical anonymity on stage, going against the ego-driven practices of mainstream theatre.[21] This practice of covering faces subverts self-identity in favor of bringing recognition and awareness to the dead persona as a reanimation rather than to the performer's own advancement in the theatre world for celebrity status. Ultimately this provides a meta-commentary due to the invisibility of women in theatre.

This concept of incongruous issues and images can be applied to Pussy Riot. Before arrest, Pussy Riot performed the song, "Punk Prayer," calling on the Virgin Mary to become a feminist and redeem society from Vladimir Putin. By using spontaneous performance tactics this group reclaims public spaces, such as a church, a mall, fashion show, and boutique, as arenas for protest. Both entertaining and enlightening, Pussy Riot's highly-charged lyrics criticizes the government and call for religious reform. The church performance comments on the role of women in the church and serves as an affront to clergy and believers. The premise that the Virgin Mary would support a punk band-turned-reformists also assumes an incongruous perspective.

The *Zapatista* of Mexico delivers militant demonstrations against discrimination and political injustice through two incongruous forms of fighting. While wearing traditional colorful and decorative Mexican folk dress, they don ski masks, used as aggressive accessories to express the serious nature of this movement. What originally began as a masculine effort against tyranny has evolved into indigenous women assuming the roles of combatants and referring to themselves as an army. They seek to eliminate their plight through demonstration, conferences, and workshops in order to improve community. But they are prepared to literally fight. They are equipped with weapons, which are also part of the costuming, evidencing their willingness to contest all forms of patriarchy, human rights violations, lack of access to health care and education, gender inequality, and land dispute. It is incongruous that these women are willing to adopt violence even as they oppose it, subverting their traditional role as caring, nurturing females. They outline their message in the Revolutionary Laws of the *Zapatista* Women (1996) which contains thirty-one demands, such as respect within family life, the prohibition of drugs and alcohol, the reclamation of indigenous societal norms, and the eradication of prostitution. Their focus pertains to issues specific to Chiapas women, as well as themes relatable to women worldwide. The image of this army of women masked and dressed femininely, carrying children, guns, and machetes is incongruous indeed. Even the use of the word "army" denotes that the women have taken on two roles: that of warrior, fighting for the cause, and advisor, seeking to create a collective of protesters. This mixture of feminine and masculine characteristics is evidenced in dual imagery:

> Irma leads one of the guerrilla columns which takes the plaza at Ocosingo.... From one of the edges of the central park, together with the soldiers under her command, she attacks the *guarnición* [garrison] inside the municipal palace until they surrender. Then Irma undoes her braid and her hair falls to her waist as though to say "here I am, free and new."[22]

Juxtaposing the harshness of war-like imagery against the softness of the final action of unfurling her braids disrupt the assumptions regarding "soldier" and combat officer. This woman, successful in battle, concludes with a feminine gesture demonstrating her success over women's subordination. The last image of her unfurling her hair emphasizes its importance and communicates the intended message.

Kenneth Burke offers a second theoretical aspect, comic corrective or framing, which appears in feminist masked activism. He demonstrates this theory with his "King of the Hill" example wherein a boy shouts, "I am King of the Ashpile."[23] This claim serves as a boast of his power as well as a challenge to others to try to usurp his right of authority. Therefore, the comedic element of the boy's play occurs in his effort to become the self-declared king to something as arbitrary as an ashpile that contains little or no value, thereby "succinctly symbolizing the comic principle of tragedy."[24] This concept evokes the polarization of rich and poor, and even the boy's assertion becomes tragic when he consequently struggles for a fleeting moment of power, with only cuts and scrapes to show for it. Burke's comic framing serves as an underpinning to incongruity by reconstituting tragic elements into comedic correctives.

Burke alludes to comic corrective or comic framing by referencing how the theory "opens up a whole new field for social criticism."[25] GGOT uses this theory precisely when it targets a serious concern or issue but facilitates it in a comic fashion. For example, the group focuses on rehabilitating notions about the dreaded F-word. While many may immediately reference the F-word as an obscenity, GGOT uses the F-word as a pun. In this context, it signifies feminism.

Myths and stereotypes about second-wave feminism led to the pejorative term "feminist" by conjuring images of bra burning, man hating, and angry, demanding, and spectacle-creating women. As a result, many in society distance themselves from the term feminist, but at the same time they espouse many of the tenets.[26] The GGOT explained that feminism clamored for change, equality, awareness, and action, but "making demands are the tactics of the '70s and let's face it, they didn't really work very well. So we decided to try another way: humor, irony, intimidation, and poking fun."[27] Essentially they reinvented feminism through a comedic lens. By making their demands more acceptable and more appealing, feminism becomes funny and not an affront. "Aphra Behn," primarily the group's "spokesgorilla," recognized the benefits of comedy, noting:

> When you make people laugh in a live performance, then you could engage people and speak to them one to one, or face to face, or mask to face, as it were. You can influence them in a different way.... So, we decided that our mission would be to create plays, and performances, street theatre, actions, that addressed women's issues.... Comedy has its own power ... comedy disarms people ... we feel we get our message across by making people laugh and think.[28]

The GGOT attacks from behind masks as a comic corrective that informs the group's work in bringing awareness to the plight of marginalized minority artists and their social, political, and cultural issues.

In contrast to mainstream theatre, the performative style of this collective uses singing, dancing, and projected images, as well as statistics and audience participation. Their overtly political stage, reminiscent of Brecht, brings these social issues to the audience. An extensive travel schedule calls for a minimalist set, which compels the audience to focus on the masked performers and message. Their repertoire of shows include: "The History of Women in Theatre," "Feminists Are Funny," "Silence Is Violence," and "If You Can't Stand the Heat: The History of Women in Food," each of which not only includes their gorilla logotype,[29] but also masks specific to the message of that particular show. Hunger, oppression, and violence are some of the themes they confront during these performances, but they frame these themes comically through the adoption of Burke's comic corrective to remedy the tragic.[30]

*Guerrilla Girls on Tour* change masks as relevant to the skit or routine and adopt half masks which allow for projection and clearer communication of the message. Humanoid masks add a fluid quality and allow performers to embody a variety of characters, regardless of gender or age. For example, in the skit "For President," George Bush and Margaret Thatcher masks provide commentary and satire. This strategy enhances the humor and the comedic elements while also addressing and targeting serious leadership and political issues. The use of slightly grotesque or distorted masks in "Feminists Are Funny" creates a dissonance from the characters, establishing the audience as onlookers. Politically-aware audiences gain an appreciation for the potential catalyst for change; hence, "the comic frame should enable people to be observers of themselves, while ... its ultimate [goal] would not be passiveness, but maximum consciousness.[31] The exaggerated facial features result in misidentification because the audience members do not see themselves on stage. This alienation technique removes the audience from the issues projected on stage, but the audience remains compelled to consider the implications of the message.

Applying a different tactic in "If You Can't Stand the Heat: The History of Women in Food," performers don realistic masks which function similarly to stage make-up, enhancing the actresses' natural facial configurations. The *Heat's* subject matter contains a more poignant message concerning body image and global hunger. Natural masks mimic how the audience views itself, which allows identification and active participation in the experience and message.

Identification serves as "one key rhetorical strategy used by those who create persuasive text—verbal or visual—to attempt to align an audience with the text's overall message."[32] Confronted with identifying themselves in the messages, the audience is more fully compelled to listen. Jill Dolan, a feminist scholar, observes that this strategy serves as "a critical social tool, [an] embodied moment of theory and practice."[33] Theory itself cannot serve as an apparatus or impetus for change. Instead, theory must work with practice to actively create social and political change. Serving as a powerful tool, realistic masks aid in identification, creating a more compelling message through performance. With a ferocious sense of humor, this binary links the rhetoric of the message to the mask.

FEMINIST HULK, a web entity, reaches a worldwide audience demonstrating Burke's comic corrective applied toward contemporary issues. Online avatars occupy a digital rather than a physical space, constituting a contemporary equivalent of masks by concealing a user's online identity. Like their physical counterpart, though, they allow anonymity and freedom of expression. The HULK avatar shows the green hero of Marvel Comics holding a copy of Judith Butler's *Gender Trouble*. This image juxtaposes two titans from two different literary genres and ideologies, and has resulted in 68,000 followers. Again, using Burke's theory, incongruity lies in the image of a comic book superhero espousing feminist theory. The HULK Twitter feed brings feminist theory and concepts to people who might not be familiar with such scholarship. In an interview conducted by *Ms.* magazine, *FEMINIST HULK* responded to the question regarding the greatest challenge facing contemporary feminism:

> WORD "FEMINISM" ITSELF. HULK LOVE FACT THAT FEMINISM REFER NOT TO A SINGLE SCHOOL OF THOUGHT, BUT MANY DIFFERENT APPROACHES TO POLITICAL ACTION. UNFORTUNATELY, MANY POTENTIAL ALLIES CLOSE THEIR EARS, MISLED BY SIMPLE, REDUCTIVE, REACTIONARY DEFINITIONS OF THE TERM. CHALLENGE IS TO REOPEN DIALOGUE, SHOW THAT FEMINIST POLITICS ARE RELEVANT TO EVERYONE! WE MAKE FEMINISM WHAT IT IS, WHAT WE NEED IT TO BE.[34]

While the term feminism has proven off-putting and many feel it is not relevant, the goal lies in opening a conversation which all can share. Wit and use of theory empower the HULK's work as does the use of ALL CAPS to demonstrate a protest against the male-imposed hierarchy of language. The rules of language and grammar were created by men, and through language regulation and power are maintained. Therefore, the use of all caps signifies a refusal to adhere to such language control. This type of humor is a tactic which the Hulk uses to make these concepts more palatable and accessible, which "can be an awfully good thing."[35]

Through this digital medium, HULK has created an online community and draws all people into a discourse that attempts to probe serious issues. Social networks are another tactic for mobilizing and sharing ideas among activists. Cyperspace has evolved into an alternative platform for expression and protest. Internet dissidents, such as HULK, endure due to the fact they are visible in the media space. This type of mask has become a powerful recruitment tool.

In relation to Burke's concept of incongruity, the choice of the green superhero is poignant. Marvel's Hulk, an easily recognizable masculine superhero driven by impulse and anger, normally has trouble with words that contain more than two syllables. *FEMINIST HULK*, though, loves applying feminist concepts to a rage-heavy life. Humor is derived "from hearing feminist theory spouted by such a hypermasculine figure."[36] Using a male avatar has its advantage over a female superhero, such as Wonder Woman, to discuss feminist dogma. The sexuality imposed on female superheroes makes the discussion readily dismissable. This big, hulking figure is as sensitive to the female plight, bakes cookies, is intellectualized. Much of the early popularity surrounded who was issuing the tweets and the alter ego of the Twitter composer. While anonymity was an initial stratagem, *FEMINIST HULK* was unmasked in 2011, which had little effect on its success or notoriety.[37] Due to this masquerade approach, the Worldwide Web has emerged as a ubiquitous forum for disseminating feminist ideology.

The presence of feminist masqueraders proves both troubling and hopeful. Masks have successfully functioned as a means of achieving political and social goals. Masks draw attention to issues in a creative and provocative manner, ultimately giving the wearer a more prominent voice. Activists reach a broader audience combating the dominant paradigm that places women in subordinate roles, and this fearless work provokes thought about the disenfranchisement experienced by groups who do not fit within the prescribed form. GGOT boldly stands outside the traditional idea of what feminist theatre looks like because they have constructed their own identity and act as their own autonomous theatrical unit of performers and playwrights. Suzanne Lustig recognizes their importance to the world, noting, "they have remained a resilient form of resistance to male dominance."[38] In terms of Mexican resistance, Subcomandante Insurgente Marcos, an early male *Zapatista* leader, states that "I will take off my ski mask when Mexican society takes off its own mask, the one it uses to cover up the real Mexico."[39] By removing the nation's mask, citizens will take a more active role in reform, bringing Mexico to its full potential. WIB, on the other hand, prefers to create a powerful imagery with silent vigil. What appears as a seemingly small step for Afghan *Niqab* women, in context is a large step for women who serve as pioneers in this effort. Pussy Riot provides feminist criticism of the modern Russian patriarchal state "with a splash of anti-clerical critique."[40] The arrest and imprisonment of three members continues to focus attention on their activist efforts.[41] *FEMINIST HULK* eludes arrest while provoking discourse from an even larger audience online. As world drama unfolds, masks and masquerade thrive as vivid performance spectacle.

# Notes

1. A fracturing occurred in 2001, dubbed the "Banana Split," resulting in three separate entities: Guerrilla Girls, Inc., a continuation of the original art-focused group; Guerrilla Girls BroadBand, a digital-media endeavour; and Guerrilla Girls on Tour, a traveling theatre collective.

2. "Aphra Behn" interview by Kyle Bachan (2010), "Reinventing the F-Word with Guerrilla Girls on Tour!" (8 April), 2.

3. Sue-Ellen Case (2009), *Feminism and Theatre* (New York: Palgrave Macmillan), 3.

4. Marsha Norman (2009), "Not There Yet: What Will It Take to Achieve Equality for Women in the Theatre," *American Theatre* (26 November): 29.

5. Ibid., 29.

6. Emily Glassberg Sands (2009), "Opening the Curtain on Playwright Gender: An Integrated Economic Analysis of Discrimination in American Theatre," Senior Thesis, Princeton University, 1.

7. Ibid., 99.

8. "Aphra Behn" interview by Cherie (2010), "Artistic Director of Guerrilla Girls on Tour," *Daily Femme* (2 June): 24.

9. Helen Krich Chinoy (1996), "Art Versus Business: The Role of Women in American Theatre," *A Sourcebook on Feminist Theatre and Performance: On and Beyond the Stage,* Carol Martin, ed. (New York: Routledge), 24.

10. Meredith Tromble (1998), The Guerrilla Girls Make Art Herstory (Again), 26 February, 4.

11. Damon, 2.

12. Maria Chehonadskih (2012), "What is Pussy Riot's 'Idea'?" *Radical Philosophy* (November/December): 3.

13. Case (2009), 5; Jill Dolan (1996), "Introductory Essay: Fathom Languages: Feminist Performance Theory, Pedagogy, and Practice," *A Sourcebook on Feminist Theatre and Performance: On and Beyond the Stage,* Carol Martin, ed. (New York: Routledge), 1, 2.

14. Suzanne Lustig (2002), "How and Why Did The Guerrilla Girls Alter the Art World Establishment in New York City, 1985–1995?" (Spring): 5.

15. Trinh T. Ming-Ha (1998), "Not You/Like You: Post-Colonial Women and Interlocking Questions of Identity," *Feminism and the Critique of Colonial Discourse,* Deborah Gordon, ed. (Center for Cultural Studies), 372.

16. Susan Jones and Suzanne Bennett (2002), "The Status of Women: A limited Engagement?" *The New York State Council on the Arts Program Report* (January): 371.

17. Lustig, 4.

18. Slavoj Žižek, "The True Blasphemy," http://chtodelat.wordpress.com/2012/08/07/the-true-blasphemy-slavoj-zizek-on-pussy-riot/, 1.

19. Mariani Lefas-Tetenes (2005), *Guerrilla Girls* (2–30 March), 2.

20. Verfrem dungseffekt, or the alienating effect, is Bertholt Brecht's technique giving familiar aspects of reality the appearance of being unfamiliar in order to arouse the spectator's critical judgment.

21. Violaine Roussel and Bleuwenn Lechaux (2010), "guerrilla Girls on Tour: Women and Anti-War Activism," *Voicing Dissent: American Artists and the War on Iraq* (New York: Routledge), 139.

22. Marco, and Ziga Vodovnik (2004), Ya basta!: Ten Years of the Zapatista Uprising: Writings of Subcomandete Insurgente Marco (Oakland, CA: AK Press), 4.

23. Kenneth Burke (1937), *Attitudes Toward History* (Berkeley: University of California Press), 250.

24. Ibid., 350.

25. Ibid., 167.

26. Aston Elaine and Geraldine Harris, eds. (2006), *Feminist Futures? Theatre, Performance, Theory* (Houndmills UK: Palgrave Macmillan), 57.

27. Anne Teresa Demo (2000), "The Guerrilla Girls' Comic Politics of Subversion," *Women's Studies in Communication* 23 (Spring): 135.

28. Roussel, 144.

29. Logotype: a graphic representation or symbol of a company name, trademark, abbreviation, etc., often uniquely designed for ready recognition.

30. Burke, 166–75.

31. Ibid., 171.

32. Wendy Hersford (2007), *Rhetorical Visions: Reading and Writing in a Visual Culture* (Upper Saddle River, NJ: Pearson/Prentice Hall), 11.

33. Dolan, 5.

34. Audrey Bilger (2010), "FEMINIST HULK SMASH EXCLUSIVE INTERVIEW WITH ME!" *Ms* (7 June): 2, http://msmagazine.com/search.asp?q=Feminist%20Hulk.

35. Ibid., 3.

36. Christopher Shea (2010), "Feminist Hulk Smash Sexism," *Boston Globe* (15 June), http://www.boston.com/bostonglobe/ideas/brainiac/2010/06/whats_big_green.html.

37. FEMINIST HULK was unmasked as 28-year-old Jessica Lawson, a Ph.D. English literature candidate at the University of Iowa, a new mother, and as she describes herself, a "white, vegan, queer, woman-identified female."

38. Lustig, 5.

39. M. Clint McCowan (2003), "Imagining the Zapatistas: Rebellion, Representation and Popular Culture," *International Third World Studies Journal and Review* Volume XIV, 29.

40. Chehonad skih, 4.

41. Recently unmasked and jailed, Maria Alekhina, Nadezhda Tolokonnikova and Ekaterina Semutsevich face charges of hooliganism for allegedly staging an anti–Putin performance in Moscow's Christ the Saviour Cathedral. They face up to seven years in prison. Interview statement after arrest: "We are

a women's group which is forced to consume the ideas of patriarchal conservative society. We experience each process that happens in this society. Besides, we are a punk band, which can perform in any public place, especially one which is maintained through our taxes" (Elena Vlasenko [2012], "Russian Punk Collective Pussy Riot Speaks Exclusively to Index" [15 May]: 1, http://uncut.indexoncensorship.org/2012/05/pussy-riot-russia-protest/).

# Works Cited

Behn, Aphra. (2010.) Interview by Cherie. "Artistic Director of Guerrilla Girls on Tour." *Daily Femme* (2 June).

Behn, Aphra. (2010.) Interview by Kyle Bachan. "Reinventing the F-Word with Guerrilla Girls on Tour!" (8 April).

Bilger, Audrey. (2010.) "FEMINIST HULK SMASH EXCLUSIVE INTERVIEW WITH MS.!" *Ms.* (7 June). http://msmagazine.com/search.asp?q=Feminist%20Hulk.

Burke, Kenneth. (1937.) *Attitudes Toward History*. Berkeley: University of California Press.

Case, Sue-Ellen. (2009.) *Feminism and Theatre*. New York: Palgrave Macmillan.

Chehonadskih, Maria. (2012.) "What is Pussy Riot's 'Idea'?" *Radical Philosophy* (November/December).

Chinoy, Helen Krich. (1996.) "Art Versus Business: The Role of Women in American Theatre." *A Sourcebook on Feminist Theatre and Performance: On and Beyond the Stage*. Carol Martin, ed. New York: Routledge.

Demo, Anne Teresa. (2000.) "The Guerrilla Girls' Comic Politics of Subversion." *Women's Studies in Communication* 23 (Spring).

Dolan, Jill. (1996.) "Introductory Essay: Fathom Languages: Feminist Performance Theory, Pedagogy, and Practice." *A Sourcebook on Feminist Theatre and Performance: On and Beyond the Stage*. Carol Martin, ed. New York: Routledge.

Elaine, Aston, and Geraldine Harris, eds. (2006.) *Feminist Futures? Theatre, Performance, Theory*. Houndmills UK: Palgrave Macmillan.

Hersford, Wendy. (2007.) *Rhetorical Visions: Reading and Writing in a Visual Culture*. Upper Saddle River, NJ: Pearson/Prentice Hall.

Jones, Susan, and Suzanne Bennett. (2002.) "The Status of Women: A Limited Engagement?" *The New York State Council on the Arts Program Report* (January).

Lefas-Tetenes, Mariani. (2005.) *Guerrilla Girls* (2–30 March).

Lustig, Suzanne. (2002.) "How and Why Did The Guerrilla Girls Alter the Art World Establishment in New York City, 1985–1995?" (Spring).

Marco, and Ziga Vodovnik. (2004.) *Ya basta!: Ten Years of the Zapatista Uprising: Writings of Subcomandete Insurgente Marco*. Oakland, CA: AK Press.

McCowan, M. Clint. (2003.) "Imagining the Zapatistas: Rebellion, Representation and Popular Culture." *International Third World Studies Journal and Review* Volume XIV.

Ming-Ha, Trinh T. (1998.) "Not You/Like You: Post-Colonial Women and Interlocking Questions of Identity." In *Feminism and the Critique of Colonial Discourse,* Deborah Gordon, ed. (Center for Cultural Studies).

Norman, Marsha. (2009.) "Not There Yet: What Will It Take to Achieve Equality for Women in the Theatre." *American Theatre* (26 November).

Roussel, Violaine, and Bleuwenn Lechaux. (2010.) "guerrilla Girls on Tour: Women and Anti-War Activism." In *Voicing Dissent: American Artists and the War on Iraq*. New York: Routledge.

Sands, Emily Glassberg. (2009.) "Opening the Curtain on Playwright Gender: An Integrated Economic Analysis of Discrimination in American Theatre." Senior Thesis, Princeton University.

Shea, Christopher. (2010.) "Feminist Hulk Smash Sexism." *Boston Globe* (15 June). http://www.boston.com/bostonglobe/ideas/brainiac/2010/06/whats_big_green.html.

Tromble, Meredith. (1998.) *The Guerrilla Girls Make Art Herstory (Again)*. 26 February.

Vlasenko, Elena. (2012.) "Russian Punk Collective Pussy Riot Speaks Exclusively to Index." 15 May. http://uncut.indexoncensorship.org/2012/05/pussy-riot-russia-protest/.

# The Fifth of November:
# Masquerade and Social Tensions

## Derrick Vanmeter

"From grains of sand to giant stars all things share one condition. The world
we see would never be except for OPPOSITION."—Tony Kushner[1]

Terry Castle wrote in her landmark work on 18th-century masquerade, that when attending a masked gathering, "one was obliged to being opposite, in some essential feature, to oneself."[2] It is vital to note that inherent to the concept of *opposition* is a sense of tension. This tension is often related to the potential effects of shifting from one end of the binary system to the other. To shift from *up* or *down* necessarily indicates *falling* or *rising*. It is this nature of opposition that makes masquerade so effective in engaging social tensions. Some social anthropologists might call masquerade a sort of "safety valve" that reaffirms the status quo by exorcising social tensions.[3] In support of this theory, history demonstrates that 18th-century masquerades did not become a revolutionary force for social change. Movements of the 20th century and beyond have been more effective in creating a society where racial, ethnic, and sexual groups can experience increasing liberties. These changes necessitate a reevaluation of the social function of masquerade as seen in contemporary society.

The study of masquerade benefits greatly from exploration of the world of graphic novels. Though some works benefit this study more than others, these novels are often set in a world ravaged by some sort of military conflict, governmental oppression, or religious dominion. True to heroic conventions, an unlikely character rises to challenge the status quo and, through an often arduous journey, defeats the oppressor. *V for Vendetta,* written by Alan Moore and illustrated by David Lyons, provides an excellent case study to explore the intersections of masquerade, the graphic novel, and social tensions. By exploring the parallels between 18th-century masquerade and *V for Vendetta* and its impact on society, one can notice the transformation of masquerade from safety valve to revolutionary force in contemporary society.

Initially published in 26 installments between 1982 and 1985, *V for Vendetta* emerged from an amalgamation of multiple ideas from Alan Moore, David Lloyd, and Dez Skinn.

Moore wanted to emulate the pulp magazine genre's "sense of mingled exoticism and familiarity" without bowing to historical accuracy of the 1930s.[4] The story takes place in the late 1990s and features a young girl who meets a Guy Fawkes–masked terrorist named V. The mask is a stylized representation of the historical figure of Guy Fawkes who tried to bomb parliament in the 17th century.[5] Nuclear war has ravaged the world. From the ashes of English society the Norsefire regime creates a sense of order. This fascist order resonates with images of Nazi Germany. Anyone who deviates racially, ethnically, or sexually from the Norsefire norm is placed in prison or a concentration camp–style facility. These elements of the story are indicative of the social tensions felt by Alan Moore and others during the early 1980s.

Just less than twenty years later, social tensions continued to morph and escalate. After the financial crisis of 2008, frustrations about economic injustices culminated in the Occupy Wall Street movement. On September 17, 2011, people began to gather in Zucotti Park in protest of income inequality and Wall Street corruption. While questions exist concerning the legitimacy of the movement's beginnings (at least as portrayed as a grass roots movement),[6] the movement grew and gained momentum worldwide. Protesters frequently used the slogan "We are the 99 percent." This posturing as a vocal majority brings light to what the group sees as income inequality in the United States. The hacker group Anonymous got involved through people like Gregg Housh (one of the few people publically associated with Anonymous) and brought with them the use of the Guy Fawkes mask from *V for Vendetta*.[7] News outlet after news outlet presented a barrage of images of masked protesters holding signs drawing attention to their concerns.[8]

Representation of a Guy Fawkes mask. The sketch illustrates a stylized representation of the historical figure of Guy Fawkes, who tried to bomb the British parliament in 1605. *V for Vendetta* later used it (episodes published in United Kingdom, United States, and France 1982 to 1989 and film adaptation, 2005), and eventually the Occupy Wall Street movement used it in crowd protests, symbolizing an anonymous army of masqueraders united against a common enemy (sketch by Derrick Vanmeter).

## Enduring Social Tensions

The social tensions experienced by 18th-century England, Alan Moore in the 20th century, and contemporary society in the 21st century have similar themes and issues. In the introduction to the 1988 DC Comics run of *V for Vendetta*, Moore writes,

It's 1988 now. Margaret Thatcher is entering her third term of office and talking confidently of an unbroken Conservative leadership well into the next century ... the tabloid press are circulating the idea of concentration camps for persons with AIDS. The new riot police wear black visors, as do their horses, and their vans have rotating video cameras mounted on top. The government has expressed a desire to eradicate homosexuality, even as an abstract concept, and one can only speculate as to which minority will be the next legislated against.[9]

These social tensions, while over 20 years old, still find places of resonance with both 18th-century and contemporary society.

The 18th century was full of governmental conflict that culminated in the American and French revolutions. Fear of plague outbreaks in other areas caused the English to establish quarantines, sometimes leading to the deaths of those who would not comply.[10] Homosexuality was clearly deviant in the minds of the general public. If on Wednesday, the 29th of November in 1780 one were to pick up *The British Mercury and English Advertiser* he/she would find this urgent message:

> The scandalous neglect of that great moral duty, which is the cement of society, Matrimony, and the growth of effeminacy in the men, and prostitution in the women, demand the most serious attention. It is of that consequence to a commercial city in a temporal sense, and our salvation in a spiritual, that some method should be adopted to promote it, and give it a free, open, and generous encouragement....[11]

Some of the encouragement mentioned in the article above included extra benefits to men with three children, reinforcing the common idea that procreation is the sole reason for human sexuality.

In the 21st century, the divide between conservatives and liberals grows increasingly wider. The number of individuals that identify as political centrists decreased from 40 percent to 36 percent from 2000 to 2011. These former centrists have chosen to align with more conservative or liberal values.[12] One of the key issues continues to be homosexuality. An October 2012 Pew research poll found that 49 percent of people said they supported same-sex marriage and only 40 percent opposed. This was a dramatic change from 39 percent in favor and 52 percent opposed in 2008.[13] Despite shifting opinions, there are those that would suggest that the United States should eradicate homosexuals by placing them in an electrified fence until they starve and fail to reproduce.[14] This sentiment, once again, regards human sexuality as primarily for reproduction. Such conflict in attitudes creates great social tension. Amidst these tensions, one may wonder how they do not frequently explode into violent conflict. The safety valve theory postulates that tensions are exorcised by brief moments of revelry that allow mounting tensions to release. Castle does an excellent job of exploring this notion in her book, but does this theory continue to prove true in the world of *V for Vendetta* and the 21st century? Exploring the similarities between the three eras illuminates two important elements: anonymity and the carnivalesque.

## Behind the Mask: Anonymity

Anonymity was an important part of 18th-century masquerade because it facilitated the notion that a person could do whatever they wished without their actions being associated with their public reputation. Castle writes,

Thanks to the anonymity of mask and costume, [masqueraders] were free to engage in otherwise taboo behavior ... verbal intimacy with strangers [was] encouraged [and] a new liberated language of gesture arose.... Women ... were as free as men to initiate verbal or physical contacts with strangers.[15]

Anonymity was central to masquerades, and the mask was the enabler of such anonymity. Detractors of masquerades railed against the loss of inhibitions brought on by wearing a mask.

*V for Vendetta* similarly recognizes anonymity for its power. V wears a Guy Fawkes mask, granting him some sense of anonymity. Outside of his home, the Gallery of Shadows, he always wears a long flowing black coat, not unlike the domino from 18th-century masquerades. The Norsefire regime refers to enforcement units as sensory organs of the body. The Eyes watch, the Nose investigates, and the Finger has Fingermen who are patrolling officers in the party. These anthropomorphic branches of government receive their orders from a leader who consults a computer system called FATE. While it is not clear whether FATE is autonomous and intelligent or has a "man behind the curtain" running the show, FATE does have a Voice: Lewis Prothero. In the 2006 film adaptation, Prothero's role seems slightly different because of his presentation. Rather than merely existing as a voice on the radio, Prothero occupies much airtime on TV. He spews vile propaganda for Norsefire, more than is found in the graphic novel. Perhaps by showing Prothero's face to the audience he loses some of the power that the character had as a mysterious and powerful voice on the radio. What is certain however is that anonymity plays a huge role in *V for Vendetta*.

Anonymity also affects society in the 21st century. In 2010, the United States Supreme Court ruled in the case of *Citizens United vs. FEC* that the federal government could not ban political spending by corporations.[16] One of the key issues in the application of this decision was the anonymity of donors. The decision suggests that a corporation can give unlimited funds to a candidate anonymously. This obviously could give a candidate an advantage in an election. However, if the candidate supports a position that many citizens disagree with, the corporation that supports the candidate is protected from any ramifications of the connection. Citizens that do not want to support companies with unethical policies are disempowered to make informed decisions in the free market. Lawmakers attempted to add disclosure as an element to the decision, but the measure failed.[17]

Another element of anonymity in the 21st century is the political activist hacker group Anonymous. These "hacktivists" have infiltrated major governmental and corporate sites, slowing them down, causing them to crash, and releasing confidential information in order to make their political point.[18] One of the most fascinating things about this group is their use of the Guy Fawkes mask as a symbol or trademark. Warner Brothers (who distributed *V for Vendetta* in 2005) had the masks produced in support of the film. The group reportedly began using the masks in 2008 at a protest against the church of Scientology.[19] Since then, the mask has become a symbol for Anonymous. The masks not only protect the identities of the protesters, but provide a sense of collective unity.

## A World Upside Down: The Carnivalesque

In her book on 18th-century masquerade, Terry Castle particularly focuses on the carnivalesque in her subtitle. Working from her understanding of Mikhail Bakhtin's analytical volume *Rabelais and His World*, she begins to identify how 18th-century masquerade was carnivalesque. "And just as the sexes mingled freely, so a carnivalesque mixing of the social ranks took place; the typical public masquerade, as its enemies were wont to complain, was a heterogenous mass of high and low, with disguise the great leveler."[20] The intermingling of social classes temporarily subverted the hierarchical system. Enabled by the anonymity, the masquerade became a place where all were equal, if only for a little while. Castle frequently calls the carnivalesque world "a world upside down" where sexual, social, and metaphysical hierarchies are rejected.[21] This carnivalesque atmosphere is accomplished by creating laughter with spectacle, parody, and various genres of coarsely abusive language.[22]

*V for Vendetta* makes use of carnivalesque imagery for some comic relief in the midst of often weighty material. The first, most obvious element is the Guy Fawkes mask itself. Within the first few frames, the mask hangs on a mirror with make-up lights around it. A previous frame shows a collage of movie posters behind the mirror and vanity. These posters, coupled with the row of lights and the Guy Fawkes mask with its wide, white smile and rosy cheeks suggest a carnival atmosphere immediately.[23] Another carnivalesque moment occurs in a chapter aptly titled "Vaudeville." V has kidnapped Lewis Prothero and taken him to Larkhill, the concentration camp where V was held prisoner. V reminds Prothero of his work at Larkhill and in a moment of carnivalesque theatricality, Prothero comes face to face with his doll collection dressed as prisoners. V has filled an incinerator (which presumably served a more sinister purpose in the past) with more of Prothero's doll collection and ignites them before his eyes. The dolls call out "ma-ma" as they burst into flames and Prothero loses his mind. He is returned to society with face painted white, like one of his dolls, and can only say "ma-ma."[24] Another important carnivalesque moment occurs when Mr. Finch, a detective trying to find V, takes LSD to "know what it's like being him."[25] He begins to see strange visions of people with skin the color of "a thousand blends of coffee." He realizes through further hallucinations that he is in control of his own destiny. He strips off his clothes and runs to Stonehenge to declare himself absolutely free.[26]

The 21st century embraces the carnivalesque as well. In creating a "world upside down" Comedy Central's "The Daily Show" makes use of parody and satire. Their website once read:

> One anchor, five correspondents, zero credibility. If you're tired of the stodginess of the evening newscasts, if you can't bear to sit through the spinmeisters and shills on the 24-hour cable news networks, don't miss "The Daily Show" with Jon Stewart, a nightly half-hour series unburdened by objectivity, journalistic integrity, or even accuracy.[27]

Ironically, "The Daily Show" has often been noted as or more informative than network news channels.[28] One Pew poll found that 54 percent of viewers of "The Daily Show" and its spin-off "The Colbert Report" scored in the same high-knowledge category as people who read newspaper websites regularly. This poll found that only 35 percent of people were in the high-knowledge category.[29] These comedy shows have quickly become more reliable sources of information than networks dedicated to providing news. This absurd opposition is classically carnivalesque.

## Practical Application of Masquerade in the 21st Century

The social tensions that permeated 18th-century England carry through to the 21st century. Society has developed new ways of engaging them, such as the graphic novel. *V for Vendetta* is one title that has been of particular interest to the study of masquerade since it features a masked character who brings down a fascist government by turning their world upside down, making it his own carnival. What does it mean in a practical sense? How do the insights gained from making these connections inform one's view of the relation between 21st-century society and masquerade?

The Occupy Wall Street movement exhibits similar tendencies toward masquerade and the carnivalesque. The use of the Guy Fawkes mask in the Occupy protests seems to constitute a new facet of masquerade in the 21st century. Instead of being a safety valve, masquerade has become a tool in the hands of a political movement. A particularly carnivalesque image used to promote the movement was a poster of the Wall Street bull with a dusty mob of people wearing gas masks and stick-like implements. On top of this bull, a dancer stands calmly poised on one foot under the slogan "What is our one demand?" Photographs of large groups of masked pro-testers call to mind some of the final images from the film adaptation of *V for Vendetta*. As the now dead V hurdles toward parliament in a train car full of homemade explosives, hundreds upon hundreds of people dressed in black robes and white Guy Fawkes masks descend on the downtown area. Without orders from their deceased leaders (killed by V of course) the soldiers stand down and the people (symbolically?) take back their government.[30] This scene never happens in the graphic novel. Instead, a young girl whom V has mentored, Evey, picks up the mask belonging to V and takes up his cause.[31] In this way, V becomes more than just a man, he becomes a symbol of rebellion against a corrupt government. The Guy Fawkes mask becomes the visual representation of V's rebellious spirit.

While there are more innocuous forms of masquerade in the 21st century such as costume-themed parties, the level of engagement with social tensions stemming from source material such as *V for Vendetta* renders the act as a potentially subversive political force rather than affirming the status quo. By using the Guy Fawkes mask, the Occupy Wall Street movement became an anonymous army of masqueraders united against a common enemy. The victorious are the arbiters of history. Occupy Wall Street continues to stand against corporate greed, but will they ultimately win? An ironic result of the 2006 film adaptation produced by Warner Brothers, Time Warner owns the rights to the visage of the Guy Fawkes mask used in *V for Vendetta*.[32] Each time protesters purchase a mask, they continue to add to the bottom line of a giant corporation.

# Notes

1. Tony Kushner (1987), *Yes Yes No No: The Solace-of-Solstice, Apogee/Pedigree, Bestial/Celestial Holiday Show*. In *Plays in Process: Three Plays for Young Audiences,* 11th ed., Vol. 7 (New York: Theatre Communications Group).

2. Terry Castle (1986), Masquerade and Civilization: The Carnivalesque in Eighteenth-Century English Culture and Fiction (Stanford, CA: Stanford University Press), 5.

3. Ibid., 88.

4. Alan Moore (2011), "Behind the Painted Smile," In *V for Vendetta* (New York: DC/Vertigo), 269.

5. Edward Lovett, (2011), "How Did Guy Fawkes Become a Symbol of Occupy Wall Street?" ABC News, http://abcnews.go.com/blogs/headlines/2011/11/how-did-guy-fawkes-become-a-symbol-of-occupy-wall-street/.

6. *Occupy Unmasked* (2012), directed by Stephen K. Bannon, perf. Andrew Breitbart, Brandon Darby, and David Horowitz, Magnolia Home Entertainment.

7. Saki Knafo (2011), "Occupy Wall Street and Anonymous: Turning a Fledgling Movement into a Meme," *The Huffington Post* (20 October), http://www.huffingtonpost.com/2011/10/20/occupy-wall-street-anonymous-connection_n_1021665.html.

8. Lovett (2011).

9. Alan Moore (2011), "Introduction," in *V for Vendetta* (New York: DC/Vertigo), 6.

10. Arnold Zuckerman (2004), "Plague and Contagionism in Eighteenth-Century England: The Role of Richard Mead," *Bulletin of the History of Medicine* 78, no. 2: 292.

11. Norton Rictor, ed. (2012), "Newspaper Reports, 1780–81," *Homosexuality in Eighteenth-Century England: A Sourcebook*, http://rictornorton.co.uk/eighteen/1780news.htm.

12. Jonathan Haidt (2012), "America's Painful Divide," *Saturday Evening Post* 284, no. 5: 35.

13. Marjorie Connelly (2012), "Support for Gay Marriage Growing, but U.S. Remains Divided." *The New York Times* (8 December), http://www.nytimes.com/2012/12/08/us/justices-consider-same-sex-marriage-cases-for-docket.html.

14. "N.C. Pastor Charles Worley: 2013: 'Put Gays and Lesbians in Electrified Pen to Kill Them Off,'" YouTube, 21 May, http://www.youtube.com/watch?v=w2839yEazcs.

15. Terry Castle (1984), "Eros and Liberty at the English Masquerade, 1710–90," *Eighteenth-Century Studies* 17, no. 2: 162.

16. Adam Liptak (2010), "Justices, 5–4, Reject Corporate Campaign Spending Limit," *The New York Times* (22 January), http://www.nytimes.com/2010/01/22/us/politics/22scotus.html?pagewanted=all.

17. "Editorial: Corporate Contributions and Disclosure" (2012), *The New York Times* (10 September), http://www.nytimes.com/2012/09/10/opinion/corporate-contributions-and-disclosure.html?_r=0.

18. "Anonymous (Internet Group)" (2012), *The New York Times*, http://topics.nytimes.com/top/reference/timestopics/organizations/a/anonymous_internet_group/index.html.

19. Rosie Waites (2011), "V for Vendetta Masks: Who's Behind Them?" BBC News (20 October), http://www.bbc.co.uk/news/magazine-15359735.

20. Castle (1984), 162.

21. Castle (1986), 6.

22. M.M. Bakhtin (1968), *Rabelais and His World* (Cambridge, MA: MIT Press), 5.

23. Alan Moore, David Lloyd, Steve Whitaker, Siobhan Dodds, Jeannie O'Connor, Steve Craddock, Elitta Fell, and Tony Weare (2011), *V for Vendetta* (New York: Vertigo/DC), 9–10.

24. Ibid., 31–36.

25. Ibid., 212.

26. Ibid., 216.

27. Rachel Smolkin (2007), "What the Mainstream Media Can Learn from Jon Stewart," http://www.ajr.org/article.asp?id=4329.

28. Andrew Beaujon (2012), "Survey: NPR's Listeners Best-Informed, Fox Viewers Worst-Informed," Poynter (23 May), http://www.poynter.org/latest-news/mediawire/174826/survey-nprs-listeners-best-informed-fox-news-viewers-worst-informed/.

29. Smolkin, (2007).

30. *V for Vendetta* (2005), directed by Larry/Lana Wachowski and Andy Wachowski, perf. Natalie Portman and Hugo Weaving, Burbank, CA: Warner Home Video, DVD.

31. Moore et al. (2011), *V for Vendetta*, 262.

32. Nick Bilton (2011), "Masked Protesters Aid Time Warner's Bottom Line," *The New York Times* (August 29), http://www.nytimes.com/2011/08/29/technology/masked-anonymous-protesters-aid-time-warners-profits.html?_r=0.

# Works Cited

Bakhtin, M. M. (1968.) *Rabelais and His World*. Cambridge, MA: MIT Press.

Beaujon, Andrew. (2012.) "Survey: NPR's Listeners Best-Informed, Fox Viewers Worst-Informed." Poynter (23 May). http://www.poynter.org/latest-news/mediawire/174826/survey-nprs-listeners-best-informed-fox-news-viewers-worst-informed/.

Bilton, Nick. (2011.) "Masked Protesters Aid Time Warner's Bottom Line." *The New York Times* (August 29). http://www.nytimes.com/2011/08/29/technology/masked-anonymous-protesters-aid-time-warners-profits.html?_r=0.

Castle, Terry. (1984.) "Eros and Liberty at the English Masquerade, 1710–90." *Eighteenth-Century Studies* 17, no. 2.

Castle, Terry. (1986.) *Masquerade and Civilization: The Carnivalesque in Eighteenth-Century English Culture and Fiction.* Stanford, CA: Stanford University Press.

Connelly, Marjorie. (2012.) "Support for Gay Marriage Growing, but U.S. Remains Divided." *The New York Times* (8 December). http://www.nytimes.com/2012/12/08/us/justices-consider-same-sex-marriage-cases-for-docket.html.

"Editorial: Corporate Contributions and Disclosure." (2012.) *The New York Times* (10 September). http://www.nytimes.com/2012/09/10/opinion/corporate-contributions-and-disclosure.html?_r=0.

Haidt, Jonathan. (2012.) "America's Painful Divide." *Saturday Evening Post* 284, no. 5: 34–37.

Knafo, Saki. (2011.) "Occupy Wall Street and Anonymous: Turning a Fledgling Movement into a Meme." *The Huffington Post* (20 October). http://www.huffingtonpost.com/2011/10/20/occupy-wall-street-anonymous-connection_n_1021665.html.

Kushner, Tony. (1987.) *Yes Yes No No: The Solace-of-Solstice, Apogee/Pedigree, Bestial/Celestial Holiday Show.* In *Plays in Process: Three Plays for Young Audiences* 11th ed., Vol. 7. New York: Theatre Communications Group.

Liptak, Adam. (2010.) "Justices, 5–4, Reject Corporate Campaign Spending Limit." *The New York Times* (22 January). http://www.nytimes.com/2010/01/22/us/politics/22scotus.html?pagewanted=all.

Lovett, Edward. (2011.) "How Did Guy Fawkes Become a Symbol of Occupy Wall Street?" ABC News. http://abcnews.go.com/blogs/headlines/2011/11/how-did-guy-fawkes-become-a-symbol-of-occupy-wall-street/.

Moore, Alan. (2011.) "Behind the Painted Smile." In *V for Vendetta.* New York: DC/Vertigo.

Moore, Alan. (2011.) "Introduction." In *V for Vendetta.* New York: DC/Vertigo.

Moore, Alan, David Lloyd, Steve Whitaker, Siobhan Dodds, Jeannie O'Connor, Steve Craddock, Elitta Fell, and Tony Weare. (2011.) *V for Vendetta.* New York: Vertigo/DC.

Norton, Rictor, ed. (2012.) "Newspaper Reports, 1780–81." *Homosexuality in Eighteenth-Century England: A Sourcebook.* http://rictornorton.co.uk/eighteen/1780news.htm.

*Occupy Unmasked.* (2012.) Directed by Stephen K. Bannon. Perf. Andrew Breitbart, Brandon Darby, and David Horowitz. Magnolia Home Entertainment.

Smolkin, Rachel. (2007.) "What the Mainstream Media Can Learn from Jon Stewart." http://www.ajr.org/article.asp?id=4329.

*V for Vendetta.* (2005.) Directed by Larry/Lana Wachowski and Andy Wachowski. Perf. Natalie Portman and Hugo Weaving. Burbank, CA: Warner Home Video, DVD.

Waites, Rosie. (2011.) "V for Vendetta Masks: Who's Behind Them?" BBC News (20 October). http://www.bbc.co.uk/news/magazine-15359735.

Zuckerman, Arnold. (2004.) "Plague and Contagionism in Eighteenth-Century England: The Role of Richard Mead." *Bulletin of the History of Medicine* 78, no. 2: 273–308.

# Section IV

Visual Art's Influence on Masquerade: Graphic and Performance Art, Branding, Photography and Comic Books

# Pop Art to Pop Masquerade—Warhol to Lady Gaga: When Does the Mask Become the Reality?

MARIANNE CUSTER AND
JOHANN STEGMEIR

What is the mask of a pop culture icon? As Andy Warhol, whose paintings of commercial products began the "pop art" movement in the 1960s once put it, "Just look at the surface of my paintings and films and me, and there I am." He says, in effect, don't read anything into this; I am the mask and the mask is me. Like the many pop stars to follow in his wake, creating and evolving the mask was necessary for commercial survival. From David Bowie's changing personae to Lady Gaga's creation of herself as a religious cult figure (*Born This Way*), these transformations were intended to keep a fickle public constantly reengaged with their icon's evolving masquerade.

Warhol, like the pop musicians who followed in his wake, consciously developed an image. It was the early sixties when the counter culture revolutionaries fell in the thrall of androgyny. Warhol and Bowie consciously cultivated images of ambiguous sexuality. In Harlem, underground ballroom culture or "vogueing" celebrated drag glamor in runway competitions among black men. The stage was being set for the development of pop music personae whose genealogy leads from Warhol to Lady Gaga and encompasses Elton John, Boy George, The New York Dolls and Madonna, and shock rockers Alice Cooper, Kiss and Marilyn Manson.

Though musically the shock rockers and pop artists may have little in common, they share the careful cultivation of personae and mask. Their influences included Andy Warhol and his Factory, manufacturing art and image, the Harlem club culture, the bizarre sado-masochistic fashions and personae adopted by Australian performance artist Leigh Bowery, and the Club Kids, a group of young New Yorkers noted for their outrageous costumes and rampant drug use. These groups desired attention and the need to separate themselves from the crowd. They desired to exact revenge on a culture in which they felt themselves to be outcasts or misfits by flaunting an outrageous persona. In some extreme cases they were motivated by a messianic impulse.

Andy Warhol, not a musician, but a cultural impresario inside the art world's crystal ball, laid the groundwork for artists of all kinds and, with his paintings celebrating the commercial and mass produced, collapsed the boundaries between high and low culture. Similarly, David Bowie created personae for himself whose influences and interests included "Christopher Isherwood's Berlin of the 1930s, Hollywood divas of the 1940s, Kabuki theatre, William Burroughs, English mummers, Jean Cocteau, Andy Warhol, French chansons, Buñuel's surrealism, and Stanley Kubrick's movies, especially *A Clockwork Orange*, whose mixture of high culture, science fiction, and lurking menace suited Bowie perfectly. Artists and filmmakers have often created interesting results by refining popular culture into high art. Bowie did the opposite: he would, as he once explained in an interview, plunder high art and take it down to the street; that was his brand of rock and roll theater."[1]

Warhol adored celebrity, he became a celebrity, and he created celebrities. His conscious superficiality was acknowledged in David Bowie's tribute to Warhol, "Andy Warhol." Bowie, who invented his own artificial images, acknowledges in his song, "Changes," this shared conscious superficiality.

One of the characteristics of rock music is that so much of it involves posing or "role playing." David Bowie, followed by a host of pop and rock musicians since the 1960s, has created serial personae. Starting with Arnold Corns, Major Tom (a fictional astronaut), Ziggy Stardust (a sexually ambivalent demigod from outer space), Aladdin Sane (a further development of Ziggy), and ending with Thin White Duke (a character impeccably dressed, emaciated, desensitized, amoral and of wavering sexual orientation). "The image cultivated by Bowie, as he became more famous, was as a complete oddity, an isolated alien, a pop deity, utterly enigmatic, freakish, alienated, but dangerously alluring."[2] With each of these personae came the invention of a new outrageous costume and mask.

The visual expression of pop and rock artists must be a factor considered entirely separately from their musical genre. While performers like Bowie create personae that they inhabit for periods of time, performers like Elton John, Alice Cooper, Kiss, Madonna and Lady Gaga create a single career persona, though often with a variety of cultural signifiers. While Bowie uses constant character reinvention, as well as outrage to maintain the interest of his public, the latter group chooses one outrageous or shocking persona that they maintain throughout their careers. In all cases, their motivation is to single themselves out from the crowd and to attain fame and money.

In an interview with Oprah Winfrey, Elton John elaborates on the evolution of his character: "When you're sitting at the piano, you're not David Bowie, you're not Mick Jagger, you're not Rod Stewart, you're not Freddie Mercury." He explains that he "just needed to put some attention" on himself.[3] He chose to attract attention to himself with humor through the adoption of wildly colored and proportioned costumes, including his famous enormous, glittery sunglasses, effectively, the Elton John mask.

Virtually every pop entertainer recounts his or her effort to single themselves out of the crowd of would be stars. Alice Cooper, originally a member of the band, Alice Cooper recalls, "We got here [California] in the midst of all the good groups, like The Doors and Love. The competition was incredible. No one would even listen to us."[4] They had to find a gimmick and Cooper's first try was to "go on in a pink satin clown costume, with blue eye makeup and a bottle of wine."[5]

While Elton John became the face of glam pop of the early '70s, Alice Cooper was helping to shape the look and sound of heavy metal. He was the first to introduce horror imagery to rock 'n roll and his stagecraft and showmanship have permanently transformed the genre. The films, *Whatever Happened to Baby Jane?* (1962) and *Barbarella* (1968) served as inspiration for the mask that is Alice Cooper. In a 2011 interview Cooper reveals that these two movies, and particularly the characters of Baby Jane and The Great Tyrant, were what shaped the whole Alice persona, with Bette Davis' increasingly cracked make-up, and the sexy evilness and whirling wrist switch-blades of The Great Tyrant striking a resonating chord that endures to this day.[6] A 1974 *People* magazine interview with Cooper, whose original name was Vincent Furnier, reveals his early relationship to his character. "To me Alice is a product. If I ever got to be Alice, I would be in real trouble. Alice on stage is a whole different thing. Offstage I'm Ozzie Nelson. It's like Jekyll and Hyde to me."[7] In a 2012 interview Christina Patterson asked if he is ever bored with Alice's unchanging persona, he replies, "My posture changes. Now, I'm this character, and for an hour and a half I do not break this character. I know Alice so well that he's my defense. People like Alice so much, why would I want to invent another character? You think I get bored with it? I don't. I think Alice is infinitely fun to play."[8]

KISS leader Gene Simmons and his band members chose their personae when they formed their band in New York City in 1973. "We said let's put together the band that we never saw on stage. We were four boys off the streets of New York. We started putting our early songs together in a loft above a Sears store. We knew how we sounded, but we needed to see how we looked, so we went down to Sears and got a mirror. Then we went to the drugstore and bought a bag of women's make up, and some white clowns' make up from a costume shop on the street. We didn't have a clue. We sat in from of the mirror with a handful of Maybelline and played around like kids, drawing, rubbing it off, drawing more. I had no idea that we were creating the four most recognizable faces in the world."[9] Each chose a character and persona based on his individual interests. Peter Criss chose a Catman. Ace Frehley adopted a Spaceman persona. Paul Stanley adopted a star over his eye because he wanted to be a Rockstar. Gene Simmons became a fire-breathing, tongue-wagging ghoul.[10] In an interview with NPR's Terry Gross on *Fresh Air* he says, "my makeup came as a result of a lot of things, all things Americana, Godzilla, horror movies, science fiction.... Black Bolt, which was an *Inhumans* Marvel comic book, and science fiction, sort of, all things sort of American Pop Culture." The former teacher at Manhattan's PS 75 went on, "I wanted to be in a band that gave bang for the buck. I wanted to be in the band that didn't look like a bunch of guys who were, you know, studying for their finals. You know, I wanted stars up on stage. And regular people just didn't look big enough. So we wore 8-inch platform heels, put on more makeup and higher heels than your mother and made more money than your banker."[11] Though the faces underneath the makeup have become puffy and lined in the intervening years, the makeup and characters Kiss created have remained the same. Gene Simmons satisfaction with the success of his masquerade reports to Terry Gross, "They've done polls where they show people a series of faces. Not everyone knows what Barrack Obama looks like, but everyone can recognize KISS."[12]

Michael Jackson transformed himself both physically and as a performer. He wanted to create a new mask that erased the memory of his days as the youthful star of the Jackson Five. In his "manifesto" scribbled in purple ink on a brown paper bag when he was 21, Jackson outlines his aspirations:

> MJ will be my new name. No more Michael Jackson. I want a whole new character, a whole new look. I should be a tottally [sic] different person. People should never think of me as the kid

who sang "ABC," [or]"I Want You Back." I should be a new, incredible actor/singer/dancer that will shock the world. I will do no interviews. I will be magic. I will be a perfectionist, a researcher, a trainer, a masterer [sic]. I will be better than every great actor roped into one.[13]

In this early plan for the persona he was to invent, the theme of "shock" emerges, as it has with Kiss and Alice Cooper. As with Bowie and John, he understood the need to attract attention to himself as an individual artist through the development of a persona. His first shocking transformations began with his own physical appearance.

Hampton Stevens wrote in *The Atlantic:* "He not only made art promoting pop's egalitarian ethos, but literally tried embody it. When that vision became an obsession, a standard showbiz plastic surgery addiction became something infinitely more ambitious—and infinitely darker. Jackson consciously tried to turn himself into an indeterminate mix of human types, into a sort of ageless arch-person, blending black and white, male and female, adult and child."[14] Michael Jackson became one of the first entertainers to use music video movies to promote his celebrity. He had already begun his physical transformation in 1983 when he made the groundbreaking video, "Thriller." Jackson's interest in the theme of transformation is evident in this video, in which he morphs from Michael Jackson, dating boy, to werewolf, to zombie, and back to Michael Jackson dating boy again.

Starting in the 1980s, Andy Warhol's influence on pop culture continues to grow. Even Alice Cooper's girlfriend at the time, Cindy Lang, was a model "chummy with the Warhol set."[15] "Madonna, who arrived in New York in the late '70s also became friendly with the artist circle surrounding Warhol. Art dealer Bruno Bischofsberger continually brought new artists to Warhol's The Factory, a ritualized event where Andy created a portrait of the artist in exchange for a piece of their art. In this way, Andy maintained a connection with younger artists who kept him in touch with emerging trends and celebrity youth."[16] Madonna's association with artists Jean-Michel Bisquiat and Keith Haring eventually led her to Warhol's circle, and in December, 1984, to the first of her many covers on Warhol's *Interview* magazine.

The Madonna of the early '80s was playfully provocative in her fashions, but by 1984, "her image became one of a blatant sexual being, in control of her sexuality and proud of it."[17] She began a series of self-reinventions that have become the signature of her stardom. Camile Paglia writes: "Feminism says 'no more masks':" Madonna says we are nothing but masks."[18] Peter Wilkinson writes: "Peel away one of Madonna's masks, and you'll usually find another."[19] As an artist, Madonna had many public incarnations, a virtual potpourri of images designed to keep her in the public eye and consciousness through both attraction and outrage. "Like Barbie, Madonna sells because, like Mattel, she constantly updates the model—Boy Toy Madonna, Material Girl Madonna, Thin Madonna, Madonna in Drag, S&M Madonna, and so on."[20] As a teenager, raised in a Catholic family by her father and a stepmother Madonna resented, she expressed her rebellion by wearing provocative clothing and make-up. She learned in her early teens that controversy could garner the attention she craved.[21] Wearing underwear as outerwear and religious iconography in the form of crucifixes in her music video, "Like a Virgin,"and her Virgin Tour, may have shocked and horrified observant Catholics around the world, but its very subversiveness attracted and delighted Madonna's growing crowd of admirers. She was making use of lessons she had learned as a teenager.

Madonna exposes femininity as a masquerade in her "parodies of *femme fatales* such as Marilyn Monroe and Veronica Lake. In the video for "Material Girl" she imitates Monroe's "Diamonds are a Girl's Best Friend" number from *Gentlemen Prefer Blondes.* The video reproduces the elements of blondness, sexuality and gold-digging, but parodies the gold-digger's self-commodification as a form of 1980s crass materialism.[22]

The post "Material Girl" incarnations see Madonna appropriating the symbolism of Indian, Asian, and Latin cultures. As her interest in all things Asian grew, she incorporated artifacts from Sufism, Buddhism, Hinduism and the Kabbalah into her image repertoire. Similarly, her interest in gay culture sees her incorporating gender bending and sexually ambiguous images into her dress and music. As she has appropriated artifacts of foreign cultures in her image, her song and video, "Vogue," reflect her appropriation of gay, black *voguing* culture. The Vogue, which Madonna dances in her music video, is based on the dance that evolved from the moves of cross dressers posing as if they were fashion models on runways in the gay black nightclubs of New York. "Like David Bowie, Madonna is a cultural sponge: 'I am not a scholar, I'm a sponge. I soak things up.' She absorbs fashions, trends, other people's artistic successes—past and present. As a postmodern icon, she seems constituted of successive layers of signifiers, gathered according to a very precise Madonnesque logic. What is then named Madonna is a collection of masks, of personae. To do drag is to wear the clothes and signifiers of the Other, to do drag is to transpose a personality."[23] In other words, it is to wear a mask.

Much has been written about Madonna and sexual identity. Her interest in the subversion of repressive societal mores is expressed in the gender ambiguity of her successive image changes. "Madonna's appropriation of both 'male' and 'female' constructs supports Judith Butler's idea of a variable construction of identity. She takes this to the extreme by dressing in drag; in the 'Express Yourself' video, she wears a suit and monocle. At one point she teasingly opens and closes the jacket to reveal a black lace bra, thus exposing gender as a put-on. Here, Madonna can be seen to mock male power and identity by reducing gender and sex to the level of fashion and style."[24]

Madonna's impact on pop culture is immeasurable. Her methods of refreshing the Madonna mask have inspired those who have come in her wake. "Madonna and the career she carved out for herself made possible virtually every other female pop singer to follow.... She certainly raised the standards of all of them.... She redefined what the parameters were for female performers."[25]

But nothing could quite prepare the world for Lady Gaga; Gaga whose work encompasses a kaleidoscope of influences from high and pop art, fueled by Madonnesque ambition and intellectual aspiration. She exists at the apex of a pyramid of artists who have come before her, issuing manifestos from her artistic promontory. Her detractors might say she has copied those who came before, but her manifestation of a single persona has been drawn from more diverse sources and she has synthesized those sources in new ways. Her Mother Monster character, the messiah of the misfits, has won her "Little Monsters" (fans) around the world. Is Mother Monster real or a mask? Lady Gaga herself said, "Have you ever loved something so much, you told a tiny little lie, a negative truth? And you believe and you love your new invention so deeply you would kill to make it true. Your visualization, your futurization, your self-masturbation is all you have—so honor it. Some say that Lady Gaga is a lie—and they are right. I am a lie and every day I kill to make it true."[26]

Lady Gaga created her Mother Monster character from constellations of influences that include: rock performers, fringe performance artists, female impersonators, fashion designers, and fashionistas, philosophers, and, of course, Andy Warhol. Early in her career, she thought Andy Warhol was guiding her career from beyond. A source for *The Sun* related that, "Her house is insane. She has spent thousands turning it into a shrine to Warhol."[27] She has tried to combine her music with art throughout a whirlwind career that has seen her become the world's most famous female singer.

Lady Gaga's most obvious source of inspiration among rock musicians is Madonna. Like Madonna, she repeatedly changes her visual image. She declares, "Madonna is a wonderful influence on me. I feel blessed to have grown up with a powerful, blonde woman to show us the ropes. It's all down to her that I'm able to do what I do."[28]

Madonna certainly broke ground for Lady Gaga's hyper-sexualized costumes when she began performing in underwear. She does not adopt multiple personae, but instead transforms herself from performer to celestial messiah, carrying the message of individual empowerment. She acknowledges having created a life for herself that exists in a place between reality and fantasy.[29] She creates a masquerade that in effect becomes her everyday reality. She theorizes that birth is an ongoing, lifelong process of becoming who you really are. In a Chicago *Sun Times* interview she explains:

> It's a process of living and it's also not ultimately a goal. It's something ever-changing. Something you can ignite at any moment. My bones have changed in my face and in my shoulders because I am now able to reveal to the universe that when I was wearing shoulder pads or when I was wearing jackets that looked like I was wearing shoulder pads, it was really just my bones underneath. My fashion is part of who I am, and though I was not born with these clothes on, I was born this way.[30]

Lady Gaga acknowledges her debt to the constellation of fringe performance artists that influence her constantly changing images. In an article in *The Guardian* in 2011, rock and pop critic, Alexis Petridis, states that she is a product of the downtown club scene that Lady Gaga describes as a "hybrid of performance art meets singer-songwriter-meets-drag-meets-theatre-meets-rock".[31] This is a mostly gay club scene in which clothing and make-up were devised to command attention and create outrage. As Stefani Germanotta, Lady Gaga learned to use shock to command attention on stage when, she worked in the bars of the Lower East Side in New York. In an interview with Barbara Walters on ABC, she says:

> Well, the name of the club was The Bitter End, and I played there all the time, but I had been gone for a while and it was my first time playing my new glam-inspired music. And nobody would be quiet. I walked into the room and before I even opened my mouth they were yelling and chatting and drinking and slamming their glasses, And I, I kept [saying], "Excuse me, hello," and nobody would stop. So, um, something just came over me and I, I took my clothes off.[32]

So, how does Stefani Germanotta transition from taking her clothes off in a bar to birthing Lady Gaga and all of her transformations and transmogrifications?

> When I was really young, I was fascinated with performance artists, Leigh Bowery, Klaus Nomi. And when I got older I became fascinated with Yoko Ono and Marina Abramovic. I grew up with them, and sort of naturally became the artist I am today. It wasn't until I started to play out in New York and my friends said, "Look how much this has influenced you," that I realized it. The one thing there wasn't on the Lower East Side was pop music. So as a pop songwriter, I thought that would be an interesting way to make a name for myself in this neighborhood. I figured if I could play the grocery store around the corner as if it was Madison Square Gardens, maybe someday I can assimilate pop music into performance art in a more mainstream way.[33]

*Voguepedia*, in reflecting upon the influences on Gaga's fashions/costumes reports, "It's in this tradition of clothing as performance art as provocation as declaration of independence—the *outré* territory blazed by New York underground artists like Candy Darling and Leigh Bowery, as well as a legion of wildly accoutered club kids during the 1980s—that won the heart of the fashion world."[34] Lady Gaga, through her use of costume as performance art, has drawn attention to her fashion designers. As Jonathan Van Meter reported in *Vogue*, "Gaga demonstrates a commitment to outrageous self-presentation that makes every crazy costume worn by Elton or Cher or Madonna look like child's play."[35] Whether in a rocker-chick Hussein Chalayan black leather jacket or a Jan Taminiau dress that seems revived from the Gothic recesses of Victorian England, Lady Gaga remains an astonishing individual. As the designer Karl Lagerfeld succinctly declared: "I hate average, and she is anything but average."[36]

From Leigh Bowery, Lady Gaga learned that it doesn't have to look good, it just has to look fabulous. Bowery, an Australian born fashion designer, model, performance artist, pop artist, club kid, and actor, became a major player in the fringe gay performance art scene in London. He was an unattractive fat man who used his size as a tool in his art form. He became an inspiration for important artists and fashion designers including the painter Lucien Freud, who whose nude paintings of Bowery that hang in the Tate Modern, and Alexander McQueen, whose last collection was a tribute to Bowery. This was the same collection that McQueen presented as a gift to Lady Gaga. Bowery's garish, sometimes clown-like, sometimes sex doll, sometimes sado-masochistic images were, like Lady Gaga's images, a constantly changing form of body art.

Lady Gaga contends that she is "born this way"; that the physical distortions of her fashion choices result in the transmogrification of her bones. "Well, first of all," she says of the protrusions on her face and shoulders, "they're not prosthetics. They're my bones. They've always been inside of me, but I have been waiting for the right time to reveal to the universe who I truly am…. It's artistic expression," Gaga says. "It's a performance-art piece. … Body modification is part of the overarching analysis of '*Born This Way*.' In the video, we use Rico, who is tattooed head to toe [including a skull on his face]. He was born that way. Although he wasn't born with tattoos, it was his ultimate destiny to become the man he is today. I am an artist, and I have the ability and the free will to choose the way the world will envision me."[37]

At the same time that Bowery was the master of ceremonies of London nightlife, Michael Alig was hosting the Club Kid scene in the Lower East Side in New York City. In the mid '80s, when New York nightlife was dominated by socialites and celebrities, clubs like Studio 54 and Andy Warhol's The Factory, disaster happened: Andy Warhol died and left a huge void in the downtown scene.[38]

"The flamboyant Club Kids, led by Michael Alig and James St. James, emerged on the New York nightlife circuit. In the wake of the 1987 stock market crash; amidst the economic gloom, this motley crew of drag queens and fashionistas—decked out in loud sartorial affairs … brought a revived spirit to the scene."[39]

While Lady Gaga is too young to have been part of the Club Kid scene, many of her ensembles can clearly be traced to Club Kid styles. Her Kermit outfit, for example appears to be homage to Club Kid, Amanda Lepore's Hello Kitty regalia. Her meat dress and blood smeared romper from *Paparazzi* likely referenced James St. James's get ups in the film *Party Monster* that chronicled the exploits of the club kids and Michael Alig's drug fueled murder of his dealer. One can also speculate that both meat dresses could have been inspired by artist Mark, Ryden's series of surrealist meat paintings.

Though Grace Jones calls her a "copycat," Lady Gaga often mentions Jones as an inspiration. Jones created her own persona by drastically transforming her appearance, and before

Lady Gaga did it, moved her shows from rock performances to "performance art." She adopted a hyper-sexualized androgyny that attracted, not only the attention of Lady Gaga, but of female impersonators. "I wasn't born this way," Jones once said. "One creates oneself."[40] Also an associate of the Warhol circle, Jones literally used her body as a canvas for graffiti artist, Keith Haring. Haring painted her angular dark body with bold white marks, giving her the appearance of an African deity.

Now that she is famous, Lady Gaga is assisted in her masquerade party by fashion designers, not only from her own House of Gaga, but from around the world. Her fashion star has risen so high as to have attracted the attention of even financial magazines. *Forbes* magazine writes, "No one can deny that her style is uniquely her own. Who else can wear a T-bone steak as a dress or show up at a baseball game in nothing but a bra and knickers? Her brand of fashion requires guts and unbelievable self-confidence."[41]

Financial magazines aside, she is certainly the darling of fashion magazines and fashion blogs. A *Harper's Bazaar* blogger writes, "Her relationship with the stylist Nicola Formichetti is one of fashion's great love affairs; she even closed his first womenswear outing as the creative director of the house of Mugler in March dressed as a club-kid bride. She also greatly admires Hussein Chalayan, who designed her 'vessel' for the Grammys and who she describes as 'an incredible mind and a genius human being. He truly leads the way in the avant-garde world.'"[42]

Seemingly all the titans of fashion have leapt to provide her with custom designs, among them Donatella Versace, Thierry Mugler, Chanel, Valentino, Frank Fernandez (meat dress), Commes des Garçon, Karl Lagerfeld, Prada, and Jean-Paul Gautier.[43]

Another of her fashion heroes is the late, great Alexander McQueen, who gave her his entire last collection. "McQueen worked with Lady Gaga, who Mr. McQueen's publicist called 'an unofficial muse.' Lady Gaga, who was about to release her album *Fame Monster*, unveiled her song 'Bad Romance' at Mr. McQueen's show, as the models walked out in their final looks."[44]

Giorgio Armani has been designing custom performance clothes for Gaga. They became a creative duet for the 2010 Grammy Awards. Of their collaboration, Armani says, "Collaborating with Lady Gaga is always an exciting experience for me. I admire the way she uses fashion as a scenic element and as a means to build a character. She is an artist of many talents and great intelligence."[45]

Creating and controlling the entertainers mask is vital to their emergence from the lower ranks of fame seekers. If they lose control of the mask and masquerade they might be forgotten, dismissed or in some cases, reviled. Emerging pop artists will continue to seek new means of drawing attention to themselves. In what has become a global entertainment culture, there is very little new under our sun. Entertainers have used nudity, gender confusion, horror images, cultural appropriation, bizarre physical transformation, and extreme glamour to mask as characters that both attract and repel. What is left in the future to shock, outrage or amaze an audience that has seen seemingly everything can only leave us in dubious anticipation.

# Notes

1. Ian Buruma (2013), "The Invention of David Bowie," *The New York Times Review of Books* (23 May).
2. Ibid.
3. Sir Elton John and Oprah Winfrey (2010), *Oprah Winfrey Show:* Oprah Fridays LIVE: Sir Elton John (16 April), http://www.oprah.com/oprahshow/Music-Legend-Elton-John/3#ixzz2TwLgqMXD.

4.  "The Preacher's Son Who Became Alice Cooper" (1974) *People* magazine, vol. 1, no. 5 (1 April).

5.  Ibid.

6.  Richard Cosgrove (2011), "An Evening with Alice Cooper's Movie Nightmares at the BFI," *Shadowlocked* (11 May), http://www.shadowlocked.com/201111052235/opinion-features/an-evening-with-alice-coopers-movie nightmares-at-the-british-film-institute.html.

7.  "The Preacher's Son Who Became Alice Cooper" (1974).

8.  Alice Cooper interview with Christina Patterson (2012), "Every Word of the Bible Is True," *The Independent* (17 October), http://www.independent.co.uk/arts-entertainment/ music/features/alice-cooper—every-word-of-the-bible-is-true-i-believe-the-old-testament-explicitly–8207597.html.

9.  Jade Wright (2010), "Gene Simmons Talks Liverpool, The Beatles," *Kiss Online* (9 April), http://www.kissonline.com/news/article/id/23033.

10.  Gene Simmons interview by Terry Gross (2001), "Interviews Gene Simmons," National Public Radio, *Fresh Air* (11 November).

11.  Ibid.

12.  Ibid.

13.  Chiderah Monde (2013), "Michael Jackson 1979 Manifesto Reveals Singer's Plan to Become the Most 'Incredible' Entertainer," *New York Daily News* (20 May).

14.  Hampton Stevens (2010), "Michael Jackson's Unparalleled Influence," *The Atlantic* (24 June), http://www.theatlantic.com/ entertainment/archive/2010/06/michael-jacksons-unparalleled- influence/58616/.

15.  "The Preacher's Son Who Became Alice Cooper" (1974).

16.  Devon Stonebrook (2012), "Intersecting Icons: Keith Haring, Madonna, Jean-Michel Basquiat, and Andy Warhol," 21 August. http://www.devonstonebrook.wordpress.com/.../intersecting-icons-keith-haring-mad.

17.  Andrew Morton (2001), *Madonna* (London: St. Martin's Press), 124.

18.  Camille Paglia (1990), "Madonna—Finally, a Real Feminist," *The New York Times*-Opinion (14 December).

19.  Kellie B. Gormly (2012), "Madonna Leads the Way," *Pittsburgh Tribune-Review* (1 November), 2.

20.  Pamela Robertson (1996), *Guilty Pleasures: Feminist Camp from Mae West to Madonna* (London: I.B. Taurus), 123.

21.  Morton (2001), 46.

22.  Robertson (1996), 126–27.

23.  George-Claude Guilbert (2001), *Madonna as Post Modern Myth* (Jefferson, NC: McFarland), 111.

24.  Cathy Schwichtenberg (1993), "Madonna's Postmodern Feminism: Bringing Margins to the Center," in *The Madonna Connection: Representational Politics, Subcultural Identities, and Cultural Theory* (Boulder, CO: Westview Press), 134.

25.  Gormly (2012), 2.

26.  Lady Gaga, "The Fame Tour," http://www.youtube.com/watch?v=Hs1u6jT3q9E.

27.  Pete Samson (2013), "Warhol's Chats with GaGa … in Her Sleep," *The Sun* (29 June): 1, http://www.thesun.co.uk/sol/homepage/showbiz/bizarre/3135455/GaGa-Andy-Warhols-talking-to-me.html.

28.  Dean Piper (2011), "Lady Gaga: There's No Problem with Madonna," *Mirror* (20 November), 1.

29.  Simon Hattenstone (2011), "Lady Gaga: Lording It," *The Guardian* (14 May), 1.

30.  Bill Werde (2011), "Gaga Rebirth an Ongoing Process," *Chicago Sun-Times* (24 February), 1.

31.  Alexis Petridis (2011), "From Yoko Ono to Lady Gaga: How Pop Embraced Performance Art," *The Guardian* (7 July), 1.

32.  Lady Gaga ABC television interview by Barbara Walters (2009), "Ten Most Fascinating People of 2009," New York, 9 December.

33.  Petridis, (2011), 1.

34.  "Lady Gaga." *Voguepedia*.

35.  Derek Van Meter (2011), "Lady Gaga: Our Lady of Pop," *Vogue* (10 February), vogue.com.

36.  "Lady Gaga." *Voguepedia*.

37.  Derek Blasberg (2012), "Lady Gaga: The Interview," *Harper's Bazaar* (13 April).

38.  Ross Kenneth Urken (2010), "Behold the Emperors: Are These New Club Kids Really Like the Old Club Kids?" *Guest of a Guest* (23 November), guestofaguest.com.

39.  Ibid.

40.  Laird Borrelli (2013), "A Monthly Look at Those Who Made History: Grace Jones," style.com (May).

41.  Blue Carreon (2011), "Does Lady Gaga Deserve the CFDA Fashion Icon Award?" *Forbes* (6 June).

42.  Laura Brown (2011), "The Real Lady Gaga," *Harper's Bazaar* (6 September).

43.  Blasberg (2012).

44.  Rachel Dodes (2010), "Lady Gaga Was Alexander McQueen's 'Unofficial Muse,'" *The Wall Street Journal* (11 February).

45.  Alicia Waite (2012), "Giorgio Armani Designs Outfits for Lady Gaga's Asian Tour," *The Telegraph* (19 April).

# Works Cited

Blasberg, Derek. (2012.) "Lady Gaga: The Interview," *Harper's Bazaar* (13 April).

Borrelli, Laird. (2013.) "A Monthly Look at Those Who Made History: Grace Jones," style.com (May).

Brown, Laura. (2011.) "The Real Lady Gaga." *Harper's Bazaar* (6 September).

Buruma, Ian. (2013.) "The Invention of David Bowie." *The New York Times Review of Books* (23 May).

Carreon, Blue. (2011.) "Does Lady Gaga Deserve the CFDA Fashion Icon Award?" *Forbes* (6 June).

Cooper, Alice. (2012.) Interview with Christina Patterson. "Every Word of the Bible Is True." *The Independent* (17 October). http://www.independent.co.uk/arts-entertainment/ music/features/alice-cooper—every-word-of-the-bible-is-true-i-believe-the-old-testament-explicitly–8207597.html.

Dodes, Rachel. (2010.) "Lady Gaga Was Alexander McQueen's 'Unofficial Muse,'" *The Wall Street Journal* (11 February).

Gormly, Kellie B. (2012.) "Madonna Leads the Way." *Pittsburgh Tribune-Review* (1 November).

Guilbert, George-Claude. (2001.) *Madonna as Post Modern Myth*. Jefferson, NC: McFarland.

Hattenstone, Simon. (2011.) "Lady Gaga: Lording It." *The Guardian* (14 May).

Monde, Chiderah. (2013.) "Michael Jackson 1979 Manifesto Reveals Singer's Plan to Become the Most 'Incredible' Entertainer." *New York Daily News* (20 May).

Morton, Andrew. (2001.) *Madonna*. London: St. Martin's Press.

Paglia, Camille. (1990.) "Madonna—Finally, a Real Feminist," *The New York Times*-Opinion (14 December).

Petridis, Alexis. (2011.) "From Yoko Ono to Lady Gaga: How Pop Embraced Performance Art." *The Guardian* (7 July).

Piper, Dean. (2011.) "Lady Gaga: There's No Problem with Madonna." *Mirror* (20 November).

"The Preacher's Son Who Became Alice Cooper." (1974.) *People* vol. 1, no. 5 (1 April).

Robertson, Pamela. (1996.) *Guilty Pleasures: Feminist Camp from Mae West to Madonna*. London: I.B. Taurus.

Samson, Pete. (2013.) "Warhol's Chats with GaGa … in Her Sleep." *The Sun* (29 June). http://www.thesun.co.uk/sol/homepage/showbiz/bizarre/3135455/GaGa-Andy-Warhols-talking-to-me.html.

Schwichtenberg, Cathy. (1993.) "Madonna's Postmodern Feminism: Bringing Margins to the Center." In *The Madonna Connection: Representational Politics, Subcultural Identities, and Cultural Theory*. Boulder, CO: Westview Press.

Simmons, Gene, interview by Terry Gross. (2001.) "Interviews Gene Simmons." National Public Radio, *Fresh Air*. 11 November.

Stevens, Hampton. (2010.) "Michael Jackson's Unparalleled Influence." *The Atlantic* (24 June). http://www.theatlantic.com/ entertainment/archive/2010/06/michael-jacksons-unparalleled- influence/58616/.

Stonebrook, Devon. (2012.) "Intersecting Icons: Keith Haring, Madonna, Jean-Michel Basquiat, and Andy Warhol." 21 August. http://www.devonstonebrook.wordpress.com/.../intersecting-icons-keith-haring-mad.

Urken, Ross Kenneth. (2010.) "Behold the Emperors: Are These New Club Kids Really Like the Old Club Kids?" *Guest of a Guest* (23 November), guestofaguest.com.

Van Meter, Derek. (2011.) "Lady Gaga: Our Lady of Pop," *Vogue* (10 February).

Waite, Alicia. (2012.) "Giorgio Armani Designs Outfits for Lady Gaga's Asian Tour." *The Telegraph* (19 April).

Werde, Bill. (2011.) "Gaga Rebirth an Ongoing Process." *Chicago Sun-Times* (24 February).

Wright, Jade. (2010.) "Gene Simmons Talks Liverpool, The Beatles." *Kiss Online* (9 April). http://www.kissonline.com/news/article/id/23033.

# Masquerades of Alexander McQueen and John Galliano

## DEBORAH BELL

---

"If masquerade costumes disguised one's true identity while covertly expressing hidden desires, much the same could be said of fashionable dress."[1]
—Valerie Steele

The late Alexander McQueen was not the first fashion designer to understand this principle. But he tops the list of designers successful in applying the principle in his practice of
using narratives to inspire his elaborate fashion runway masquerades. Historical- or folkloric-
based accounts served as a primary influence on his runway creations, ultimately drawing strong
interest to his collections. The sheer theatricality of these dramatizations morphed into grand
masquerade presentations that shocked, provoked, and mesmerized his viewers. McQueen's
design predecessor, John Galliano (another graduate of London's Central Saint Martins School
of Art and Design) also used narrative in his work emphasizing spectacle with a notable theatrical, albeit more deconstructive edge.

This essay compares and contrasts the motivations behind their uses of narrative. It also
explains how their separate approaches to narrative affected contrasting notions of theatricality
and masquerade. Both designers gained significant inspiration for their collections from historical, literary, legendary, or operatic figures. Moreover, I will suggest ways in which the curtain
call appearances of the designers also resembled masquerade. Perhaps McQueen's understated
street wear that he wore at his curtain calls functioned more as masquerade than even McQueen
himself would have consciously perceived. Conversely, for several years Galliano presented
himself to the public as an eclectic mix of historic and cultural figures as part of his curtain
calls. At least initially he relished these colorful, raucous, and even gaudy masquerades.

Noël Palomo-Lovinski contrasts the two designers, describing Galliano as a postmodernist
while placing McQueen in the category of "conceptualist." McQueen as conceptualist "saw

clothing as a metaphor for survival, and occasionally examined the complex relationship between victim and aggressor." He repeatedly explored several common themes, "including the relationships between men and women, the tensions between humans and nature, and the dynamics between aggression, anger, and submission."[2] Palomo-Lovinski suggests that McQueen was a "bridge between the old sense of fashion, as seen in his respect for Savile Row tailoring ... as he helped to propel fashion forward in terms of artistic statement and concept."[3] Judith Thurman also recognizes McQueen's conceptualist propensity, noting his "deeper sense of identity with the broken and martyred women who stirred his fantasies, and whom he transfigured." She suggests that "the real agenda of his romance with fragility may have been hiding in plain sight, tattooed on his arm [declaring] ... 'Love looks not with the eyes but with the mind.'"[4] McQueen's vision for the runway invariably attracted considerable attention because of his skill in creating emotional responses to universal issues of identity, aggression, and vulnerability as he created fashion statements more as intellectual commentary rather than as predictable eye candy.

Museum of Modern Art curator Andrew Bolton writes that McQueen's runway shows "suggested avant-garde installation and performance art, [and] provoked powerful, visceral emotions" that "were a consequence of their dramatic scenarios, ... often hinged on subjects that tapped into our cultural anxieties and uncertainties." He placed "particular emphasis on awe and wonder, fear and terror, emotions closely aligned with the concept of the Sublime."[5] His models exemplified the performance art quality of his shows, generally appearing as theatrically masquerading characters from diverse narration rather than simply strutting and showing off his collection. Brenda Polan and RogerTredre describe his fashion shows as "artistic events, sharpened through McQueen's interest in historical references, shot through with spectacle, mystery, violence, tenderness and beauty."[6]

Galliano has also used narrative as inspiration for his work, but differently from McQueen. His interpretations of narrative are more celebratory and light-hearted and less emotional. Lady Amanda Harlech once said that part of what thrilled her (and Galliano's audiences in general) was that

> ... his clothes didn't come out of nowhere. They always had an implicit story, a beyond-just-spectacle theatricality in which Galliano invested each garment with the sense it had been designed not for some abstract size 4 but for an actual, specific woman, a character drawn from history, art, culture, or his imagination—sometimes all at once.[7]

Ingrid Sischy writes that Galliano's 1994–95 collection, which was presented at the mansion of famed Parisian hostess São Schlumberger, reflected East-West dynamics. She describes the entire show as using "basic rolls of black fabric, using both the matte and the shiny sides. Models came out in jackets that morphed into tine kimonos with floral-patterned obi sashes."[8] She acknowledges, however, that his "themes," although "ambitious," could be "superficial," such as when he "reduced the weighty topic of Christianity's 17th-century mission to convert a millennia-old Native American culture" for his 1998–99 Dior Haute Couture Collection into essentially "color versus stark black and white; with *Pocahontas* fringe versus ruffs and ecclesiastical collars; loose shapes versus strict silhouettes."[9] Furthermore, Polan and Tredre cite Galliano biographer Colin McDowell and historian Farid Chenoune in pointing out Galliano's "love of historicism and the exotic allure of Orientalism," as well as his propensity toward "postmodern" design and his frequent "decontextualized" references.[10]

Clearly both designers discovered tremendous potential for unifying as well as inspiring their fashion shows by applying narrative, but ultimately each approached the use of narrative with quite different intentions. McQueen's narratives functioned primarily to unify his message. Andrew Bolton also notes the profoundly autobiographical quality of McQueen's elaborate narratives, especially exemplified in the romantic version of historic narrative found in his *Highland Rape* (1995–96) fashion show and its sequel, *The Widows of Culloden* (2006–07).[11] This might have been one reason why his narratives could provoke such strong emotional responses. In contrast Galliano's narratives have not been autobiographical, and they functioned (at least at Givenchy and Dior) primarily to unify the visual look of his designs.

The *Guardian*'s Imogen Fox wrote, "Some people think a catwalk show is all about the clothes, others think the real spectacle is in the audience, but ... [for] John Galliano ... the best bit of the show is the designer's appearance on the catwalk at the end."[12] During his fifteen years at Dior, Galliano would usually appear at his curtain call as a character that inspired or resembled part of his collection. For example, the theme of one of his haute couture shows was *Madama Butterfly*. He masqueraded as Lieutenant Pinkerton at the end of the showing. But his personal masquerades did not always follow a linear logic. Fox observed, "Sometimes he will take the audience by surprise ... emerging at the end of the show that trumpeted a particularly wearable Joan-of-Arc-meets-punk-rocker look dressed as an astronaut.... You have to hope his tongue is in his cheek."[13]

Neither designer dramatized stories didactically. Seldom could the audience recognize any of their narratives in their entirety. Nathalie Khan describes McQueen's themed narratives as "resisting the temptation to ascribe his shows any obvious or predictable message."[14] Still, McQueen saw significant value in contextualizing narrative as an important avenue that could lead beyond his actual fashion statements toward provocative political or cultural messages for viewer discussion long after the fashion show had ended. Galliano has contented himself with mixing narratives out of context and letting the viewer see whatever s/he wanted to see. Galliano's postmodern approach could more easily lead to pastiche. His approach has not been as message-oriented as McQueen's.

If an artistic experience transports the viewer to another state of reality, then McQueen was surely as much an artist as he was a fashion designer and artisan. Sarah Burton, his longtime assistant, struggled to define McQueen in an interview after his death:

> He used to say, "This is the last big one we're doing," but he couldn't help himself.... He was a showman more than anything. Still, when you think about the way he designed, it did feel more about art. It was never, "oh, is that comfortable?" It was all about the vision and the head to toe look of it. When you saw the models lined up, it was so clear and so direct. Lee [McQueen] was a designer who was making a world and telling a story. Sometimes it was on such a level that maybe the fashion audience wasn't the right audience to tell it to, but what audience was right? That's the problem I think he had. The stigma: Is it fashion? Is it art? ... Lee did care about the commercial side of the industry, but what most people remember are the shows.[15]

Examples from McQueen's uniquely dramatic fashion shows were enthrallingly exhibited at the Metropolitan Museum of Art from May to July in 2011. The frozen figures "masqueraded" (as they would have as models on the runway) as elaborate, contextualized, spectacular "characters," allowing the mannequins on display to project compelling themes and commentary. A number of mannequins wore masks over their faces or as painted/woven detail on their apparel, which McQueen had incorporated in a number of his runway shows.

A typical reviewer of McQueen's work would note the complexities of whatever theme he was working with. For example, Thurman describes highlights of his *Highland Rape* fashion runway as masquerading "bare-breasted disheveled girls [staggering] down the runway (recalled in great detail at the MMA exhibit) in gorgeously ravaged lace, sooty tartan, and distressed leather." She adds, "According to feminist critics, the show eroticized violation. According to McQueen, it commemorated the 'genocide' of his Scottish ancestors."[16]

Galliano had quite different strategies and intentions for incorporating and manipulating narrative in his work. Part of Galliano's genius lies in his ability to add new visual dimensions by assimilating a range of past and present imagery. Pamela Church Gibson cites Colin McDowell and Robert O'Byrne's description of how Galliano "mixes up historical and geographical references, famously putting Naomi Campbell in a ballgown reminiscent of the Belle Époque, but then adorning her face and hair with paint and feathers evocative of a Native American."[17]

Like McQueen's, we can consider Galliano's shows as "themed-collections," and like McQueen, he favored "complex fictional tales with [a] heroine at the centre." But Galliano typically used such narrative as a way of pursuing "flights of fancy"[18] and not necessarily to comment on dark contemporary tensions in society—as McQueen did. Galliano's collections could certainly provoke commentary but essentially as showcases created by a wizard of spectacle. Polan and Tredre observe that Galliano's work could be "laced with unsettling elements and references (although rarely pushed as far as Alexander McQueen)."[19]

Both designers consistently created opulent theatricality in their themed-narrative presentations, though some might consider Galliano's use of theatrical showmanship more blatant. A single Galliano show can comment simultaneously on a range of different historical and cultural references with great wit. His broad understanding of fashion styles will continue to marvelously inform his intense, bombastic runway looks that present characters brought to life with his costumed models displaying astonishing originality and flare. But McQueen demonstrated a more complex understanding of masquerade in his shows, in part by his tendency to create imagery that could be interpreted in a variety of ways, depending on how he exploited the context of his chosen narrative and how viewers might interpret that context.

Galliano's literal sense of theatricality is especially evident in his famed "showstopper" curtain call masquerades. These whimsical masquerading "costume bows" that crowned his fashion shows became legendary. But Ingrid Sischy writes that "by 2007 Galliano ... was dealing with a marked dependency on alcohol and self-medication [and] stopped these "crowd-pleasing performances that had him dressing up as a sailor, a matador, Napoleon, the Marquis de Sade, and Madame Butterfly's Lieutenant Pinkerton. Galliano himself remarked that "what had started out as self-expression turned into a mask." Galliano's persona as an omnipotent celebrity designer was also evolving into a more obvious masquerade. Sischy writes that even though Galliano maintained a charming and polite demeanor, he admitted that "I would be backstage and there would be a queue of five people to help me. One person would have a cigarette for me. The next person would have the lighter. I did not know how to use the A.T.M."[20]

Sischy concludes that Galliano never lost his passion for the work, but that "his sense of [creative] burden increased."[21] The light-hearted masquerading images of Napoleon or Pinkerton finally became formulaic charades. Galliano could no longer support the notion that his artistry in creating these masquerades (and perhaps ultimately his collections) was authentic, improvisatory, and self-driven.

Galliano has presented himself as a celebrity in the manner of many top fashion designers who maintain readily identifiable images that clearly relate to the distinct personae they carefully cultivate. Like Galliano, designers such as Vivienne Westwood, Alber Elbaz, Donatella Versace, and Karl Lagerfeld recognized and embraced the branding power of exaggerating their personae early in their careers. The public immediately recognizes Lagerfeld's signature outfit with his pony-tail, dark, fitted clothing, and glasses. Church Gibson mentions his fan that "has latterly been replaced by extraordinary leather fingerless gloves, and the collars are now high and starched."[22] She describes Alber Elbaz' signature outfit as "a tuxedo jacket, cropped trousers, round-toed shoes and large floppy boy tie," and describes Galliano as a combination of "traditional dandy with the piratical and the tribal through his inventive hairstyling and bold stripes of make-up."[23]

Galliano's brilliant, gregarious personality has allowed him to easily project the splashy, glamorous demeanor of a celebrity designer who publically masquerades with exaggerated clothing effects. His public image has looked much like his illustrious fashion shows: he wears an eclectic range of sexy clothing silhouettes along with hats in white, black and vivid accent colors, varied hair colors (often with the aid of wigs in a range of lengths), often along with a restrained Cavalier moustache and beard.

Unlike many of his flamboyant contemporaries, including Galliano, McQueen seemed content to make his fashion runways the supreme center of his theatrical fashion apparel universe even as he typically presented himself in very casual wear before an adoring—and occasionally perplexed—public. McQueen would never wear either blatant "masquerade attire" or "celebrity attire" at the end of his shows, even though boldly masquerading fashion models theatrically dominated his shows. He preferred understated street clothing, such as black tank shirts, blue work shirts, Dockers, blue jeans, tennis shoes, and the occasional trench coat. No doubt his preference reflected his practical artisan sensibilities, but we might wonder if his casual image subliminally suggests a kind of masquerade. Imogene Fox interprets his curtain calls as resembling "a bad boy, [who] favors running down the catwalk, as if the cops have come for him."[24] McQueen in casual street wear at his curtain calls could conceivably indicate "an outsider's" attempt to simulate a look that could more easily blend in with a crowd on a London or Paris street corner—essentially as a masquerade, though much less obvious as masquerade than Galliano's costume bows.

McQueen generally thought of himself as an outsider and loner more than as a typical urban citizen. He acknowledged his identification with and preference for outsider status in a 2007 *Harper's Bazaar* when he explained that he came to terms with not fitting in a long time ago: "I never really fitted in. I don't want to fit in."[25] He had earlier referred to this notion when he spoke in 2000 about his regrets after taking the major design position at the House of Givenchy in 1996. While acknowledging that he learned a lot about the experience at the atelier, he could not "mold in with the atelier's concept of couture and [its] hierarchy.... I think it looks stupid when designers play these bourgeois characters. At the end of the day, I'm left with the real me. What you see is what you get."[26]

Andrew Bolton cites *Guardian* journalist Alix Sharkey's musings on how McQueen intentionally manipulated messages of authenticity—especially in the fashion world:

> Despite his seeming lack of guile, his what-you-see-is-what-you-get stance, McQueen is a deft and subtle media player. He knows how easy it is, speaking his mind, to send shudders of delight and horror through the kissy-kissy world of fashion—where bitching about others is always done behind their backs.... Beyond this is a need to put others' sincerity to the test. Despite all the mouth and swagger, you can tell McQueen wants to be liked but his insecurity leads him to adopt this spiky, provocative attitude. It's a classic emotional defense mechanism: rather than waiting for someone to disappoint, he provokes them [via his fashion shows] into a hostile reaction, which confirms his worst suspicions and justifies his own behavior.[27]

Drawing on a collection of interviews with people who worked closely with him, Bolton writes that McQueen "wasn't at ease in many social situations." There were times when "the designer's fragility appeared obvious." People talked about him as "a private person," "a closed shop," and observed that he was "increasingly withdrawn" and "more introverted." Even so, many close friends and peers commented over the years that he had a "truly romantic side" that complemented his "dark side."[28] But Judith Thurman ponders the complexities of his "romantic side" when she writes about his retrospective at the MMA, quoting him as saying, "I hate it when people romanticize Scotland." She adds that "The idea of its bleakness, though, seems to have warmed him—it resembled the climate of his mind."[29]

Dramatically contrasting with Galliano's extroverted personality, McQueen's introverted personality could translate into the "dark," "romantic," and often "Sublime-oriented" themes of his fashion shows, making me wonder why he did not present himself to his viewers in some sort of punk attire at the end of his shows. If he were truly authentic, would he not wear apparel that looked "more" the way he "felt?" For example, wouldn't something Gothic and reclusive in appearance be more in line with his feelings of isolation? (His fashion shows frequently indicated dark, Gothic themes.) Or why did he not choose to wear "clothing as armor," like clothes he created for so many of his female heroine/victim characters?

His propensity for wearing ordinary street clothes at the curtain calls of his highly theatrical fashion events created its own unique dramatic contrast. Perhaps he "masqueraded" not by appearing as one of the elite (which he certainly was as a celebrity fashion designer)—nor as an outsider (the persona he generally felt himself to be)—but as one of society's everyday people or as the anonymous artisan persona he felt perhaps most comfortable projecting.

## Conclusion

On the runway, McQueen's narratives, often autobiographical, dramatized emotionally charged themes that were illustrated by the masquerading characters brought to life by his costumed models. At variance with the substance and emotional impact of McQueen's shows is the multi-dimensional beauty and sheer wit found in Galliano's fashion shows, whose narratives project a different type of theatricality. Galliano's runway models also frequently masquerade as characters, but they function to unify his fashion looks rather than to present and unify a message with *gravitas*.

Galliano's "informed" approach on his runways provides as an artistic foil to McQueen's more "emotional and deeply personal" approach. Interestingly, Parsons New School of Design invited Galliano to teach a course in 2013, entitled "Show Me Emotion."[30] Perhaps he intended to explore ways to achieve more emotional and less intellectual responses in his own future shows as he examined these issues with his students.

Ultimately even the public personas of these two contemporary designers can be interpreted as versions of masquerade. McQueen's subdued public persona dramatically contrasted with Galliano's deliberately sparkling, showy public persona. Galliano's image suggests an intentional type of public masquerade, while McQueen's public persona was more nuanced, depending on more subtle messages of how his personal clothing might have suggested or countered hidden traits and intentions.

Claire Wilcox notes that we readily understand the idea of fashion as a "performance," especially within the context of "the elaborate catwalk presentations staged by many a fashion house." But we are less inclined to "recognize the idea of simply wearing fashionable street clothes as performance." She points to Gilbert and George's "living sculpture" shows, which demonstrate the performance aspects of actually wearing street attire, describing how Gilbert and George wear everyday suits (in these living sculpture performances) as they slowly revolve like musical automatons. "While the suits have helped to craft their identity, the concept of how they function while wearing their suits ultimately suggests that life and performance are in many ways, congruent," she concludes.[31]

McQueen's emotional make-up was dark enough—simultaneously romantic and nihilistic—to recognize this congruence. While McQueen's public will continue to speculate regarding the motivations behind his suicide, perhaps he simultaneously feared and yearned for more authenticity and less masquerade in his life and work.

Just as McQueen might have finally succumbed to masquerading fantasies too powerful to ignore or to live with, might Galliano's 2011 staggering public self-destruction have to do with his inability to recognize the emotional repercussions of relying too much on public and private masquerades? The House of Dior suspended him from his $5 million-a-year position after learning of his drunken tirades directed at several patrons on different nights at a Parisian bar. After hurling a series of vicious and vulgar anti–Semitic and racist insults he "reportedly struck his signature runway pose—a bow with a touch of flamenco in it, one hip jutting out, stance ever so proud, albeit wobblier ... and mumbled, 'I am the designer John Galliano!'"[32]

This culmination of his considerable demise, caused in part from years of alcohol and drug abuse, might well have masked anger more with himself than with the people he verbally attacked. Perhaps Galliano, like McQueen (though in opposite ways), had lost sight of the need to savor the artful guise of masquerade while maintaining respect for the consequences of its potential repercussions if taken too seriously—in one's life as well as in one's career.

# Notes

1. Phyllis Galembo (2002), *Dressed for Thrills* (New York: Harry N. Abrams), 12.

2. Noël Palomo-Lovinski (2010), *The World's Most Influential Fashion Designers* (London: Barron's Educational Series), 160.

3. Ibid., 177.

4. Judith Thurman (2011), "Dressed to Thrill," *The New Yorker* (16 May), 119.

5. Andrew Bolton (2011), *Alexander McQueen: Savage Beauty* (New York: The Metropolitan Museum of Art), 12.

6. Brenda Polan and Roger Tredre (2009), "John Galliano," in *The Great Fashion Designers* (New York: Berg Publishers), 245.

7. Ingrid Sischy (2013), "Galliano in the Wilderness," *Vanity Fair* no. 635 (July): 77.

8. Ibid., 78.

9. Ibid., 78, 119.

10. Ibid., 213.

11. Bolton (2011), 14.

12. Imogen Fox (2007), "How Fashion's Big Names Cut a Dash at Their Shows," *The Guardian* (23 January), http://www.theguardian.com/lifeandstyle/2007/jan/24/fashion.imogenfox..

13. Ibid.

14. Nathalie Khan (2000), "Catwalk Politics," in *Fashion Cultures: Theories, Explorations, and Analysis,* Stella Bruzzi and Pamela Church Gibson, eds. (New York: Routledge), 118.

15. Bolton (2011), 231.

16. Judith Thurman (2011), "Alexander McQueen at the Met," *The New Yorker* Dressed to Thrill (16 May), 119.

17. Pamela Church Gibson (2012), *Fashion and Celebrity Culture* (New York: Berg Publishers), 193.

18. Polan and Tredre (2009), 244.

19. Ibid., 213.

20. Sischy (2013), 120.

21. Ibid., 120.

22. Church Gibson (2012), 187.

23. Ibid., 193.

24. Fox (2007).

25. Polan and Tredre (2009), 245.

26. Ibid., 244.

27. Bolton (2011), 18.

28. Ibid., 26.

29. Thurman (2011), "Alexander McQueen at the Met," 116.

30. Thomson Reuters (2013), "John Galliano to Teach Master Class at Parsons," *The Business of Fashion* (22 April), http://www.businessoffashion.com/2013/04/john-galliano-to-teach-master-class-at-parsons.html.

31. Claire Wilcox (2001), *Radical Fashion* (London: V&A Publications), 41.

32. Sischy (2013), 74.

# Works Cited

Bolton, Andrew. (2011.) *Alexander McQueen: Savage Beauty*. New York: The Metropolitan Museum of Art.

Church Gibson, Pamela. (2012.) *Fashion and Celebrity Culture*. New York: Berg Publishers.

Fox, Imogen. (2007.) "How Fashion's Big Names Cut a Dash at Their Shows." *The Guardian* (23 January). http://www.theguardian.com/lifeandstyle/2007/jan/24/fashion.imogenfox.

Galembo, Phyllis. (2002.) *Dressed for Thrills*. New York: Harry N. Abrams.

Khan, Nathalie. (2000.) "Catwalk Politics." In *Fashion Cultures: Theories, Explorations, and Analysis*, Stella Bruzzi and Pamela Church Gibson, eds. New York: Routledge.

Palomo-Lovinski, Noël. (2010.) *The World's Most Influential Fashion Designers*. London: Barron's Educational Series.

Polan, Brenda, and Roger Tredre. (2009.) "John Galliano." In *The Great Fashion Designers*. New York: Berg Publishers.

Sischy, Ingrid. (2013.) "Galliano in the Wilderness." *Vanity Fair* no. 635 (July).

Thomson Reuters. (2013.) "John Galliano to Teach Master Class at Parsons." *The Business of Fashion* (22 April). http://www.businessoffashion.com/2013/04/john-galliano-to-teach-master-class-at-parsons.html.

Thurman, Judith. (2011.) "Alexander McQueen at the Met." *The New Yorker* Dressed to Thrill (16 May).

Thurman, Judith. (2011.) "Dressed to Thrill." *The New Yorker* (16 May).

Wilcox, Claire. (2001.) *Radical Fashion*. London: V&A Publications.

# The Drama of Identity:
# Masking and Evolving Notions
# of Self in Contemporary Photography[1]

## M. Kathryn Shields

In contemporary photo-based work, masking allows artists to subversively, often playfully, challenge accepted norms; to reveal certain elements and conceal others; to assume and then discard roles; and to engage variable, even unstable notions of identity. Shearer West wrote in her 1992 book *Portraiture*:

> During the last decades of the twentieth-century role-playing became prevalent and even more self-conscious. Role-playing has become a method of exploring fluctuating aspects of identity in portraiture, but it has also been used ironically, as a means of undermining the idea that identity can be encapsulated in representation.[2]

Contemporary artworks that employ masking challenge established notions of self and address the fact that identity is dependent on peoples' perceptions, as embodied in the concept of the "social constructions of reality" identified by Peter Berger and Thomas Luckman in 1966.[3]

## Masking as Concept and Artistic Strategy

In order to understand the concept of masking in contemporary art, an historical consideration of the terms "mask" and "masking" may be helpful. A mask is, by definition, a form of disguise. As an object, usually worn over or in front of the face, masks simultaneously conceal and reveal the identity of the wearer. Masks are also frequently conceived to establish another entity during performance.[4] Masks may be seen as objects of deception (as in a façade or an alter-ego) or masks may be viewed as revelatory (a conduit between the physical and supernatural realms). Simply stated, masking is the process of activating a mask

As cultural objects, masks have been used throughout the world in all time periods. They vary in appearance as well as in their use and symbolism. Since its inception, the medium of photography has recorded such masks as reminders of cultural practices and mysticism beyond visual comprehension. Edward S. Curtis, for example, photographed Native Americans from 1900 to 1930. As he documented ways of life passing into extinction due to the westward expansion of European settlers, he captured masks as objects along with ritual clothing and maskers in performance. Curtis's body of work not only gives us access to the physical presence of an entire spiritual realm but also indicates the fascination of such metaphysical potential possible through the ostensibly empirical technology of the camera.

The appearance of a mask often signals the layering of meaning characteristic of both masking and photography. Masking can be literal (showing an actual mask or a face that looks like a mask), technical (involving intentional manipulation), or metaphorical (emphasizing the underlying meaning rather than the surface appearance of the image).[5] Masking in the creation, presentation, and reception of a photograph highlights masquerade as the time in which the image comes to life—when it accrues meaning, engages the imagination, and generates its own reality. As laden with meaning as masking is, its most important characteristics embrace complexity, ambiguity, and mystery.

In his 1991 essay "The Crisis of the Real," Andy Grundberg discusses masking as a key component in postmodern photography: pastiche and simulacrum call attention to "internal inconsistencies" and question the assumptions of dominant discourses, stereotypical notions of identity, and previously accepted modes of image-making.[6] By the same token, Grundberg discusses appropriation as postmodern photography's tendency to "unmask" the complex nature of both form and content.[7]

## Act 1: Diane Arbus, Exploring the Margins (aka "The Grandma")

The work of Diane Arbus has been seminal to the history of photography because of the ways her art deals with identity. This essay will consider her photographs as precursors for two generations of artists working from the 1970s to the present. Arbus made very direct pictures of separate groups of people she called "freaks" and "normals," in the parlance of her time. A preoccupation with notions of identity pervades her work as she interacted with people she found fascinating, resulting in photographic moments of frozen dialogs and visual interactions. As she said,

> Everybody has that thing where they need to look one way but they come out looking another way and that's what people observe. You see someone on the street and essentially what you notice about them is the flaw. It's just extraordinary that we should have been given these peculiarities. And, not content with what we were given, we create a whole other set. Our whole guise is like giving a sign to the world to think of us in a certain way but there's a point between what you want people to know about you and what you can't help people knowing about you. And that has to do with what I've always called the gap between intention and effect. I mean if you scrutinize reality closely enough, if in some way you really, really get to it, it becomes fantastic. You know it really is totally fantastic that we look like this and you sometimes see that very clearly in a photograph. Something is ironic in the world and it has to do with the fact that what you intend never comes out like you intend it.[8]

Her statement indicates a fascination with the "gap between intention and effect," which populates her pictures and allows both visions to exist simultaneously. Her choice of photography as her medium also allows her to focus on the boundary between reality and fantasy in ways that each extreme complicates and compliments the other. People wear masks of both the labels we give them and the labels they give themselves. According to Friedrich Nietzsche, "What things *are called* is incomparably more important than what they are."[9] In Arbus' work, the photograph itself operates as a mask, which literally becomes what we see, whether she depicts a dwarf, a giant, a transvestite, or a masquerader.

Arbus' independent photo career from 1958 to 1971 coincided with the Civil Rights and Second Wave Feminist movements. Groups of people were publically acknowledging individualities in ways that had been previously overlooked. According to scholars Rory Dicker and Alison Piepmeir, 1960s feminist efforts differed from those of the late 19th and early 20th centuries because, "in addition to focusing on attaining social justice and equal rights for women, feminists were inspired by the Civil Rights movement and countercultural protests to critique 'the notion of biological or inherent differences between the sexes, contending instead that these differences are socially constructed.'"[10] Arbus' photographs of people wearing masks actively question some of the binaries that had been culturally entrenched, adding normal/unfamiliar to the feminist male/female dichotomy.

Her photographs of lesbians, transvestites, and hermaphrodites in addition to beauty queens and body builders issue a challenge to societal norms about gender binaries. Even when people are not wearing masks in Arbus' photographs, they seem to be performing their identity because her photographs emphasize the spectacle of unique individuals on display at the same time they capture an everyday quality that could be seen as quite ordinary. Images like *Naked Man Being a Woman* (1968) and *Hermaphrodite and Dog in a Carnival Trailer* (1970) challenge our experience of these individuals, which initially remains on the level of surface observation. At the same time, these pictures suggest how complicated identity truly is, basically subverting or even reversing stereotypical expectations.

Arbus's *Young Man in Curlers at Home on W 20th Street NYC* (1966) directly confronts traditional societal expectations as he confidently looks out at the viewer with his manicured nails and make-up, in a momentary pause during an intimate conversation. In a 1929 essay called "Womanliness as a Masquerade," British psychoanalyst Joan Riviere noted that "Womanliness ... could be assumed and worn as a mask, both to hide the possession of masculinity and to avert the reprisals expected if she was found to possess it."[11] Though she was speaking specifically of women wearing the mask of womanliness, Riviere also noted that in her day, in order to have any position of power, a woman must impersonate a man, transcend existing sexual identification and become what she called a masculine "homosexual woman"[12] or what might later be called a "transvestite."[13] Arbus' subjects have actually moved beyond such a state of repression and openly redefine gender by showing both women and men in feminine and masculine roles.

Arbus was invested in the exploration of difference, both intentional and unexpected, sometimes to the point where revelation borders on exploitation. In order to push the boundaries of "normal," she sometimes stared social definitions in the face. In photographs like *Young Man in Curlers at Home*, the construct of male and female was destabilized by direct engagement with the reality of transgenderism. The photo records a direct interaction between the photographer/viewer and the subject that exemplifies what John Gage has called "confrontational" pose.[14] The dialogue suggested through the "confrontational" composition bespeaks the social and political concerns of the time while inciting further dialogue by raising questions about spectatorship and viewing dynamics.

Although she was clearly impacted by both the feminist and Civil Rights initiatives,[15] Arbus' images were not propaganda. The viewing dynamics she explored were similar to those discussed by feminist scholars in the 1980s, in part because there was not much perceived latitude in terms of representation or viewing agency at the time of feminism's second wave. Viewers were gendered male and women functioned as passive subjects of the male gaze, in keeping with societal power structures.[16] In Mary Ann Doane's 1982 essay "Film and the Masquerade: Theorising the Female Spectator," she explores structures of film in the context of feminist psychoanalysis and proposes that female masquerade is based on the system of repression in which women have no agency within this scenario. Masquerade creates "distance between oneself and [one's] image" and a seeing/ knowing/thinking woman "poses a threat to an entire system of representation."[17]

These limitations were also recognized by critics like Ann Kaplan, who wrote "Is the Gaze Male" in 1983. Kaplan noted that culture in the early 1980s was "deeply committed to clearly demarcated sex differences, called masculine and feminine, that revolve on, first, a complex gaze-apparatus; and second, dominance-submission patterns."[18] She continues, "The problem with all these arguments is that they leave women trapped in the position of negativity— subverting rather than positing."[19] Kaplan ends her essay with a call to "move beyond long-held cultural and linguistic patterns of oppositions: male/female (as these terms currently signify); dominant/submissive; active/passive; nature/civilization; order/chaos; matriarchal/patriarchal."[20]

Arbus' photographs set the stage for later photographers to answer Kaplan's call. As a matter of fact, in the 1970s-80s the feminist movement itself would draw attention to race, ethnicity, class, and sexuality as crucial markers of identity for women, "reminding us that ... not all women's lives and experiences are identical."[21] Ultimately, Arbus was inspired to follow her photography teacher's advice that "a photograph has to be specific," saying, "I remember Lisette Model telling me, 'The more specific you are, the more general you'll be.'"[22]

## Act 2: Cindy Sherman and the Social Construction of Identity

Cindy Sherman represents a subsequent generation of artists that was committed to exploring identity, specifically notions about women that had been generated during and up to the modernist 1950s. While Arbus opened the door to visually exploring difference and non-mainstream individuals, Cindy Sherman turned the camera lens onto herself. As writers like Jennifer Dalton (2000) and Phoebe Hoban (2012) have written, self-portrait photography was forever changed by Sherman's contribution and influence, so much so that a whole new genre emerged from her practice.[23] Sherman is also part of a "generation" of artists working from 1975 to 1990, who used photography to explore femininity as it relates to gender, sexuality, and race by "borrowing iconic representations and stereotyped images from mass culture" to create "ironic signifiers and mediators of female identity."[24] About her work Sherman said,

> I think I was part of a movement, a generation, and maybe the most popular one of that movement at the time, but it probably would have happened without me.... The art world was ready for something new, something beyond painting. A group of mostly women happened to be the ones to sort of take that on, partly because they felt excluded from the rest of the [male] art world, and thought. 'Nobody is playing with photography. Let's take that as our tool.'[25]

The group Sherman refers to was part of second wave feminism and, as Lucy Soutter points out in her 2008 essay "Enigmatic Spectacle," the notion of the postmodern constructed self includes the "potentially freeing ... idea that a woman could present herself wearing a number of masks, and that existing stereotypes might be unmasked along the way." Soutter further explains, "feminist film theorists describe this dynamic as 'masquerade.' The notion of masquerade is potentially subversive and can be extended to encompass characters constructing their own sense of self by playing different roles, trying on different styles."[26]

In the *Untitled Film Stills* series (1977–80) Sherman assumes the guise of Hollywood heroines from fictional films. These pictures reveal the construction of women in the 1950s, through female types that had become readily identifiable by the 1970s, such as housewife, starlet, runaway, country-girl-come-to-the-city, secretary, etc.[27] The story behind these works, though, cannot be as easily understood just by looking at them. From the vantage point of a feminist, Sherman's role-play creates a framework for exploring and critiquing stereotypes about women, their position in society, and the constructions of their identities. Throughout her career Sherman has brought attention to the boundary between physical appearances from "reality" and their representations, not unlike the fascination that the blurring of reality/fantasy held for Arbus. Andy Grundberg asserts that the masks Sherman manufactures for herself in the *Untitled Film Stills* not only "[unmask] ... the conventions ... of *film noir* but also of woman-as-depicted object. The stilted submissiveness of her subject refers to stereotypes in the depiction of women and in a larger way, [question] the whole idea of personal identity, male or female."[28]

In her "History Portraits" series (1989–90), Sherman impersonated works of art, sometimes generally, sometimes specifically. The act of appropriating is important because the creative agency shifts between the artist and the viewer.[29] No longer does the artist illustrate an idea or give the narrative fully formed. The viewer is expected to fill in gaps and make connections. Informed viewers who know that a previous artwork exists and that a reference is being suggested have a very different experience from those who do not notice the connection. In *Untitled #224* (1990) Sherman assumes the appearance of an historically important painting, Caravaggio's *Young Sick Bacchus* (1593–94). *Young Sick Bacchus*, in turn, is Caravaggio's own self-portrait in the guise of the god Bacchus. The masks in both artworks signify a metaphorical layering of meaning and indicate a dialogic relationship embracing and building on historical references rather than denying or downplaying them. Our attention focuses on identity and sexuality (as in the "Untitled Film Stills"). The Bacchus figure is said to be androgynous and in both pictures we are tempted to ask, are we seeing a feminine male or a masculine female? Even though we know Sherman is a woman, the question of gender is not resolved visually. Sherman's self-conscious examination here reveals the self-portraits to be simultaneously the portrait of someone else.

A statement Sherman made in the early 1980s about the *Untitled Film Stills* is also appropriate for the portraits of female types she has made since that time:

> These are pictures of emotions personified, entirely of themselves with their own presence-not of me. The issue of the identity of the model is no more interesting than the possible symbolism of any other detail.... I'm trying to make other people recognize something of themselves rather than me.[30]

Even though she downplays her own presence, it is a fact that informs the image and our experience of it. Similarly, by using photography as her medium she calls attention to both a reality that precedes the creation of the artwork and the artifice involved in its making.

Recalling Arbus' desire to make universal pictures by focusing on individuals, Sherman realized as early as 1982 that she "had to become more specific in details, because that's what makes a person different from other people."[31] Since that time specificity in her work often blurs the distinction between life and art, whether the subjects are derived from film, art, or fairy tales. In some of her more recent work she has continued to engage socially constructed types of women related to contemporary life. Around 2003 Sherman was using neon colors and exaggerated make-up like Ganguro and Yamamba, who provoked Japanese fashion fads of the 1990s. These styles took appearance to the level of an exaggerated disguise, not unlike the type of masking in Sherman's *Clown* series. As she has throughout her career, Sherman embraced stereotypes in order to draw attention to them. In 2011 she used the MAC cosmetics line in a series of promotions photos for the company.[32] In the MAC ads she showcases make-up as a tool for transformation, not relegated to hiding flaws and spots but as an implement for creating a new persona. These pictures do not make her look "beautiful" or "ideal" in the traditional sense but call attention to the masking she has undertaken. More recently Sherman has used incorporated digital technology to create additional masks of multiple selves and disembodied environments.

## Act 3: The Younger Generation—Kimiko Yoshida, Nikki S. Lee, Gillian Wearing, and Jillian Mayer

A third wave of feminism, which began in the 1990s, expanded on the assumption that identity is complex and multifaceted, furthering ideas raised in Sherman's (and other artists') works. Among the broad spectrum of issues existing in the late 20th century are "a world of global capitalism and information technology, postmodernism and post-colonialism, and environmental degradation"[33] About the same time another generation photographers, working from 1990 to at least 2005, combined the generative approaches of role-playing and subjective documentary to portray "truths" about gendered identity.[34] In their essay "Fashioning Feminine Identity in Contemporary American Photography," Susan Sterling and Kathryn Wat state that these younger photographers, following in the wake of Sherman's generation, "have effectively collapsed the old boundaries between postmodern and documentary photography ... without the outright critique of the status quo found in the first generation [feminist's] work."[35] Rather than a bridge, we could see this divide as a focal point, a mask, drawing our attention to the way that photography can both emphasize and question approaches that once seemed antithetical.

## Act 3, Scene i: Brides

Kimiko Yoshida, who was born in Tokyo (1963) and has lived in France since 1995, is part of this younger generation of artists; in our drama of identity it is the third generation. She follows Sherman's example in numerous ways, including her exclusive creation of self-portraits and the elaborate set up for the purpose of making one single photograph. Inspired by the ritual dressing of the bride and the geisha in Japanese culture, she began a full-fledged artistic venture with the picture *Birth of a Geisha* (2001). This photograph shows her in profile applying the distinctive white, red, and black geisha make-up in front of a stark black background. Yoshida explains that make-up in Japan was traditionally intended to make the wearer disappear, to erase identity. Yoshida identifies the use of light as one of the distinctly Japanese qualities of her work: "I have a typically Japanese sensitivity to the way light arrives and settles on an object.... There are no shadows, no contrast, it is extremely flat.... My primary reason for using mono-chromes is to express the infinity of time, timelessness."[36] The square format from her Hassel-blad 6" × 6" camera and the monochromatic palette offer an additional "meditative silence."[37]

Her fascination with the Japanese ritual of crafting appearance led her to explore similar traditions in other countries and she made *Bride* images based on various existing customs and fabricated brides from about 2001–2006. For example in *El Dorado Bride* (2005) she wears ancient Peruvian artifacts borrowed from a museum on a gold ground and in *Afghan Bride* (2005) the black background and chador surround the intricate white lace covering her face. Neither of these brides wears historically accurate regalia, but, in keeping with third wave fem-inism, they draw attention to Yoshida's interest in the individuality of women within the pursuit of set cultural aesthetic standards. According to the catalogue of her self-portraits enti-tled *All That Is Not Me,* "Yoshida truly thinks *identity* does not exist ... there are only *identi-fications*."[38] Similarly, the artist says her own identity is not the focus of these pictures. She

Kimiko Yoshida, *The Bride with the Mask of Herself: Self-Portrait/La Mariée au masque de soi: Auto-portrait*, 2002 (copyright Kimiko Yoshida, reproduced with permission).

"becomes the 'idea of woman' rather than the 'ideal woman.'"[39] By transforming her own identity in light of the cultural identity of women all over the world, "The Intangible Brides" uncover a fabricated world filled with *Nô* masks, Pokémon costumes, Bauta adornments, and fashions created by Paco Rabanne. At the same time, the resulting images are connected to the promise of a deeper truth animating these potentially lifeless objects.

Some of Yoshida's brides acknowledge artistic predecessors and in them she offers her own interpretations. Some sources refer to her series as "Bachelor Brides," referencing Marcel Duchamp's *Bride Stripped Bare by Her Bachelors, Even* (1915–23). *Bachelor Bride Stripped Bare* (2002) consists of a monochromatic white background and veil that are punctuated by the artist's bare breasts. She references other artists in pieces like *The Harlequin Bride: Remembering Picasso* (2006)—which includes the hat, collar, and sad expression characteristic of the *commedia dell'arte* figure that Pablo Picasso returned to throughout his career—in a monochromatic black scene interrupted only by the stark white lips and faint outlines of Yoshida's body and costume. The artistic references convey the accumulated meaning of the images while acquiring a new layer of inquiry into the formation of identity:

> I do recognize in their concentrated, dynamic and universal presence, all the faces of the women I know. In the overturned bubble of Time recaptured, the "Self-Portraits" incorporated all kinds of forgotten rituals and timeless mythologies. ... They take upon themselves the entire history of the portrait and absorb it. "[40]

Several of the brides offer very conceptual references to identity. In *The Bride as a Work of Art* Yoshida's body is encased inside a tube of bubble wrap so thick that we can no longer see her face. The backdrop consists of the same bubble wrap, stamped repeatedly with the word "fragile." The image does not clarify, however, whether the wrapping is protective or a trap. In *The Bride with a Mask of Herself* Yoshida wears a mask printed with her own features, though the mask has been lifted to rest on the top of her head, revealing her face with the same white make-up and red lipstick and covered with a veil. Images like these emphasize the personal nature of Yoshida's brides series. In a 2012 interview Yoshida said:

> Since I fled my homeland to escape the mortifying servitude and humiliating fate of Japanese women, I amplified through my art a feminist stance of protest against contemporary clichés of seduction, voluntary servitude of women, identity and the stereotypes of gender.[41]

Like Arbus's photographs of people wearing masks highlighting the "gap between intention and effect" the lifted mask draws attention to the masking to the self-reflexivity of Yoshida's process and, by extension, the art making process. The reference to identity formation in her work also recalls Sherman's oeuvre and its connection to feminist discourse.

## Act 3, scene ii: Persona

Another member of the present study's younger generation, Nikki S. Lee, was born Lee Seung-Hee in South Korea in 1970. While in graduate school at NYU, Lee was struck by the vast array of U.S. cultural groups compared to the homogeneity of South Korea, which led her to explore a variety of social identities and to invent her own. Jennifer Dalton notes the performative aspect of Lee's work recalls Cindy Sherman's "types," and requires her to "look beyond the surface markings that define us to one another and keep us separated while simultaneously riffing on those very markings."[42]

For the *Projects* series (1997–2001), Lee observed over a dozen groups of people and got to know them well enough to mix in rather than appear as an outsider. Her goal for each of these prolonged interactions was to have a snapshot taken of her with the group in which she appears to be (and is now) a part. Although she told the people she met that she was an artist, not all of them believed her.

Scholars have noted a spiritual component in the approach Lee used for "Projects" series due to its similarity to the Buddhist lack of concern with self. The artist has said, "Essentially life itself is a performance. When we change our clothes to alter our appearance, the real act is the transformation of our way of expression—the outward expression of our psyche."[43] By contrast, Lee's "Parts" series almost aggressively focuses on the individual self, though she is still interested in the formation (and dissolution) of relationships. She carefully staged and set up images rather than having random stranger make a snapshot as she had for "Projects." She also altered the carefully composed pictures after they were taken. The original scenes showed Lee next to another person, presumably a man (in a pool looking up at him, in the back seat of a car looking out the window, or posed for a wedding portrait, on vacation, etc.). In the final versions, the man has been cut out of each picture, leaving her alone, though his former presence is still clear. Like a giant album of bad breakups in which the same woman is featured, the series raises questions about identity being determined by one's relationship status, both during and afterwards.

Lee's 2006 mockumentary *A.K.A. Nikki S. Lee* features the artist in two distinct personae, a quiet intellectual and a bubbly socialite. As Carol Kino pointed out, "both Nikkis are fake."[44] Lee also plays multiple roles in the film: director and subject, interviewer and interviewee. The complexity of the film is compounded by the fact that some scenes are filmed as they actually happened, while others are pure fabrication. Ultimately the reality might be seen as fantasy, yet it might be more accurate to say that fact and fiction inform one another. In her exploration of masquerade Wang Ping noted, "masquerade bridges the gap between fantasy and reality, magic and secularity, taboo and order."[45]

Wang further notes a "magic moment of going beyond the body of the self to enter the other, of blending the two into one," which can also be seen in the various guises Lee takes on. Her "Layers" series (2007–09) includes sketches on Mylar that she commissioned by different street artists all over the world in cities like Rome, Bangkok, Prague, Seoul, and New York. She then created composites of the sketches by layering the set of drawings made in the same location and enlarging them. Like the other artists in the third generation discussed here, Lee's navigations on the border between art and life recall Nietzsche's sentiments in *The Birth of Tragedy*:

> Art is not merely the imitation of the reality of nature, but in fact a metaphysical supplement to the reality of nature.... Tragic myth ... participates in this transfiguring metaphysical purpose of art in general. What does it transfigure? ... Least of all the 'reality' of this phenomenal world, for it says to us: 'Look at this! Look carefully!' It is your life! It is the hour-hand of the clock of your existence![46]

Employing the questioning inherent in postmodern practice, Lee's "Projects," "Parts," *A.K.A. Nikki S. Lee*, and "Layers" together transcend the notion of codifiable identity and our contemplation of it through the vehicle of art. Lee and Yoshida follow in the footsteps of Sherman and Arbus by inspiring us to ask questions rather than become passive receptors of the imagery, the characterizations, and the scenarios they have constructed in their work.

# Act 3, scene iii: Self and Other

A third member of the younger generation of artists is Gillian Wearing (British, born in 1963). In 2003 Wearing created an updated family album in which she plays all the parts. She reconstructed old family photographs of her mother, father, sister, and brother in addition to herself at various ages. The silicone prosthetic masks meticulously copy the facial features of each person, mimicking the appearance of the photograph, whether it was a black and white studio portrait of her mother Jean Gregory as a young woman, or a snapshot of her brother Richard brushing his long hair in his bedroom. *Self-Portrait as My Sister Jane* (2003) is a head-on color portrait from the shoulders up, composed like the "confrontational" posture identified by John Gage and discussed previously in relation to Arbus' photographs. The figure wears a black sweater interlaced with red ribbon, a slight smile, and shoulder length reddish-brown hair that has been curled. The picture is virtually seamless, looking like a direct picture of Jane, until one notices the edges of the mask, especially around the eyes. Also like Arbus, the gaps between reality and artifice are revealed, raising questions about the identity of the subject and about the certainty of our relationship to her. According to Wang Ping, "Simulation is much more dangerous than open defiance. It suggests that law and order, gender and sex, class and hierarchy could be constructed as simulation as well."[47] Not only does this scenario induce possible fear of not being able to tell real from fake, it also indicates a failure to comply with a binary world structure. Masquerade encourages acceptance of situations with less certainty.

Much of Wearing's work deals with social masks by engaging scenarios in which interactions are featured, personal stories are told, and the tension between private and public selves is emphasized. Her shyness has played a big role in artworks she has created. Wearing explained in a 2000 interview, "I'm actually quite a shy person, but I like seeing if you can be able to be more outrageous than you are, being able to be disinhibited, see if you can feel like not being so shy."[48] Her art is thus somewhat of an inversion of her experience in daily life.

In addition to the "confrontational" composition possible through still photography, Wearing also introduces the element of dialogue by using video. The format of a figure looking out of the frame towards the viewer, familiar from Arbus' oeuvre, suggests interaction and dialogue between the subject and the viewer. This

Gillian Wearing, "Self-Portrait as My Sister Jane Wearing," 2003. Framed c-type print, 141 x 116 cm (55 ½ x 45 ⅝ inches) (copyright the artist; courtesy Maureen Paley, London).

scenario has become increasingly common since Arbus' day due to its ubiquity on television (newscasters) and webcam, Skype, and FaceTime interactions. This scenario has become so ubiquitous, in fact, that it was parodied by David Foster Wallace in *Infinite Jest* when he describes "High Definition Masking" developed to offset the stress, or "Video-Physiognomic Dysphoria" induced by video telephone and "teleputer" interfacing.[49] Two of Wearing's series, "Confess all on video. Don't worry you will be in disguise. Intrigued? Call Gillian" (1994) and "Secrets and Lies" (2009), capitalize on the suggestion of interface, though actual interaction is ultimately deferred by the subject's mask and the video format. People wear commercial costume masks and tell their own secrets because their identities are concealed. The stories are very dark and related to events witnessed, sexual deviance, and even murders. Both the individuals and their stories intrigued Wearing: "I'm more interested in how other people put things together, how people can say something far more interesting than I can."[50]

In 1995 Wearing made a video inspired by a chance interaction she had with a woman on a busy city street that had her entire face bandaged. She never knew the woman's actual story, but she could not get the woman out of her mind so she made up one for her. *Homage to the woman with the bandaged face I saw yesterday down Walworth Road* consists of shots taken from two different perspectives along with Wearing's spoken and subtitled narration. In some scenes Wearing impersonates the woman as she walks down a crowded street with her head covered in white bandages. Other shots were taken from a different vantage point, showing the reactions of the people she is passing, recorded by a camera she has hidden from view. Crowds part in front of her, people lean in to stare, they whisper to one another, and shout insults to her as she walks down Walworth Road. Clearly the mystery of the woman's condition and her bravery to face the world captured Wearing's attention. The piece certainly reflects her interests in another manifestation of the gap between intention and effect; as Wearing has said, "I'm transfixed by people that I see that do stand out, whether they want to or not."[51]

Several of Wearing's more recent self-portraits show her embodying the artists she considers her "spiritual family."[52] The composition and appearance of *Me as Andy Warhol in Drag with a Scar* (2010) combines two portraits of Warhol by Richard Avedon and Christian Markos. The stance and resulting image reflect an interest in him as an artist and public personality at the same time highlighting his own fascination with celebrity and surface. Wearing adopted a similar framework for *Me as Diane Arbus* (2008), with a white backdrop and Arbus' characteristic Rolleiflex in hand. Like the "Family Album" pictures, the masks emulate facial definition with an eerie accuracy. Wearing brings their pictures to life only to have them frozen in a new photograph all the while announcing the impersonation in the very slight misalignments of the mask on the cheeks or near the eyes.

Three years before she made the tribute self-portrait, Wearing emulated Arbus's style in *To Diane Love Gillian (Homage to Diane Arbus)*. She met a young teenage biker girl in Southend on Sea and restyled her to recreate the look and feel of a 1960s Diane Arbus street portrait. Like a composite of several of Arbus's photographs (the woman in *A Young Brooklyn family going for a Sunday outing, N.Y.C.* (1966) and *Blond Girl with Shiny lipstick, N.Y.C.* (1967), the resulting photograph was made using the same medium format Rolleiflex camera with flash that Arbus used. One reviewer wrote: "The resulting portrait is remarkable in capturing the same sense of intimacy and exposure that Arbus was known for. Both an inspiration and influence on Wearing's work, this photograph is a true homage to the continued legacy of Diane Arbus."[53]

# Act 3, scene iv: Self-Portrait, Future Tense

The fourth artistic granddaughter in our drama is Jillian Mayer (Miami-based artist born in 1984). Her video "I Am Your Grandma" premiered at the Borscht Film Festival on April 23, 2011. It subsequently went viral. By October 2011 it was viewed over two and a half million times on YouTube[54]; featured on the TV Show "Web Soup"; parodied in two YouTube videos called "I Am Your Father" and "I Am Your Lawyer"; and "officially" remixed by Limp Bizkit's Wes Morland. "I Am Your Grandma" is a montage of 13 repeated scenes in which the artist wears a selection of masks along with elaborate costumes. The introductory dialogue and narrative of the video indicate that the woman is making a video diary for a future unborn grandchild:

> One day, I'm gonna have a baby. And you will call her mom. That baby will have a baby and you will have this song to know that I am your grandma.... This is a gift I give to you, like I already said, that there was a time I was aware that one day I'd be dead.... I wish we could have met, I would have loved you so, but you are in the future, you get love by video. I am your grandma....[55]

In each clip, Mayer's modulated voice says a line of the catchy song as she makes corresponding gestures. The plain backdrop and confrontational pose correspond to those seen frequently in the work of Arbus, Sherman, Yoshida, and Wearing (also in Lee's "Layers"). A distinct difference for this project is the medium of video, which allows a series of still images to come together in one piece. The suggestion of interaction becomes even more fully realized with the added components of music, the passage of time, and interspersing of images.

Mayer was inspired to make this piece after spending time with a close family member who is obsessed with genealogy and ancestry.[56] The family member had a program that traced their family lineage back to the 1700s and presented small glimpses of all these people: "Martin, a butcher, married to a seamstress." As the accounts got more contemporary there was more information and eventually photos illustrating members of the family tree. Mayer started thinking about who these people were and wondering what aspects of themselves they passed on. There was one photo of "this lady with a smirk" and when she saw it Mayer thought, "she must have been funny ... maybe that's where my kookiness comes from."[57] She also realized that we generally only know our grandparents as old. Mayer wondered about the life her ancestors had before they became those older relatives. She wishes she had a way to know who they were as people, so she decided to use technology to tap into that curiosity and foster a connection. Her "Video Diary" might tell her future family something about who she was in her late 20s. She also happened to work for a friend's entertainment company and dressed up for parties for side money, so the idea of masks and costumes made sense.

Mayer intended her appearance to be non-traditional and so she used crazy masks that are startling, even shocking. When asked about the masks, she said that many of them were based on styles she "hadn't seen too much of."[58] For Mayer "It is more about image and identity shifting and not as much about the masks."[59] As each of the 13 masks is shown, some of the spoken words resonate with deeper meaning. We can however, uncover myriad meanings in the masks that represent an array of possibilities for identity, including playful, fun, sad, emergent, dark, historical, glitzy, potential, and forgotten.

There are numerous art historical references embedded in the video. While she says the word "video," she wears a brightly colored, neon-painted face in blacklight with a distinctively-shaped yellow hat recalling Picasso's Harlequin (also referenced in Kimiko Yoshida's *Brides* series). There is a direct quotation of Edvard Munch's *The Scream* in her gesture as she tilts

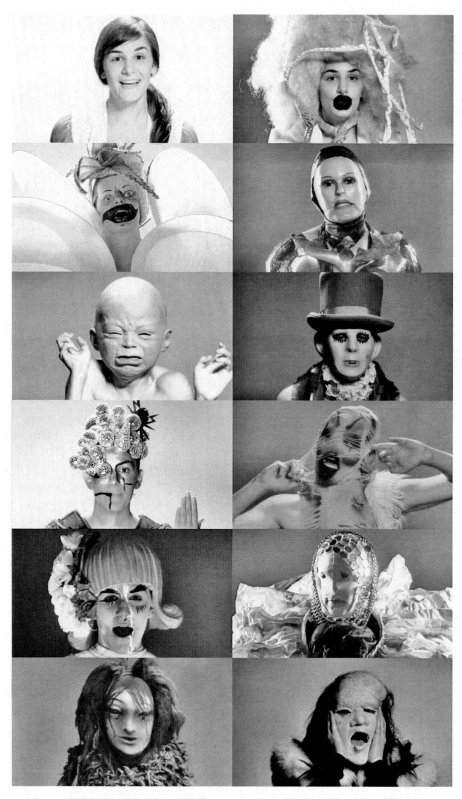

Jillian Mayer, stills from "I Am Your Grandma," 2011, video, 1 minute, edition of 5 (courtesy the artist and David Castillo Gallery, Miami, Florida).

her head and holds the side of the mask while she says "dead." This mask has a markedly more neutral palette, in keeping with the face itself rather than the overall scene in Munch's iconic painting, known for its vibrant color. A skin-like mask she stretches to the sides away from her face at the word "said" might reference an illustration by Gerald Scarfe for Pink Floyd's "The Wall" in which the screaming face seems to morph at the sides and smaller screaming faces appear to echo in the mouth.

The first mask to appear in the video shows up several times along with the lines "and you will call her mom," again (with eyes closed) "and you will have this song." In this mask Mayer wears a giant off-white wig wrapped haphazardly with frilly white satin wire, a bright red necktie inside the collar of her white shirt and bold black lipstick. This mask bears a direct resemblance to "The Apprentice" character played by Barney in his film *Cremaster 3*. The ninth mask, where a flesh colored cloth covers her face, is surrounded by mirrored disks and a giant purple ruff that flares out around her neck. It accompanies the words "So this is a gift I give to you." This image recalls Lady Gaga's "Eternal Mother" character from her video for "Born this Way." While some of these references were surely intentional, others were likely the result of being raised in a culture saturated with fictional characters and media images. As Mayer noted of her childhood, "Growing up I was over saturated with cartoons and sitcoms. I had much difficulty separating the dilemmas of real life with those from scripts of mock families crafted for my weekly entertainment."[60]

Mayer explained the individual masks were not that important to her, but noted that the one surrounded by white fans and bold turquoise headdress has a name. "I call that one Coral because it looks like corallimorphs, a specific type of coral that my scientist friends research in their lab that is known for cloning itself."[61] It turns out that corals are marine animals that look like plants, thus using disguise as a survival strategy. This organism has interesting implications for the malleability of identity and image shifting so crucial to this piece. In addition to criss-crossing the boundaries of fact and fiction, Mayer engages the mediated nature of contemporary culture. Like the other cast members of the Drama of Identity, the identity of the subject as the artist is equally important in "I Am Your Grandma," yet she is fabricating a story about herself in the present to be told to unborn relatives, intentionally projecting her own personal narrative into the future.

During her October 2013 residency at Elsewhere Art Collaborative in Greensboro, Mayer discussed the importance of "technology to deal with identity" as a means of "legacy leaving" to more intentionally impact the digital and virtual self that determines what "your great grandchildren will know about you."[62] The metanarrative of Mayer's 2011 video *Giving Birth To Myself* even more directly evokes the recently coined the term "parafiction, " which describes a whole category of artwork that resides on the boundary between fact and fiction with each mode enhancing and shaping the other. In the video Mayer took the videotape of her own birth, superimposed her face over her mother's, and transcribed/rewrote the script spoken by her parents.[63] Art historian Carrie Lambert-Beatty defines "parafiction" in a 2009 essay:

> ... like a paramedic as opposed to a medical doctor, a parafiction is related to but not quite a member of the category of fiction as established in literary and dramatic art. It remains a bit outside.... [Parafiction] has one foot in the field of the real. Unlike historical fiction's fact-based but imagined worlds, in parafiction real and/or imaginary personages and stories intersect with the world as it is being lived. Post-simulacral, parafictional strategies are oriented less toward the disappearance of the real than toward the pragmatics of trust. Simply put, with various degrees

of success, for various durations, and for various purposes, these fictions are experienced as fact."[64]

As a method of defining, examining, and questioning identity, parafiction threatens to destabilize certainty. Narratives employing parafiction, like the ones in the present study, embrace play and ambiguity as generative forces rather than considering them contradictions to authentic "reality." Reminiscent of storytelling, identity no longer has to be relegated to past actions or even to verifiable events.

## Dénouement

In the Drama of Identity, metaphorical masking in contemporary art is often indicated by the presence of a mask. In addition, the artists' work roughly corresponds to the three waves of feminism. Diane Arbus set the stage by calling our attention to the "gap between intention and effect." She utilized structuralist binaries prominent at the time of the First Wave in order to call them into question, making the perceptive viewer aware of the biases and inequities rampant in society, perhaps in the hopes of inspiring change. Cindy Sherman followed suit by turning the camera on herself and exploring the nuanced nature of identity. In her work both, the presentation and the interpretation of self are revealed to be multiple and complex, bringing to life the Second Wave's realization that gender roles are in fact socially constructed. The younger generation in this narrative—represented here by Kimiko Yoshida, Nikki S. Lee, Gillian Wearing, and Jillian Mayer—further the investigation of personal, social, and artistic identity.

This younger generation of contemporary artists is part of a wider circle that "recognize that they are speaking with a constructed voice, mediated by internal needs and external demands along an axis between a realized and idealized self."[65] Their work calls attention to the fact that "understanding one's role and its mutability in the face of the world at large—a significant aspect of identity formation—has been central to the art and social function of contemporary American photography from the 1980s to the present day."[66] Yoshida defines herself through cultural investigation or ritual practice across the globe, past, present, and imagined—while Lee assumes different personae to suggest fictional possibilities that expand on her own identity and experience. Wearing recreates the visage of close family members at different times in their lives and cathartically engages the secrets of disguised strangers. Mayer proposes a fabricated self of the future that reflects the dynamism of contemporary life, technology, and popular culture. These artists embrace the multiplicity not always visible in reality. In her examinations of masquerade, Wang Ping noted:

> The point is that on the stage of the masquerade the enigma is not about who or what is hiding under the outward appearance. When the mask falls, it reveals nothing but the very fact of the masquerade itself. All the value and meaning of the mask reside on the surface alone: it is the coexistence of masculine and feminine, the original and reproduction, the real and simulacrum, all in one single body, the body that is neither male nor female, the belongs to the space of desire.[67]

In this family of artworks, masking is used a metaphor to self-consciously reference the malleability of identity (both gendered and non-gendered), representation and the act of art-making, and a simultaneous emphasis on both underlying meaning and surface appearance.

# Notes

1. Some of the research in this essay has been presented at Weatherspoon Art Museum, December 1, 2011, as part of the programming for the "Persona: A Body in Parts" exhibition; during an Alumni Workshop at Virginia Commonwealth University on March 22, 2013; and in a public lecture at Virginia Tech December 3, 2013. I am grateful for a 2012 Guilford College Faculty Research Grant that enabled research for portions of this essay.

2. Shearer West (1992), *Portraiture* (New York: Oxford History of Art), 206.

3. See further, Peter L. Berger and Thomas Luckman (1966), *The Social Construction of Reality: A Treatise on the Sociology of Knowledge* (New York: Anchor Books, Doubleday).

4. See further, David Napier (1986), *Masks, Transformation, and Paradox* (Los Angeles: University of California Press).

5. See further, M. Kathryn Shields (2001), "Masking and the Art of Diane Arbus and Ralph Eugene Meatyard," PhD Thesis, Virginia Commonwealth University; and M. Kathryn Shields (2005), "Masking," *Encyclopedia of Twentieth-Century Photography* (New York: Routledge).

6. Andy Grundberg (1990), "The Crisis of the Real: Photography and Postmodernism," in *Crisis of the Real: Writings on Photography Since 1974* (New York: Aperture), 7–9.

7. Ibid., 9.

8. Diane Arbus (1972), *Diane Arbus* (New York: Aperture), 1–2.

9. Friedrich Nietzsche (1882), *The Gay Science: With a Prelude in Rhymes and an Appendix of Songs*, Book 2, section 57, translated with commentary by Walter Kaufmann (1989) (New York: Vintage Books), 121.

10. Rory Dicker and Alison Piepmeir (2003), "Introduction," *Catching a Wave: Reclaiming Feminism for the 21st Century* (Boston: Northeast University Press), 9.

11 Joan Riviere (1929), "Womanliness as a Masquerade," *International Journal of Psychoanalysis* 10: 306.

12. Ibid., 305.

13. Mary Anne Doane (1982), "Film and the Masquerade: Theorising the Female Spectator," *Screen* 23, 3–4: 81.

14. John Gage (1997), "Photographic Likeness," in *Portraiture: Facing the Subject*, Joanna Woodall, ed. (New York: Manchester University Press), 125.

15. See, for example, Diane Arbus's photographs Peace Protesters Passing through New Jersey (published in Esquire, November 1962) and Germaine Greer/Feminist in Her Hotel Room (1971).

16. Laura Mulvey (1975), "Visual Pleasure and Narrative Cinema," *Screen* 16, 3 (Autumn): 6–18.

17. Doane (1982), 82–83.

18. E. Ann Kaplan (1983), "Is the Gaze Male?" *Women and Film: Both Sides of the Camera* (New York: Routledge), reprinted in E. Ann Kaplan, ed. (2004), *Feminism & Film* (New York: Oxford University Press), 129.

19. Ibid., 130.

20. Ibid., 135.

21. Dicker and Piepmeir (2003), 9.

22. Arbus (1972) *Diane Arbus*, n.p. Also referenced in Patricia Bosworth (1984), *Diane Arbus: A Biography* (New York: Knopf), 305. Arbus's often-quoted statement about Model's advice was transcribed from a tape made by Arbus's student. According to *Diane Arbus: Revelations*, "Ikko Narahara ... The class was given from January to March 1971 in a public room at Westbeth, the artist's residence where Diane lived in New York City" (*Diane Arbus: Revelations* [New York: Random House, 2003], 332). According to Bosworth, Model stressed that "the most mysterious thing is a fact clearly stated" (Bosworth, 187).

23. See Jennifer Dalton (2000), "Look at Me: Self-Portrait Photography after Cindy Sherman," *PAJ: Performance Art Journal* 22.3, 200: 47–56; and Phoebe Hoban (2012), "The Cindy Sherman Effect," *ARTnews*, 111.2 (February): 76–85.

24. Susan Fisher Sterling (2008), "Preface," in *Role Models: Feminine Identity in Contemporary American Photography* (Washington, D.C.: National Museum of Women in the Arts), 7.

25. Hoban, 76.

26. Lucy Soutter (2008), "Enigmatic Spectacle: Key Strategies in Contemporary Staged Photography," in *Role Models: Feminine Identity in Contemporary American Photography* (Washington, D.C.: National Museum of Women in the Arts), 11–22.

27. See Untitled Film Still # 35, Untitled Film Still #10, Untitled Film Still #7, Untitled Film Still #48, Untitled Film Still #21, and Untitled Film Still #5.

28. Grundberg (1990), 8.

29. Michael Baxandall (1985), *Patterns of Intention: On the Historical Explanation of Pictures* (New Haven: Yale University Press), 58–62.

30. Cindy Sherman (1982), "Untitled Statement," *Documenta* 7 (Kassel: Documenta), 411; reprinted in *Theories and Documents in Contemporary Art: A Sourcebook of Artists' Writings* (1996), Kristine Stiles and Peter Selz, eds. (Berkeley: University of California Press), 791.

31. Cindy Sherman (1982), "Interview with Els Barent," in *Cindy Sherman* (Munich: Schirmer and Mosel); reprinted in *Theories and Documents of Contemporary Art*, 793.

32. Her previous ad campaigns include Balenciaga and Marc Jacobs.

33. Dicker and Piepmeir (2003), 10.

34. Sterling, 7.

35. Susan Fisher Sterling and Kathryn A. Wat (2008), "Fashioning Feminine Identity in Contemporary American Photography," in *Role Models: Feminine Identity in Contemporary American Photography* (Washington, D.C.: National Museum of Women in the Arts), 40.

36. Kimiko Yoshida (2006), interview with Barbara Oudiz, *Eyemazing*, http://www.kimiko.fr/text/16-meeting-with-kimikoby-barbara-oudiz-eyemazing-2006/.

37. Ibid.

38. Jean-Michel Ribetts (2007), "All That's Not Me," translated by Charles Penwarden, in *Kimiko Yoshida: All That's Not Me* (Arles, France: Actes Sud), not paginated.

39. Yoshida (2006), interview with Barbara Oudiz.

40. Ribetts (2007).

41. Myles Little (2012), "Ceremonies of Disappearance: Kimiko Yoshida's Critique of Identity," *Time Lightbox* (June 19), http://lightbox.time.com/2012/06/19/ceremonies-of-disappearance-kimiko-yoshidas-critique-of-identity/#ixzz2ba6ONasV.

42. Dalton (2000), 47 and 49.

43. Nikki S. Lee, "Nikki S. Lee," Museum of Contemporary Photography, http://archive.mocp.org/collections/permanent/lee_nikki_s.php.

44. Carol Kino (2006), "Now in Moving Pictures: The Multitudes of Nikki S. Lee," *The New York Times* (1 October): Art & Design.

45. Ping Wang (2002), "Fabric of Masquerade," *Aching for Beauty: Footbinding in China* (New York: Anchor), 200.

46. Friedrich Nietzsche (1872), *The Birth of Tragedy*, reprinted in *The Philosophy of Nietzsche* (1927) (New York: The Modern Library), 1084.

47. Wang (2002), 220.

48. Miranda Sawyer (2000), "Daring Wearing," *The Guardian/The Observer*, 6 September.

49. David Foster Wallace (2006), *Infinite Jest* (New York: Back Bay Books), 144–151.

50. Gillian Wearing (1999), "Donna De Salvo in Conversation with Gillian Wearing," in *Gillian Wearing* (London: Phaidon), 11.

51. Gillian Wearing (2000), in Miranda Sawyer, "Daring Wearing," *The Guardian/The Observer*, 6 September.

52. www.artonair.org.

53. http://www.countereditions.com/diane-love.

54. There had been 2,527,440 views on November 22, 2013.

55. Jillian Mayer (2011), lyrics from "I Am Your Grandma."

56. Jillian Mayer, interview with the author, 27 November 2011.

57. Ibid.

58. Ibid.
59. Ibid.
60. Amanda Cruz (2011), "Jillian Mayer's Love Trip, November 2011-February 2012," *World Class Boxing: Exhibitions*, http://www.worldclassboxing.org/exhibit_love_trip.php.
61. Jillian Mayer (2011), e-mail to author, 27 November. See www.coralmophologic.com for more information.
62. Jillian Mayer (2013), Artist Talks at Elsewhere Art Collaborative, Greensboro (October 4 and 16).
63. Ibid.
64. Carrie Lambert-Beatty (2009), "Make-Believe: Parafiction and Plausibility," *October* 129 (Summer), 54.
65. Sterling and Wat, 43. See this essay for further similarities to a 2008 exhibition called *Role Models* at the National Museum of Women in the Arts.
66. Ibid.
67. Wang (2002), 228.

# Works Cited

Arbus, Diane. (1972.) *Diane Arbus*. New York: Aperture.
Arbus, Diane. (2003.) *Diane Arbus: Revelations*. New York: Random House.
Baxandall, Michael. (1985.) *Patterns of Intention: On the Historical Explanation of Pictures*. New Haven: Yale University Press.
Berger, Peter L., and Thomas Luckman. (1966.) *The Social Construction of Reality: A Treatise on the Sociology of Knowledge*. New York: Anchor Books, Doubleday.
Bosworth, Patricia. (1984.) *Diane Arbus: A Biography*. New York: Knopf.
Cruz, Amanda. (2011.) "Jillian Mayer's Love Trip, November 2011-February 2012." *World Class Boxing: Exhibitions*, http://www.worldclassboxing.org/exhibit_love_trip.php.
Dalton, Jennifer. (2000.) "Look at Me: Self-Portrait Photography after Cindy Sherman." *PAJ: Performance Art Journal* 22.3, 200: 47–56.
Dicker, Rory, and Alison Piepmeir. (2003.) "Introduction." In *Catching a Wave: Reclaiming Feminism for the 21st Century*. (Boston: Northeast University Press).
Doane, Mary Anne. (1982.) "Film and the Masquerade: Theorising the Female Spectator." *Screen* 23, 3–4.
Gage, John. (1997.) "Photographic Likeness." In *Portraiture: Facing the Subject*, Joanna Woodall, ed. New York: Manchester University Press.
Grundberg, Andy. (1990.) "The Crisis of the Real: Photography and Postmodernism." In *Crisis of the Real: Writings on Photography Since 1974*. New York: Aperture.
Hoban, Phoebe. (2012.) "The Cindy Sherman Effect." *ARTnews*, 111.2 (February): 76–85.
Kaplan, E. Ann. (1983.) "Is the Gaze Male?" *Women and Film: Both Sides of the Camera*. New York: Routledge.
Kaplan, E. Ann, ed. (2004.) *Feminism & Film*. New York: Oxford University Press.
Kino, Carol. (2006.) "Now in Moving Pictures: The Multitudes of Nikki S. Lee." *The New York Times* (1 October), Art & Design.
Lambert-Beatty, Carrie. (2009.) "Make-Believe: Parafiction and Plausibility." *October* 129 (Summer): 51–84.
Little, Myles. (2012.) "Ceremonies of Disappearance: Kimiko Yoshida's Critique of Identity." *Time Lightbox* (June 19), http://lightbox.time.com/2012/06/19/ceremonies-of-disappearance-kimiko-yoshidas-critique-of-identity/#ixzz2ba6ONasV.
Mayer, Jillian. (2011.) E-mail to author, 27 November.
Mayer, Jillian. (2011.) Interview with the author, 27 November.
Mayer, Jillian. (2013.) Artist Talks at Elsewhere Art Collaborative, Greensboro (October 4 and 16).
Mulvey, Laura. (1975.) "Visual Pleasure and Narrative Cinema." *Screen* 16, 3 (Autumn): 6–18.
Napier, David. (1986.) *Masks, Transformation, and Paradox*. Los Angeles: University of California Press.

Nietzsche, Friedrich. (1872.) *The Birth of Tragedy*, reprinted in *The Philosophy of Nietzsche.* 1927. New York: The Modern Library.

Nietzsche, Friedrich. (1882.) *The Gay Science: With a Prelude in Rhymes and an Appendix of Songs,* Book 2. Translated with commentary by Walter Kaufmann. 1989. New York: Vintage Books.

Ribetts, Jean-Michel. (2007.) "All That's Not Me." Translated by Charles Penwarden, in *Kimiko Yoshida: All That's Not Me.* Arles, France: Actes Sud.

Riviere, Joan. (1929.) "Womanliness as a Masquerade." *International Journal of Psychoanalysis* 10.

Sawyer, Miranda. (2000.) "Daring Wearing." *The Guardian/The Observer* (6 September).

Sherman, Cindy. (1982.) "Interview with Els Barent." In *Cindy Sherman.* Munich: Schirmer and Mosel.

Shields, M. Kathryn. (2001.) "Masking and the Art of Diane Arbus and Ralph Eugene Meatyard." PhD Thesis, Virginia Commonwealth University.

Shields, M. Kathryn. (2005.) "Masking." In *Encyclopedia of Twentieth-Century Photography.* New York: Routledge.

Soutter, Lucy. (2008.) "Enigmatic Spectacle: Key Strategies in Contemporary Staged Photography." In *Role Models: Feminine Identity in Contemporary American Photography.* Washington, D.C.: National Museum of Women in the Arts.

Sterling, Susan Fisher. (2008.) "Preface." In *Role Models: Feminine Identity in Contemporary American Photography.* Washington, D.C.: National Museum of Women in the Arts.

Sterling, Susan Fisher, and Kathryn A. Wat. (2008.) "Fashioning Feminine Identity in Contemporary American Photography." In *Role Models: Feminine Identity in Contemporary American Photography.* Washington, D.C.: National Museum of Women in the Arts.

Stiles, Kristine, and Peter Selz, eds. (1996.) *Theories and Documents in Contemporary Art: A Sourcebook of Artists' Writings.* Berkeley: University of California Press.

Wallace, David Foster. (2006.) *Infinite Jest.* New York: Back Bay Books.

Wang, Ping. (2002.) "Fabric of Masquerade" In *Aching for Beauty: Footbinding in China.* New York: Anchor.

Wearing, Gillian. (1999.) "Donna De Salvo in Conversation with Gillian Wearing." In *Gillian Wearing.* London: Phaidon.

West, Shearer. (1992.) *Portraiture.* New York: Oxford History of Art.

Yoshida, Kimiko. (2006.) Interview with Barbara Oudiz. *Eyemazing.* http://www.kimiko.fr/text/16-meeting-with-kimikoby-barbara-oudiz-eyemazing-2006/.

# The (Super) Hero's Masquerade

## RON NAVERSEN

Contemporary America's most prevalent exposure to masks and masquerades is in the form of fictional superheroes. The appearance of Superman in *Action Comics*[1] spawned a wave of costumed mystery men, women, children (even pets) as gaudily clad, masked defenders of the weak and oppressed. These costumed crime fighters, along with their rogues gallery of super villains, appear in comic books, newspaper strips, graphic novels, short stories, novels, web blogs, literary criticism, cartoons, television shows, wide screen movies, direct sale videos, pop songs, posters, stickers, trading cards, video gaming, toys, action figures, bed linens, t-shirts and clothing, lunch boxes, candy wrappers, fast food packaging, stationary supplies, parades, Halloween costumes, Cosplay conventions[2] and even two hit Broadway musicals. In his *The Myth of the Superhero* Marco Arnaudo speculates that there are between 2,471,040 and 2,851,200 pages of comic book stories from the two mainstream publishing giants DC and Marvel Comics.[3] Considering the superhero genre is a relatively recent phenomena (Superman is just celebrating his 76th anniversary this year), this is an astounding feat of storytelling and art. Add to Arnaudo's calculations the scores of characters and stories by the smaller publishing houses, animated cartoons, and all the other venues the superhero genre migrated to has resulted in a a rich, intricate, often contradictory mythology that rivals the combined works of Greek, Norse, Asian, African and Native American mythologies, especially since the pantheons of these myths were and continue to be a fruitful source of many characters for the comics.

Originally conceived as cheap escapist entertainment for young boys, single issues of the National Comics Publishing Company's (now DC Comics) *Action Comics* and *Superman* sold over a million copies at the height of its popularity. The market demanded and the publishing **industry** (emphasis mine) rallied to supply hundreds of characters and stories "in a never ending battle for truth, justice and the American way."[4] Literary and artistic merits of these early comic books aside, their stories tapped into the wish fulfillment fantasies of scores of powerless children allowing them to imagine themselves as mighty heroes. This was especially true of little Billy Batson who just by speaking the magic word "Shazam" was transformed into "earth's mightiest mortal": Captain Marvel.[5]

As the first generation of superhero-inspired child readers grew to adulthood some followed their dreams creating their own gaudily clad heroes for the flourishing comics industry. Each succeeding generation advanced the genre by creating new champions and scoundrels embellishing and reinterpreting older protagonists to create a fertile and extensive superhero mythos. But why is America in the throes of the current "superheromania"?

The comic book's genesis lies in the ancient cave paintings of the Trois-Frères and Lascoux, Egyptian hieroglyphics, Greek and Roman bas-relief friezes, and stained glass windows of gothic cathedrals. These visual forms of storytelling depicted hunters, warriors, kings and gods in significant societal events through static dumb show. With the modern printing press the comic book combined images with words to create a unique form of storytelling filled with dialogue, narration, and colorful action. Film took these series of still images and projected them rapidly in succession onto a screen creating the illusion of motion complete with soundtrack.

In his blog *Beyond the Veil, The Mask of the Superhero: Ritual Portrayal in the Comics,* Joe Muszynski provides a persuasive and fascinating argument that America has turned to its entertainments including comic books and movies as a source for myth and ritual experience to fill a need in our daily lives. Muszynski quotes from noted crime author, Harold Schechter's *The New Gods: Psyche and Symbol in Popular Art,* "Far from being 'mindless escapism' or 'worthless junk,' popular art is a projection of the collective unconscious—an expression of the deepest, myth-producing level of the human psyche."[6]

When the Western cowboy genre was popular, American children loaded their Red Ryder BB-guns while slipping on their cowboy boots and white hats to battle black-hearted (and hatted) desperados. With the coming of World War II, they put on plastic combat helmets, lined up their toy army soldiers and waged fierce battles in the backyard sandbox. Now with the ascendance of superheroes as leading characters in blockbuster movies, hit TV shows, video games and adult-oriented comic books and graphic novels these meta-human marvels have become the latest exemplars of our archetypal heroes. Who among us hasn't fantasized about "leaping tall buildings with a single bound"[7] or drinking a super serum to become Captain America "the first Avenger"?[8] But we no longer need to pin a simple red towel to our t-shirts to become Superman. Children and adults can purchase fully equipped costumes complete with padded muscles, molded masks and props to become Captain America, Batman, Thor, Iron Man, Wonder Woman, Supergirl or any number of costumed crime fighters and villains. And we do this because?

In our contemporary society where the individual seems to have little power over the corporate, political, and cultural tides, acts of viewing, playing, and becoming the powerful hero or wily anti-hero give us a sense of hope and some measure of control. The ongoing battle between good and evil helps provide a mythic experience. Muszynski blogs that "When readers interact personally with a text as closely as reading a comic, utilizing the built-in structure of gaps between panels to interject their own thoughts into the narrative ... such works function in a manner similar to classic myths."[9] Perhaps television, film and video gaming versions of these costumed adventurers fill imaginative gaps for their viewers preventing us from participating as fully as Muszynski suggests. However the visceral impact of these moving images enhanced as it is with computer generated images (CGI) has a remarkable stimulating power all its own.

The common assumption is that superheroes and villains wear masks simply to conceal their secret identity thereby preventing their enemies from striking back at them in person or by harming the ones they love. In *Batman: The Masks of the Gods*, Michael A. Rizzotti recognizes that a major function of a mask is "to hide the identity of the wearer allowing him to break everyday rules," allowing him "to avoid exposure and personal condemnation by the world."[10]

This is certainly true of heroes like Batman, Captain America and Spider-Man. Steve Ditko, the artist credited with devising the first full-face mask for Spider-Man, wanted not only to conceal his identity but also to hide the fact that he was just a teenager.[11] In the film *Spider-Man 2* the web-slinger is unmasked by Dr. Octopus as they fight on top of an elevated subway train. The movie-goer fully experiences Toby McGuire's anguished features as he heroically strains to stop the runaway subway. When the train comes to a halt mere inches from a precipice and Spider-Man collapses from the exertion the train car's grateful passengers lift him Christ-like into the car remarking "He's just a kid."[12]

The literary trope of the hero with a secret identity begins long before superheroes take to the skies. One of the first of these adventurers was Baroness Emmuska Orczy's the Scarlet Pimpernel who appeared as the title character in her play and subsequent novels. Although the Pimpernel was not known to wear a specific mask he is credited with being a master of disguise, often depicted on book jackets and in film publicity posters wearing an embroidered domino mask. The Pimpernel's alter ego, Sir Percy Blanckney, established the archetype of the ineffectual, foppish, ne'er-do-well as a disguise to misdirect attention away from his swashbuckling personae. This trope became a mainstay in many superhero origin stories.[13]

The first truly masked man-of-mystery appeared in "The Curse of Capistrano", a serialized story in the pulp magazine *All-Story Weekly*. Nobleman Don Diego de la Vega, living during California's colonial period, finds he must adopt the mask, sword and the sobriquet "Zorro" (Spanish for fox) to defend the peasants against the tyranny of their Spanish overlords. The cover art depicts a cloaked man wearing a sombrero with black cloth mask hanging from the inner brim. Quickly adapted into the silent film *The Mark of Zorro*, Douglas Fairbanks in the title role established the convention of the mask as a flowing black sash with eye holes wrapped tightly around Don Diego's smiling face. The appeal of this black-clad swashbuckler continued through cartoons, television shows and recent movies with Latin heartthrob Antonio Banderas in the title role.[14]

The Shadow debuted first as narrator on the radio program *Detective Story Hour* before being spun into the titled character of his own pulp magazine, *The Shadow Magazine*. In the pulps wealthy man-about-town, Lamont Cranston developed psychic powers that allowed him to "cloud men's minds" rendering him invisible to the human eye. Despite this invisibility the Shadow wore a theatrical costume consisting of a crimson-lined black opera cloak over a black suit while his face was masked by a wide brimmed fedora, upturned collar, and a crimson scarf that covered his mouth.[15]

*The Lone Ranger* and *The Green Hornet* first appeared on radio before being spun into comic books, movie serials, television shows, and films. In each incarnation they wore clothing contemporary to their times and a simple domino mask to hide their identities. In recent films *The Green Hornet*'s domino mask is cast in metal, while in *The Lone Ranger* his mask was a strip of leather cut from the bloodstained vest of his murdered brother, its eye holes marking the spots where bullets entered his brother's body. As these characters evolved their simple masks were heightened by both their material and their psychological significance.[16]

The masked crime fighter moved from pulps, and radio to strips with the introduction of Lee Faulk's *The Phantom*. The Phantom is the first hero to wear the skintight costume of tights, trunks, skullcap cowl and a domino face mask that hid the eyes giving him an "inhuman, awe inspiring appearance." The muscular heroic silhouette and costume serves as the archetype of the superhero costume to the present day. The mask and costume, while concealing Kit Walker's identity, also allowed the Phantom to pass on the mantle of "the ghost who walks" from father to son over generations creating an ageless symbol of justice.[17] This too becomes a heroic theme of the champion imperiled in countless cliff hangers is able to survive and continue their quest for justice due to their powers, ingenuity or the assistance of a plucky sidekick.

This short history illustrates how mask and costume evolved to become essential elements of the superhero's masquerade. These dynamic elements make the hero easily recognizable to the general public by condensing the character into a distinctive idea or concept. Costumes are often colorful enhancing the character's visual appeal and frequently incorporating the superhero's theme whether it is bat, spider, the stars and stripes or emblematic initial.

While concealment of identity is a significant function of the mask, not all heroes wear masks and many do not have a secret identity. Although the "Man of Steel" was the first great comic hero, as Superman, he did not wear a mask. As a symbol of "truth, justice and the American way" his handsome unmasked face exemplified his honesty and openness.[18] The same is true for his female counterpart, Wonder Woman.[19]

The Fantastic Four live openly in their Baxter Building wearing blue uniforms with the large "4" emblazoned on their chests to identify and unify them as a team. The original X-Men wore identical costumes and masks, but as newer heroes were recruited they adopted unique costumes and masks each sporting the "X" allowing more individuality like the Avengers but still identifying them as a team. Unlike the comic book's Tony Stark who used his mask and armor to conceal his identity, Robert Downey, Jr.s' egocentric entrepreneur declares in a national press conference that "I am Iron Man" forever linking the two personalities.[20]

Hal Jordan, as a member of the Intergalactic police force the Green Lantern Corps, wears a domino mask to conceal his identity. Yet when in outer space battling intergalactic menaces he continues to wear this mask. In both the movie and *Green Lantern: The Animated Series* the other Lanterns tease Hal for wearing the mask out in space where the chances of being recognized are literally astronomical.[21] So why does the "Emerald Knight" wear a mask when it isn't necessary?

As to their foes, masked super villains like Catwoman, Electro, Red Skull, Madame Masque, Scarecrow, and Mirror Master are routinely defeated and incarcerated, their masks removed revealing, their secret identities to the world. Yet when they escape (which they seem to do with alarming regularity) and venture forth to commit further crimes (recidivism seeming to be the habitual condition of the super villain) they slip on their masks as if nothing has changed. Why do these formidable crooks continue this masquerade when their secret identity is known? Obviously there are other reasons for masks and costumes.

Rizzotti explains that masks also function to protect the wearer through their ability to "illicit fear in the enemy" and "frighten away malevolent spirits."[22] Fear was clearly the motivation behind the design of Batman's cape and cowl. In his origin story young Bruce Wayne was orphaned in a traumatic robbery gone horribly wrong. As he grew to manhood Bruce obses-

*Opposite*: Artist Mike Wieringo shows the iconic transformation of Clark Kent into Superman in a telephone booth (from *The Adventures of Superman*, Issue 598, New York: DC Comics, January 2002; courtesy Marvel Comics).

sively trained his body and mind to become an instrument of justice and avenge his murdered parents. When he wonders how to set about on this quest, he reasons that "Criminals are a superstitious and cowardly lot. So my disguise must be able to strike terror into their hearts. I must be a creature of the night, black and terrible—a..." As Bruce searches for an appropriate symbol a bat flies in the open window and he exclaims "A bat! That's it! It's an omen. I shall become a bat!" And thus was born "this weird figure of the dark. This avenger of evil, 'The Batman.'"[23]

Super villains also utilize their masks to scare civilians and police allowing them to commit their crimes without interference from the general populous. The world knows that it is the pitiless Victor Von Doom who resides behind the riveted iron mask, armor, and cloaked hood of Dr. Doom while the Joker's macabre features send chills down the spine. But a mask doesn't require scary features to cause fear. Any mask that hides the wearer's identity and physical expression can cause unease and illicit fear. Walking down a deserted street and bumping into a figure cloaked under a hooded sweatshirt could set any citizen's heart racing. It is only at sanctioned events like Halloween or costume balls where we can relax when encountering a masked character.

Rizzotti also credits masks with facilitating "rituals of initiation and rites of passage."[24] The ritual of donning a special costume or uniform whether it is endowed with magic, weaponry, or is a symbolic representation of an animal or country is a familiar leitmotif in the superhero's world. Like soldiers gearing up for battle or a football squad suiting up for scrimmage, heroes ritually abandon their civilian lives of safety and comfort to become warriors facing their nemeses. Transformed into demigods they protect the social order, balance the scales of justice, and change the course of destiny (or at least "mighty rivers").[25] Villains on the other hand transform themselves into fearsome agents of chaos and misrule to challenge the status quo.

Traumatic events such as loss or death of loved ones or abandonment are often catalysts that set an individual on their path to becoming a hero or villain. The murder of his brother and resurrection from a death-like state becomes the rite of passage for The Lone Ranger, the only survivor of a massacre. His mask symbolizes his isolation from the rest of humanity allowing him to fulfill his solitary destiny. Peter Parker, an ordinary teenager filled with the angst and frustration characterized by adolescents the world over, is unlike the teenage superhero sidekicks of the 1940s. Accidently bitten by a radioactive spider Peter gains miraculous powers but this is not what transforms him into a hero. He is only interested in how his spider powers can earn him money and fame. Only when his beloved uncle Ben is murdered due to Peter's failure to act does the ineffectual boy don the mask and costume to become a powerful hero capable of dealing with formidable criminals. The boy becomes a Spider-**Man** (emphasis mine).[26]

In their beautifully illustrated book *Masks: Faces of Culture* John W. Nunley and Cara McCarty explain that masks help "to insure a sense of renewal—of abundance, vitality, and fertility."[27] They submit that professional sports function as a renewal masquerade ritual that metaphorically supports "national renewal, as regional [uniformed] teams from the same country compete to prove who is the fastest and the strongest."[28] Superheroes also function as agents of renewal in the social order by defending the common man against uncommon threats and balancing the scales of justice time after time. Heroes and anti-heroes often portray themselves as counterparts to one another. The physically powerful and attractive Superman dramatically contrasts with the chubby, balding intellect of Lex Luthor. The obsessively controlled Batman faces off against the madcap chaos of the Joker. The upright and noble American patriot, Captain America, and the vicious psychopath, Red Skull seem eternally locked in a battle of opposites: one side representing liberty and individualism, the other tyranny and totalitarianism. As the Skull expounds during one of their many struggles, "What mattered was the DANCE: the perennial interweaving of light and darkness! And we have danced as few others have, Captain! Oh it has been magnificent!"[29]

Nunley and McCarty additionally recognized the offensive and defensive functions of the mask.[30] Iron Man is essentially a contemporary knight whose armor is enhanced by sophisticated technology. The conceit behind his armor is effective. Underneath Iron Man's shining, nearly invulnerable metallic skin is a deeply conflicted, flawed and vulnerable individual. His heart, damaged during his kidnapping, is kept beating by the technology in his breastplate. As a man he suffers from an oversized ego, the heartbreak of lost love, the loneliness of the hero's journey all leading to bouts with alcoholism. His armor protects him from physical harm, extremes of temperature, provides oxygen, enhances his senses, allows him to shoot "repulsor" blasts all the while concealing his less than sterling character.[31]

Rizzotti attests to the mask's function as a vehicle "to make the gods manifest," and to become an "apparition of the mythical being that it represents."[32] This is certainly true of Wolverine, Hawkwoman, The Blue Beetle, The Wasp, Black Panther and others whose liveries are designed to make them appear as avatars for the creatures they embody. Like many animal inspired heroes and villains they become totemic figures when wearing their ceremonial dress which helps them manifest the power of their spirit helper and become powerful, fearsome, and god-like symbols.

There are literally hundreds of animal/insect/bird/fish/reptile/men, women, boys and girls in the comic book pantheon. But these guardians and reprobates can also embody nature and abstract concepts. Storm is the elemental goddess of the sky while the Flash embodies the very idea of speed. Bane is the bane to all who oppose him and Bizarro is—just that!

Comic books often play with the notion that some characters are so deeply affected by the spirit entities found in masks that they totally surrender their individuality to the spirit. As an example Kent Nelson becomes the sorcerer Dr. Fate when he places the helm of Nabu over his head. Nabu, a Lord of Order, seems to have no qualms about completely dominating his human host in his struggle against the Lords of Chaos often sacrificing the host's physical health and sanity in the process.[33] Henry Pernet, author of *Ritual Masks: Deception and Revelations,* feels that our Western interpretation of masking too often characterizes the sacrifice of one's ego to the will of the mask thereby transforming the wearer into a supernatural slave. Pernet maintains this is a simplistic and naïve concept and as proof points out the masker "generally remains aware and responsible" for his actions.[34] He further explains how the mask wearer "must often submit himself to a long apprenticeship" and "demonstrate great concentration" in order to prepare to wear the mask.[35] This is certainly true of Batman who trained himself to ultimate human perfection and maintains a rigid control over his emotions.

The necessity of specialized regalia as part of the hero's masquerade points to the deep psychological underpinning for the creation of their identity. Rizzotti once again helps us understand this by pointing out the mask's ability to assist in creating a "persona." Psychiatrist and therapist Carl Gustav Jung also uses personae to describe how the mask serves as a metaphor for the interaction between the individual self and the social world. Rizzotti and Jung's insightful use of personae utilizes the Latin concept for mask, of which Greek and Roman actors took advantage in order to portray their characters. Many theater and film scripts still refer to characters as "dramatis personae" or "dramatic characters."

After his arrival on Earth, Superman appears as a foundling baby lifting a large chair over his head. As an adult he appears raising steel girders with one hand, leaping up to "1/8 of a mile" and racing a speeding express train. Realizing his great powers can benefit humankind he assembles the iconic red and blue costume with the emblematic "S" to become Superman. After he becomes Superman he chooses to become a reporter so he can be close to breaking news. Only then does he adopt the timid alter ego of Clark Kent by putting on a mask of thick eye glasses.[36] The irony is that this nonpareil being chooses to act like an ordinary human by placing a symbol of human frailty on his face and embracing a masquerade of shy ineptness. In effect, the **super** man masquerades as the **common** man and through this charade he comes closer to his humanity. In John Bryne's *The Man of Steel* limited series, reinterpretation of the Superman origin Lex Luthor assembles a team of investigators to discover Superman's identity. But when they reveal to him that Clark Kent is Superman, Luthor, with his own insatiable desire for power, can't believe that anyone with god-like gifts would chose to live like a human.[37] In the television series *Smallville* the iconic eye glasses do not appear until the 10th and final season when Lois conceives the idea to hide Superman's identity by wearing glasses and taking on a restrained personality.[38] Whenever he performs the ritual of removing his glasses and sheds his outer garments, he is reborn like a chrysalis into the "Man of Tomorrow" and renews the struggle for "truth and justice and the American way."[39]

In the recent film *Man of Steel*, on his heroic quest to discover where he came from and the source of his powers, young Clark Kent learns his true name Kal-El and, accepting his heroic responsibility, dons the ancestral suit to battle the evil Zod. The "S" shaped symbol on his chest, which on Krypton means "hope," is misinterpreted by humans who name him Superman. In the last frames of the movie, he appears with the iconic eye glasses and assumes the human persona of Clark Kent.[40]

The Bat-Man first appeared in *Detective Comics* #27. Part Pimpernel, part Zorro, Batman was immediately popular with readers. Batman's backstory emerged slowly issue after issue. With each story his creators added to his arsenal of bat-themed gimmicks including the Bat (autogiro) Plane, Batarang and utility belt. It is not until *Detective Comics* #33 his origin as the traumatized child was finally revealed. Over the last 70 years Batman's origin story has been continually refined and enhanced. Ensuing comics and movies added themes that suggest that as a child Bruce was traumatized by an encounter with bats and so either channels their spirit to conquer his own fears or uses this terror as an inspiration for the fear to intimidate the criminal element. With each succeeding incarnation the Batman persona has been fleshed out into a deeply psychological study of obsession and determination. In "Shaman" *Batman: Legends of the Dark Knight* writer Dennis O'Neil deepened the psychological association with the bat by creating a mystical experience for Bruce, who near death, is saved by a shaman wearing a Pacific Northwest transformation mask. These ingenious masks open to reveal a mask within the mask metaphorically foreshadowing his transformation into Batman.[41]

Batman's mask serves to create his persona as the "Dark Knight" and also distinguishes him as a member of a secret society of powerful shaman heroes. In this way the superhero emulates African secret societies also protected by masks. The mask allows them to stand apart from humanity and serve as protectors of the social order. In his fanatical pursuit of the justice denied him Batman helps to renew and balance social order.

The Joker introduced in *Batman* #1 was originally killed in his second appearance. However his madcap personality and ability to match the Batman made him so popular he was

The young Bruce Wayne in the throes of a fever dream is approached by a shaman wearing a Pacific Northwest Native American transformation mask which opens to reveal a bat inside (from *Batman: Legends of the Dark Knight,* Issue # 1, New York: DC Comics, November 1989; (courtesy DC Comics).

quickly revived to challenge Batman again and again. Originally portrayed as a homicidal maniac he commits murder for his own amusement. Over the years the Joker mirrored Batman's myriad interpretations. In the 1960s he was portrayed as a comic figure interested only robbing banks and outwitting Batman. In recent incarnations he has reverted to the violent sociopath crippling Batgirl and even murdering the second Robin, Jason Todd.[42] Some might quibble that the "Crown Prince of Crime" doesn't wear a mask, but masks and personae can also be fashioned by altering facial features through plastic surgery or scarification. The Joker's clownish features weren't explained until Detective Comics #168 when it was revealed he fell into a toxic vat of chemicals permanently coloring his face, lips and hair.[43] Tim Burton's film *Batman,* offered an interesting twist to this origin by revealing that Batman and the Joker played a role in each other's creation. Jack Nicholson portrayed Jack Napier, the hood that murdered Bruce Wayne's family. Unaware of his identity, Batman scars Napier's face with his batarang and then is unable to prevent him from falling into the vat of chemicals that permanently colors his features.[44] His jester's grin is the result of a botched underworld doctor's operation resulting in his caricatured "Glasgow smile."[45]

Christopher Nolen revisited the Joker's origin to match the gritty realism of his *The Dark Night*. Heath Ledger's Joker is an in-depth study of the psychopathic personality whose origins don't involve comic book acid vats and bungled surgeries. As Ledger's Joker explains,

> Wanna know how I got these scars. My father was a drinker and a fiend. And one night he goes off crazier than usual. Mommy gets the kitchen knife to defend herself. He doesn't like that. Not ... one ... bit. So me watching, he takes the knife to her, laughing while he does it. He turns to me and he says 'Why so serious?' He comes at me with the knife. 'Why so serious?' He sticks the blade in my mouth. 'Let's put a smile on that face.'[46]

Interestingly the Joker tells an entirely different story later in the film confirming his psychopathic persona.

Lindy Hemming, costume designer for Nolan's trilogy, designed the Joker to be edgy, gritty, and grungy drawing upon images of punk rockers, Iggy Pop and Johnny Rotten.[47] With the horrific smile carved permanently into his face by his father, the Joker intensifies his masquerade through shambolic white face, confused rouged lips and green streaked unkempt hair.

Neurologist Paul MacLean has postulated a neuropsychological function of the human brain that may help understand the relationship between masks and the creation of identity and help validate Rizzotti and Jung's concepts of masking and masquerades. MacLean suggests that the human brain is composed of three evolutionary segments. This "Triune Brain" is composed of the reptilian brain, the paleo-mammalian brain, and the neo-cortex. Each section developed sequentially during the evolutionary stages of the human species. But these three brains are interrelated and continually interact with each other to create personality.

The reptilian brain is the oldest and regulates breathing, body temperature, sexual desire, survival instincts, and functions that do not require conscious thought. It is also the center for primitive instincts and base emotions such as our fight or flight response. The paleo-mammalian brain is thought to have developed in the evolutionary stage between reptiles and mammals and is the source of our more complex emotions of love, hate, envy, and even those in our dreams. It is also considered to be the root of our senses of morality and ethics. These first two brain sections seem to be the foundation of Jung's "collective unconscious."

The third and final brain section to evolve, the neo-cortex, is what separates humanity from the rest of the animal kingdom. The neo-cortex is the center of our rational thought, logic, language and self-awareness. It allows us to create an outward persona by controlling our baser actions and emotions. It is the Apollonian balance to the more primitive Dionysian reptilian and pre-mammalian systems.

MacLean suggests that these two earlier brains can assert dominance over the neo-cortex when provoked by stimuli like physical threats, powerful memories, intoxication and possibly the mask. When a person puts on a mask the sense of anonymity it produces reduces the wearer's risk of public condemnation. As a result the control over our outward persona relaxes allowing the masquerader to do things he or she wouldn't think of doing as their public self. The outward persona won't be held accountable for the inner self's actions. So the mask may be more than just a physical object placed over the face. It is a vehicle that transforms us into another being. Early cultures without knowledge of psychological and neurological concepts saw the mask as a totem that sanctions the spirit to enter the body of wearer. Contemporary comic writers and artists use this psychological dimension as a means of expressing the often dual nature of their characters occasionally permitting them to lose themselves entirely in the masquerade.[48]

The physical nature of the mask including its color, shape, and construction also influences the interpretation or performance in a masquerade. In comic books and cartoons the mask is simply composed of lines and colors drawn to suit the needs of the character and the temperament of the artist. Masks and costumes in comic books are very flexible and expressive as the artist can exaggerate the eye slots, muscles, mouth and draw waves of expression lines around the head. Steve Ditko often divided Spidey's face in two with one half showing Peter's startled human emotions, the other half the enigmatic mask.

But film and television versions of superheroes are problematic and must deal with real actors and real materials. Past attempts at making dynamic character costumes have been at best campy and more often than not unmitigated failures. The masks of past films and television clearly reflected materials and budgets available at the time. In the *Batman* Columbia Pictures serials the mask appears to be made of a stiff felt-like fabric with pointy devil horns attached.[49] In the television series *Batman* Adam West credited his tongue and cheek performance of the "bright knight" to the pop-art inspired costume with lavender tights and black three-piece tailored cowl of satiny fabric accented with painted eye brows and nose edging. The iconic bat ears were reduced to small, silly appendages on the sides of the cowl.[50] Burton's dark revisionist film *Batman* and subsequent sequels introduced new technology and materials to the superhero masquerade. According to costume designer, Bob Ringwood, "the problem was to make somebody who was average-sized and ordinary-looking into this bigger-than-life creature."[51] The solution was to create the muscular molded latex "bat-suit" and cowl. Burton explained that the costume was not simply visually impressive but also helped Keaton create his character, "Michael is a bit claustrophobic, which made it worse for him. The costume put him in a dark, Batman-like mood though, so he was able to use it to his advantage."[52] Additionally the heavily molded cowl prevented Keaton from turning his head so he had to turn his shoulders to be able to see to the sides. This added a stoic movement that became part of future Batman characterizations in both animated and live action movies.

Lindy Hemming created the character designs for Christopher Nolan's *Batman Begins* and *The Dark Knight* and *The Dark Knight Rises*. This bat-suit required more flexibility to allow the actors to perform demanding stunts and fight sequences. As the series evolved the designers examined high-tech sportswear and protective motorcycle suits to create a menacing and a realistically plausible combat outfit with a molded under-suit covered with segmented plating. The molded cowl was redesigned with a series of protective neck bands that flexed allowing greater movement. The eye slits were even given white lenses like the comic book whenever the character used his sonar detection. The bodies of the Christian Bale and his stunt doubles had to be life-cast so the sculptors could develop the design based upon their individual physiques.[53]

As the superhero continues to evolve costumes may become entirely computer generated animations much as video games. The character of the Hulk was reproduced using motion capture technology for his first two film outings as well as *The Avengers* movie.[54] As the sophistication of CGI generated characters evolves we may see a new generation of superheroes no longer constrained by the limitations of human bodies and faces returning the character and costume entirely over to the artist's imagination much like the original comic books. How then will this affect the Halloween and Cosplay costumes? Will we reach a time when once again we puny mortals cannot replicate the flickering images of the designer's imaginations?

*I would like to thank John Russell for opening up his extensive comic book collection to me and helping me to research images.*

# Notes

1. Superman was created by teenagers Jerry Siegel and Joe Shuster and premiered in *Action Comics* #1 (1938).

2. Cosplay is short for "costume play." It is categorized as a form of performance art in which contestants dress in costumes and props to masquerade as a character in literature and popular culture.

3. Marco Arnaudo (2013), *The Myth of the Superhero*, translated by Jamie Richards (Baltimore: Johns Hopkins Press), 7.

4. *Adventures of Superman* (1952–1958), syndicated.

5. Captain Marvel was created in 1939 by artist C. C. Beck and writer Bill Parker. He first appeared in *Whiz Comics* #2 (February 1940).

6. Harold Schechter (1980), *The New Gods: Psyche and Symbol in Popular Art* (Bowling Green, OH: Bowling Green University Popular Press), 9. Quoted in Joe Muszynski (2009), "The Mask of the Superhero: Ritual Portrayal in the Comics," *Beyond the Veil* (20 September), http://joemuszynski.blogspot.com/2009/09/mask-of-superhero-ritual-portrayal-in.html.

7. *Adventures of Superman* (1952–1958), syndicated.

8. Captain America was created by writer Joe Simon and artist Jack Kirby and appeared first in *Captain America Comics* #1 (1941) published by Timely Comics. Captain America is now a character in Marvel Comics. The film *Captain America: The First Avenger*, was released on 22 July 2011.

9. Joe Muszynski (2009), "The Mask of the Superhero: Ritual Portrayal in the Comics," *Beyond the Veil* (20 September), http://joemuszynski.blogspot.com/2009/09/mask-of-superhero-ritual-portrayal-in.html.

10. Michael A. Rizzotti (2013), "Batman: The Mask of the Gods." *The Net Age,* http://netage.org/2010/03/01/batman-the-masks-of-the-gods/,

11. *In Search of Steve Ditko* (2007), Dir. Peter Boyd Maclean, London, BBC 4.

12. *Spider-Man 2* (2002), Marvel Studios.

13. Orczy Emmuska (1903), *The Scarlet Pimpernel*. First staged in 1903. The novel of the same name was published in 1905.

14. Johnston McCulley (1919), "The Curse of Capistrano," *All-Story Weekly*, vol. 100, #2 (August 6,), New York: Grosset & Dunlap. *The Mark of Zorro* (1920), United Artist Studios.

15. David Chrisman, William Sweets, and Harry Engman Charlot (1930), *Detective Story Hour. The Shadow* was adapted for *The Shadow Magazine* by Walter B. Gibson (New York: Conde Nast, 31 July).

16. George W. Trendle and Fran Striker (1933), *The Lone Ranger,* Chicago: WXYZ Radio (1936), *The Green Hornet,* Chicago: WXYZ Radio. *The Green Hornet* (2011), Columbia Pictures. *The Lone Ranger* (2013), Walt Disney Studios.

17. "The Phantom: Comic Strip Crusader" (1996) *Biography*, Arts & Entertainment Channel, 31 May.

18. *Adventures of Superman* (1952–1958), syndicated.

19. William Moulton Marston (1941), *Sensation Comics*, #1 (New York: DC Comics). Princess Diana exchanged identities, including a pair of glasses, with nurse Diana Prince to be closer to the wounded Steve Trevor.

20. *Iron Man* (2008), Marvel Studios.

21. *Green Lantern: The Animated Series* (2011–13), DC Entertainment. *Green Lantern* (2011), DC Entertainment.

22. Rizzotti (2013).

23. Bob Kane and Joe Finger (1939), *Detective Comics* #27 (New York: DC Comics). His origin story was first published in *Detective Comics* #33 (1939).

24. Rizzotti (2013).

25. *Adventures of Superman* (1952–1958), syndicated.

26. Stan Lee and Steve Ditko (1963), *The Amazing Spider-Man* #1 (New York: Marvel Comics).

27. John W. Nunley and Cara McCarty (1999), *Masks: Faces of Culture* (New York: Harry N. Abrams), 68.

28. Ibid., 128.

29. Jack Kirby and Joe Simon (1984), *Captain America* # 298 (New York: Timely/Marvel Comics, 1 January).

30. Nunley and McCarty (1999), 275.

31. Stan Lee, Jack Kirby, Larry Lieber and Don Heck (1963), *Tales of Suspense* #39 (New York: Marvel Comics, March).

32. Rizzotti (2013).

33. Gardiner Fox and Howard Sherman (1940), *More Fun Comics* #55 (New York: DC Comics).

34. Henry Pernet (1992), *Ritual Masks: Deception and Revelations,* translated by Laura Grillo (Eugene, OR: Wipf & Stock), 125.

35. Ibid., 162.

36. Jerry Siegel and Joe Schuster (1938), *Action Comics* #1 (New York: DC Comics, June).

37. *Man of Steel* (2013), DC Entertainment and Legendary Pictures.

38. "Masquerade," (2011), *Smallville,* episode 209, WB Television Network (18 February).

39. *Adventures of Superman* (1952–1958), syndicated.

40. *Man of Steel* (2013), DC Entertainment and Legendary Pictures.

41. Dennis O'Neil and Edward Hannigan (1998), *Batman: Shaman* (New York: DC Comics).

42. "A Death in the Family" (1988–1989), *Batman* #426–429 (New York: DC Comics).

43. Bill Finger, Bob Kane and Jerry Robinson (1951), *Detective Comics* #168 (New York: DC Comics). Bill Finger introduced the story of a criminal named the Red Hood who is disfigured after falling into a chemical vat which transforms him into the Joker. The Joker was created by Jerry Robinson, Bill Finger and Bob Kane.

44. *Batman* (1989), Warner Brothers Studios.

45. Oliver Harvey (2009), "If the Booze Doesn't Get You, The Blade Will," *The Sun* (London; 16 October). A Glasgow smile is a wound "where victims are slashed from mouth to ear" causing the cuts to extend the mouth into an elongated smile.

46. *The Dark Knight* (2008), DC Entertainment & Legendary Studios.

47. Dan Jolin (2008), "Fear Has a Face," *Empire Magazine* (January): 87–88.

48. Paul D. MacLean (1990), The Triune Brain in Evolution: Role in Paleocerebral Functions (New York: Plenum Press), 8–18.

49. *Batman* (1943), Columbia Pictures Serial.

50. "Superheroes" (2013), *Pioneers of Television*, PBS, 29 January.

51. Jody Duncan (1990), "Building the Bat-suit," *Cinefex: The Journal of Cinematic Illusions*, 16–24.

52. Ibid., 16–24.

53. Jeff Jensen (2007), "Batman's New Suit," *Entertainment Weekly* (15 June), http://www.ew.com/ew/.

54. *Hulk* (2003), Marvel Studios; *The Incredible Hulk* (2008), Marvel Studios; *The Avengers* (2012), Marvel Studios.

# Works Cited

*Adventures of Superman.* (1952–1958.) Syndicated.

Arnaudo, Marco. (2013.) *The Myth of the Superhero*. Translated by Jamie Richards. Baltimore, MD: Johns Hopkins Press.

*The Avengers*. (2012.) Marvel Studios.

*Batman*. (1943.) Columbia Pictures Serial.

*Batman*. (1989.) Warner Brothers Studios.

*The Dark Knight*. (2008.) DC Entertainment & Legendary Studios.

Duncan, Jody. (1990.) "Building the Bat-suit." *Cinefex: The Journal of Cinematic Illusions*.

Fox, Gardiner, and Howard Sherman. (1940.) *More Fun Comics* #55. New York: DC Comics.

*Green Lantern*. (2011.) DC Entertainment.

*Green Lantern: The Animated Series*. (2011–13.) DC Entertainment.

Harvey, Oliver. (2009.) "If the Booze Doesn't Get You, the Blade Will." *The Sun* (London; 16 October).

*Hulk*. (2003.) Marvel Studios.

*In Search of Steve Ditko*. (2007.) Dir. Peter Boyd Maclean. London: BBC 4.

*The Incredible Hulk*. (2008.) Marvel Studios.

*Iron Man*. (2008.) Marvel Studios.

Jensen, Jeff. (2007.) "Batman's New Suit." *Entertainment Weekly* (15 June). http://www.ew.com/ew/.

Jolin, Dan. (2008.) "Fear Has a Face." *Empire Magazine* (January).

Kane, Bob, and Joe Finger. (1939.) *Detective Comics* #27. New York: DC Comics.

Kirby, Jack, and Joe Simon. (1984.) *Captain America* # 298 (1 January). New York: Timely/Marvel Comics.

Lee, Stan, and Steve Ditko. (1963.) *The Amazing Spider-Man* #1. New York: Marvel Comics.

Lee, Stan, Jack Kirby, Larry Lieber and Don Heck. (1963.) *Tales of Suspense* #39 (March). New York: Marvel Comics.

MacLean, Paul D. (1990.) *The Triune Brain in Evolution: Role in Paleocerebral Functions*. New York: Plenum Press.

*Man of Steel*. (2013.) DC Entertainment and Legendary Pictures.

*The Mark of Zorro*. (1920.) United Artists Studios.

Marston, William Moulton. (1941.) *Sensation Comics* #1. New York: DC Comics.

McCulley, Johnston. (1919.) "The Curse of Capistrano." *All-Story Weekly*, vol. 100 #2 (August 6), New York: Grosset & Dunlap.

Muszynski, Joe. (2009.) "The Mask of the Superhero: Ritual Portrayal in the Comics." *Beyond the Veil* (20 September), http://joemuszynski.blogspot.com/2009/09/mask-of-superhero-ritual-portrayal-in.html.

Nunley, John W., and Cara McCarty. (1999.) *Masks: Faces of Culture*. New York: Harry N. Abrams.

O'Neil, Dennis, and Edward Hannigan. (1998.) *Batman: Shaman*. New York: DC Comics.

Pernet, Henry. (1992.) *Ritual Masks: Deception and Revelations*. Translated by Laura Grillo. Eugene, OR: Wipf & Stock.

Rizzotti, Michael A. (2013.) "Batman: The Mask of the Gods." *The Net Age*. http://netage.org/2010/03/01/batman-the-masks-of-the-gods/.

Schechter, Harold. (1980.) *The New Gods: Psyche and Symbol in Popular Art*. Bowling Green, OH: Bowling Green University Popular Press.

Siegel, Jerry, and Joe Schuster. (1938.) *Action Comics* #1 (June). New York: DC Comics.

*Spider-Man 2*. (2002.) Marvel Studios.

"Superheroes." (2013.) *Pioneers of Television*. PBS. 29 January.

Section V

_____

The Universality of
Digital Masquerade for a
Global Audience

# Animators as Professional Masqueraders: Thoughts on Pixar

## HEATHER L. HOLIAN

As early as the 1930s studio animators were viewed as "actors with pencils" and "cast" for particular shots or characters accordingly.[1] The same attitude is widely held in the field today and dictates everything from the assignments given to animators at Pixar Animation Studios, to the curriculum of American animation schools, to the advice supplied online to budding practitioners. Following this logic to its rational conclusion, animators are then arguably the most sophisticated, versatile and total—that is entirely masked and anonymous— professional masqueraders working in the entertainment business today. In essence the characters they bring to life are complex, highly pliable digital "masks" or "suits"[2] briefly inhabited by the animator, who "is really an actor performing in slow motion, living the character a drawing [or frame] at a time."[3]

At Pixar and other computer animation studios, the digital "mask" visible on the movie screen in the form of a fully developed character, initially exists on an animator's computer as a digital model, or to use the words of veteran Pixar animator Adam Burke, "a string-less marionette" that animators skillfully and painstakingly manipulate with highly sophisticated computer animation software to create a performance that is projected at 24 frames per second.[4] Throughout this process, performance and acting is *especially* foregrounded, since computer or 3D animation does not require thousands of hand drawn images like its 2D counterpart. According to Pixar animator, Jaime Landes, "That's not our focus anymore, the draftsmanship, it *is* a little bit, but it's mostly the acting and the performance."[5] The computer in this dynamic is simply a tool, or as Pixar director, writer and animator Angus MacLane observed, "just a big, dumb pencil," through which the performance is realized by the animator.[6]

Approximately 120 animators currently work at Pixar, where productions run concurrently and as many as 45 animators typically contribute to a feature-length film. Over the studio's more than 25 year history, Pixar has always adhered to sequence or shot assignments for its animators whereby three to five seconds of film, or 72 to 120 frames, are distributed to an animator for completion.[7] Animators typically receive several such assignments over the course of a production, and ultimately complete between 90 seconds to less than ten minutes of final footage, which is usually scattered throughout the film.[8] This method of assignment is valued for the internal chemistry a shot is more likely to contain since the same animator works on all the characters involved in that single three to five second sequence. "The big challenge for us as animators, and as performers, is to very calculatedly and by sophisticated engineering come up with a performance that seems spontaneous and organic. I mean, what we're doing—it's orchestrated spontaneity—which is like a contradiction of terms, but it's what we're doing as animators because we work so incrementally."[9]

Given the huge collaboration necessary to make an animated film, twenty to thirty animators frequently contribute incrementally to the same character throughout the course of a production. These same animators will often contribute to the performance of other characters as well. Therefore, being an animator is also in large part about being able to deftly put on and take off a persona or "mask" at will, and at times, wear more than one should the shot demand it. Long time Pixar animator, Andrew Gordon, likened the task, which he described as "pretty natural" to play-acting.

> Ever play with an action figure? You've got to play different parts. It's similar to that, only animation is a hundred million times more detailed in what you can get out of that little action figure. You're *really* putting the performance into it.[10]

At the start of the animation process on any Pixar project, part of the conversation centers upon what character or characters an animator *wants* to animate. At Pixar animators are encouraged to be vocal in this regard and "a lot of us already come into a project feeling strong about a certain character and we'll ask for it," explains Gini Cruz Santos, an animator at Pixar since 1996.[11] Some animators excel at or prefer animating one character, while others want to contribute a performance for every character in the film. The animator's individual strengths, or "cast-ability,"[12] are the other primary factors guiding assignments. "You've got animators who are really good at quiet moments, solid work, more human-like acting," observes Andrew Gordon. "And you've got people who are really into cartoony, and you've got guys that are great at physicality and good at action scenes, and so *every* animator has their specialty."[13] Therefore, Pixar animators don the digital "mask" of a character at specific moments where *that* particular animator is proven to excel at the performance required of the story and/or the character. The mask is then passed on and shared with other animators gifted at different emotional "beats."

Although several Pixar animators noted they "don't over think" the action of switching character "masks," they do often follow an initial process of preparation similar to a live-action actor.[14] For example, Adam Burke explains,

> As I think about my shot I would sort of explore my ideas similar to how an actor sort of would flesh out what his or her performance might be, but after that you aren't going to find animators doing immersive character work like Daniel Day Lewis. You won't see one of us walking down the hall being Carl (Frederickson from *Up*)! That aspect of it isn't, I think, a very conscious or calculated thing with us.[15]

While the act of switching character "masks" is perhaps not overly conscious, Jamie Landes observes it *is* a fundamental part of the job,

> It's something that's expected for you to be able to do—that range—to be able to switch (characters), but then again, of course it's a challenge. You always have to do this mind switch like,

"Right now I'm working on *this* character," and collect all your reference[16] and all your materials and really embody that character all over again before you feel comfortable, like stepping in, that's how I work anyway. It's like method acting, in a way, you know, embrace it.[17]

Indeed, animators at Pixar often prepare to animate their assigned sequence by video recording themselves or a friend acting out the scene as they imagine the character might. This footage becomes part of the important preparatory materials an animator can later reference, especially for the more subconscious gestures or body movements that endow a performance with believability.

All Pixar animators interviewed noted that much like live-action actors, animators are also frequently "type cast," because they excel at a certain kind of performance or masquerade. Many animators choose to challenge themselves by requesting at least one assignment per film that breaks their usual casting. "I think on *Ratatouille*," Landes recalls, "I did a lot more physical stuff, which was really exciting, really challenging, not my comfort zone, but I enjoy that part of it. I love pushing myself to do more cartoony, physical stuff so I always ask for it no matter which show I'm on." She calls this "a little break, to switch it up, keep it fresh,"[18] so that she can continue to excel at the emotional, quiet, subtle performances for which she is known, such as her Annie-nominated work on Elinor in *Brave* (2012).[19] Changes in casting also enable an animator to bring a "fresh perspective" to a character they have not consistently animated on a project.[20]

Perhaps not surprisingly, the dozens of animators who work to bring one character to life over the course of a Pixar film leave a bit of themselves behind through their performance. "A lot of what we are and who we are [as people] actually comes out through our character," observes Santos. "So a lot of the times we have to kind of police ourselves into reminding us of how a character is, so that it's consistent."[21] Or in other words, so the mask maintains its integrity as it's worn and seamlessly inhabited by several individuals. Predictably, communication is essential to this goal, as Santos also notes, "It is very important that we always have a dialogue with each other. Nobody really works isolated or else your shot's going to look funny with the rest of the film."[22] The fundamental need for individually animated scenes not to look "funny" or call attention to themselves requires not only consistency of performance and style, but also total on-screen artistic anonymity from the animator. According to Adam Burke,

> Our job is to try to have the performance be consistent and uniform regardless of who touched it. You may have over the course of the film 20 to 30 people animating Sulley (of *Monsters University* [2013] and *Monsters Inc.*) and it has to feel and look consistent regardless of whose hands touched those shots, so we're almost initially taxed with *not* standing out. Everything is about serving the character and how that performance fits within the context of the story.[23]

Angus MacLane also observed that if he does his job well as an animator his work will not be noticeable, "since the nature of animation is to cover up what the animator actually does."[24] As such "showboating" or the pure demonstration of artistic virtuosity for the sake of individual expression or skillful display has no place in the performances of studio animation. Indeed, as Burke notes "the most successful artists of our medium are the ones that blend in *and* stand out at the same time,"[25] due to their amazing skill and acting range. And yet, their work blends seamlessly into the homogenous stylistic fabric of the film, which, like all other parts of a Pixar production, are ultimately in service to the story. "Yes, as animators we *do* masquerade, because," as Burke explains, "we have to be flexible, versatile—but ... *everything* we do is secondary to the story. We are basically serving that greater purpose." The great success of Pixar animators at such dissimulation and masquerade is born out by John Goodman's reaction to viewing animated footage, which accompanied his previously recorded sessions for James P. "Sulley" Sullivan, the character Goodman voiced in both *Monsters* films. As Burke recalled, during a recording break for *Monsters University*,

> John's watching the footage and he says, "How do you *do that*? He [Sulley] looks worried! He looks pensive! How do you do that?! His facial expressions are communicating everything that is going on!" ... It made a connection. He [Goodman] saw an actor. He saw the person performing Sulley. He wasn't seeing the 10 to 15 animators involved in that progression of shots that they showed. He saw Mike. And he saw Sulley. And when we're doing our job well, that's what happens.[26]

Not surprisingly, however, the performances of especially gifted Pixar animators *are* recognizable to their colleagues who are familiar with their work from dailies,[27] but the general public is unlikely, and in most cases, unable, to identify the artistry with a particular individual. The current method of shot assignment at Pixar, makes specific film credit for each animator's individual contribution impossible and as a result, they are alphabetically credited *en masse*. This includes those animators who "organically" assume the role of "character lead" at Pixar and oversee the animation of a single character throughout a film, often contributing key sequences to that character's performance, while also monitoring its consistency.[28] The strong collaborative culture of Pixar also embraces a collective, rather than an individual approach to celebrating achievement and thus the group method of acknowledgment simultaneously upholds important studio values.

Traditional 2D animation, however, provides an important contrast on both fronts. Beginning no later than the production of *Three Little Pigs* in 1933, Walt Disney set a precedent by carefully casting his animators for specific roles.[29] These assignments often corresponded with particular characters, and as the years passed, the Disney Studios established character leads.[30] The drawn work of these individuals was both published and exhibited over the years enabling the interested public,[31] to learn who chiefly created the performance for Cruella De Vil, Madame Medusa, Belle and a whole host of other Disney characters.[32] "You would *read the books* and see they (the individual animators) did it! With computer animation you don't really get that. It's *a lot* more anonymous because on the one hand they're [the animators] not being promoted the way that Disney did it, *and* there's a lot more people doing it," observes Andrew Gordon. "It's not like you really are the lead on the Beast [of *Beauty and the Beast*]. It's different. Everybody's working on these things."[33]

The characteristic anonymity of an animator created, perpetuated, and necessitated by the medium impacts contemporary practitioners in a variety of ways, some surprising. As we have seen, the studio animator's individual *artistic* identity must remain sublimated to insure both the story's primacy and the required consistency of style necessary within such large collaborative projects. Furthermore, an animator's artistic anonymity is also perpetuated by assignment and crediting methods. However, the complete and total on-screen masquerade of an animator *also* guarantees the benefits of *physical* anonymity outside the walls of the studio. Therefore, while a Pixar animator contributes to well-known, award winning, blockbuster productions, which feature highly recognizable digital "stars," the "masked" animators responsible for the performances remain essentially un-recognizable. According to several Pixar animators this is the positive side of animation anonymity—no physical recognition means no harassment, no paparazzi and the freedom to do what they love, accompanied by a private life of peace. "Just hearing about all the people who come through the Lucky 7 and their issues with fame, you know, I would *not* want to be famous," Gordon reflects. "When you're an animator—most everybody here has no egos—and people didn't get into it (animation) to be in front of the camera. They're just nerds or geeks, you know. They're into performance or into animation and so it's *great* being anonymous."[34] Indeed, as Gini Cruz Santos notes, "... As much as we feel (animating) *is* an acting thing, we're not really the types to go up on stage and want to perform."[35] Their chosen medium gives them the opportunity and space to perform, fully masked and free of the limelight with all that implies. "There are *a lot* of downsides to being famous [so] it's really nice to work on projects that everybody sees and people enjoy, *but not* have to deal with that (the price of fame)," says MacLane, who adds with a laugh, "but the flip side of course is that you're fairly expendable and the pay isn't equal (to stars), but that's a fair trade."[36]

Also on that "flip side," is the public lack of recognition for what an animator does, both individually and collaboratively. "Where it [the anonymity] goes to the extreme, to a bad point," Adam Burke observes, "is that with *that* anonymity comes a certain amount of non-recognition and maybe like invalidation."[37] Burke quickly adds, however, that for him this sense is trumped by the many moments when he's outside of Pixar, anonymous, and people discover what he does for a living, and they immediately share with him all the times they have seen a Pixar movie with their children, or they describe a cherished Buzz and Woody backpack their daughter takes to school every day. "It evens out in the wash," Burke confided. Besides, he continues, "I don't think you'll find any animator pining to be a Kardashian ... if you want to be famous the last place you want to go is animation! If you want to be seen, and seen by the world, do *not* get into animation. This just isn't where you should be."[38]

Angus MacLane's 2009 "Chart of Fame" only reinforces Burke's more recent assessment. MacLane created the characteristically self-deprecating and humorous visual commentary on the enigmatically linked phenomena of fame and recognition for a class or public talk. As MacLane recently recalled, the presentation was on this very issue, "don't go into this business to *be famous* because there's *no value* there. If you're chasing that you're going to be disappointed."[39] Not surprisingly the diagram circulated among animators, eventually making its way onto the web, where it was posted on Andrew Gordon's Spline Doctors website with the explanation, "We always joke how animators are one of the least recognized people in the entertainment industry."[40] MacLane's Chart, which he thinks is "still accurate," also unconsciously highlights a perceptible existential dilemma that appears to exist for some animators and involves a tension between the beneficial, characteristic anonymity of 3D animation and the frustrating drawbacks of non-recognition.[41]

Social media, like Facebook and especially Twitter, provide a public space where the animator's mask can be removed. In fact, in the last few years social media, fueled by a growing and increasingly tech savvy animation fan base, has in effect turned being an animator into "its own celebrity," to use the words of Jaime Landes, who has watched the phenomenon of social media take hold and transform the relationship between some of her colleagues and the world outside Pixar.[42] "*It is* a celebrity in a way. People want to be known for, 'I am an animator.' It's an identity. 'It's cool to be this!'" Landes continues, "but in the end if you just say where you work, 'DreamWorks, Pixar, Disney ... people will follow (on Twitter). People will want to listen to those people and they'll be banging on your door asking for advice and help.... Some people love it and some people just want nothing to do with it."[43]

Landes's observation points to a powerful reality. As we have seen, due to the necessarily large-scale collaborative nature of 3D studio animation, individual credit for specific elements of a film is nearly impossible, including the animation. Therefore, instead of individuals, it is the studio, as a collective or ensemble, which garners the fame. Indeed, the indisputable cachet of "Pixar" is readily apparent, again, from social media, where several studio artists and animators who previously left the company still identify themselves as former employees on Twitter, rather than shedding the connection. The aura of Pixar attracts not only employable talent, but also fans and recognition.

But does the masquerade and subsequent anonymity of animation's performers impact the seriousness with which animation, as a medium, is taken by the larger world of cinematic entertainment? The Academy Awards seem to pose an unfortunate, if indicative example. An animated film has never received an Oscar nomination for Production Design, despite the inescapable fact that an *entire* animated film and *every* detail of that film must be designed and then created by artists. Before 2009, when the nomination pool was expanded from five to ten honorees, only one animated feature was ever nominated for Best Picture—Disney's *Beauty and the Beast* (1991)—and none have won in this category.[44] Does the physical recognition of an actor's (human) body on screen therefore make live action films somehow more legitimate to Hollywood and critics? Does that "star appeal" matter? According to MacLane it just might.

> You know, I think there's not a lot of respect for animation because you don't see the people. There's something magical about seeing someone on the screen and already they have an allure the same way a musician does when you see them on stage. There's something that's unnaturally *or naturally* highlighting them to your attention and that's hypnotic and inescapable and there's something really human about that, and that *can* be distracting to the narrative of the thing you're watching, but there is no such thing with animation unless you're *really* an animation fan.[45]

Obviously the "distraction" of *physical* recognition is not an issue for animation. And as MacLane further observes, "The characters are, in a way, *more* complete because there's not a person. I mean there *is* a voice talent, but it's easier to kind of exist as a one-off, like Nemo's not starring [as another character] in another movie."[46] Indeed, a character "mask" is only ever inhabited by animators who consciously work to *maintain* a consistent range of behavior that an audience associates with that character's development and personality. And in fact, as Adam Burke explains, it is precisely Pixar's highly recognizable and "more complete" characters that ultimately provide the star power.

> I mean animators aren't public figures, just because they work behind the scenes. But if we're making the equivalent to live-action stars, no one knows Angus MacLane, no one knows Adam Burke or Andrew Gordon or Ralph Eggleston. *Everyone* around the world knows what Buzz and Woody look like, everyone knows Mike and Sulley, *those* are the stars. So, animation does have its icons it's just not the people involved with actually producing the work, it's the product itself that's the star.[47]

And so, it appears that for the immediate future, at least, the studio collective, and the characters or "masks" the animators bring to life through a sophisticated, collaborative performance will remain decidedly more recognizable (and famous) than their makers. But, as one might expect from true masqueraders, animators routinely speak of performing and entertaining as their goal, rather than the attainment of personal recognition or fame. Indeed, they easily joke about the incompatibility of the two in animation? However, one cannot help but wonder if the swift cultural shift brought on by social media within the last five years will ultimately chart a permanent new path, and what that might look like. In the meantime, however, and before the masks are entirely removed, the performances of animators serve to broaden the definition of what it means to masquerade in contemporary culture.

# Notes

1. Finch, Christopher (2011), The Art of Walt Disney: From Mickey Mouse to the Magic Kingdoms and Beyond (New York: Abrams), 67.

2. When discussing animation and masquerade with the author, Pixar animator Andrew Gordon described the dynamic this way, "You're putting on a mask, but it's more like a *suit*, you're *really feeling* the physicality of *that* thing." Andrew Gordon, interview with the author, 24 April 2013. Andrew Gordon studied character animation at the Vancouver School of Animation (now VanArts) where his strong student work earned him a job at Warner Bros. in 1994. In 1997 Andrew started at Pixar with contributions to *A Bug's Life* (1998). Over his sixteen years at Pixar, Andrew has animated performances in nearly a dozen short and feature film projects, including *Monsters Inc.* (2001), *The Incredibles* (2004), *Jack-Jack Attack* (2005), *Brave* (2012) and *Finding Nemo* (2003), for which he won a 2004 Visual Effects Society (VES) Award for Outstanding Character Animation in an Animated Motion Picture. Most recently he served as a directing animator on *Monsters University* (2013).

3. Lasseter, John (2009), "Moving Pictures," In *Animation*. The Archives Series, Walt Disney Animation Studios. New York: Disney Editions), 7.

4. Adam Burke, interview with author, 23 April 2013. Adam Burke attended the Character Animation program at CalArts, where he trained as a 2D animator before working more than a decade in Los Angeles at a series of animation studios, including DreamWorks and Warner Bros. In 2003 Adam began at Pixar with his first assignment on *The Incredibles* (2004). During the following ten years Adam has contributed animated performances to seven Pixar productions, including most recently, *Monsters University* (2013), where he served as supervising animator of crowd scenes. Adam has also worked on various projects for the theme parks division of parent company, Walt Disney.

5. Jaime Landes, interview with author, 23 April 2013. Jaime Landes graduated in 2004 with a BFA in computer animation from the Ringling College of Art and Design. After graduation Jaime interned in the Pixar Animation Department where she was officially hired in October 2004 to work on *Cars*. During her nine years at the studio Jaime has contributed animated performances to several projects including *Mater and the Ghostlight* (2006), *Wall•E* (2008), *Toy Story 3* (2010), *Brave* (2012) and *Ratatouille* (2007) for which she won the Visual Effects Society Award for Outstanding Animated Character in an Animated Motion Picture for her work on the character of Colette.

6. Quoted in Liu, Ed (2008), "Toon Zone Presents a Virtual Roundtable with *BURN-E* Director Angus MacLane," *Toon Zone*. http://www.toonzone.net/2008/11/toon-zone-presents-a-virtual-roundtable-with-burn-e-director-angus-maclane/#.UcC8P46Ci9Y, 18 November. Angus MacLane earned a BFA from the Rhode Island School of Design, where he studied 2D animation and illustration. Shortly after graduation in 1997, he was hired at Pixar, and his first project for the studio was the Academy Award winning short, *Geri's Game*. Since 1997, Angus has contributed animated performances to nearly every feature Pixar production, including *The Incredibles* (2004) for which he won an Annie award for Outstanding Achievement in Character Animation. In the last five years Angus has taken on additional responsibilities as a director and writer for a variety of Pixar short productions, including *BURN•E* (2008) and the *Toy Story Toon: Small Fry* (2011). He is also the director for the upcoming 2013 television release, *Toy Story of Terror*.

7. This method of assignment contrasts with its parent company, Disney, which for much of its history assigned individual animators to specific characters based upon particular acting talents.

8. Two to three minutes of final footage per animator per feature length film is the Pixar average. During production, a typical Pixar animator completes approximately 100 frames every one to two weeks, depending on the number of characters involved.

9. Adam Burke, interview with author, 23 April 2013.

10. Andrew Gordon, interview with author, 24 April 2013.

11. Gini Cruz Santos, interview with author, 22 April 2013. Gini Cruz Santos holds a BFA in advertising from the University of Santo Tomas in the Philippines and an MFA in computer art, with a specialty in computer animation from the School of the Visual Arts (SVA) in New York City. In 1996, following her graduation from SVA, Gini began at Pixar on her first project, *Toy Story 2* (1999). During her seventeen years at Pixar, Gini has contributed animated performances to more than twelve short and feature-length projects including, *Finding Nemo* (2003), *The Incredibles* (2004), *Up* (2009), *Brave* (2012) and *Lifted* (2006), where she served as a supervising animator.

12. Andrew Gordon, interview with author, 23 April 2013.

13. Ibid.

14. Ibid.

15. Adam Burke, interview with author, 26 April 2013.

16. Animation reference may include a variety of things from a self-made video of the animator acting out their sequence, to the character's voice track and voice recording video, to notes made by the animator outlining the emotional or mental subtext of the shot. Some animators also like to make "thumbnails" or small, active sketches that briefly lay out the shot's action.

17. Jaime Landes, interview with author, 23 April 2013.

18. Ibid.

19. The Annie Awards are annual industry awards, which honor various facets of animation production and design. Landes was nominated for Outstanding Achievement in Character Animation for her contributions to *Brave* (2012).

20. For example, on *Monsters, Inc.* (2001) Andrew Gordon spent most of his time contributing to the animated performance of Mike Wazowski, but Gordon remembers that when given the opportunity to switch "masks" and animate Mike's girlfriend, Celia, in a shot, he did so and his performance was praised for bringing a "fresh perspective" to that character. Andrew Gordon, interview with author, 24 April 2013.

21. Gini Cruz Santos, interview with the author, 22 April 2013.

22. Ibid.

23. Adam Burke, interview with the author, 26 April 2013.

24. Angus MacLane, interview with the author, 21 October 2008. He expressed the same concept to Tim Hauser. See Hauser, Tim (2010), *The Pixar Treasures*, New York: Disney Editions, 36.

25. Adam Burke, interview with the author, 23 April 2013.

26. Ibid.

27. "Dailies" are animation reviews held daily at the studio and involving the director and the animation crew for a project in production.

28. As Adam Burke explains, "We don't have the classic Disney model of Character Leads. [Well] we have that, but ... it's definitely more organic or kinda done by proxy, where it's not, 'this person is on paper solely responsible for the consistency and quality of this character's performance.' We don't have that model. That's not us." Adam Burke, interview with the author, 23 April 2013.

29. Barrier, Michael (1999), *Hollywood Cartoons: American Animation in its Golden* Age. Oxford: Oxford University Press), 88. Although as Barrier notes, for economic and scheduling purposes the kind of "thoughtful casting" employed for *Three Little Pigs* could not be employed on every Disney project in the early 1930s. Barrier, 109. Eventually this method would become the Disney Studio norm and the studio's first feature film, *Snow White and the Seven Dwarfs* (1937), was cast in this manner. Finch, Christopher (2011), *The Art of Walt Disney, From Mickey Mouse to the Magic Kingdoms and Beyond*. New York: Abrams), 124. For more on the animation assignments of *Three Little Pigs* see Maltin, Leonard (1987), *Of Mice and Magic: A History of American Animated Cartoons*. New York: Penguin Group), 40–41.

30. At times the Walt Disney Studios broke away from this model as well as the casting of "specific animators for specific characters." *Bambi*, for example, involved sequence assignments. Finch, Christopher, 189.

31. For example, the first edition of Christopher Finch's *The Art of Disney*, published in 1973 is well illustrated and also credits the artist or animator by name in some cases. An arguably more important text, *The Illusion of Life: Disney Animation*, written by longtime studio animators, Frank Thomas and

Ollie Johnston remains the seminal guidebook for animating in the "Disney style." *Illusion of Life* is extensively illustrated and credits artists by name throughout. Thomas, Frank and Ollie Johnston (1981), *The Illusion of Life: Disney Animation*. New York: Hyperion.

Early exhibitions often did not give credit to the individual artists or animators responsible, this changed dramatically in 1981 with the Whitney Museum of Art's exhibition, "Disney Animations and Animators," where the work of twenty Disney animators were showcased and identified. Mikulak, William (1996), *How Cartoons Became Art: Exhibitions and Sales of Animation Art as Communication of Aesthetic Value*. University of Pennsylvania, Ph.D. diss., 258–59, 262. Subsequent exhibitions have continued the practice of identifying responsible artists.

32.  Many of these animators belong either to the group known collectively as the Nine Old Men, who contributed animation to Walt Disney Studios productions from the 1930s through the 1970s, or they number among their later successors at the studio, such as Glen Keane or Eric Goldberg. For more on the Nine Old Men and their careers see, Canemaker. John (2001), *Walt Disney's Nine Old Men and the Art of Animation*. New York: Disney Editions.

33.  Andrew Gordon, interview with author, 24 April 2013.

34.  Ibid. The Lucky 7 Lounge is the brainchild of Andrew Gordon. The posh bar is a must-see destination for select studio visitors, including celebrity guests. The Lucky 7 sits hidden in a narrow space adjacent to Gordon's office, behind a moving bookcase activated by a "secret button" hidden inside a nearby portrait bust. Gordon's Lucky 7 guest book documents the long and distinguished list of famous visitors.

35.  Gini Cruz Santos, interview with the author, 22 April 2013. Jaime Landes expressed the same sentiment in her April 2013 interview with the author.

36.  Angus MacLane, interview with the author, 21 October 2008.

37.  Adam Burke, interview with the author, 23 April 2013.

38.  Ibid.

39.  Angus MacLane, interview with the author, 1 July 2013.

40.  Posted January 10, 2010 on the Spline Doctor's animation blog, founded and managed by Andrew Gordon. *http://splinedoctors.com/2010/01/*

The relative position of the last two entries on Angus's chart: "The Computers that render an animated film" and "Animators" addresses a notorious and persistent public misunderstanding of the computer's role within the 3D animation process. As MacLane's 2008 Toon Zone interview (see note 6) makes clear, Pixar animators have, through the years, made a valiant effort to elucidate the public on this point during interviews, press events and public talks.

41.  Despite becoming a director, MacLane maintains an emphatic lack of interest in fame. As he recently observed, "I value my privacy. What we do is really public anyway ..." Angus MacLane, interview with the author, 1 July 2013.

42.  Jaime Landes, interview with the author, 23 April 2013.

43.  Ibid.

44.  Since 2009, Pixar has earned two nominations in the Best Picture category for *Up* (2009) and *Toy Story 3* (2010).

45.  Angus MacLane, interview with the author, 1 July 2013. Here Angus refers to a studio outsider's ability to recognize the work of individual animators within a film, however, as noted above, this is particularly challenging in 3D animation.

46.  Ibid.

47.  Adam Burke, interview with the author, 26 April 2013.

# Works Cited

Barrier, Michael. (1999.) *Hollywood Cartoons: American Animation in its Golden* Age. Oxford: Oxford University Press.

Burke, Adam. Interviews with the author, 23 and 26 April 2013.

Canemaker. John. (2001.) *Walt Disney's Nine Old Men and the Art of Animation*. New York: Disney Editions.

Finch, Christopher. (2011.) *The Art of Walt Disney: From Mickey Mouse to the Magic Kingdoms and Beyond*. New York: Abrams.

Gordon, Andrew. Interviews with the author, 23 and 24 April 2013.

Hauser, Tim. (2010.) *The Pixar Treasures*. New York: Disney Editions.

Landes, Jaime. Interview with the author, 23 April 2013.

Lasseter, John. (2009.) "Moving Pictures." In *Animation*. The Archives Series, Walt Disney Animation Studios. New York: Disney Editions.

Liu, Ed. (2008.) "Toon Zone Presents a Virtual Roundtable with *BURN-E* Director Angus MacLane." *Toon Zone* (18 November), http://www.toonzone.net/2008/11/toon-zone-presents-a-virtual-roundtable-with-burn-e-director-angus-maclane/#.UcC8P46Ci9Y.

MacLane, Angus. Interviews with the author, 21 October 2008 and 1 July 2013.

Maltin, Leonard. (1987.) *Of Mice and Magic: A History of American Animated Cartoons*. New York: Penguin.

Mikulak, William. (1996.) *How Cartoons Became Art: Exhibitions and Sales of Animation Art as Communication of Aesthetic Value*. Ph.D. diss., University of Pennsylvania.

Santos, Gini Cruz. Interview with the author, 22 April 2013.

Thomas, Frank, and Ollie Johnston. (1981.) *The Illusion of Life: Disney Animation*. New York: Hyperion.

# Post-Feminist Radical: Jenna Marbles and the Digital Masquerade

## Ted Gournelos

On August 17, 2013, Eminem performed what was probably a well-produced, slick, and fan-pleasing concert to thousands of screaming fans at Slane Castle. I say "probably" because neither Eminem nor the music generated as much attention as did the photographs taken of a 17-year-old girl performing oral sex on at least one male. The images went "viral," as did the social media firestorm on Facebook and Twitter in which users harassed and abused the girl to a massive (and sickening) extent. Additional information included assertions that the victim of the abuse (and of what would be called "statutory rape" in the U.S.) actually reported being sexually assaulted to a police tent at the site, a video depicting her being pushed and verbally abused by a group of young men while kissing another young man, and reports that she was hospitalized due to the extreme stress of her harassment online and her unintentional foray into the public sphere. The social media condemnation of the girl was soon joined by angry and disgusted responses, both in support of the victim and in response to the harassment. The sheer hypocrisy of the negative spotlight on the girl rather than the men was covered in an editorial by noted journalist Sarah Ditum for the *New Statesman* (2013).[1]

This raises a number of interesting and disturbing questions regarding gender and the Internet, many of which are encapsulated in Angela McRobbie's brilliant book *The Aftermath of Feminism* (2009), in which she critiques what she calls a movement towards "post-feminism" that "undoes" the feminist project as it is more traditionally known. Drawing from her 2008 article "Pornographic Permutations," McRobbie responds to "how little serious scholarly debate there is about what widespread participation in sex entertainment by women means for the now out-of-date feminist perspectives on pornography and the sex industry,"[2] and reflects critically on her own work and its place in both the feminist and more broadly cultural studies literature. Noting that her previous work was "far removed" from the work of other feminists who were simultaneously "troubled and intrigued" by the pleasure they took from Dominant media,

McRobbie asks herself several key questions: "Just how oppositional were these seemingly subversive practices? How far did they reach? What value did they deliver to women in the context of the relations of power and powerlessness within which they still found themselves inscribed? How did they articulate with other activities beyond the interface with popular culture?"[3]

In the context of the "Slane Girl" incidents and media furor, McRobbie's questions take on a broader set of implications, in which we must investigate the importance of digital media, especially social and mobile, for the establishment/enforcement of gender and sexuality norms and messages, while at the same time searching for areas not just of oppression, but also agency. In other words, this is not an abstract conversation about feminism. It is a set of realities we are actively living and shaping from day to day, and those realities have very powerful repercussions that are both specific, such as the suicide of Amanda Todd (perhaps the most well-known and well-publicized example of digital bullying and "slut shaming") and general negotiations of the presence and influence of sexuality and/or pornography in everyday life. In this essay, I will discuss two videos produced by "Jenna Marbles" on her YouTube channel that directly engage with, and are often simultaneously critical of and complicit in, contemporary gender politics. I suggest that through explorations of her own gender and sexuality, as well as the context in which those exist and become intelligible, Jenna Marbles is indicative of one form of contemporary post-feminism that acknowledges the necessity of mobilizing the "masquerade" to operate outside of both the "culture wars" and the dominance and restrictions of post-feminism.

## Case Study: Jenna Marbles and Ambivalent Disruption

Unlike the aspects of digital media which I will discuss more extensively later, YouTube offers vloggers (video bloggers) an opportunity to consolidate their voices in Channels. My personal YouTube channel, for instance, provides tutorials to students on media production skills so they can prepare for class. Users less interested in making their own videos, in contrast, often create playlists relating to a certain type of joke assembled from many different posts from other users, like the "My New Haircut" videos. These two uses both demonstrate a tendency to perform a sustained identity that can then be fragmented with different versions of the self, expanded on through new material, and combined through references to others. This reflects the spirit of both true web 1.0, which was based on the idea of not only the circulation of ideas, but of the constant linking (hyperlinking) to other ideas and web pages, as well as web 2.0, which emphasizes participation, creation, and shareability. Web 2.0 functions on the assumption that its material will be horizontally integrated in both production and consumption. It foregrounds the idea that many videos online are direct responses to contemporary culture and thus operate not just as exhibitionism or circulation without thoughts for the implications, but also as a willing and knowing relationship to the Dominant.

One example that demonstrates the power and perils of digital media is the Jenna Marbles YouTube channel, which is one of the top ten most popular channels on the site. It has over 10 million subscribers and its videos have received over one billion total views. A video blog started by a young (24 years old) woman named Jenna Mourey in 2010 introduced the Jenna Marbles phenomenon, beginning with a video called "How to Trick People into Thinking You're Good Looking," which was her comedic rendition of getting ready for work as a go-go dancer. In her *New York Times* article on Mourey, Amy O'Leary (2013) calls it a sort of "reverse burlesque," and notes that "while few people older than 30 probably know who Jenna Marbles is, her popularity is unquestioned among teenage girls who live on the Internet. She has more Facebook fans than Jennifer Lawrence, more Twitter followers than Fox News and more Instagram friends than Oprah."[4] She is, in other words, perfect for the present discussion on post-feminism and the digital masquerade.

This essay will examine issues related to post-feminism and the masquerade in two of Jenna Marbles' videos. These cases are not cherry-picked. In fact, it was difficult to choose *which* videos made the most sense to analyze simply because so many of them apply to the topic. The videos are performances of a stereotypical "girl" (in this case, Marbles plays herself) and "boy" (also played by Marbles) as they surf the Internet. Both are recorded from a computer webcam; unlike many of her videos, in which Marbles looks directly at us (into the camera), and speaks directly to us, here she looks "through" us, into the world of the computer itself, and her commentary is self-directed.

Marbles begins all of her videos with her splash screen, which portrays her in what appears to be football pads (with accompanying eyeblack) and nothing else. The image plays with sexuality and the appropriation of masculinity, both of which it then plays with ironically as her logo pops up (her name in a futurist/techno font with one of her chihuahua's heads above it) accompanied by the sound of squeaker dog toys. Marbles' videos are visually distinctive not for what she wears or her background (which is often a sparse office or bedroom), but rather for their staccato rhythm. She at times jumps from concept to concept, but mostly this is a visual technique, in which she sharply cuts a longer video into a shorter video with no transitions and often with broken sentences and positions. This adds a do-it-yourself (DIY) feeling to the videos, which makes them feel personal as well as low tech enough to be relatable.

*What Girls Do on the Internet* takes the perspective of a performed "Jenna," and *What Boys Do on the Internet* takes the perspective of a performed "everyday guy," which is Marbles with a drawn-on curled mustache, backwards baseball cap, and parodically deepened voice. Both videos are extremely funny and use intricate imagery and voiceovers (neither character actually speaks, but only "thinks.") But for the sake of space I will point out only a few of the defining parallel moments in each of the films: the dominant preoccupation of each gender, the attitude towards pornography and blurred sexual lines, and the attitude towards one's own body. In "girls"' narrative, Marbles is trying to get some work done, but is constantly distracted by other things. Celebrity gossip, pictures of cats, standing upside down, Twitter, and her ex-boyfriend's new girlfriend's Facebook profile, are all sources of interest and often anxiety. In other words, Marbles is portraying the classic, ditzy, sexualized stereotype of a young woman critiqued by McRobbie above. Similarly, one could view the way she portrays her body, whether that is poking her breasts gleefully while she sings "boobies boobies boobies" to herself or sadly obsessing over the size of her butt (at which point she writes it a note asking it to look better and won't let herself eat cake). At the same time, she fragments that understanding, implicitly critiquing those concepts through parody while also recognizing that there is a degree of truth to them. This is most explicit in a short scene in which she says "fucking thong is making my butthole itch" before wiggling around in her chair and saying "should *not* have shaved so close to my butthole!" Marbles takes a similar approach to sexuality. When prompted to pay for three months of lesbian porn, she considers and says "okay!," upon which she wonders "am I gay?" and responds, laughing, "I don't know!" When she looks at the pornography, she's obviously enjoying herself as a spectator, but then realizes "nah, I like boys." When she turns to male pornography, however, she spends her time not enjoying it, but being horrified at men's bodies, with disgusted comments like "what is *wrong* with that guy's dick?," an ironic "sick tat, bra ... what's that, the tribal sign for 'douche?,'" and a happily teasing singsong "homeboy's got a dangly ballsack!"

Unlike the laughingly parodic version of female use of the Internet, *What Boys Do on the Internet* has a definite edge to it, if still a funny one. The main activity/distraction of the "boy" is masturbation, and "his" primary challenge is not how to get work done over distractions, but to find something "suitable" for masturbation. He begins on ESPN.com, before wondering if that is "right," and decides to look at porn instead. His attempt to connect to "real" women, like Marbles, is to look at an ex-girlfriend, at which point he becomes angry at seeing a new man in her life and begins to look at other girls' profiles. While the "girl" obsesses over the new girlfriend herself, and vacillates between anger at her ex and despair that he doesn't like her anymore, the "boy" looks for new sexual partners, before failing as he is bewildered by their stereotypical self-portrayals such as making "duck faces" and "throwing up deuces" as if they're in some kind of secret "gang for hot girls." Like the "girl," the "male" character is also dissatisfied with his body, which is sparked by an advertisement to buy pills to grow his penis 15 inches in size. Excited, he says it's "going to be like a weapon, I'm gonna like hurt bitches with it," and buys a lifetime supply (before reading a testimonial and finding out that it doesn't work). The constant portrayal and emphasis on masturbation and pornography is particularly interesting, however. Like the "girl," he is at times horrified by female sex organs (for example, "her vagina looks like an Arby's sandwich"), but that does not deter him long from masturbating. Neither does "tranny porn," and his insistence that he not "look at the dick." After he orgasms to the imagery of the transvestite, he opens a beer, says that he is "so ashamed," and then shrugs and says "well, better go eat something!"

These two videos directly engage the way in which critical cultural studies scholars discuss gender, sexuality, and pornography. An emphasis on insecurity regarding one's sexual appearance is divided into self-disgust on the female's part and an ego-supportive desire for power (represented by domination) on the male's. Insecurity regarding one's sexual desires, moreover, is largely connected, although the male is represented as far more horrified and insecure about his homoerotic arousal than the female, and interestingly enough is the one who actually ends up pursuing that desire. In other words, these are both homages to cultural stereotypes containing gender and sexuality, while they are also pointed criticisms of our preconceptions and hypocrisies. I find this particularly interesting in the "boys" video, in which transvestism by Jenna Marbles (even if it is only nominally so) allows her to critique the construction of the male Self. While Doane wonders if this is possible for women, in that it is "not understandable ... why a woman might flaunt her femininity, produce herself as an excess of femininity ... because it constitutes an acknowledgment that it is femininity itself which is constructed as mask—as the decorative layer which conceals a non-identity,"[5] I suggest that within the post-feminist schema it is absolutely vital that women construct, and acknowledge and critique the construction of themselves as masks. In other words, to engage one's own femininity and the broader socio-political aspects of that femininity, it is important to decenter it, grasp it, and perform it in order to use it strategically and push it towards egalitarianism without foreclosing opportunities for agency or disregarding the lives and contexts of the women who are *forced* to retain that construction in their everyday lives.

Marbles is certainly exceptional in terms of the depth and mastery of the medium. Of course she is absolutely hilarious and has a huge market appeal. However, she is not rare on the Internet. Thousands of other films take similar approaches to popular culture, identity, gender, and social politics (and this is not restricted to gender—race, disability, ethnicity, or politics all manifest in this way online). In fact dozens of films take similar approaches to the above vlog entries. What these videos should remind us is that feminism and the feminist project is far from over. Indeed it is a very real, and much *lived* reality for most young women.

Although scholars like McRobbie do, in fact, at times lament that feminism has been "undone," and that young women have not only abandoned feminism but are living a corrupted version of it, I would argue that we are witnessing not just an undoing of feminism. We are actually witnessing an invigoration of feminism in which many of the central questions the movement forced society to ask, including whether women deserved equal pay, whether they should be able to choose their path through sexuality, and whether they should be able to openly critique and fight for different representations for themselves without anyone telling them "no," are actually internalized into the culture. The issue is not just that they are embattled, or that the project is over, but that post-feminism is a representation of a negotiated identity that at once recognizes many of the goals of the project and the constraints (market constraints, social constraints, and constraints of desire) that women are under. As Banet Weiser (2011) has argued,

> The construction of the self is not an insular, isolated activity, but is rather situated in a media and cultural context that involves a dynamic between the self and others, or in the case of YouTube, between video content and user feedback. Of course, this is not only a generational dynamic but also a gendered one. That is, if kids are "living online," part of this everyday life means, among other things, negotiating power relations and crafting gendered identity. In particular, the practices of "living online" are often similar to those central to post-feminism: Empowerment and constraint need to be understood in the particular context which not only validates their specific logic, but indeed makes specific definitions of power and constraint legible in the first place.[6]

In fact, this is borne out at least in part by a 2013 article from, believe it or not, *Glamour* magazine. In a section on "dos and don'ts," which is at least in part on fashion, one of the "dos" is to "call yourself a feminist," and critiques what it calls "feminots" (that is, women who claim to not be feminists, but assert "the strength of women" or female equality.) Citing statistics on the growing number of women (especially young women) who identify as feminists, it follows up with an interview with feminist-chic online magazine Jezebel.com editor-in-chief Anna Holmes, in which she argues that

> Not only are women's websites thriving, but I am also seeing lively and regular discussions of feminist issues in mass media–pop culture and news. Things like rape culture, pay equality, and gender discrimination in the workplace, conventional standards of beauty, and quality child care. We discuss these things *as* a matter of course now, and we didn't in the past.[7]

So while Jenna Marbles might not look anything like what the feminist movement often envisioned as an enlightened woman, I would argue that her YouTube channel in fact serves a vital function as a forum for discussion in the public sphere, as well as a pedagogical function in which we begin to break down not only gender, but what constructs it. For me, it is hard to imagine something more feminist, "post" or not.

## Post-Feminism and the Masquerade

McRobbie laments that she has been "complicit" in a "compromise position" due to her students' desire for and interest in aspects of media and culture that she herself might find conservative or reactionary.[8] Throughout the book, in fact, she connects us to what she perceives (rightly, in my experience) to be a hesitancy and at times outright hostility to "feminism" on the part of both young women and young men. McRobbie doesn't fully explain *why* this might be the case, but simply points it out as a reality[9] even when she is engaging it through the literature (for example, her discussion of Faludi and Stacey's work).[10] McRobbie continually relies on a nostalgia for a feminism *that might never have actually existed*, and laments cultural turns to a "subtle renewal of gender injustices" as if the focus on the beauty myth and beauty industry are a new invention, or as if women and girls have not been viewed as sexual objects for thousands of years of patriarchy.[11] This is not to suggest that the current culture of hypersexualization, age compression, and beauty construction are not particularly exploitative. It rather suggests that framing it in comparison to halcyon days of feminist success versus an anthropomorphized Dominant might be more indicative of the failure of feminism to either gain/retain a broad appeal to women, or to articulate itself or its project in the anti-racist, anti-inequality, human rights vein that McRobbie and many other feminist scholars see as primary.

In many ways, McRobbie is quite right in her critiques, and she is certainly accurate in her connections (drawing on Wendy Brown and Lisa Duggan among others) between a neoliberal market and the establishment of a neoliberal identity that can foreclose emancipatory politics. However, what she does not engage is the possibility that women might feel that feminism *itself* was a movement that often seemed to (in reality or not) foreclose agency and gender flexibility. In other words, for many women "feminism" could easily be interpreted in one of two ways, first, advocating a "state of injury," to borrow Wendy Brown's (1995) terminology, that foregrounded gender identity and politics as victimization, and second, of advocating a hard line of gender-reimagining, in which every day women's desires and realities were diminished in favor of an ideal of "equality" that de-emphasized culturally-determined "femininity" and characterized women who, for instance, dress in "spindly stilettos and 'pencil' skirts," as complicit in the patriarchy.[12]

The latter point in particular is key for the present discussion, as it suggests that images of women in popular culture determine our reality and, most importantly, shape not only how women *can* act within society, but how they *should* act as women responsible for combating the Dominant's portrayal of the gender. It takes a stance reflected in much feminist literature stemming from the second wave, especially surrounding images and representation of women. This important area of study deserves a great deal of criticism and thought. However, it also correlates to the hostility McRobbie and others notice in young women's relationship to the movement, not only because it is judgmental about women's everyday desires and pleasures, but also because it takes a position that in large part stems from a position of privilege. In other words, it is all very well and good to speak as an economically secure, White, tenured, academic feminist about what women's lives and attitudes should be in an ideal world. It is very different for women who might view their sexuality or consumption as a source of pleasure, fantasy, or escape *even if* and perhaps even *because* it reflects broader power structures in society. Women might see their sexuality in terms of a strategic essentialism, or a de Certeauian tactical response to power. Or women might simply want to seem taller in order to be more confident when working with male colleagues, or women who see a foregrounding of their femininity as such an important political statement *in and of itself* within a masculine-dominated environment.

I do not advocate here that McRobbie herself is taking this stance due to privilege. To the contrary, her oeuvre is pivotal precisely in its movement beyond such issues. She makes an important point about what she calls the "post-feminist masquerade," which "would seemingly re-locate women back inside the terms of traditional gender hierarchies." She suggests that this form of the masquerade is only on a surface level "a matter of choice rather than obligation," which forces women into the rituals of a "feminine totality" represented by practices of grooming and other self-maintenance.[13] McRobbie explicitly suggests this as an update to Joan Riviere's (1929) discussion of the masquerade, adding an awareness of the importance of "images of femininity found in the cultural realm" rather than everyday women and their encounters.[14]

The "Slane Girl" example mentioned at the beginning of this essay suggests that the old feminist adage that "the personal is political," or that the public spheres and private spheres are blurry for women in particular, is amplified exponentially on the Internet. Therefore, it is important that while we take the criticism of the images and representation of women as a primary area of critique, we also emphasize how daily life and everyday encounters are in many ways *themselves* the images and representations we see online, and are examples of both the "self-branding" of the gendered body and the "*branding*" of that body by external forces. In other words, outside of film, television, and advertising, it is precisely the everyday portrayals of women, and increasingly their *self-portrayals*, that are the meat of online representation.

In Riviere (1929), femininity is a strategic identity worn to diffuse tensions connected to women taking roles and positions culturally attributed to men: "womanliness therefore could be assumed and worn as a mask, both to hide the possession of masculinity and to avert the reprisals expected if she was found to possess it."[15] If we go back to the masquerade as an event, however, the masquerade is not just a cultural trope, it is a way for women (and men) to interact in a quasi-public sphere. Masquerades were parties that emphasized the carnivalesque using masks to conceal identity. Particularly for Victorian women, as Terry Castle (1987) argues, the masquerade could be considered a "masked assembly as a kind of machine for feminine pleasure."[16] Moreover, rather than an "index to female degeneracy," the "pleasure seeking" of the masquerade could be "an altogether comprehensible reaction to the horrific erotic repression enjoined upon respectable women by 18th-century culture" and in which they "had access to a unique realm of sexual freedom, and a psychological latitude reserved normally reserved for men." They could enter into a "temporary if problematic release from such prescriptions" as sexual desire that was at best contained only within marriage and a disregarding of class absent from all other areas of society.[17] Because unlike other areas of the public sphere, women could attend masquerades unescorted, and because prostitutes often masqueraded as "women of quality" and vice versa, this was not only an aspect of freedom but also of potential violence. "Masquerading women ... invariably illustrated the misogynist theme that every woman was at heart a rake. Any woman at a masquerade might be viewed as a 'prostitute in disguise'—at once hyper sexualized, hypocritical, and an exploiter of innocent men."[18] Interestingly enough, Castle also argues that in literature, "women writers seem unwilling to grant to their heroines the same sexual or professional success they have achieved themselves."[19] Indeed, in these narratives women were often abducted from masquerades and raped, sometimes due to men pretending to be trusted family members, and the women are then ostracized by the family.[20]

As a middle ground between these concepts of the masquerade, Doane (2003) suggests that it "involves a realignment of femininity, the recovery, or more accurately, simulation, of the missing gap or distance."[21] To masquerade is the ability to move between how one views oneself and one's role and the image produced for us, by the Symbolic in general and in interpersonal or media power relationships more specifically. McRobbie echoes this in some ways, and her rhetoric highlights the tension here between emphasizing power and a discontent with (young) women's (self-) portrayals, and their instinct and desire to seek agency and activity in both media and everyday life. While she suggests that the post-feminist masquerade is a representation of "nervousness" and a lack of power of young women because they are "still unused to power, it ill-befits them, they are inexperienced, they cannot afford for it to be relaxed or casual, they are anxious it will make them unfeminine."[22] She also immediately questions this with her rhetoric afterwards, as she uses words like "adopts this style," "the air of," and "to help her navigate."[23] In other words, McRobbie acknowledges that the masquerade, even in a post-feminist context, is at the very least unconsciously strategic.

The tension between agency and constructed representation is of course highly present in debates within the feminist movement itself, as Attwood (2007) argues.[24] When Attwood discusses the role of Riot Grrrl as "an attempt to refashion femininity from existing items, a form of bricolage that insists there is no essential meaning 'underneath' and that meaning depends precisely on intent, placement, combination and performance,"[25] she is highlighting the fact that media in many forms is completely entwined in our everyday lives, and that we live our lives at least in part through the breakdown and (re)formation of images. This is particularly important when we speak about young women, who might have internalized *both* the gains made in gender equity (in the U.S. context, we have Title IX), but also the increasing assumption by young women that if there is gender inequity, that fact is both wrong and changeable). Moreover we find the dangerous emphasis on hyper-sexualization and age compression in the media and young women's self-identification with femininity such as the growing influence of Victoria's Secret as cultural icon rather than the more overtly or admittedly sexual Playboy brand.[26] The masquerade, then, represents a series of social and cultural foreclosures, but also an increasingly internalized assumption of the ideal of gender equity and the acknowledgment that femininity could be employed strategically to navigate or fight the dangers of contemporary misogyny.

## The Online Masquerade

Because our identities are increasingly shaped and circulated online, we need to recognize the specific challenges that the Internet poses for any discussion of gender performance, or the potential transgressions and negotiations of the Dominant present in the masquerade. As I argued with David Gunkel in *Transgression 2.0* (2011), the Internet is a location, a medium, a cultural product, a mode of distribution and consumption that often simultaneously takes emancipatory/progressive and reactionary/conservative forms. Gender, sexuality, and the masquerade are no exceptions to that rule. Internet theorists have pointed this out for decades, in fact. For instance, while scholars like Herring (1993) and Kendall (1998) identified stereotypical performances of gender online in terms of use of language used, modes of address, and even links (in addition to more visual design elements), other scholars like Baym (2000) and Witmer and Katzman (1997) argue that this is extremely context dependent, and relies on a reified assumption regarding (the separation of) "male" and "female" behavior. In the early text-based worlds of interaction on the Internet like Internet-Relay-Chats (IRC) and Multi-User-Domains (MUD), scholars like Danet (1998), Stone (1996), and Turkle (1995) have argued that the performance of identity is particularly interesting on the Internet, as it is *always* performed apart from notions of authenticity, decentered, and multiplied. This allows it to be hidden or altered, as Danet argues, or rewritten as a construct both online and, particularly interesting, offline as well. As Turkle argues, "Having literally written our online personae into existence, we are in a position to be more aware of what we project into everyday life. Like the anthropologist returning home from a foreign culture, the voyager in virtuality can return to a real world better equipped to understand its artifices."[27]

The idea that the Internet serves such a progressive function is challenged, however, by many other scholars, notably Wynn and Katz (1997) and Kendall (2002). Wynn and Katz question whether "the fragmentation of self would ever be the basis of cultural change," since humans will prefer metanarratives (especially the further decentered or alienated they feel.)[28] Kendall argues that people are more prone to resist views of themselves as performative constructs than to embrace it, as being a construct is far more difficult to grasp than being a coherent, logical individual with a clearly defined social place and mentality. Kendall takes this further, in fact, suggesting that "The electronic medium that makes gender masquerade possible and conceivable for a wider range of people also enables both the masqueraders and their audiences to interpret these performances in ways that distance them from a critique of *real* gender."[29]

## Conclusion

Jenna Marbles' digital masquerade reminds us of the gap in our understanding about how women *should* present themselves as consistent with a feminist tradition, and how they currently *are* presenting themselves on a more active level in their interactions with the Dominant. Even if we consider stereotypically "feminine" media, what about women's responses to gossip, fashion, and celebrity "news," which at least in everyday life often appear quite critical and oppositional (or at least takes a negotiated view of ideology)? What about women's discussions about their families like Anne-Marie Slaughter's public discussions on her life choices negotiating the contradictory pulls of her family and her diplomatic career? What about the increasingly public discourse surrounding women's portrayals of their sex lives, or their feelings about romantic partners? These are issues that are front and center in women's media (meaning, media created *by* women as well as media created *for* women), even in productions like fashion magazines that are considered to be largely reactionary and thus are routinely ignored as a potentially transformative space in feminist scholarship. When we think about the masquerade, in particular, this is problematic. The masquerade is not how women are presented, after all, but how they strategically present *themselves* in order to function in certain ways within certain contexts.

## Notes

1. Sarah Ditum (2013), "Why It's Different for Girls: Slut Shaming in the Digital Age," *New Statesman* (19 August), http://www.newstatesman.com/voices/2013/08/why-its-different-girls-slut-shaming-digital-age.
2. Angela McRobbie (2009), *The Aftermath of Feminism: Gender, Culture and Social Change* (Los Angeles: Sage Publications), 3.
3. Ibid.
4. Amy O'Leary (2013), "The Woman with 1 Billion Clicks, Jenna Marbles," *The New York Times* (13 April).

5. Mary Ann Doane (1982), "Film and the Masquerade: Theorising the Female Spectator," *Screen* 23, 3–4: 65–66.

6. Sarah Banet-Weiser (2011), "Branding the Post-Feminist Self: Girls' Video Production and YouTube," in *Mediated Girlhoods: New Explorations of Girls' Media Culture*, Mary Celeste Kearney, ed. (New York: Peter Lang), 281.

7. "The New Do: Calling Yourself a Feminist" (2013), *Glamour* (September), http://www.glamour.com/inspired/2013/09/the-new-do-calling-yourself-a-feminist.

8. McRobbie (2009), 3.

9. Ibid., 14–15.

10. Ibid., 33–35.

11. Ibid., 55.

12. Ibid., 65.

13. Ibid., 65–66.

14. Ibid., 64.

15. Joan Riviere (1929), "Womanliness as Masquerade," *International Journal of Psychoanalysis* 10: 306.

16. Terry Castle (1986), Masquerade and Civilization: The Carnivalesque in Eighteenth-century English Culture and Fiction (Stanford, CA: Stanford University Press), 254.

17. Ibid., 44.

18. Ibid., 33.

19. Ibid., 288.

20. Ibid., 45.

21. Doane (1982), 66.

22. McRobbie (2009), 66.

23. Ibid., 67.

24. Feona Attwood (2002), "Reading Porn: The Paradigm Shift in Pornography Research," *Sexualities* 5, 1: 241.

25. Ibid., 240.

26. Ibid., 242.

27. Sherry Turkle (1997), *Life on the Screen: Identity in the Age of the Internet* (New York: Simon & Schuster), 263.

28. Eleanor Wynn and James E. Katz (1997), "Hyperbole over Cyberspace: Self-Presentation and Social Boundaries in Internet Home Pages and Discourse," *The Information Society* 13, 4: 303.

29. Lori Kendall (2002), *Hanging Out in the Virtual Pub: Masculinities and Relationships Online* (Berkeley: University of California Press), 107.

# Works Cited

Attwood, Feona. (2002.) "Reading Porn: The Paradigm Shift in Pornography Research." *Sexualities* 5, 1.

Banet-Weiser, Sarah. (2011.) "Branding the Post-Feminist Self: Girls' Video Production and YouTube." In *Mediated Girlhoods: New Explorations of Girls' Media Culture,* Mary Celeste Kearney, ed. New York: Peter Lang.

Castle, Terry. (1986.) *Masquerade and Civilization: The Carnivalesque in Eighteenth-century English Culture and Fiction.* Stanford, CA: Stanford University Press.

Ditum, Sarah. (2013.) "Why It's Different for Girls: Slut Shaming in the Digital Age." *New Statesman* (19 August), http://www.newstatesman.com/voices/2013/08/why-its-different-girls-slut-shaming-digital-age.

Doane, Mary Ann. (1982.) "Film and the Masquerade: Theorising the Female Spectator." *Screen* 23, 3–4.

Kendall, Lori. (2002.) *Hanging Out in the Virtual Pub: Masculinities and Relationships Online.* Berkeley: University of California Press.

McRobbie, Angela. (2009.) *The Aftermath of Feminism: Gender, Culture and Social Change.* Los Angeles: Sage Publications.

"The New Do: Calling Yourself a Feminist." (2013.) *Glamour* (September), http://www.glamour.com/inspired/2013/09/the-new-do-calling-yourself-a-feminist.

O'Leary, Amy. (2013.) "The Woman with 1 Billion Clicks, Jenna Marbles." *The New York Times* (13 April).

Riviere, Joan. (1929.) "Womanliness as Masquerade." *International Journal of Psychoanalysis* 10.

Turkle, Sherry. (1997.) *Life on the Screen: Identity in the Age of the Internet*. New York: Simon & Schuster.

Wynn, Eleanor, and James E. Katz. (1997.) "Hyperbole over Cyberspace: Self-Presentation and Social Boundaries in Internet Home Pages and Discourse." *The Information Society* 13, 4.

# Cosplay: Masquerade for the Millennials

## Laura Crow

---

Cosplay is arguably the masquerade for the millennial generation. As with other generations in other worlds, dressing-up and assuming another persona has often been regarded with suspicion, but also titillation. Eighteenth-century Venetian aristocrats would live dangerously by masking themselves to venture into a forbidden public at night. When the general public began to mask themselves as well, to pretend what they were not, it became all the more anonymous and exciting. The masquerading allowed time to explore many things not permitted in one's milieu, including sexual dalliances. Many 18th-century aristocratic women in particular ventured into a world that they had never even seen, let alone interacted with. Cosplay today has created a similar culture that levels out society and allows people to develop a fantasy alter ego, but it is not in the streets, and is a bit more about bonding than sexuality. Cosplay happens in enormous halls and convention centers that are so populated that they feel a bit like a city existing in an alternative reality, probably a lot like Venice at Carnival time in the 18th century and even today.

Cosplay has grown out of a number of influences, including the incredible popularity of Japanese animated television cartoons and video games spurring the growth of *Nerds*, Comic-Con conventions celebrating science fiction and encouraging "fan dressing," and Halloween. Halloween in the United States has traditionally been a time when anyone can feel free to wear a mask and still retain social respectability. After World War II, this holiday sanctioned children to dress up with parents in tow. Sometimes the adults would wear a token costume piece in order to take part of the ritual of candy gathering when they thought the masquerading might venture into unsafe territory. Parents would lag behind in the shadows and live vicariously through their children with the excuse that they should not wander the neighborhood alone.

This essay examines in more detail how traditional Halloween celebrations after World War II have morphed into the big business of convention masquerades now established across the country. Those in turn have greatly influenced the Cosplay masquerade phenomenon. We could easily start this exploration with the onset of the mid '70s well-attended annual Halloween parades on Christopher Street in Greenwich Village. This was less of a parade, than a giant six-block long gathering of people in adult dress-up that had a party atmosphere and the same rather illicit undertones that existed in 18th-century Venice *Carnevale*. Adult dress-up in that instance still had an air of danger and sexuality.

New York City also had performance artists at that time who were moving beyond costume into themed wearable objects. In 1973, a store that opened in New York City on Madison Avenue titled "Julie: Artisans' Gallery" specialized in expensive hand crafted wearable art. The owner of the shop, Julie Schaffer Dale had connections to the entertainment industry through her husband, the actor Jim Dale. She received a lot of publicity for dressing rock stars with her garments.[1] Another shop in Manhattan that was more retro in its offerings, with a range of masquerading looks post World War II, was titled "Early Halloween," by the owner Joyce Ostrin. "Halloween" was becoming an adult term and wearing something that went beyond contemporary clothing into period costume was becoming a trend. Dressing in second-hand store clothing continue to be very popular throughout the 1970s and the looks grew more and more theatrical, typified by the extremely popular Beatles album cover, *Sergeant Pepper's Lonely Hearts Club Band*, that exemplified Army surplus on acid.

In Seattle, Washington, an organization of performance and fiber artists who called themselves, "Friends of the Rag," was founded in the late '60s. They regularly peppered the streets of Seattle with wearable art that was sometimes not recognizable as clothing at all. That grew out of the arts and crafts movement during the "Hippie Era," in the late '60s and early '70s. These were not amateur embroiderers, but artists working in this new medium of wearable art.

Simultaneously "Star Trek" conventions were popping up around the United States and attendees started to wear the standard "Trekker" uniforms. By the mid-'70s, at the "Star Trek" Convention in Seattle, there were many costumes that went far beyond Captain Kirk and his crew. In addition to "Trekkers" and "Whovians," the followers of the legendary "Captain Who" other futuristic space costumes or aliens began to appear. Comic-Con was a direct outgrowth of the "Star Trek" Conventions, but Cosplay has grown even beyond the huge Comic-Con events. There are now 4000 Cosplay Clubs on university campuses across the United States. They grew out of Sci Fi clubs into Anime clubs, but now as Cosplay clubs they are enormously popular because they are far less restrictive.

Many of those who gravitated towards the Comic-Con conventions might be described as "Nerds." The word "Nerd" originated in the Dr. Seuss book *If I Ran the Zoo*, published in 1950. It was a typical whimsical Seussical creature, who was a bit odd. The term was popularized in the 1970s by the sitcom *Happy Days,* and generally referred to an overly intellectual and socially-impaired person. Since the advent of the computer age, "Nerd" is strongly identified with someone skilled at computer technology and/or computer gaming. It gained more power and credibility as the computer age developed social media, where each could masquerade as their own fantasy persona on the Internet. Sports-challenged people could move beyond socially negative labels, since they could live vicariously through video-game heroes. Intellectual prowess was on the rise, especially as it related to skill at computer games. "Geek Chic" came into fashion following the grunge movement in Seattle in the early 1990s and by 2013 in Paris a fashion-based Anime/Cosplay movement had fully developed. The "Hipster" fashion movement evolved out of the Nerd Culture, and the bulk of Comic-Con attendees fall into this category where it is cool to be ugly.

The first Comic-Con occurred in Great Britain in August of 1968 in Liverpool around the same time as the "Trekkies" were meeting in conventions in the United States. It grew out of the parents of the millennial generation, who were raised on comic books. The convention in Great Britain carried on until 1981 in various locations, and focused on British comic book art. They had comic book collector's items handled by dealers, and various other saleable objects. By 1979 one of the highlights, a contest of costumes based on comic book characters, was renamed as the "Comic Art and Fantasy Convention."[2] These events usually occurred during a weekend so working people found them accessible and could afford to build elaborate costumes for the contests allowing them to parade around incognito as someone far from the working class drudgery. About this same time, heading into the '80s, Lee Bowery and the "Glam Rock" club era was about to begin along with David Bowie and "Ziggy Stardust."

In the United States the earliest Comic-Con convention was in San Diego, California, and called "San Diego Comic-Con International." This "fan convention" started with a crowd of some 300 persons in 1970. In San Diego, a little more than 40 years later in 2012, that number had risen to more than 130,000 people.

> Comic-Con International: San Diego is a nonprofit educational corporation dedicated to creating awareness of, and appreciation for, comics and related popular art forms, primarily through the presentation of conventions and events that celebrate the historic and ongoing contribution of comics to art and culture.[3]

In 1972, Chicago Comic-Con had begun under the name, "Wizard World Chicago," and had about 2,000 patrons, and that became 70,000 by 2010.[4] In the early 1970s, The Organic Theatre Company operating out of the Body Politic in Chicago produced a comic book science fiction piece titled *Warp*, the brainchild of Chicago director Stuart Gordon and writer Lenny Kleinfeld (a.k.a. Bury St. Edmund). It displayed comic book style characters, both women and men, equally muscled from trips to the gym. It grew into a trilogy and was hugely successful and influential in Chicago, especially in light of Comic-Con.[5] With the emergence of Women's equality appearing in many forms, the comic conventions encouraged women warriors. These empowered young adults were not old enough to vote for John F. Kennedy, but were part of a whole generation who believed in him and in space travel following the 1969 landing on the moon.

Since the turn of the new millennium Comic-Con conventions began to take place all over the United States. Beyond the mega mother Comic-Con in San Diego there is a very popular Convention in New York City large enough to inhabit the huge Jacob Javits Convention Center in Manhattan, and yet another Convention in Boston. Between these two sites resides the Connecticon in the Hartford Connecticut Convention Center which doubled its attendance from 5000 to 10,000 from 2011 to 2012, and in 2014 increased to 15, 000. Connecticon was given an award for bringing the most business to Hartford through contracts with bars and movie theatres as well as eight hotels supported with shuttle buses.[6] This continues to be a rapidly developing industry.

Hollywood discovered the population of fans in San Diego's Comic-Con and began to exploit the potential publicity for upcoming science fiction films, sending actors in costume from past hits, such as the movie, *Star Wars*. When *Lord of the Rings* was about to be released, the director Peter Jackson was there at the Comic-Con to talk about his work and the upcoming film.

Fan tables at Comic-Con encourage people with similar interests to meet and converse. In San Diego, Legendary Pictures has its own table, and in 2012 featured directors such as

Guillermo del Toro pushing *Pacific Rim* before its release.[7] In that instance fans of Legendary Pictures seek out their fan table to see what's coming out next. Comic-Con has become about big business and Hollywood continuing to push films while the gaming industry promotes new games. Comic-Con International is itself a big business at this point in its development. It also runs APE, the Alternative Press Expo in San Francisco that is not a Cosplay event, but a graphic novel convention, and WonderCon, a convention at the Anaheim Convention Center near Disneyland. BlizzCon is also at the Anaheim Convention Center in November and caters specifically to Blizzard Entertainment buffs of games such as "World of Warcraft." Dragon Con occurs annually in Atlanta and exploits all things dragon plus Cosplay.

A huge Cosplay movement in Japan supports the "World Cosplay Summit." It really started in Japan in Akihabara, a pop gathering site in Tokyo inspired by fans of the Otoku no Video, a product that kids watched in 1991. It is a comic video about Otoku who are obsessed with media, and particularly Anime and Manga.

Cosplay is equally popular in other parts of Asia, including the Philippines and Taiwan, and developing in China. There is even "Japan Expo-Sud" in Marseilles, France. Among many others, there is a huge Anime Convention at the MCM Convention Center in London on Canary Wharf that pushes comics and films. Clearly, it is a world phenomenon.

Cosplay evolved out of the Comic-Con movement and supports a myriad of costumes, many of which are fan-based. The fan bases can represent a broad spectrum of animated television and film characters, video games, and comic book characters. Anime cartoon characters are the most prominent, but video games also provide a lot of ideas particularly for young men. In 2013 the *Doctor. Who* revival brought back "nerdy" space suits. The *Sherlock Holmes* BBC television series as well as other films gave rise to more steampunk costumes. *X-Men* the television animated series has been reborn as live action film, providing roles. Io9 is a website that pushed science, movies, television and concept art. World Com showcases World Combat games that have grown up through the video game industry and they provide characters as well. One important rule does not allow nudity or beachwear when dressing up for Cosplay. This is not so much about showing off the body as it is about showing off the intellect. It appears innocent on the surface but the characteristics displayed are quite sophisticated. Most people want to be recognized. It is flattering to be photographed, so there is ample opportunity through Facebook and on the Internet to see what options are available and acceptable.

The generation that populates these conventions was the first generation to embrace Halloween extensively. The children of a generation of hippies and artists were dressed up in very elaborate costumes for Halloween. The idea of the Halloween parade came about, not only on Christopher Street in New York City, but in every elementary school in the country. By 1985, each "little darling" had their own moment to shine in their exotic costumes.

This Halloween costume event seemed to grow exponentially through the 1980s and really took off in the 1990s. Their mothers increasingly worked to create award-winning Halloween costumes for their children. The paper pattern companies such as Simplicity, McCalls and Butterick jumped into the fray and created patterns for moms to make elaborately constructed costumes for their children, often based on Walt Disney cartoon characters. In addition, the market was flooded with cheap costumes made in China for those who didn't know how to sew or didn't care to sew. These young people continued to dress up for Halloween far beyond their childhood years and continue to have enormous Halloween parties where each person will devote hours to the creation of their Halloween persona. Not surprisingly the Halloween parade that began on Christopher Street with a very particular social group of gay men has spread to become a parade in New York City on 6th Avenue, larger than the Macy's Thanksgiving Parade that now crosses all social boundaries.

Comic book characters with their large strokes were easy to reproduce and easily identified even if the costume was not particularly well-crafted. Young people in their late teens and twenties began to recreate the characters from television and their favorite video games. Marvel Comics (Spider-Man, The Hulk, Iron Man, Thor and Loki, Captain America) and DC Comics (Superman, Batman and Robin, Wonder Woman, Green Hornet, the Flash, Aquaman) heroes and nerds were sourced, but more commonly used were the animated cartoons that the Millennials watched in the '80s, '90s, and early 2000s that came out of Japan. Rainbow Brite, Ninja Turtles, Transformers, Powerpuff Girls, Adventuretime's Finn—a human boy with a bear hat and Princess Bubblegum of the Candy Kingdom whom he protects—and more complex, Revolutionary Girl Utena who cross-dresses as a Prince to save Anthy, the Rose Bride are Japanese cartoons that are part of a sub-genre known as Anime, with a specific drawing style called "Manga" and the various characters created became extremely popular.

Also popular were favorite video game characters from games such as Kingdom Hearts, Final Fantasy, Street Fighter, Mortal Combat, Mario Brothers—used often for gender swap— and Legend of Zelda with Princess Zelda & Link. All of these various characters on television and in video games became popular collectible figurines. This provided something for the boys to embrace dressing-up as video game characters or geek versions of helmeted heroes in brightly colored spandex leotards from live action series such as The Power Rangers. The Power Rangers are particularly easy to duplicate with spandex and motorcycle helmets. The helmet adds to the masquerade. The nerd factor is illustrated also in the elaborate costumes that took technology to produce, such as Optimus Prime from the Transformers series. This costume at Connecticon in 2012 had mechanized parts so that it could partially convert its body and had eyes that lit up red with LEDs.

The "Steampunk" movement grew out of Seattle and added another eccentric look for role playing. "Steampunk" is a way of making a theatrical statement using Victorian clothing and industrial waste in combination. Frock coats and the elegant proportion created are sleek and imposing on young men and the top hats add height, but the grungy side of old garments and industrial metallic pieces (like those from steam engines) had a "Punk" quality. Sunglasses were common masks whether mirrored as in *The Matrix* movie characters, or almost gogglelike crazy scientist glasses that had a retro look to them.

Halloween dress up had become so popular that other outlets for "dress up" were needed to spark up mundane lives and take them into the realm of fantasy. The Millennial generation embraced fantasy figures of all types and sizes, particularly warrior women at the Comic-Con conventions alongside very childlike and girlish Anime characters. The boys seem to favor the robot phenomenon or helmeted heroes in spandex leotards and brightly-colored tights rather than the pumped up heroes of the video games, perhaps because Comic-Con embraces the *Nerd* factor and super-muscled sports jocks are not as intellectually appealing. There are always a fair number of wizards, but not much crossover from other "Renaissance Fair" role-playing.

Masquerade is a way to seduce with a false appearance; a way to hide the actual person

*Opposite*: **Optimus Prime inspired by The Transformers, at Connecticon 2013, Hartford, Connecticut (courtesy Laura Crow).**

behind a costume or a mask. In Cosplay, however, the person wants to identify with the character and hopes that it brings out their true persona. This is not theatre costume, but costume that brings out the alter ego hidden in the person. This is masquerade that does not include masking. The character embodied is hopefully crystal clear. As such, another masquerader in the same costume champions those characteristics, facilitating an instant bond between the two. Gender-bending, another important element in Cosplay, allows for cross-dressing interpretations from female to male in a safe atmosphere. Furthermore, a woman may take on a male character, but make a female version of that same character. These masquerade options are far more common than males taking on female roles.

Another phenomenon coming out of Cosplay promotes the concept of group costumes. "Shipping" signifies the activity of joining two Cosplay characters together. A whole team of people will dress up like each of the characters in a television series. "Sailor Moon" seems particularly prone to this kind of group costuming, as an Anime cartoon showing the magical transformation of an average Japanese schoolgirl in a sailor blouse and short skirt who masquerades as "The Princess of the Moon," who will save the earth. She has a magical wand that she uses to ward off evil enemies. Sailor Moon has two blond ponytails that twist into a bun before hanging down, that look a bit like mouse ears. She is clumsy at first and gets girl power. She is attended by others bearing names of planets from the solar system. Coming as a couple or just two characters from the same series safely sanctions a way to go to the convention. With 10,000 people it is safer to come in with friends by your side rather than attempt to find anyone. However, when the costumed team meets another in similar gear, they become an instant fan club with similar interests. These groups question reality itself, and the relationship between reality, staging and performance. In some ways this is performance art, but during a convention that embraces Cosplay, this is reality as much as it is masquerade.

Comic-Con has become synonymous with Cosplay. Comic book characters are all around, including many warrior alter egos. At the Connecticon each person has to go through a weapons check to make sure that the weapons brought in are harmless. Swords are generally made of elaborately cut cardboard shapes covered with foil and they are there as props rather than for usage. On the expo floor however there are plenty of real, or semi real, weapons to be purchased. It is difficult to know whether convention participants view these props as works of art to hang on the wall or whether they might be used. On the flip side beyond the chain *maille*, dragon, dagger, and sword makers are the "Plushies." Frequently a very odd juxtaposition occurs when the childish soft plush animals are placed next to evil-looking pointed swords. Not to confuse the "Plushies" with toys, they often range in price from $100 to $250. This points out that to some degree these Cosplay enthusiasts are trying to hold on to childhood with soft stuffed animals. The "Plushies," however, are two-dimensional, more like throw pillows for display rather than cuddly toys. There are also myriad models for purchase or in kits ready for assembling. Some are collectible cartoon super heroes or video game characters and some are beautifully crafted "Dungeons and Dragons" fantasy figures.

Masqueraders easily flatter each other's costumes. There is a fair amount of camera clicking by those who wish to record another's costume and to remember the event and the friendship found. The event fosters the fan base with posing and taking on the alter ego. With the advent

*Opposite*: **Sailor Moon inspired by Pretty Guardian, Connecticon 2013 (photographer: Kellie Wagner; courtesy Laura Crow).**

of Facebook, the fan base can find each other and continue the friendships. Those who have an interest in the same character, or a television series or game, have a common interest and can potentially form a fan base. Problems can occasionally ensue when someone who is not really wanted insists on "glomping" on to a person or a group. Those who embrace the character and the fan base know when another is merely trying to join the group without having the correct characteristics. Cosplay does not imply consent to sexual behavior. Alternatively, people with similar interests can rapidly hook up anonymously if that is their desire.

Facebook pages all over the Internet facilitate those trying to attach to a fan base, or simply to show off a costume that took a lot of time to prepare. Comic-Con gatherings have expanded to four-day weekends from Thursday through Sunday, but then the event concludes, and participants find themselves longing for that alter ego to come back to life. Many now travel to various cities to enjoy the event and find the comfort of a fan base again. A Facebook page for "WeAreNerdCaliber," serves as one of many places to post photos from Comic-Con events.

There are important self-help websites. "Operation Hammond," a website for networking and helping nerds, says, "We are a non-profit organization of like-minded individuals within the Anime, Sci-Fi, fantasy and pop culture convention community dedicated to bringing awareness of first aid, emergency preparedness and training to people who attend and staff Anime, Sci-Fi, fantasy and pop culture conventions. We are nerds helping nerds in times of need."[8]

CosplayNation.net is another very popular website particularly for women:

> Cosplay is more than just pretty women in outfits. Cosplay is an art form where the subject attempts to take on the characteristics and mannerisms of a chosen character. Most often this in the form of comic book characters but can range to film/television or video game characters. Some get it right, others get it wrong. Some may even just be outright weird. But when done correctly, their work speaks for itself.[9]

In addition to WeAreNerdCaliber's Facebook page, there is a magazine on line at http://nerdcaliber.com/. This is a statement for the generation to come and expresses the importance of Comic-Con and Cosplay in their lives:

> We are living in a world where change is constantly happening. Definitions of what is steampunk, Cosplay or even nerd and geek are constantly in flux. Our goal at Nerd Caliber is to explore our culture and not only question its definition but to see where it will lead us years from now. This magazine is about your identity. It's about finding a place in this world.[10]

## Conclusion

We might consider Cosplay the current frontier for masquerade extravaganzas. It has certainly encouraged a type of masquerade that has never before appeared in the history as extensively and indeed, as globally as today. Cosplay works across nationalities. The same Anime figures are equally embraced not only in the United States, but in Japan, Germany, France, the United Kingdom, the Philippines, and now in China as well. Cosplay works across gender lines. Men need to be in costumes as well as women although there are definitely more women involved. A woman can cross-dress as a favorite male character or she can adapt a male character

*Opposite*: **Cosplay girl warrior, Connecticon 2013. Hartford, Connecticut (photographer: Kellie Wagner; courtesy Laura Crow).**

to a female persona. It is significant that the new world icon is rather childlike despite having special powers. This generation will find its own way to a more pure and optimistic future that values mind over body, with serious empowerment granted to women. Cosplay provides a pretend violent world with cardboard weapons as opposed to semi-automatic rifles—a much healthier world to live in. Fantasy has its place and reality is attached to machines. The Millennial Generation will have to embrace machines as an integral part of life. Cosplay allows a place for a generation to interact with each other rather than through machines, even if it is done with the magic of masquerade.

## Notes

1. Julie Shafler Dale (1986), *Art to Wear* (New York: Abbeville Press).
2. http://dezskinn.com/fanzines-3/copywrite 2013, Dez Skinn, WorldPress MU, hosted by UK2. net and http://en.wikipedia.org/wiki/British_Comic_Art_Convention.
3. http://www.comic-con.org *and http://en.wikipedia.org/wiki/San_Diego_Comic-Con_International.*
4. http://en.wikipedia.org/wiki/Chicago_Comicon.
5. http://www.organictheater.com/Organic/news/history/index.shtml. "History: 1971." Organic Theater Company (official site). Archived from the original 2 April 2007 and http://web.archive.org/web/20070402221220/http://www.organictheater.com/Organic/news/history/index.shtml.
6. *Cori Leyden-Sussler, interview with the author, April 2013. Weapons check and management assistant at Connecticon.*
7. David S. Cohen (2013), *Pacific Rim: Man, Machines, and Monsters,* foreword by Giullermo del Toro (San Raphael, CA: Insight Editions).
8. operationhammond.com/wp/ (2013), *Responsive Theme powered by WorldPress.*
9. http://cosplaynation.net (2013), The Mystique Theme *Blog at WordPress.com.*
10. http://nerdcaliber.com/ (2013), Copyright © 2013 Nerd Caliber All Rights Reserved.

## Works Cited

Cohen, David S. (2013.) *Pacific Rim: Man, Machines, and Monsters.* Foreword by Giullermo del Toro. San Raphael, CA: Insight Editions.
Dale, Julie Shafler. (1986.) *Art to Wear.* New York: Abbeville Press.
Leyden-Sussler, Cori. Interview with the author, April 2013.

*Opposite*: **Dollies on the sidewalk in Tokyo, Japan, 2011 (courtesy Laura Crow).**

# Appendix: Masquerade in Selected Plays, Broadway Musicals and Operas

---

## Plays

COMPILED BY KEITH CUSHMAN

John Arden, *Serjeant Musgrave's Dance*
Richard Bean, *One Man, Two Guvnors*
Bertolt Brecht, *The Good Person of Szechwan*
Pierre Corneille, *The Liar*
Thomas Dekker, *The Shoemaker's Holiday*
Oliver Goldsmith, *She Stoops to Conquer*
Carlo Goldoni, *A Servant of Two Masters*
Ludvig Holberg, *Masquerade*
Naomi Iizuka, *Polaroid Stories*
Ben Jonson, *The Alchemist*
Ben Jonson, *Volpone*
Mikhail Lermontov, *Masquerade*
Thomas Middleton, *The Revenger's Tragedy*
Molière, *The Doctor in Spite of Himself*
Molière, *The Imaginary Invalid*
Molière, *Tartuffe*
N. Richard Nash, *The Rainmaker*
Eugene O'Neill, *The Great God Brown*
Eugene O'Neill, *Lazarus Laughed*
Luigi Pirandello, *Enrico IV*

Luigi Pirandello, *Right You Are (If You Think So)*
Edmond Rostand, *Cyrano de Bergerac*
William Shakespeare, *All's Well That Ends Well*
William Shakespeare, *As You Like It*
William Shakespeare, *The Comedy of Errors*
William Shakespeare, *Measure for Measure*
William Shakespeare, *A Midsummer Night's Dream*
William Shakespeare, *Much Ado About Nothing*
William Shakespeare, *The Taming of the Shrew*
William Shakespeare, *The Tempest*
William Shakespeare, *Twelfth Night*
Bernard Shaw, *The Devil's Disciple*
Bernard Shaw, *Pygmalion*
Bernard Shaw, *You Never Can Tell*
Richard Brinsley Sheridan, *The School for Scandal*
Brandon Thomas, *Charley's Aunt*
John Vanbrugh, *The Provok'd Wife*
Oscar Wilde, *The Importance of Being Earnest*
William Wycherley, *The Country Wife*

## Broadway Musicals

### Compiled by Matthew Teague Miller

*Annie*
*Anything Goes*
*Assassins*
*Big*
*Big River*
*The Boys from Syracuse*
*Cabaret*
*La Cage aux Folles*
*Catch Me if You Can*
*Chicago*
*Damn Yankees*
*Dirty Rotten Scoundrels*
*A Funny Thing Happened on the Way to the Forum*
*Guys and Dolls*
*Hedwig and the Angry Inch*
*How to Succeed in Business Without Really Trying*
*Kiss Me, Kate*
*Kiss of the Spider Woman*
*Les Misérables*
*Man of La Mancha*
*The Music Man*

*My Fair Lady*
*110 in the Shade*
*Pacific Overtures*
*Phantom*
*The Phantom of the Opera*
*Pippin*
*She Loves Me*
*Sweeney Todd*
*Sweet Charity*
*Thoroughly Modern Millie*
*Victor/Victoria*
*Where's Charley?*

## Opera

### COMPILED BY KEITH CUSHMAN

Auber, *Le Domino noir*
Birtwistle, *Punch and Judy*
Britten, *A Midsummer Night's Dream*
Dvořák, *Rusalka*
Janáček, *The Makropulos Affair*
Leoncavallo, *Pagliacci*
Massenet, *Cendrillon*
Mozart, *Così fan tutte*
Mozart, *Don Giovanni*
Mozart, *Die Zauberflöte*
Nielsen, *Maskarade*
Nikolai, *The Merry Wives of Windsor*
Puccini, *La Fanciulla del West*
Ravel, *L'Enfant et les sortilèges*
Rimsky-Korsakov, *The Golden Cockerel*
Rossini, *La Cenerentola*
Shostakovich, *The Nose*
Johann Strauss II, *Die Fledermaus*
Richard Strauss, *Ariadne auf Naxos*
Stravinsky, *The Rake's Progress*
Verdi, *Un ballo in maschera*
Verdi, *Falstaff*
Verdi, *Nabucco*
Verdi, *Rigoletto*
Verdi, *I vespri siciliani*

## TROUSER ROLES IN OPERA

A selection of male characters performed by female singers

| | |
|---|---|
| Adès, *The Tempest* | Ariel |
| Bellini, *I Capuletti e i Montecchi* | Romeo |
| Catalani, *La Wally* | Walter |
| Corigliano, *The Ghosts of Versailles* | Cherubino |
| Donizetti, *Anna Bolena* | Smeton |
| Glinka, *Ruslan and Lyudmila* | Ratmir |
| Gounod, *Faust* | Siebel |
| Humperdinck, *Hänsel und Gretel* | Hänsel, The Sand-Man, The Dew-Man [often the witch is sung by a tenor] |
| Janáček, *From the House of the Dead* | Aleja |
| Massenet, *Chérubin* | Chérubin |
| Mozart, *La clemenza di Tito* | Sesto, Annio |
| Mozart, *Idomeneo* | Idamante |
| Mozart, *Le nozze di Figaro* | Cherubino |
| Offenbach, *Les Contes d'Hoffmann* | Nicklausse |
| Ravel, *L'Enfant et les sortileges* | The Boy, The Shepherd |
| Rossini, *Le Comte Ory* | Isolier |
| Rossini, *La donna del lago* | Malcolm |
| Rossini, *Guillaume Tell* | Tell's son Jemmy |
| Johann Strauss II, *Die Fledermaus* | Count Orlovsky |
| Richard Strauss, *Ariadne auf Naxos* | The Composer |
| Richard Strauss, *Der Rosenkavalier* | Octavian |
| Verdi, *Un ballo in maschera* | Oscar |
| Wagner, *Parsifal* | Two novices in the all-male society are sung by sopranos |
| Wagner, *Tannhäuser* | The Shepherd |

# About the Contributors

Loyce L. **Arthur**, an associate professor at the University of Iowa, has designed costumes for numerous productions, including the U.S. premiere of *Peter Pan & Wendy* at the Prince Music Theater, Philadelphia. She has studied mask making with Donato Satori in Italy; ritual and mask performance in Ghana, Côte d'Ivoire, Bali, and India; and world carnival traditions in Cuba, Trinidad and Tobago, Colombia, Brazil, Canada, the United Kingdom, and the Netherlands.

Hilary **Baxter** is the program director for Theatre and Screen at Wimbledon College of Art, University of the Arts, London. Her costume research has been funded by the AHRC and the British Academy. She was the principal investigator for the Oral History of British Theatre Design, part of the National Life Stories Collection at the British Library. Her research interests are focused on the influences and working practices of professional costume practitioners.

Deborah **Bell** is a professor of costume design at the University of North Carolina at Greensboro. A member of United Scenic Artists, she has exhibited design work at the Prague Quadrennial and received the United States Institute for Theatre Technology's Herbert D. Greggs Award and American College Theatre Festival's Faculty Recognition Award. Her book *Mask Makers and Their Craft: An Illustrated Worldwide Study* (2010) is based on interviews with mask makers in ten countries.

Laura **Crow** is a professor of costume history at the University of Connecticut. She was a Fulbright Senior Research Scholar in the Philippines in 2002, studying multi-culturalism in festival costumes. She continues to design for professional theatre, and in 2012 her costume designs were on display at Lincoln Center in the exhibition *Curtain Call: Celebrating a Century of Women Designing for Live Performance*. She was the resident designer for Circle Rep for thirteen years, where she designed many of Landford Wilsin's plays.

Marianne **Custer** is a professor of costume design at the University of Tennessee. She is resident costume designer at the Clarence Brown Theatre, and her design credits include Broadway, Theatre Les Halles, Avignon, and the National Theatres of Germany and Hungary. Her designs have been included in juried exhibitions, including the 2005 World Stage Design exhibit. A winner of the Helen Hayes Award for Outstanding Costume Design, Custer has published several articles based on her research on Central and Eastern Europe costume designers.

Richard **Fallis** is a professor emeritus of English at Mercer University, where he also served as the dean of the College of Liberal Arts. While on the faculty at Syracuse University, he edited some sixty titles in the university press's Irish studies series. He is the author of *The Irish Renaissance* (1977).

Ted **Gournelos** is an assistant professor of critical media and cultural studies at Rollins College. A scholar of media and oppositional culture, his 2009 monograph *Popular Culture and the Future of Politics* was followed in 2011 with two edited collections, *A Decade of Dark Humor* and *Transgression 2.0*. He is researching the cultural politics and social implications of digital culture.

Heather L. **Holian** is an associate professor of art history at the University of North Carolina at Greensboro. Her animation research centers on the collaborative process of Pixar Animation Studios and the role of the individual artist within this studio structure. In addition to a forthcoming essay on studio animation as a fine art form, she has published on a range of topics addressing Florentine portraiture of the 16th and 17th centuries.

Kara **McLeod** has taught the history of costume and decor at the Fashion Institute of Design and Merchandising for 12 years. Since the 1980s she has worked in professional theater and the Halloween industry for a wide variety of companies, theaters, and educational institutions, including Cal Arts, UCLA, Disney Imagineering, and Center Theater Group.

Ron **Naversen** is a professor of scenic design at Southern Illinois University Carbondale and a member of United Scenic Artists. He also maintains a freelance career, designing for several professional and university theaters. A mask scholar and designer, he has written numerous articles on masks and recently received an After Dark Award (Chicago Area Theater Awards) for for his mask for the Vitalist's production of *A Passage to India.*

Art historian John Wallace **Nunley** has conducted research in both rural and urban West Africa since 1972 and on the African Diaspora in the West Indies since 1983. Interested primarily in social crises and the arts of performance, especially masquerades, he has published four books, including *Moving with the Face of the Devil: Art and Politics in Urban West Africa* and *Caribbean Festival Arts*. In 2008, he received a Guggenheim Fellowship in support of his research for a book entitled *African Art and the Experience of Slavery.*

Peter **Probst** is a professor of anthropology and African art history at Tufts University. He has written extensively about African art and visual culture and his research interests include the materiality of religion, aesthetics and agency, and heritage and public memory. His most recent book is a study on heritage politics in Nigeria, *Osogbo and the Art of Heritage*. He recently edited a special issue of *African Arts* entitled "Iconoclash in the Age of Heritage."

Mary **Robinson** recently received her master's degree from the Department of Drama and Theater at Tufts University. Her research focuses primarily on performance styles in America and England from the late 19th century to the present day. Other areas of interest include costuming, burlesque, cinema, and anthropology, often from the perspective of feminist and gender theory. An ongoing emphasis is the intersection of many of these interests in the life and career of the great French actress Sarah Bernhardt.

M. Kathryn **Shields** is an assistant professor of art history and serves as the chair of the Art Department at Guilford College. Her writings have appeared in *Mosaic: A Journal for the*

*Interdisciplinary Study of Literature, The Encyclopedia of 20th-Century Photography,* and *A History of Visual Culture.* Most recently she co-authored *Gateways to Art: Understanding the Visual Arts.* She previously taught at the University of Texas at Arlington and served as a curatorial assistant at the Virginia Museum of Fine Arts.

Johann **Stegmeir** is an assistant professor of theatre at the University of Richmond. Recently he collaborated with Bruce Beresford on costumes for the feature film *Peace, Love, and Misunderstanding,* starring Jane Fonda. He designed costumes for "Tecumseh's Vision," the second episode of the PBS documentary *We Shall Remain*; *Pagliacci* for Teatro Verdi in Sassari, Sardinia; and *A Streetcar Named Desire* at the Kennedy Center. He has also designed for the Washington National, Los Angeles and Pittsburgh operas, among others.

Vincent **Stephens**, the director of the Office of Multicultural Student Services at Bucknell University, writes about depictions of social pluralism in post–World War II American popular culture. He has published articles in *African-American Review, American Music, Popular Music,* and *Popular Music & Society.* He has taught at Bowling Green State University, the University of Maryland, and Syracuse University.

Marta **Turok** is an anthropologist who serves as a curator of the Ruth D. Lechuga Folk Art Collection at the Franz Mayer Museum in Mexico City and heads the research department of the School of Crafts at the National Institute of Fine Arts. She has curated numerous national and international exhibitions displaying various Mexican crafts, the most recent being *1001 Faces of Mexico: Masks.* Her numerous books and articles include several related to masks and festivities.

Derrick **Vanmeter** is an assistant professor of costume design at Youngstown State University. He received the Atlantic World Research Network's First Place Award for scholarship in 2013 and the Southeastern Theatre Conference Graduate Costume Design Award for *The Threepenny Opera* in 2012. His academic pursuits converge at the intersection of theatre, postmodernism, and religion.

# Index

Numbers in **_bold italics_** indicate pages with photographs